THE DAWN OF EMPIRE

Rome's Rise to World Power

BY

R. M. ERRINGTON

Cornell Paperbacks

CORNELL UNIVERSITY PRESS
ITHACA, NEW YORK

First published 1972 by Cornell University Press
First published, Cornell Paperbacks, 1973

International Standard Book Number 0-8014-9128-2
Library of Congress Catalog Card Number 75-176296

PRINTED IN GREAT BRITAIN

RBE
IWE

CONTENTS

PART FOUR

WORLD POWER

MAPS

(drawn by Patrick Leeson)

PREFACE

The importance of Rome's rise to world power as a major development in the history of the Mediterranean world was recognized as
early as the second century B.C. by Polybius of Megalopolis. Polybius
was a contemporary of and participant in many of the crucially for-
mative events of that century; and I can provide no better explanation of the existence of this book than to echo Polybius' justification
of his own work: 'Who is so incurious or idle as to have no interest
in knowing the constitutional qualities and the methods which
enabled Rome to subject the whole known world to her sole rule in
less than fifty-three years?' Polybius' fifty-three years run from
220 B.C. to 167 B.C.; but—as he himself recognized—the history of
these crucial years must be prefaced by some background to set it in
context and completed by some supplementary material, to examine
its immediate effect. Hence I have followed Polybius' pattern
(though not his dates), and have begun my account with Rome's
first overseas venture in 264 B.C., and continued it (where appropriate) until 133 B.C.

Polybius was the first critical historian to attempt to write a
coherent account of Rome's rise to world power. His example—and
his text—have been followed by many subsequent writers, both
ancient and modern. It would be invidious and impertinent to single
out individuals among them for praise or criticism. The most
important works will be found listed in the notes and the bibliography. But it would be wrong not to acknowledge the fact that this
book owes such merits of interpretation as it has chiefly to the stimulus of one outstanding modern follower in Polybius' path, Professor
Ernst Badian, and in particular to his ground-breaking book,
Foreign Clientelae.

Since I have not been writing primarily for the professional
classicist, but rather for the interested general reader who is likely,
like Shakespeare, to have little Latin and less Greek, I have cited
in the text no Latin without translating it and no Greek at all except
in translation. Even in the notes, I have tried to make discussions

intelligible to readers who cannot read the original classical languages, though their chief purpose is to give the main references to the major ancient and modern writers for the aid of those who may wish to follow up particular matters beyond the scope of this book. Similarly, the bibliography is not intended to be comprehensive, but merely to give a guide to what seem to me to be the most useful recent modern works, chiefly (but not exclusively) in English, on Roman imperialism and related subjects. I have also provided a short glossary of the most common technical terms.

Many friends have helped me with advice and discussion. I should particularly like to mention Professor A. E. Astin, Professor E. Badian and Mr. J. B. Salmon, all of whom read sections of the book in draft and made comments and suggestions which produced many improvements. My wife has read the whole work from the point of view of the general reader, and in addition has provided indispensable help with proof-reading and indexing. To all I am deeply grateful.

Heidelberg   R.M.E.
January 1971

PART I

BEFORE HANNIBAL

PART I

BEFORE HANNIBAL

CHAPTER I

ROME IN 264 B.C.

I Rome and Italy

ROME'S rise to world power was one of the most important accidents in European history. It was not a deliberately engineered process; Rome's empire was not created by any initial desire to rule or to exploit others. Rather it evolved through a continual process of responding to threats, real or imagined, to Rome's ever-widening sphere of interests. Expansion proceeded by a series of steps which aimed to achieve, first and foremost, merely the security of Rome. Security might be interpreted (as it was at first) as lying quite simply in the physical protection of the city of Rome; or it might be interpreted (as it was later) as protecting Rome's wider interests elsewhere, which were nevertheless regarded as essential to the prevailing concept of Roman security. Thus the process which produced the Roman empire overseas was accidental in the sense that it was not deliberately begun with the aim of achieving empire or (in the early stages) deliberately continued. It was not dissimilar to the way in which, since the Second World War, the security interests of the USA have spread, half unwillingly, to embrace the greater part of the so-called 'free' world.

We begin our examination of this process in 264 B.C., when it had already started, but had not yet taken Rome beyond the mainland of Italy. By 264 Rome was already pre-eminently powerful within Italy. Though a casual glance at a map might suggest that Italy is a geographical unity, it was in fact inhabited in the third century B.C. by a large number of different races: to the north of Rome were the Etruscans, and beyond them the Celtic Gauls; to the east, in and beyond the Apennines, were the Samnites; to the south-east a hotch-potch of races including Oscan-speaking Campanians and a large number of Greek-speaking cities scattered along the coast. Originally the only speakers of Latin were the comparatively few inhabitants of the plain of Latium, of which Rome was one small community.

The process of Rome's expansion within Italy is not clear in detail and does not concern us here as such. The fact, however, must be recorded. The political theme of Rome's expansion within Italy was the search for mutual protection. Those communities physically closest to Rome were in due course incorporated into the Roman state in various forms of citizenship; those situated too far away for this to be practicable or desirable were customarily bound to Rome by a formal treaty (*foedus*) which regulated their relationship with Rome: they thus became allies (*socii*). Since these alliances were formed primarily for reasons of security, they involved a mutual military commitment but no tribute or taxation.

As Rome became more powerful within Italy, an increasing number of smaller communities became prepared, when facing attack by a third party, to surrender themselves to Rome's care and protection, in return for a treaty of alliance which, most urgently, bound Rome to help them in their present emergency, but which also bound them to help Rome in the future. Such unconditional surrender by a small state to Rome's good faith (*deditio in fidem*)— which might come voluntarily from the need for protection, or under compulsion from being fought to a standstill—tended to be resolved by a form of treaty which, as far as the formulation of the terms was concerned, made both parties equal (*foedus aequum*). But the fact of the real difference of power between the smaller state and Rome, which had produced the unconditional surrender in the first place, meant that in practice and in the long term Rome's allies tended to become little more than her satellites. In law they were equal; but in power—which was what ultimately mattered—Rome's protection entailed Rome's predominance.

The chief burden of Rome's allies was to provide troops for Rome's annual levies. For although Roman religious law (the 'fetial law') forebade Rome's undertaking a war other than in her own defence (thus establishing the proud principle that Rome fought only 'just wars'), the accepted concept of her own defence had, by the end of the fourth century B.C., broadened to the point where assistance to an ally who was attacked, or even just threatened, might for the purposes of fetial law be regarded as defensive action. Thus by 264 in northern Italy Rome was looked upon as a protector against the Gauls;[1] in the south, when in 282 the Greek town of Thurii was hard-pressed in a war with her neighbours the Lucanians, it was Rome which was called upon for help.[2] By acceding to this kind of request and (within Italy) by deliberately taking measures to increase her influence and her power, Rome had established by 264, through her widespread net of alliances, a controlling interest over the greater part of Italy. Moreover, it seems that her Italian allies were on the whole content to pay the necessary price for Rome's protection, for even during the first war with Carthage—which, since it was fought outside Italy, many of them must have regarded as foreign to their own interests of security which had originally bound them to Rome—there is little evidence of dissatisfaction with their status.

II Rome

Throughout the period of Rome's expansion within Italy the city was governed by an exclusive body of some 300 aristocrats, the Roman Senate, which had originally been the council of the kings of Rome. After the expulsion of the last king, Tarquinius Superbus, in the sixth century B.C. the Senate had become the effective government, although the mass of the Roman People formally retained the right to the last word on most matters affecting the state. To express these opinions the People were collected into various assemblies, the most important of which was the *comitia centuriata*, organized into 193 voting units called '*centuriae*'. This was not a democratically organized grouping, but was so arranged that the assembly could normally be controlled by the wealthy—in practice these included the senators—if they were united. The main functions of the *comitia centuriata*, as far as this book is concerned, were to elect the chief magistrates—the annual pair of consuls and (in 264) single praetor—and to decide on peace and war.[3]

I have stated that the rich could in practice (if united) normally control the decisions of the *comitia centuriata*. This was in part due to the arrangement of the centuries which gave a built-in majority to the rich. But it was also affected by the operation of the moral code of social behaviour known as *clientela*. *Clientela* was the mutual relationship of client and patron. It was sanctified in the religious and moral code of the Roman Republic, and it operated at all levels of society. On the broadest interpretation it consisted of the expressed willingness of the patron to protect his client—whether from physical, economic or other pressures of life—in return for which he expected support. The client and patron were thus bound together by mutual moral obligations. To be effective, a patron needed to be rich and influential. The rich and influential at Rome customarily had political ambitions, in which case the support they required from their clients could best be given in terms of votes and canvassing. This would obviously be most important at elections; but it might also be needed in connection with legislative or policy-making measures in which the patron was interested. Thus while the assemblies of the Roman People legally had the last word on any measure, the far-reaching moral obligations of *clientela*—it was not a *legal* relationship—meant that in practice the decisive factors in most political situations were the political alliances and enmities of the patrons who were members of the upper class, the most import-ant and influential of whom, the politically active aristocrats, formed the Roman Senate. In practice, therefore, the Senate virtually con-trolled the most important aspects of Roman government if it could control the *clientelae* of its own members.

No Roman could achieve political importance without being a member of the Senate. Most senators were ex-magistrates; and all had to pass a scrutiny by two censors (who were elected by the *comitia centuriata* every five years, from the body of existing senior senators) before they were allowed entry to the Senate. The Senate was therefore a self-perpetuating and exclusive oligarchy, and as a class it tended to close ranks against newcomers. The chief reason for senatorial exclusiveness was the characteristic of Roman political life which laid great stress on the clan (*gens*) and the family; and this has reasonably been compared with English politics in the eighteenth century. At Rome the chief personal aim of political life was honour acknowledged by one's equals; and such honour and respect could be most readily and traditionally achieved by attaining the consulship, which made its two annual holders joint heads of state for their year. For this reason the electoral competition for the consulship was great: it brought high honour and status both to the holder in person and to his family. Consequently politics at Rome tended to be family politics; family influence was exerted, particu-larly through *clientela*, to gain consulships for family members.

The internal politics of Rome in this period is therefore on the whole not the politics of popular movements led by the chosen leaders of the masses, nor the politics of conflicting doctrines or ideologies: it is the politics of the governing class, the politics of the Roman Senate. The senatorial families were comparatively few. Between 264 and 220, for instance, all the 104 known senior magis-trates—consuls and praetors—come from only thirty-four *gentes*;

and since eleven *gentes* are each represented only once, the remaining twenty-five *gentes* average more than four magistrates each. The decision-making of the Senate was therefore effectively in the hands of a comparatively small number of men, the leaders of the family groups within the Senate. For within the Senate seniority ruled. The leading senatorial families dominated the senior magistracies; those who held or who had held the chief magistracies dominated the decision-making in the Senate. By virtue of their prestige, their *clientela*, and the organization of the *comitia centuriata* they were usually (though not always) able to ensure that decisions reached in the Senate would be approved by the appropriate assembly of the People. Thus when we say 'the Senate decided' or 'the Senate thought', what we mean in practice is that a majority of the leaders of the senatorial families decided or thought.

III Rome and the Mediterranean World

While Rome was achieving pre-eminence in Italy under the guidance of the Senate, the peninsula was naturally not isolated from the broader context of Mediterranean politics. The Greek cities of the south, in particular, maintained close links with the older cities of the Greek world, and as Rome's contact with and influence over the Greek cities within Italy increased, so she inevitably became more conscious of the existence of Greeks outside Italy. But Rome had as yet no important interests overseas. She was prepared to bind the Greeks of Italy to her by alliances because their geographical proximity made their friendship an essential part of Rome's scheme for her own security within Italy. But contacts with overseas states were so slight that, where they existed at all, they were in most cases not regulated by formal treaty. For instance, as early as the beginning of the fourth century—and perhaps even earlier—Rome had developed informal friendly relations (*amicitia*) with the western Greek city Massilia.[4] Shared hostility to their common neighbours, the Gauls, ensured that this friendly connection survived; but it was many years before a treaty formalized the friendship.

Later in the fourth century Rome's contacts with other overseas states—so far as we know them—only emphasize that, while Rome was widely known as a great power within Italy, she had little interest in affairs outside Italy. When in 333/2 Alexander of Epirus —the brother-in-law of Alexander the Great—crossed the Adriatic and came to southern Italy to help the Greek city of Tarentum against its neighbours, Rome made some kind of alliance with him.[5] Since he was murdered before the alliance became operative we do not know what, if anything, Rome ultimately intended by it. But we may confidently assume that the Senate would not have been at all bothered about Alexander had he not involved himself in Italian affairs. At about the same time Alexander the Great is said to have complained to Rome about pirates operating from the Latin town of Antium, a Roman colony which was therefore technically in Roman control. Again we do not know what Rome did, but Alexander's distant complaint can certainly have had no long-term effect, for a few years later the Macedonian Demetrius I Poliorcetes ('The Besieger') complained of the same annoyance.[6] Some ancient writers also believed that a Roman embassy was among those which greeted Alexander the Great at Babylon on his return from the east in 324 B.C.[7] And although many modern scholars regard this incident as a later invention, it is possible that the recent intervention in Italy of Alexander's like-named brother-in-law, Alexander of Epirus, made the Romans sufficiently interested to investigate the attitude of the great conqueror, whose reputation they obviously will have known, and whose future plans—if they could judge by those of Alexander of Epirus—might affect them.

Around 306 the Greek island of Rhodes, which already had trading contacts with some of the Greek cities of southern Italy, seems to have become a friend (*amicus*) of Rome.[8] In 306 Rome would get little advantage from friendship with Rhodes; but Rhodes must have been interested in making sure that Rome, by now the most powerful state in Italy, would not interfere with her established trade with the Italian Greeks. Rome had no reason to refuse Rhodes' friendship.[9] Similarly in 273 the current king of Egypt, Ptolemy II Philadelphus, took the initiative in sending ambassadors to Rome. He was perhaps impressed by the way Rome had recently managed (though, in fact, not without some difficulty) to defeat the invasion of Italy by another king of Epirus, Pyrrhus. Perhaps, like Rhodes a little earlier, Ptolemy was anxious simply to establish good relations with the most powerful Italian state to protect his commercial interests. We know that Rome returned the diplomatic courtesy by sending ambassadors of her own to Alexandria; but the novelty of the situation for Rome is nicely illustrated by the fact that when Ptolemy followed the usual hellenistic practice of giving expensive presents to the ambassadors, the Roman Senate held a special discussion before it allowed its ambassadors to accept them.[10] Apollonia, a Greek city in Illyria, just across the Adriatic from Italy, was perhaps not treated so courteously when it sent ambassadors to Rome some time after 270: the Senate probably did not even bother to send a counter-embassy, thus showing its essential indifference, though it no doubt considered that informal friendly relations (*amicitia*) had been established.[11]

The only formal treaties which we know Rome had with a non-Italian state before 264 were with Carthage, a Phoenician city in north Africa. Following the long-established Phoenician tradition, Carthage derived her wealth chiefly from commerce; and the physical situation of the city was excellent both for contacting and controlling the peoples of the interior of north Africa (including other Phoenician settlements there) and for trading in all directions throughout the Mediterranean. Already by the end of the sixth century B.C. Carthage had formed close links with—amounting in practice to effective predominance over—the originally independent Phoenician colonies in western Sicily, Motya, Panormus and Solus; she also had settlements of her own in Sardinia and in Ibiza. The chief reason for her westward exploration was the search for metals, in which the Iberian peninsula is particularly rich. Modern Cadiz (Roman Gades) was an early Phoenician settlement, and Carthage quickly established her own colonies on the south coast of Spain.[12]

Carthage's interest in trade with Spain was so important for her prosperity that she soon tried, with some success, to prevent any other state from trading there. In Sicily also, Carthage tried to increase her influence, chiefly at the expense of the numerous Greek cities in the island. The first attested contact between Rome and Carthage goes back to this period. When writing of the outbreak of Rome's war with Hannibal in 218, Polybius reviewed all past treaties between Rome and Carthage; and the first of these, he says, dated from the first year of the Roman Republic (509/8 B.C.).[13] The terms indicate the current pre-occupations of Rome and Carthage, and these, conveniently enough, were mutually exclusive. The Etruscans, who had ruled Rome until 509/8 B.C., had been interested in trading, and Carthage had needed a treaty with them; but the new Roman Republic had other interests and other priorities. The treaty nevertheless safeguards Carthage's commercial claims and restricts Roman commercial activity, particularly in Africa and Sardinia; and this suggests that the initiative for it came from Carthage. But since Rome had at this early date almost certainly no commercial (or other) interest in Africa or Sardinia, we may readily assume that the Senate was willing enough to accept this restriction. In return, the Carthaginians accepted limitations on their activities in Latium.

Polybius' second treaty, which probably dates from 348,[14] shows Rome accepting much wider trading restrictions to the west—complete exclusion from Sardinia and north Africa (except in emergencies) and perhaps from Spain also. These terms suggest that the initiative for the treaty again came from Carthage. But Rome's acceptance shows clearly that the Senate was still happy enough to undertake to confine Roman interests to Italy. In return Carthage guaranteed to establish no permanent post in Latium, though the treaty allowed the legitimacy of some attacks on persons and property. Agreement not to damage areas subject to each other and a statement of mutual trading rights in the cities of Carthage and Rome conclude the terms.

Rome's earliest treaties with Carthage, therefore, far from suggesting that formal overseas contacts necessarily imply active overseas interests, show exactly the opposite: just as Rhodes and Ptolemy Philadelphus seem to have taken the initiative in becoming friendly with Rome, so it was Carthage, not Rome, which took the initiative in formulating the terms of the treaties. And Polybius' third treaty, probably to be dated to 279/8, confirms that Rome still had no desire to extend her formal interests beyond Italy.[15] For part of the new treaty simply repeated terms already agreed in 348, despite the fact that Rome was now much more powerful within Italy than she had been then. The difference—and indeed, the reason for the new treaty—arose from an immediate crisis which affected both Rome and Carthage, the invasion of Italy by king Pyrrhus of Epirus. The Senate negotiated with Pyrrhus after he had beaten a Roman army at Asculum in 279; and Carthage was worried about repercussions which an agreement between Rome and Pyrrhus might have on her Sicilian interests. The terms reveal Carthage's anxiety, for they amount to little more than an attempt to keep Rome and Pyrrhus mutually hostile: 'If either Rome or Carthage should make a written alliance with Pyrrhus, they shall make it with the explicit provision that each might provide military help to the other in the territory of whichever is attacked. The Carthaginians shall provide ships for transport, whichever of the two states requires aid, but each state shall provide subsistence for its own men. The Carthaginians shall also help the Romans by sea if necessary, but the crews shall not be compelled to land against their will.'

This, then, is the sum of what we know about Roman contacts outside Italy before 264 B.C.: by that date Rome had contracted no important political interests or commitments outside the Italian mainland. She had some overseas contacts, but these involved no obligation. Friendship with Massilia, Rhodes, Ptolemy Philadelphus, Apollonia—and perhaps a few other states which we do not know about—seems to have begun in each case on the initiative of the external state, not on that of Rome. We have seen exactly the same general Roman attitude in her more formal relationship with Carthage; for Roman advantages from the treaties had remained essentially unchanged for more than 200 years, while the Senate had willingly accepted increasing restrictions from Carthage's widening aspirations. The Senate clearly must have thought that these restrictions cost Rome nothing.

In Italy, of course, the situation was very different. For in Italy Rome's very existence had been threatened; and there the Senate's view of the best way of procuring Rome's safety gradually developed wider limits as the Latins, the Etruscans, the Samnites, the Greek cities of southern Italy, were either beaten into submission or more peacefully brought to accept that Rome's interests were supreme. By 264 the chief work in Italy had been done; Rome now regarded all Italy except the area between the Apennines and the Alps (Cisalpine Gaul) as her sphere of influence. We shall see in subsequent chapters how the same kind of attitude which had brought her to pre-eminence within Italy led logically to a view of her essential interests—aimed, in the last resort, at the preservation of the security of the city of Rome—which gradually came to embrace most of the coastlands of the Mediterranean.

CHAPTER II

THE FIRST PUNIC WAR

I Into Sicily

FROM 264 B.C. the chief energies of Rome and Carthage were absorbed for more than twenty years in war with each other; yet the incident from which the war arose did not at first seem to contain the prospect of such massive confrontation. We have seen that the two states had allied against their common enemy Pyrrhus a mere fifteen years before; and after Pyrrhus' departure from Italy no conflict occurred between them which need have disturbed their friendly relationship. Yet a brief series of incidents and accidents soon bred mutual suspicion and quickly produced a major conflict.

Appropriately perhaps, the scene of the crisis was the border between their respective spheres of influence. The Sicilian Greek city of Messana, which overlooks the narrow straits between Italy and Sicily, had at some time between 288 and 283 been captured and occupied by some Campanian mercenaries, recently demobilized from service with Syracuse. Once in full possession, they called themselves *Mamertini*, 'sons of Mars'.[1] Initially this event did not affect Rome at all, since she had no interests in Sicily. But the Mamertines' example quickly found its imitators; and Rhegium, the Greek city opposite Messana on the Italian side of the straits, was soon afterwards seized by a similar group of Campanian mercenaries, whom Rome had initially employed as a garrison. Rhegium, being on the Italian mainland, was a Roman ally; its government therefore appealed to Rome, whereupon the Campanians were ejected and the city restored to its grateful inhabitants. For Rome the exercise was a convenient demonstration of the value of alliances with her and of the reliability of Roman good faith (*fides*).[2]

The superficial similarity between the situations of Rhegium and of Messana did not mean that the Romans now intended to interfere at Messana. Far from it. From the Roman point of view the situations of the two cities were quite different. Rhegium was a Roman

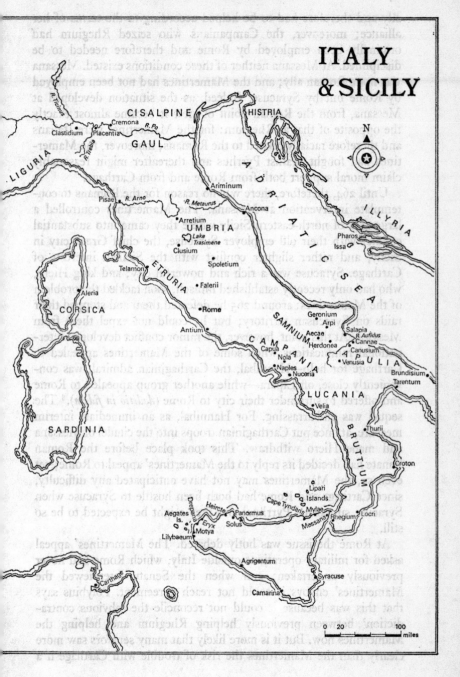

ally and therefore had to be helped according to the terms of her alliance; moreover, the Campanians who seized Rhegium had originally been employed by Rome and therefore needed to be disciplined. At Messana neither of these conditions existed. Messana was not a Roman ally; and the Mamertines had not been employed by Rome but by Syracuse. Indeed, as the situation developed at Messana, from the Roman point of view it became almost exactly the opposite of that at Rhegium: for the Mamertines were Italians and therefore racially related to the Romans; moreover, the Mamertines had fought against Pyrrhus and thereafter might reasonably claim moral support both from Rome and from Carthage.

Until 264, therefore, there was no reason for the Romans to contemplate intervention at Messana. The Mamertines controlled a large area of north-eastern Sicily where they came into substantial conflict with their old employer Syracuse, the chief Greek city in Sicily, and rather slighter conflict with the Sicilian interests of Carthage. Syracuse was a rich and powerful city; and king Hiero, who had only recently established himself, soon tackled the problem of the Mamertines: around 265 he defeated them and stopped their raids on Syracusan territory; but he could not expel them from Messana. At this point, however, the minor conflict developed international ramifications when some of the Mamertines appealed to Carthage for help—Hannibal, the Carthaginian admiral, was conveniently close, off Lipara—while another group appealed to Rome and offered to surrender their city to Rome (*deditio in fidem*).[3] The sequel was embarrassing. For Hannibal, as an immediate interim measure, at once put Carthaginian troops into the citadel of Messana and made Hiero withdraw. This took place before the Roman Senate had decided its reply to the Mamertines' appeal to Rome; yet even so, the Mamertines may not have anticipated any difficulty, since Carthage and Rome had both been hostile to Syracuse when Syracuse supported Pyrrhus; and they might be expected to be so still.

At Rome the issue was hotly debated. The Mamertines' appeal asked for military operations outside Italy, which Rome had never previously undertaken; and when the Senate interviewed the Mamertines' envoys it could not reach agreement. Polybius says that this was because it could not reconcile the 'obvious contradiction' between previously helping Rhegium and helping the Mamertines now. But it is more likely that many senators saw more clearly than the Mamertines the risk of trouble with Carthage if a

Roman army crossed to Sicily to help the Mamertines. For Sicily had been a Carthaginian sphere of influence now for nearly 300 years; and while Carthage had never previously maintained influence as far east in the island, the step to Messana was clearly much smaller for her than it was for the Romans, who would be officially entering Sicily for the first time. The extension of Roman protection across the straits would be such a great innovation in Sicilian affairs that Carthage might easily interpret it as a challenge, an indication that Rome had aspirations which stretched beyond simply bringing aid to those who had appealed to her.

In the Senate wiser counsels prevailed. The Mamertines' appeal was not accepted. Rome had no intimate interest in Sicily; there was no good reason for believing that Carthage viewed Messana as a step towards influence in Italy; and there was no point in unnecessarily seeming to provoke her by interfering in Sicily. But in the last resort the matter did not rest with the cool-headed Senate. The People technically had the last word; and one of the consuls of 264, Appius Claudius Caudex, doubtless eager for military success without which his consulship would be undistinguished, raised the question of the Mamertines' appeal before them. He particularly emphasized the rich booty which would accrue from a war in Sicily, and the Roman People were easily persuaded by his disreputable short-sighted arguments. The Mamertines were thus accepted into Roman protection.[4] This decision meant that for the first time Rome was committed to military action outside the Italian mainland. It was a small step in terms of distance—the straits are very narrow—but in terms of the character of the Roman involvement it was vast. For the first time Rome could not simply march her troops to the scene of action; for the first time naval transport was necessary; and— most important—for the first time non-Italian powers had to be faced. The step was lightly taken. The Mamertines were Italians and (in principle) friends: false logic put them into the same category as Rome's other Italian friends who, in the face of external threats, had from time to time been received into Rome's protection. It was the superficial logic of the situation, coupled with the desire for booty—which Appius Claudius' military ambitions led him to emphasize—which ensured that the Roman People took the simple but momentous decision to accept the appeal of the Mamertines.

Moreover, before Appius left Rome the *comitia centuriata* seems to have given him discretionary powers to declare war on Carthage if he thought this necessary. Once Roman *fides* embraced the

Mamertines, the Roman People clearly intended to share any profits from the war with no other state; and since the Carthaginians already had a garrison in Messana, it obviously might be necessary to declare war before ejecting it. But we have nothing to indicate that at this stage anybody at Rome contemplated a *major* war with Carthage. Rome's technique in the past, when she had accepted appeals from threatened states, had been to take as much (or as little) action as was necessary to make the hostile power drop its threats. So also in the present case. The intention was to fight only until Hiero and the Carthaginians recognized that the Mamertines were in Rome's protection and that Rome would take all necessary steps to make that protection effective.

In accordance with this limited objective Appius left Rome in summer 264. On arriving at Rhegium he learned that the Mamertines had themselves already expelled their Carthaginian garrison[5]— its commander was subsequently crucified by the Carthaginians for his incompetence—and were now besieged by a joint army of Syracusans and Carthaginians. The alliance between Syracuse and Carthage was recent, but its purpose is self-evident: it was in the long-term interests of neither of them that the unprincipled Mamertines should retain Messana and continue their plundering. Moreover, the danger they posed will doubtless have been further emphasized when it became known that the Mamertines preferred Roman help to Carthaginian. Polybius says that Hiero used his alliance with Carthage to try to drive out the Mamertines from Sicily: we may add that he must have hoped to do this before their prospective Roman help materialized. In this he failed. Appius began negotiations as soon as he arrived at Rhegium—though his communication was probably more like an ultimatum than a negotiating position. Perhaps not surprisingly no point of agreement emerged. Appius then formally declared war, as he himself clearly wanted to do and as he had been authorized by the *comitia centuriata*. He immediately crossed with his army to Messana, where he engaged the Syracusans and Carthaginians in separate encounters and relieved the pressure on Messana.[6]

Subsequently, when it became clear that Appius Claudius' crossing to Messana was the active origin of the massive hostility between Rome and Carthage, which lasted in some form for almost 120 years, some people on each side attempted to justify their own country's conduct by blaming the other for beginning the war. The Carthaginian effort seems to have been more formal, perhaps even more effective (since their task was, of course, rather easier). The Sicilian Greek Philinus, a native of Agrigentum, wrote a monograph on the First Punic War—which has not survived—which Polybius used (though he criticizes Philinus for being a Carthaginian partisan).[7] Philinus' Carthaginian sympathies led him to record an almost certainly fictitious treaty between Rome and Carthage, according to which, he claimed, the Romans agreed to keep out of Sicily and the Carthaginians out of Italy, and which the Romans therefore broke when they crossed to Sicily. In Philinus' version the Romans were treaty-breakers and were thus in the wrong; and the Carthaginians were justified in fighting to defend not only themselves but the sanctity of their international treaties. Law, Philinus argued, was on Carthage's side.[8]

Polybius could discover no trace of this treaty in the Roman archives, where he found the full texts of the other treaties with Carthage; and he concludes that it is apocryphal. His disbelief is almost certainly justified, and it can be supported by other considerations. It is very difficult to see when such a treaty could have been made, for none of the existing treaties explicitly excludes Rome from Sicily, neither do they exclude Carthage from Italy. And even if it was a secret unpublished clause to one of them, there is no place for it earlier than the treaty against Pyrrhus; and it cannot have been in that, since it explicitly envisaged the possibility of Rome's intervening in Sicily against Pyrrhus, and Carthage in Italy.[9] Philinus' treaty therefore probably represents Carthaginian wishful thinking. The purpose of the invention will no doubt have been to provide propaganda—perhaps in the battle for the 'hearts and minds' of the Sicilian Greeks—against the Roman intervention. If so, it is easy to understand how Philinus, himself a pro-Carthaginian Sicilian Greek, was prepared to swallow the propaganda and indeed, if we may believe Polybius, to make the treaty one of the most important features of his anti-Roman polemic.

Some Romans also seem to have tried to obscure the real issue and to find legalistic excuses for Rome's action. A later tradition apparently interpreted Philinus' false treaty in Rome's favour. In 272, while Rome was besieging Tarentum, a Carthaginian fleet had appeared off the harbour.[10] The simplest interpretation of the incident is that the Carthaginians were acting in accordance with their treaty against Pyrrhus (which allowed them to interfere in Italy), and that the commander of the fleet was seeing whether the Romans wanted his help. Later Romans, however, retorted that the presence of this fleet at Tarentum was a clear breach of Philinus' treaty, and hence that Carthage was to blame for the war. The Roman historian Livy, writing some 250 years after the event, even invented a speech for one of the Carthaginians at the outbreak of the Second Punic War in 218, which attributed the first war to the appearance of this fleet at Tarentum![11]

Such was the propaganda. The facts, as we have seen, were much simpler. An ambitious consul, exploiting the People's desire for booty, unscrupulously underestimated the risk of war with Carthage which was inherent in putting into practice in Sicily the Roman technique, by now well-tried in Italy, of accepting into her protection appellants whose interests seemed to coincide with Rome's. Neither Appius Claudius nor the Roman People realized the enormous cost of their decision.

II Escalation

The original purpose of the war was to protect the Mamertines, to gain booty, and to win strategic advantage. But although Appius Claudius' eagerness was one of the causes of the war, his military success did not match the ambitiousness of his innovation; and his year as consul ended without his winning a triumph, the coveted civic celebration of military success. His successors improved on Appius' performance. Manius Valerius Maximus was a member of a family traditionally hostile to the Claudii—indeed, he may have been elected through reaction against Appius Claudius' mediocre achievement. He and Manius Otacilius Crassus, the consuls of 263, were duly sent out to Sicily with a full regular levy of four legions (with contingents from Rome's Italian allies, about 40,000 men in all). Valerius was particularly successful. He fought battles both against Hiero and against the Carthaginians, and induced Hiero to make peace after many Sicilian cities, impressed by Roman power, had chosen to join Rome. So far so good. It must have already seemed that Rome's technique of accepting the Mamertines' appeal was succeeding, just as similar operations in Italy had succeeded. Half the war, it must have seemed when Hiero made peace, was over. On his return to Rome Valerius celebrated a well-deserved triumph over Hiero and the Carthaginians, and added 'Messalla' (derived from Messana) to his name.*

---

* Just as Field-Marshal Montgomery added 'of Alamein' to his name.

Hopes must then have been high that the Carthaginians might equally easily be induced to sue for peace; and the Romans' first intention for 262 was to send only two legions to Sicily. But Carthage had scarcely begun serious preparations for the war when Hiero made peace. The main reason for this dilatoriness was that Carthage had only a comparatively small citizen population. She therefore recruited her armies largely from her subjects in the African hinterland; and if she needed extra troops she employed mercenaries.[12] The chief result of this military system was that Carthage was habitually slow to put large armies into the field. Thus it was not until Hiero had already capitulated that Carthage even began to raise extra mercenaries. At the same time she began to establish a military base in southern Sicily, at Agrigentum, the home of Philinus the historian.[13] The main reason for Carthage's determination, when Hiero had already made peace, was that Carthage's interest in Sicily was entirely different from Hiero's. Hiero acknowledged Rome's right to interfere in Sicily because he realized that in the last resort he was too weak to resist, and because the war would be fought in and would do severe damage to the territory where he and his people lived. Carthage's interest in Sicily, however, was wholly commercial. Any activity which threatened the long-term commercial equilibrium in Sicily automatically threatened Carthage's prosperity, on which her power—in the last resort, even her existence—depended. Thus while Hiero could acquiesce in Rome's presence because he lived in Sicily, Carthage, though based in Africa, could not afford to allow the possibility of Roman expansion in Sicily. In the Carthaginian view, Rome's occupation of Messana was a strong indication that political conditions in Sicily might easily develop in the same way as they had in Italy. It was a development which Carthage's commercial interests dictated should be strangled at birth.

When news of Carthage's continuing preparations for war arrived at Rome, it ensured that both consuls of 262 once again led the full Roman levy of four legions into Sicily.[14] Their obvious tactical objective was now Agrigentum, the new Carthaginian base, and their year was spent in besieging the city. Eventually Agrigentum fell. It was destroyed with characteristic Roman brutality, but not before the Carthaginian defenders (led by the Hannibal who had first garrisoned Messana) had escaped.[15] The fall of Agrigentum was nevertheless a major event. It forcefully showed the Carthaginians the extent of Rome's commitment to the Mamertines, and it is difficult to blame Polybius for seeing in it one of the crucial events which shaped the future course of the war. But while it was certainly important tactically, the Roman Senate perhaps did not think it was as vital strategically as Polybius does, for neither of the consuls who conducted the siege won a triumph.[16]

Polybius regards Rome's success at Agrigentum as a turning point in Roman policy: hereafter, he says, the Romans no longer limited their aims to protecting the Mamertines, but now hoped to drive the Carthaginians from Sicily. And since Carthage controlled the seas and prevented Rome from exerting pressure on the coastal cities, the Senate's changed overall purpose (he claims) was responsible for their first building a fleet which could challenge the Carthaginian navy.[17] Polybius' view, however, seems too schematic: it is almost certainly his own interpretation and does not go back to any contemporary source which might have known the Senate's real considerations. As the Senate does not seem to have regarded the capture of Agrigentum as being in itself worthy of a triumph, we must therefore find a different reason for Rome's building a navy: for Polybius is certainly right to regard this as a major development.

A direct response to a threat from the Carthaginian navy would be a much more likely reason for Rome's building a navy of her own; and there is fortunately some evidence that such a threat not only existed in 262 but that it also showed itself, quite independently of events at Agrigentum. We know from sources other than Polybius that Carthage's forces in Sardinia were reinforced, even before Rome attacked Agrigentum, and that later in the year the Carthaginian fleet under Hannibal and Hamilcar ravaged the Italian coast.[18] This was obviously part of Carthage's response to Rome's initial intervention in Sicily; but since Rome was by now fully committed to the struggle in Sicily, she could now only react to this new development by meeting it in kind: by challenging Carthage's fleet on its own element. Thus another stage in the escalation of the war was reached. Once Rome was committed to a full-scale naval policy, to a direct confrontation with Carthage at sea—where Carthage had for generations claimed pre-eminence over all other powers in the western Mediterranean—Carthage was in turn committed to fighting to the end, if necessary. If Carthage was prepared to resist violently the apparent threat to her commercial livelihood from Roman intervention in Sicily, she could certainly not afford to ignore the clear and direct challenge to her naval supremacy which Rome's building a navy must have seemed to imply.

After this decision events seem to have gathered their own momentum; and it is difficult to avoid Polybius' conclusion that Rome's aims had now indeed become more comprehensive, that they were no longer simply to protect the Mamertines and to obtain limited Roman advantage from that. The impending confrontation with Carthage, both on land and on sea, clearly would end only with the capitulation of one of the antagonists. A Carthaginian victory would certainly require Rome's evacuation of Sicily; a Roman victory, now that the Senate had realized the implicit threat to Italy if the island were firmly in the hands of a hostile naval power, could not require less from Carthage.

III The War for Sicily

Rome had never previously possessed a fleet. From 311 she had maintained a squadron of about twenty small ships; but by 264 this was so feeble, if it still functioned at all, that when Appius Claudius first crossed to Messana he had needed to requisition ships from local Greek cities—Tarentum, Locri, Velia and Naples—which were Roman 'naval allies' (*socii navales*).[19] During Appius' crossing a Carthaginian quinquereme was captured, a large heavy warship rowed by some 300 men, five to each oar. Thus when the consuls of 260, Gnaeus Cornelius Scipio Asina and Gaius Duilius, were instructed to build ships to combat Carthage's fleet, their naval architects showed commonsense in first studying this quinquereme, for the new Roman ships would obviously have to fight against ships of the same kind. Later Roman legend (in this case recorded and accepted by Polybius) liked to emphasize Rome's naval inexperience, and turned this admirably practical approach into a straight imitation of the Carthaginian ship by the Roman land-lubbers, since (the legend alleged) they had otherwise no idea of how to build ships. It then went on to glorify their subsequent success against the expert Carthaginians.[20]

In fact Rome's new ships were almost certainly built and mostly manned by her 'naval allies', the Greek cities who had a long seafaring tradition but little, if any, experience of quinqueremes; their normal warship was the trireme, a much lighter ship which required a totally different technique. But since Rome's new navy included only twenty triremes, the crews for the quinqueremes needed preliminary training on land. One new feature of the Roman ships, the invention of which was doubtless made possible by having the captured Carthaginian ship to test it on, was the boarding-bridge known as the 'raven' (*corvus*). This consisted of a long heavy board mounted upright in the bows which was fitted with an iron spike on the underside towards the upper end—this was the 'beak' of the 'raven' which perhaps gave the device its name. At close quarters the board was intended to be dropped on to the enemy's deck, the spike would fasten it into position, and marines could then use it as a bridge for boarding.[21]

The new fleet sailed immediately towards Sicily. Scipio, living up to his name 'Asina' ('the Ass'), incompetently managed to get himself and seventeen of his new ships captured almost at once; but soon afterwards Duilius met a Carthaginian fleet under the command of Hannibal (who had led the Carthaginians at Agrigentum)[22] at Mylae, on the north coast of Sicily. The Roman 'ravens' made carrion of the Carthaginian fleet, and Carthage lost fifty of her 130 ships. Duilius' victory was Rome's first at sea. Not surprisingly, it was heavily celebrated and long remembered: in addition to his triumph (in which Duilius was also the first Roman to lead free-born Carthaginians) he was rewarded with a column in the forum decorated with the beaks of Carthaginian ships.[23]

Duilius' victory did not, of course, mean that the war was over: paradoxically, perhaps, it rather ensured that it would continue. Had Rome been seriously defeated and lost a large number of ships, the Senate might conceivably have cut its losses and given up the naval policy as an experiment which had failed. If this had happened, a compromise settlement in Sicily might have been possible, as long as Carthage was willing. Mylae however ruled this out. Carthage could not tamely acquiesce in Rome's powerful naval challenge. And the very next year the danger from Rome's navy became even clearer; for one of the consuls, Lucius Cornelius Scipio, won a triumph over Carthage for victories in Sardinia and Corsica, where Carthage had previously been unchallenged. Events of 258 followed the same pattern: another triumph for fighting in Sardinia was awarded, this time to Gaius Sulpicius Paterculus.[24] By the end of 258 therefore the Carthaginians must have thought that Roman strategy was aimed not merely at conquering Sicily but at massively weakening Carthage's influence—and particularly her naval power —wherever it might be found in the proximity of Italy.

This impression was fostered by the comparative stalemate on land in Sicily during 259 and 258, and by the naval triumph which

Gaius Atilius Regulus won for yet another Roman naval victory in 257 at Cape Tyndaris, not far from Mylae.[25] Not surprisingly these naval successes stimulated the Senate to build more ships; the Carthaginians, despite their long naval experience, obviously could not afford to be seriously outnumbered, and they also joined the arms race. The two enlarged fleets (probably 230 Roman and between 200 and 250 Carthaginian ships) then engaged at Ecnomus, off the south coast of Sicily. The Romans, commanded by their consuls Marcus Atilius Regulus (probably a brother of the consul of 257) and Lucius Manlius Vulso, sank more than thirty and captured sixty-four Carthaginian ships for the comparatively small loss of only twenty-four Roman ships.[26]

Rome's chief and most obvious gain from this unexpected naval superiority was much freer mobility. And just as Carthage, before Rome possessed a fleet, had used naval superiority to ravage the coasts of Italy, so now Regulus and Manlius began a new phase of the war by crossing to Africa to attack Carthage's home territory. Regulus landed with forty ships, 15,000 infantry and 500 cavalry, while Manlius returned to Rome to celebrate a triumph for their victory at Ecnomus. Regulus had some initial success. The Romans did severe damage to property, captured Tunis, and defeated such forces as were sent against them; and the Carthaginians then offered to begin negotiations. Unfortunately Polybius does not give us the terms which Regulus proposed and which Carthage rejected (though he tantalisingly blames Regulus for their severity). But they must have included a demand that Carthage evacuate Sicily—a demand which Regulus could hardly expect to be acceptable at this stage. Indeed, it is difficult to see how any lasting peace could have been achieved in the prevailing conditions, and Polybius' condemnation of Regulus' foolish severity is perhaps merely a reflection of Philinus' pro-Carthaginian point of view.[27]

But however this may be, it soon became clear that Regulus had lost the initiative by negotiating; and Carthage's situation rapidly improved. A competent Spartan mercenary captain, Xanthippus, soon led them to a major victory, in which Regulus himself was taken prisoner and all but 2,000 of his troops were lost, most of them victims of Carthage's war elephants. Regulus subsequently died in captivity. Polybius knows nothing of the incident which later Roman legend made famous, that after his capture Regulus travelled to Rome under oath to return, in order to negotiate with the Senate about peace and the freeing of prisoners, that he advised against acceptance, honourably kept his oath and returned to a martyr's death by torture in captivity.[28] Polybius' silence about this story—though he does discuss Regulus' change of fortune—strongly suggests that it is false; and a reasonable explanation of its growth can be found. For a well-attested account has Regulus' widow brutally torturing two Carthaginian captives, one of whom died. Since later versions of this torture story connect it with Regulus' alleged mission, it seems possible that Regulus' noble action was invented by interested parties in order to excuse his widow's disreputable treatment of the Carthaginian prisoners.[29]

The few survivors from Regulus' débâcle were evacuated the following year. The Roman relief fleet easily beat off Carthaginian opposition; but as it returned to Sicily, 284 of its 364 ships were wrecked in a storm near Camarina, in western Sicily. Rome was discouraged but not despairing, and a crash ship-building programme quickly produced another 220 ships, which at once sailed to Sicily under the consuls of 254—a pair with sufficient experience to meet the sudden crisis in Rome's affairs, Gnaeus Cornelius Scipio Asina (consul in 260) and another of the prominent Atilii, Aulus Atilius Caiatanus (consul in 258). They soon managed to capture Panormus, the economic capital of Carthaginian Sicily, an achievement for which Scipio celebrated a triumph. This success was indeed some recompense for Rome's massive losses in the two previous years; but it was balanced out in 253 by yet another crippling disaster by storm, which this time sank more than 150 Roman ships.[30]

Encouraged by these debilitating Roman losses Carthage sent a new commander, Hasdrubal, son of Hanno, to Sicily with 140 war elephants, which the Carthaginians had used so successfully against Regulus in Africa. For the present Rome conserved her resources and concentrated on her land forces. But a battle with Hasdrubal meant facing his elephants, and Regulus' disastrous experience made the Roman commanders timid. The result was that until 250 no engagement took place. Roman inactivity drove Hasdrubal to take the initiative; and about June 250 he attacked the consul Lucius Caecilius Metellus at Panormus. The engagement produced a Roman victory which became famous, for Hasdrubal's dreaded elephants were made harmless by Metellus' skilful refusal to fight a formal pitched battle, in which the elephants' sheer weight would destroy his troops. Attacked from the safety of the city fortifications by missiles and light troops, the elephants were never allowed to reach close quarters, and all which were not killed—something over 100—were captured; these were laboriously taken to Rome where they were bloodily slaughtered in the circus. Henceforth coins issued by the Caecilii Metelli often commemorate this success by showing elephants.[31]

Also in 250 the experienced naval men—another of the Atilii, Gaius Atilius Regulus (consul in 257), and Lucius Manlius Vulso (consul in 256)—began a new phase of the naval war with their re-election to the consulship; and news of Metellus' success encouraged the Senate to persist. The new consuls optimistically began to besiege the chief remaining Carthaginian stronghold in Sicily, the naval base of Lilybaeum. But this was more easily begun than ended, for Lilybaeum was both naturally strong and comparatively easily reinforced. The slow siege accordingly continued into the next year, when Publius Claudius Pulcher was consul. Pulcher was probably the son of the irresponsibly ambitious Appius Claudius who in 264 had started the war by persuading the People to accept the Mamertines' surrender; and when he arrived in Sicily he determined to be active at whatever cost—clearly a family characteristic—and attacked neighbouring Drepana. A rapid series of blunders resulted in his losing ninety-three ships and their crews, for which he was personally blamed on his return to Rome and heavily fined. His colleague, Lucius Junius Pullus, proved equally incompetent with a second fleet, and later in the year was outmanoeuvred by the Carthaginian admiral Carthalo and lost all his transports and 105 warships in a storm.[32] It was to be six years before Rome tried again to compete at sea.

Once again Rome's apparent superiority had been suddenly swept away; and as in 253, the Carthaginians responded to Rome's sudden weakness by sending a new commander to Sicily. This time it was Hamilcar Barca, a representative of one of the most famous and prominent Carthaginian families. In 247 Hamilcar ravaged the coast of southern Italy, following up similar raids by Carthalo, before occupying the coastal strongpoint of Heircte near Panormus. Fighting continued inconclusively around Heircte until 245, when Hamilcar cut off a Roman garrison which occupied the nearby hill of Eryx. The stalemate was clearly becoming expensive for Rome; and Hamilcar's success in producing it alarmed the Roman Senate. Accordingly, during winter 243/2 they ended their six years of naval inactivity and decided to build another fleet.[33]

200 quinqueremes were constructed on a new pattern, again

based on a Carthaginian original of a rather superior type which had been captured during the siege of Lilybaeum. Gaius Lutatius Catulus, consul in 242, commanded the new fleet. He soon engaged the Carthaginian admiral Hanno near the Aegates Islands, off Lilybaeum, on March 10, 241 (by the defective Roman calendar), and routed Hanno. Fifty Carthaginian ships were sunk, seventy more captured along with their crews. The battle, as it turned out, was decisive for the whole war, and Hamilcar, who was still in Sicily, was instructed to begin negotiations for peace.[34] For although Hamilcar could probably have prolonged the stalemate on land in Sicily almost indefinitely, Carthage now saw little prospect of gain from that. Sicily had been worth fighting for only for as long as it continued to offer commercial prospects. The war prevented this, and any foreseeable settlement would do the same. It was sound commercial commonsense which at last prevailed at Carthage, which persuaded her senators to cut their losses in Sicily and to recognize the battle of the Aegates Islands as decisive.

Given the circumstances, the final terms of the treaty which Hamilcar and Lutatius negotiated were fairly predictable: Carthage must evacuate Sicily and the islands lying between Sicily and Italy (the Aegates and Lipari islands); the allies of both states were to be free from attack by the other state; neither state might levy tribute, construct public installations, collect mercenaries or form alliances with allies of the other on territories subject to the other; Carthage must pay 2,200 talents over ten years, of which 1,000 were to be paid at once; Carthage must give up all Roman prisoners of war without ransom.[35]

IV The Effect of the War

So the war ended. Polybius is not wholly accurate when he says that it was the longest war known up to his time—the Peloponnesian War between Athens and Sparta in the fifth century B.C. was longer —but the facts support his view that it was the fiercest and the most expensive. The direct cost to the combatants in men and materials for the naval war alone was huge. Rome lost something like 600 ships, Carthage around 500 (in so far as these figures can be reliably calculated from inadequate data): in terms of manpower, this means that Rome lost something like 250,000 men and Carthage 210,000. And while many of these, on both sides, will no doubt have been taken prisoner and later returned home, we must remember that these figures take no account at all of losses on land, for which no remotely reliable calculation can be made.[36]

The protagonists did not, of course, bear all these losses themselves. Carthage traditionally relied on her subjects and on mercenaries to man her forces; Rome, through her network of carefully constructed alliances throughout Italy, could draw troops from virtually the whole population of Italy; and her Italian allies will inevitably have borne the brunt of the losses. Nevertheless, it is reasonable to assume that the comparative lethargy of the last few years of the war must have resulted largely from the inability of either side to raise more than a normal complement of troops.

The destruction and disruption in Sicily must also have been substantial. Although we have no reason to believe that this troubled the combatants very much while the war was in progress, it may in the end have been an important factor in persuading Carthage to admit defeat. For even if the war continued and even if Carthage eventually won—which seemed very unlikely—and retained her traditional influence in Sicily, the Sicily which she would win might be much less prosperous than before, and therefore much less valuable commercially. And commercial value was what chiefly mattered to Carthage in Sicily. Thus from her point of view, the longer the war continued, the less did Sicily become worth fighting for. Rome's view of Sicily, however, was quite different. By now it was purely strategic. The early years of the war had shown that she must control the island to prevent Carthage (or any other power in the future) from threatening Italy from it. From Rome's point of view, therefore, it mattered little if the island's prosperity declined as a result of the war: for Rome, Sicily would have remained valuable even if the fighting had reduced it to an unpopulated desert.

Rome's non-commercial attitude was evident in the way she treated Sicily after the war. There is no sign of any attempt to exploit systematically the island's resources. Indeed, rather the opposite. Rome had fought the war in the last resort for strategic reasons, however faulty and blundering in their initial conception. It should not therefore be surprising to find that the only Roman official to serve regularly in the island seems to have been responsible for arranging the contributions of the Sicilian communities to the Roman fleet. This, at least, is suggested by his title, 'naval quaestor' (*quaestor classicus*), and by his place of residence, Lilybaeum, the chief Carthaginian naval base in Sicily; and we have no further information about his duties beyond his title.[37]

Although again the facts are not altogether clear for this early period, Rome probably continued to collect the tithe which Carthage had levied: since the Sicilians were used to paying, the pragmatic Romans would see little point in changing the system, which would cover their administrative costs. They certainly collected the tithe later, and probably did so from the beginning. This is also suggested by the appearance of an entirely new status for some privileged Sicilian communities, that of the 'free state' (*civitas libera*), which had played no part in the Roman system of control within Italy.[38] At a later time when Sicily was more formally and systematically organized, these 'free states' were 'free' chiefly in not having to pay the tithe. Since their 'free' status almost certainly originated in the settlement of 241, its existence obviously implies that other Sicilian communities were not free in this sense, and therefore that the tithe was generally collected except from these few exempt communities.

The status of the 'free state' was new. It was unknown in Italy, where Rome's usual procedure in the case of newly acquired communities, for which no form of citizenship seemed applicable or desirable, was to sign a formal treaty of alliance (*foedus*).[39] At first in Sicily also this established practice was followed, and the formal alliance was the usual form of friendly relationship: such a treaty regulated Rome's relations with the Mamertines; and a treaty which formally recognized the Syracusans as friends and allies of Rome was concluded with Hiero.[40] But the application of this diplomatic technique seems to have stopped there; for other Sicilian cities which subsequently joined Rome voluntarily were not given treaties, but were simply declared 'free' (*liberae*). Unfortunately most of our evidence about the organization of Sicily comes from Cicero, who wrote more than 150 years after this settlement, during which time there were two major upheavals which altered some of the original arrangements. But five such cities still had the privilege of being 'free and tax-free' (*civitates liberae et immunes*)—their later formal title—in Cicero's day, a fact which suggests that there may originally have been more of them before the revolt during the Second Punic War.

Freedom without a treaty to guarantee it or to define mutual obligations was a new concept for Rome; and its invention no doubt reflects the Senate's consciousness that it was now dealing with a new, overseas, problem to which Italian solutions might not be applicable (or desirable). The 'free states' were clearly privileged over the mass of the Sicilians in being free from the tithe (and from any other obligation which a treaty might have imposed), and this will probably have been because they joined Rome voluntarily. But the new status and the 'freedom' which it conferred did not signify that Rome intended to forego all her claims to influence in these privileged communities. Far from it. She was certainly foregoing regular tribute and the formal legal obligations of a treaty. But the moral obligations to which she felt herself entitled from the beneficiaries of her gift of freedom might, in practice, prove just as useful a means of exerting influence.

In private relationships the Romans had long operated the practice of *clientela*. The powerful patron gave protection and help (in general terms, called 'good works', *beneficia*) to the client, who in return was expected to perform such 'duties' (*officia*) as his patron required. These obligations were not legally enforceable contractual obligations; nor, since both client and patron were equally free men, were they in any way similar to the duties of a slave to his owner. They were moral obligations, built on custom and reinforced by social pressures. And it was this characteristic feature of Roman social life and internal politics which found its first full expression in foreign policy with the formation of the Sicilian 'free states'. For with these states there were no treaties, no formal lists of obligations to be enforced by the sanctity of law. The client was a free man: the client state was a free state, and bound to Rome as its patron by moral obligations—and *only* by moral obligations—in the same way as the client was morally bound to his patron in Roman social and political life. It was in Sicily that the concept of *clientela* was first fully exploited in Roman foreign policy. It was not so long before it became Rome's basic means of controlling the greater part of the Mediterranean coastlands.

CHAPTER III
BETWEEN THE WARS

I Sardinia

THE First Punic War both demonstrated to Rome the strategic value of Sicily and the associated small islands and placed them in Roman control. Rome had always been suspicious of strong neighbours, and her progress within Italy had been largely stimulated by this motive. However, until Carthage's violent reaction to Rome's championing the Mamertines—emphasized especially by the attacks on Italy in 262—Rome had not been much aware of danger from her neighbours outside the Italian mainland, however physically close they might be. It was Carthage's misfortune to have heightened this awareness; and Carthage was the first to suffer from it.

Thereafter Rome fought for Sicily, as we have seen, basically for strategic, not for commercial or economic, reasons. In 238 Sardinia fell to the same strategic bogey. Sardinia, like parts of Sicily, had for generations been under Carthaginian influence. By the time of the First Punic War Carthage treated the island as a Carthaginian possession, and she held it with a standing garrison of mercenaries. Sardinia's importance to Carthage is illustrated by the fact that one of the first things Carthage did when war broke out in Sicily in 264 was to reinforce her garrison in Sardinia. Sardinia, as a result, became the scene of some of Rome's earliest naval activities; but although triumphs were won there, Rome's only longstanding success in the area was her capture of Aleria in Corsica. This was apparently not a Carthaginian possession, but it was a useful base from which to attack Sardinia.[1] Despite Rome's efforts, Carthage managed to keep control of Sardinia, and the island was not mentioned in Lutatius' peace treaty in 241. It had not been prominent in the recent fighting; and if the Romans thought about it at all, they were certainly not prepared to risk pressing Carthage to continue the war by insisting on its being ceded.

Sardinia became prominent again over the next three years. In her peace treaty with Rome Carthage had agreed to evacuate Sicily. This was a large operation, since the whole Carthaginian army had to be transported to Africa; and it was badly mismanaged. Arrears due to the mercenaries were foolishly not paid as soon as the troops landed at Carthage; and as time passed the unpaid mercenaries became mutinous. Carthage soon had a full-scale war on her hands against them. The details of this war do not concern us, but it is important to notice that it lasted for three years and four months, until the early summer of 237, and that the city of Carthage and all Carthaginian possessions in Africa were in the gravest danger for the whole of that time. The war with the unpaid mercenaries might easily have entirely destroyed Carthage.[2]

It is against this background that we must look at the affair of Sardinia. During the war in Africa, perhaps in 239, the Carthaginian mercenary garrison in Sardinia emulated the mercenaries in Africa and mutinied against their Carthaginian commander Bostar. Bostar and his fellow Carthaginian officers were soon killed. Reinforcements sent from Carthage joined the insurgents as soon as they arrived, and the enlarged rebel force purged the island of Carthaginians. Carthage, fighting for her existence in Africa, could do no more in Sardinia at present. The native Sardinians now took their chance. The mercenaries had helpfully killed off the Carthaginians, but were likely to prove dangerous masters. The Sardinians therefore launched a rebellion of their own and succeeded in expelling most of the mercenaries, who took refuge in Italy.[3]

This immediately involved Rome. So far she had shown no wish to take advantage of Carthage's internal difficulties: they did not affect Sicily and therefore did not concern Rome. The Senate could therefore afford to be sympathetic. A firm Roman tradition has it that the Carthaginians were so hard-pressed that the Romans relaxed the terms of Lutatius' treaty—for this occasion only—and allowed supplies and mercenaries to be gathered in Italy and Sicily; they even sent envoys to try to negotiate peace in Africa.[4] This tradition is possible, though unlikely. Polybius does not mention these details, presumably because he thought them false. He does say, however—and this is more reasonable—that the Romans turned down an early request from the mutineer mercenaries in Sardinia for an alliance;[5] and that when relations between Carthage and Rome were threatened with a breach by the activities of Italian blockade-runners ferrying supplies to the insurgents in Africa, Rome unexpectedly recovered the 500 Italians whom Carthage had captured, and in return restored the rest of the Carthaginians who were still prisoners after the war in Sicily—the Roman tradition, perhaps exaggerated, said there were 2,743 of them.[6] There can thus be no doubt that during the greater part of Carthage's war with the mercenaries Rome stuck firmly to the terms of Lutatius' treaty and did not provoke Carthage. Further evidence is that when Carthage's neighbour Utica offered to surrender to Rome, the Senate scrupulously refused, for Rome had no interest in breaking the treaty to gain useless territory in Africa.[7] Rome, as we have seen, only accepted appeals from states whose interests seemed to coincide with hers.

A tempting opportunity, however, was not far away. While the Sardinian mutineers were still in the island, their appeal to Rome was turned down: had it been accepted it would, of course, have involved Rome in a breach of the clause of Lutatius' treaty concerning the allies of either side—the Carthaginians would be bound to take the view that the mercenaries and the Sardinians, even in insurrection, were still Carthage's 'allies'. By the time the Sardinians had expelled the mercenaries and the mercenaries had taken refuge in Italy, Carthage had practically ended the war in Africa. The mercenaries expelled from Sardinia by the Sardinians, as a last hope, offered unconditional surrender (*deditio*) to Rome, since they were, after all, seeking refuge from Carthage in Roman-controlled territory. Rome need not have accepted their offer; nor, having accepted it, need she have acted to help the mercenaries. But she did accept; and she did act, and at once prepared an expedition to Sardinia, in unprovoked breach of the peace treaty of 241.

It is not easy to see why the Senate so quickly changed its mind, and now chose to break Lutatius' treaty, since none of the ancient sources provides any information about the Senate's discussions. To Polybius—as to us—it was a clear case of unprovoked aggression, imperialism of the most blatant sort, which did not hesitate to break a treaty to gain its ends; but Polybius does not say *why* Rome acted so. Unfortunately we are very badly informed about the internal politics of Rome at this time—we do not even know for certain whether the expedition to Sardinia was conducted by a consul of 238 or of 237.[8] The fact which does stand out, however, is that at last Rome had become actively aware of the possible strategic importance of Sardinia. No doubt this had been emphasized by the fact that the Sardinian mutineers, when expelled, had immediately come to Italy without difficulty; and the Senate determined that if annexation might eventually prove desirable, it was better done now when an arguable pretext was presented by the offer of surrender by the mercenaries, and when—the vital point—Carthage was still enfeebled as a result of the war in Africa.

Carthage of course objected. The Sardinians were Carthaginian allies and therefore it was her right, acknowledged by the treaty of Lutatius, to restore them to their loyalty. She prepared accordingly and made representations at Rome. As if it were not disreputable enough for Rome to have broken the treaty and to have interfered in Sardinia in the first place—the specious argument was, no doubt, that Carthage had already lost Sardinia—the Senate chose to interpret Cathage's preparations for intervention in Sardinia as a hostile act against Rome. The Senate and the *comitia centuriata* approved a conditional declaration of war, an ultimatum, which senatorial envoys took to Carthage. When faced with the certainty of war with Rome if they persisted with their plans to recover Sardinia—a war which, in their present weakness, they could not hope to win—the Carthaginians bowed to the inevitable. The price of avoiding war was a rider which the Romans now added to the treaty of Lutatius, whereby Carthage agreed to abandon Sardinia and to pay a further 1,200 talents indemnity.[9] The Romans then set to work to gain control of both Sardinia and Corsica, tasks which occupied the next few years.[10]

Blatant imperialism of this kind was not Rome's custom. The reason for it was, no doubt, strategic. But for the first time (probably) strategic considerations had led to the breaking of a treaty; and the acceptance of the mercenaries' surrender was so poor an excuse for this, even though the technique, in different circumstances, was by now traditional, that it did not figure largely in the apologetic tradition of Roman history favoured by later Roman annalistic writers. We have noticed that a firm, though probably false, Roman tradition emphasized Rome's sympathy with and concession to Carthage during the mercenary war in Africa. The purpose of this emphasis in the earliest historiography seems to have been to underline by contrast Carthage's ingratitude in connection with the Italian 'merchants' whom Carthage captured in Africa during the war and, according to some accounts, killed. Sardinia was then surrendered when Rome threatened reprisals.[11] Polybius' version of the incident is almost certainly more reliable, though it obviously did not prevent the growth of the subsequent apologetic version: that the 'merchants' were in fact Italian blockade-runners serving the insurgent mercenaries. And he shows clearly by implication that it had nothing whatever to do with the Sardinian business.[12] Those Roman writers who, perhaps aware of Polybius' version, could not accept these conventional apologetics, preferred to record, wrongly, that Sardinia had been included (perhaps, by a convenient stretch of the imagination, as one of the 'islands between Sicily and Italy') in the treaty of Lutatius.[13]

Thanks to the survival of Polybius' book there can be no disguising the essential facts. Rome's seizure of Sardinia was a piece of unscrupulous opportunism by which the treaty of Lutatius was, on any reasonable interpretation, well and truly broken. Rome's technique of accepting surrender and then going to the help of the new distressed ally is no justification for this act of naked aggression contrary to the treaty of Lutatius. Roman apologists clearly found it difficult to explain in terms of a 'just war': we need not follow them in their distortions of the facts.

II Illyria

The seizure of Sardinia shows that by now Rome no longer allowed her ideal of fighting only 'just wars' to hinder her interests. The ideal had become elastic. This also emerges from the Senate's first experiment east of the Adriatic when Rome extended her sphere of influence to Illyria in 230. It was easy enough to intervene, easy enough, after her experience with Carthage, to conjure a threat which made intervention seem necessary. But once the Senate's conception of Rome's essential interests reached Illyria, Rome was gradually but inevitably dragged deeper and deeper into Balkan affairs. Just as intervention in Sicily was both a physical and psychological stepping-stone to empire in the west, so Illyria turned out to be the same kind of stepping-stone to empire in the east.

The Illyrian episode was of course, like the Sicilian, not in the first instance simply caused by Rome's wish to control any larger territory: indeed, for more than eighty years after her opening moves in the Balkans Rome showed herself extremely reluctant to undertake any formal responsibility for directly ruling the territories which progressively came under her influence. The Senate's real motive for intervening in Illyria was its by now habitual suspicion of strong neighbours. This may seem odd in the case of Illyria, for the real threat which Illyria could present to Rome seems, at this distance,

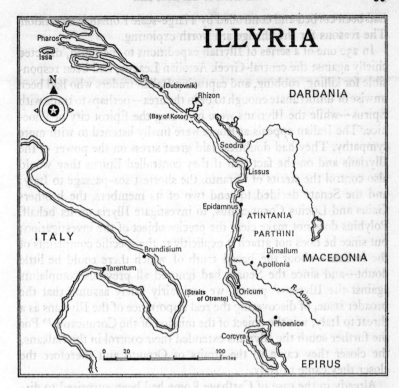

Pharos
Issa
N
(Dubrovnik)
Rhizon
(Bay of Kotor)
Scodra
DARDANIA
Lissus
Epidamnus
ATINTANIA
PARTHINI
ITALY
Brundisium
Dimallum
Apollonia
MACEDONIA
Tarentum
(Straits
of Otranto)
Oricum
R. Aous
Phoenice
Corcyra
0   20   100
miles
EPIRUS

ILLYRIA

to be minimal. By 230 the chief Illyrian tribe, the Ardiaei, controlled under its active king Agron most of the coastline of Dalmatia as far south as Corcyra—the coast of what is now Jugoslavia and Albania, southwards from near Split. The authority of the Ardiaei was based on their strong fleet—a necessity for any Dalmatian power, for until as recently as the 1960's much of that coast has been negotiable with ease only by boat.

Even with their strong fleet, however, the kings of the Ardiaei had great difficulty in controlling the large and intractable population of this immensely difficult country; and a rapidly developing tradition of piracy and coastal raiding was a characteristic which made the Illyrians well-known, but also feared and hated, by the Greeks.[14] All this, of course, affected Rome only slightly—only when Italian ships from communities allied with Rome brushed with the Illyrian pirates. Before 230 such incidents had been ignored. We do not know how regular they were, but in any case Rome had no inclination to become policeman of the Adriatic. Yet by 228 the Illyrians had been curbed and controlled by a large-scale Roman intervention. The reasons for the change are worth exploring.

In 230 one of a series of Illyrian expeditions to the south, directed chiefly against the central-Greek Aetolian League, had been responsible for killing, robbing, and capturing Italian traders who had been unwise or unfortunate enough to be in the area—perhaps to trade with Epirus—while the Illyrians were besieging the Epirot city of Phoenice. The Italian appeals at Rome were finally listened to with more sympathy. They had doubtless laid great stress on the power of the Illyrians and on the fact that if they controlled Epirus they would also control the straits of Otranto, the shortest sea-passage to Italy; and the Senate decided to send two of its members, the brothers Gaius and Lucius Coruncanius, to investigate Illyria on its behalf. Polybius does not make clear the precise object of the investigation; but since he does not attach it explicitly to the specific complaints of the Italians—about the broad truth of which there could be little doubt—and since the Senate had ignored all previous complaints against the Illyrians' piracy, we can fairly safely assume that the broader issue, of discovering the real importance of the Illyrians as a threat to Italy, was the object of the mission of the Coruncanii.[15] For the further south the Illyrians extended their control in the Balkans, the closer they came to the straits of Otranto and therefore the closer they came to Italy.

Already in the case of Carthage Rome had been surprised to discover the threat which a neighbouring naval power might present to her position in Italy. Was Illyria another Carthage? or might it become so? Was Illyria expanding southwards to secure the straits of Otranto so that she could threaten Italy? There is no good evidence that such a threat existed in fact or was likely to develop. But the important thing is what the Senate *thought* might happen; and at this time its view was based only on information from those Italian trading communities which were disturbed about the loss of their ships and their men, and which would no doubt exaggerate the threat and stimulate the Senate's suspicions in order to provoke it into taking action.

It is clear from the sequel that a preventive war was already being considered by the Senate—though no decision, even in principle, had yet been taken—when the Coruncanii set out on their investigation. King Agron, who had initiated the southward expansion of the Ardiaei, had recently died, leaving his widow Teuta as regent for his infant son Pinnes (by another wife, Triteuta). It was therefore

Teuta who received the Coruncanii. When they arrived, she was besieging the Greek island of Issa, the only Dalmatian island which had not yet submitted to the Illyrians.

Illyrian success and energy was on lavish display and seems to have confirmed the worst fears of the Roman ambassadors. Furthermore, they clearly did not like dealing with a woman, and their hostility to Teuta shows through even in Polybius' brief account[16] (which may go back, perhaps through Fabius Pictor, to the official report of the mission to the Senate). Teuta listened to the Roman case—Polybius, reflecting the prejudiced Roman viewpoint, says she listened 'arrogantly and insolently' (whatever that might entail!)—but her reply was conciliatory: she would ensure that Rome suffered no damage from official Illyrian action, though she could not undertake to curb the pirates who acted, by Illyrian tradition, in their private capacities (indeed, it may have been beyond her power to prevent this unofficial piracy, had she wished to).[17] There was room for negotiation; but the Coruncanii seem to have been determined to feel insulted. They had clearly already decided that Illyria was, or might soon become, a threat to Roman security; and the younger Coruncanius, in a virtual declaration of war—for which he had no authorization from the Senate—replied, in effect, that if Teuta was unwilling to control her pirate subjects, the Romans would force her to do so. The Coruncanii then left, and on their way home the younger brother, who had made the provocative speech to Teuta, was assassinated.

In the circumstances it was bound to be said at Rome, whatever the truth—which we cannot know—that Teuta had ordered the assassination; and this Roman version appears in Polybius and our other sources, flavoured with anti-feminist comments about the typical thoughtlessness of women.[18] In one sense the assassination was convenient for the Senate, for now it need look no further for an excuse for war: the insult must be avenged. Had it not occurred, the Senate would no doubt have claimed to be interfering on behalf of Rome's Italian allies. Later apologetic writers went even further and invented a surrender to Rome (*deditio*) by the beleaguered island of Issa so that they could depict Rome's intervention as being in the traditional Roman pattern, a 'just war' on behalf of her threatened ally.[19] But Polybius knows nothing of this and his silence condemns it as an invention. It seems clear however—whatever was *said* in justification—that the report of the Coruncanii, had the assassination not taken place, would still have recommended Roman action.

That the surviving Coruncanius grossly overstated the power and potential of Illyria and made the Senate act—not, indeed, for the first time—through a misapprehension, is further clarified by the great strength of the expedition which was sent out: both consuls participated, commanding in all some 200 ships, 20,000 troops and 200 cavalry.[20] It was saturation coverage; and it has sometimes been thought that the size of the force indicates that fear of Macedon, Illyria's eastern neighbour, was the real reason for the Senate's massive deployment in Illyria. But Macedon was particularly weak at this time; and in any case, no ancient source, not even a later Roman apologist, even hints at this motive. Macedon clearly played no part in the Senate's thinking: Rome's actions suggest that the Coruncanii and the Senate, following their report, had quite simply overestimated the power of Illyria.[21]

Teuta was far from losing her head. Intelligently anticipating the Roman expedition, she tried to secure the coastal fortresses which had so far eluded the Illyrians, Epidamnus and Apollonia, and the island of Corcyra. Had she succeeded in taking these important harbour towns, as she nearly did, the Romans might have found their military operations made extremely difficult on that dangerously rugged coast without a firm base for their fleet; and their large numbers might even have been a disadvantage. Teuta duly captured Corcyra in spring 229 before the Roman fleet arrived under the consul Gnaeus Fulvius Centumalus; but she was betrayed by a trusted subordinate, Demetrius of Pharos, whom she had made governor of the captured island. Almost as soon as Fulvius arrived Demetrius contacted him. His chief motive seems to have been personal ambition to replace Teuta as guardian of the infant king Pinnes; and to eject the highly competent queen-regent he needed outside help. Demetrius and the Corcyreans offered unconditional surrender (*deditio*), which Fulvius was glad to accept; and with his acceptance Rome's first responsibility of protection across the Adriatic was contracted.[22]

With Demetrius' help and advice the war was soon over. At Apollonia, where the other consul, Lucius Postumius Albinus, joined Fulvius with the Roman army, the inhabitants at once surrendered themselves into Roman protection; similar surrenders occurred at Epidamnus and at Issa; and envoys from the powerful inland tribes, the Parthini and the Atintanes, also had their offers of surrender accepted. By the end of 229 it was clear that although Teuta had not yet formally capitulated this was merely a matter of time.

Fulvius therefore returned to Italy with most of the Roman troops, and after some delay he celebrated a triumph on June 21, 228.[23]

Postumius stayed in the Balkans and wintered at Epidamnus. In spring 228 he received Teuta's expected capitulation. The agreed terms were that the cost of the war to Rome would be met by Teuta in the form of an indemnity, payable in instalments, such as had been imposed on Carthage after the First Punic War (but presumably much smaller, though we do not know the precise amount).[24] The Illyrians also undertook not to sail south of Lissus with more than two ships, and those unarmed. Polybius says nothing about a land frontier; and, indeed, there was no need for one, since the Illyrians were formidable to Rome solely as a result of their navy. The restriction on sailing south of Lissus will therefore have been a perfectly satisfactory means of curbing these naval activities. Furthermore, those communities which had surrendered to Rome—Apollonia, Epidamnus, the Parthini and the Atintanes on the mainland, and Corcyra and Issa of the islands—though they were given no treaties and were left as 'free states', like the privileged communities in Sicily, were likely (if Rome chose to honour her self-imposed obligations as protector and patron) to be effective reminders to the Illyrians that the settlement was supported by Rome's prestige and power. There is no evidence for—and no good reason for believing in—the modern hypothesis of a continual coastal strip of formal 'Roman Protectorate' between Lissus and Corcyra.[25]

Moreover, Demetrius of Pharos, through his capitulation at Corcyra and his subsequent co-operation, had like the 'free states' also become a Roman friend and client. His exact position after the settlement of 228, however, is not altogether certain. We know that at some time he married king Pinnes' mother Triteuta and became guardian of Pinnes;[26] that Pinnes was nominally left in control of Illyrian territory except for the places and tribes which had surrendered to Rome;[27] and that Teuta gave up all but a few strongpoints.[28] Perhaps the most likely explanation of this evidence is that Rome's friend and client Demetrius was rewarded for his helpfulness during the war by having his marriage with Triteuta and guardianship of Pinnes arranged while Postumius was still at Epidamnus; and that Teuta in effect undertook to restrict herself to a few castles, perhaps around Rhizon on the bay of Kotor, where she had spent the winter, and to give up her guardianship of Pinnes.

If this is in fact what happened it would fit well with the rest of the settlement. For while the sting of the Illyrian pirates was pulled by

the embargo on their sailing south of Lissus, the sting of the
Illyrian monarchy was pulled (it was hoped) by having friends of
Rome scattered along the coast and by having a friend of Rome, in
the person of Demetrius, installed as regent of the whole kingdom.
Demetrius and the communities which had surrendered were now,
from Rome's point of view, clients (though the full implications of
this status were not spelled out, and this caused subsequent misunderstandings). Though they were in every sense entirely free
legally, just like the 'free states' of Sicily, Rome expected, in return
for her interest, favour, and protection, that they would conduct
themselves in general and act, if necessary in particular instances, as
Rome wished: in short, that they should, as client to patron, give
every assistance to what Rome considered her interests. The concept
of *clientela* had been first employed in Roman foreign policy with the
Greek 'free states' of Sicily. Twelve years later in Illyria it has become the automatic and obvious way of dealing with this new overseas situation.

The Illyrian war gave Rome a bridgehead of responsibility and
influence—no more than this—across the Adriatic, and confirmed
her in her method of treating friendly overseas communities. At the
same time, as an act of diplomatic courtesy, Postumius sent to the
Aetolian and Achaean Leagues (which had been particularly active
against the Illyrians before Rome's intervention), announcing the
terms of the settlement.[29] Similar courtesy dispatched other Roman
envoys to the influential Greek cities of Corinth and Athens—at
Corinth the courtesy was returned by admitting the Roman envoy to
the Isthmian Games.[30] The Greek states, as Polybius makes clear,[31]
will have been immensely grateful to Rome for the curbs placed on
Illyrian piracy. The Roman embassies mean no more than that the
Roman commander thought that the most important Greek states
should know to whom they owed their good fortune.

III Italy

The population of Italy was, as we have seen, firmly under Roman
control before the First Punic War. During the war there was no
appreciable trouble in Italy: the revolt of Falerii immediately after
the peace settlement—an isolated incident, quickly crushed—only
served to emphasize the strength of Rome's control.[32] The war accustomed Rome to look beyond Italy for threats to her security: the pre-

cautions taken against Carthage in Sardinia and Corsica and against Illyria are symptoms of the wider awareness of danger which the First Punic War had aroused.

Italy, much as Rome might regret it, was not an island. Rome might feel threatened by overseas neighbours in the south; but her chief fear—which she continued to be aware of, long after she had become pre-eminent among the civilized powers of the Mediterranean coastal fringe—was of the Celtic Gauls, Italy's northern neighbours who lived in the plain of the river Po (which the Romans called 'Cisalpine Gaul'), and in and beyond the Alps. Roman history had been regularly punctuated by Gallic invasions, the most serious of which, in 387/6, had resulted in the occupation and near-destruction of the whole of the city of Rome except for the citadel of the Capitol, which was saved, tradition records, only by cackling geese. By the end of the First Punic War, there had been no Gallic invasion of Italy for over forty years; but the Gauls were now becoming restive. Fortunately for Rome, Carthage had neglected to recruit this powerful potential ally. A threatened incursion in 237 reached only the Latin colony of Ariminum before the Gauls dispersed their energies in internal squabbling.[33]

Rome was lucky to have escaped so lightly, and she soon took measures to strengthen Ariminum. The territory south of the colony as far as the river Aesis, near Ancona—the so-called *ager Gallicus*— had been officially unoccupied since Rome had expelled the Gallic tribe, the Senones, in 283. It was now decided to settle this territory, and thus to make support readily available to Ariminum. In 232 a tribune of the plebs, Gaius Flaminius, against strong opposition in the Senate, carried a law in the assembly of the plebs (*concilium plebis*) distributing the *ager Gallicus* in allotments to individual citizens. Opposition among the senators was so strong that Flaminius' father, himself a senator, attempted to stop the bill by dragging his son forcibly from the temple where the meeting was being held. But despite the drama, the law was carried.[34]

The Senate's violent opposition and Flaminius' persistence show that a serious issue was at stake. Yet it is difficult to believe, in view of the threat from the Gauls to Ariminum in 237, that the Senate opposed the settlement of the *ager Gallicus* as such. It is more likely that the opposition was against Flaminius' proposed method, of giving allotments to individual citizens. For this raised immense problems, particularly in connection with the Italian allies who had co-operated in expelling the Senones, and many of whom may have been exercising squatters' rights on the officially unoccupied 'state land' for more than a generation. Moreover, Rome's traditional way of securing new territory in Italy was to found 'Latin colonies'—such as Ariminum itself—in which her Italian allies could participate and thereby obtain the partial citizenship called 'Latin Rights'. Such a colony formed a new municipal centre and a self-sufficient military unit, in effect, a garrison. Thus not only was Flaminius' method, of distributing his allotments piecemeal to full Roman citizens, likely to offend the allies: it was also likely to be ineffective against the Gauls.

The Senate's opposition therefore had a well-found basis. Flaminius' support, however, is not difficult to see. The people who benefited from his bill were citizens; citizens alone could vote in the *concilium plebis*. They clearly wanted the land. Small farmers and tradesmen will have been adversely affected by the ready availability of slaves after the war with Carthage, and many of them may have been ready and willing to make a new start in the 'virgin lands' of the *ager Gallicus*. Flaminius clearly gave them what they wanted. He was an ambitious man—although his father was a senator no member of his family had ever reached the consulship—and his tribunate gave him the chance of making himself popular among the electors by getting a reputation for proposing popular measures. The popularity with the people which Flaminius won with his land bill stayed with him throughout his life: by it he had, in effect, made a large part of the Roman People his clients. His subsequent career shows that the Senate's traditional *clientela* was unable to prevent him from capitalizing on his support.

Flaminius' popularity with the plebs and the Senate's open hostility to his land bill and the method by which he had it passed—without consulting the Senate, which liked to discuss and approve all legislation before it came to the People—had a disastrous effect on Flaminius' reputation, which was not improved by the events of his later career. Polybius probably reflects the attitude of the Roman historian Fabius Pictor—himself a senator and one of the Fabii, a family which persistently opposed Flaminius—when he calls Flaminius the originator of the policy of working through the People, and the author of the People's moral disintegration.[35] What Polybius means—and what Fabius Pictor meant—is that over the next few years (until the disastrous battle of Cannae in 216) the People were less willing to accept without question the Senate's opinion on affairs and its chosen representatives as leaders; and that

Flaminius' method of opposing the wishes of the Senate and failing to consult it over his land bill—a measure which involved a serious matter of (virtually) foreign policy—was the origin of this unfortunate and, in the end, almost fatal trend.

There is clearly some truth in the basic judgment, that a popular politician, a man who is good at winning elections, may not necessarily be good at winning wars: Flaminius' career ultimately ended in military disaster in 217 and seemed to give substance to the point (though he had previously had his share of military success, which made him the first consul chosen specifically to fight against Hannibal in Italy in 217). But it does not necessarily follow from this that a man approved by and selected from an unrepresentative élitist clique, such as the Roman Senate was, will inevitably be good at winning wars. The Senate's real objection to Flaminius was not that he ultimately presided over a Roman disaster, but that he had ignored its opinions and flouted its authority. For this he was never forgiven; his mistakes were exaggerated, his successes depreciated. An example follows immediately. Polybius, still following the judgment of Fabius Pictor, goes on to blame Flaminius for provoking the dangerous Gallic invasion of 225 by his land law.[36] But this is quite unjust. If, as has been suggested, the Senate as a whole had agreed in principle that the *ager Gallicus* should be settled, and if its objection to Flaminius' bill was merely because of its untraditional and less efficient method, it follows that the Gauls would have been just as easily provoked by new colonies of the traditional type as they were by individual allotments. It was not therefore really Flaminius' settlement of the *ager Gallicus* as such which provoked the Gauls, but the whole policy—of which the Senate probably approved—of strengthening the northern frontier.

The invasion, however, when it came, was extremely serious. A Gallic army of some 70,000 men crossed the Apennines in spring 225 and had reached Clusium, only 100 miles from Rome, before they were stopped by a Roman army. The decisive battle, fought at Telamon in Etruria, found the Gauls sandwiched between the armies of the two Roman consuls of 225, Lucius Aemilius Papus and Gaius Atilius Regulus (the son of the consul Regulus who was captured in Africa in 255). The Gallic casualties were enormous—the Romans claimed to have killed 40,000 and to have captured 10,000—largely because of the Gallic tradition of fighting naked, which allowed the Roman javelins to play havoc. The immediate threat of the invasion was thus disposed of, and Aemilius displayed the Gallic prisoners, standards and decorations, in his splendid triumph in March 224.[37]

The Romans were not content to let matters rest there, and both consuls of 224 operated in Cisalpine Gaul, south of the river Po. The same pattern was followed in 223, when one of the consuls was Gaius Flaminius. Since his tribunate, Flaminius had distinguished himself by being the first praetor to spend his year in Sicily: in 227 for the first time four praetors were elected (instead of two, which had been the previous practice), two of whom were sent overseas, Flaminius to Sicily, Valerius Laevinus to Sardinia and Corsica.[38] As praetors, they had *imperium* (which included the right to command an army); and since the sphere in which a magistrate exercised *imperium* was his 'province' (*provincia*), the overseas territories directly under the control of Rome gradually became known as Roman provinces. In 227 for the first time they were directly administered by regular Roman magistrates, therefore for the first time could be called provinces. Whether Flaminius had used his popular support to have these new posts created and, by implication, to make the Senate adopt a more formal administrative procedure in Sicily, Sardinia and Corsica, is not attested: but it will certainly have helped to secure his election as praetor and in due course as consul.

Militarily his consulship was a great success, although the senatorial tradition which Polybius followed gives him no credit for it. A major victory against the Gallic tribe, the Insubres (who lived near modern Milan), draws from Polybius the second-hand criticism that 'he was thought to have mismanaged affairs'; and Polybius credits the victory to Flaminius' officers.[39] But the fact that Flaminius was one of the first pair of consuls specially chosen to fight Hannibal in Italy in 217 is a strong indication that senatorial hostility has deliberately concealed his earlier military success—since after his disaster at Trasimene in 217 allegations of earlier incompetence, however false and far-fetched, would seem plausible enough. Polybius, however, omits the more sensational details of the hostile senatorial tradition which appear in other sources: that Flaminius ignored a letter from the Senate recalling him and his colleague Furius, allegedly because of unfavourable omens, and demanding their resignation. When they did return, Flaminius' claim for a triumph was predictably opposed in the Senate; but again a vote of the People secured the reward for his victory. After his triumph was time enough to heed the omens: their year's work accomplished and their triumphs celebrated, Flaminius and Furius at last obeyed the Senate's wish that they should resign.[40]

After the campaigns of Flaminius and Furius the peril from the Gauls was, for the immediate future, almost crushed. The consuls of 222 again campaigned against the Insubres and took their capital at Milan. The most spectacular achievement of the year was Marcus Claudius Marcellus' victory at Clastidium, in which he personally killed the Insubrian chief.[41] But his was the last triumph won over the Gauls in this period of fighting. More important affairs soon absorbed Rome's energies. The seriousness of the initial Gallic threat, however, cannot be over-emphasized. Yet its defeat led inevitably—as had every such Roman success in the past—to Rome's adopting a wider view of her interests. No territory was immediately occupied; but the decision taken in 219 to establish Latin colonies at Cremona and Placentia on the river Po, when war with Carthage was already threatening, was a direct result of the wider awareness of danger implanted in the Roman Senate by these Gallic wars.[42]

their triumphs celebrated, Flaminius and Furius at last obeyed the Senate's wish that they should resign.[40]

After the campaigns of Flaminius and Furius the peril from the Gauls was, for the immediate future, almost crushed. The consuls of 222 again campaigned against the Insubres and took their capital at Milan. The most spectacular achievement of the year was Marcus Claudius Marcellus' victory at Clastidium, in which he personally killed the Insubrian chief.[41] But his was the last triumph won over the Gauls in this period of fighting. More important affairs soon absorbed Rome's energies. The seriousness of the initial Gallic threat, however, cannot be over-emphasized. Yet its defeat led inevitably—as had every such Roman success in the past—to Rome's adopting a wider view of her interests. No territory was immediately occupied; but the decision taken in 219 to establish Latin colonies at Cremona and Placentia on the river Po, when war with Carthage was already threatening, was a direct result of the wider awareness of danger implanted in the Roman Senate by these Gallic wars.[42]

PART II

THE WAR WITH HANNIBAL

CHAPTER IV

THE CAUSES OF THE
WAR WITH HANNIBAL

I Hamilcar and Hasdrubal

THE First Punic War and Roman opportunism during Carthage's subsequent war with her mercenaries deprived Carthage of her influence in Sicily and in Sardinia. Her earlier interests in southern Spain seem to have also been virtually abandoned—perhaps under pressure of the war with Rome—by the middle of the third century B.C. But after the shattering blows of the struggle with the mercenaries, Hamilcar Barca, who even at the end of the war with Rome had been undefeated in Sicily and who had increased his prestige in the war with the mercenaries, persuaded the Carthaginian Senate to support his plan to regain Carthage's earlier influence in Spain.

In spring 237 he set out with a substantial army, accompanied by his son-in-law Hasdrubal and his nine-year-old son Hannibal, crossed the straits of Gibraltar, and made his base at the long-standing Phoenician foundation Gadeira. Little is known of his subsequent activities. Polybius' account is imprecise: 'He spent about nine years in these parts (i.e. until winter 229/8) during which he subjected many of the Iberians to Carthage, some by diplomacy, some by war. His death, which he met in battle with one of the most warlike and powerful tribes, exposing himself bravely to danger, was worthy of his great achievements.'[1] Diodorus adds a few details, the most important of which is that Hamilcar founded a city called 'Acra Leuce' (White Rock), which is usually identified with Alicante.[2] In themselves these brief accounts and few details tell us very little about Hamilcar's activities. But they do seem to show that he laid a firm base for the renewal of Carthaginian power in the south of the Iberian peninsula.

On Hamilcar's death, the Carthaginian Senate confirmed Hamilcar's son-in-law Hasdrubal as his successor, since Hannibal was as yet barely nineteen. Hasdrubal's major contribution to Carthaginian expansion was his foundation, on the site of the old Phoenician colony Mastia, of New Carthage. The chief importance of New Carthage is that it possessed the best harbour on the east coast of Spain and an immensely strong site for the new city. Hasdrubal's foundation at once became the capital of the new Carthaginian empire in Spain.[3]

Not surprisingly, the Roman Senate took little notice of what Carthage was doing in Spain. Southern Spain was, on average, a good month's journey from Rome, quite far enough for the Senate to be unconcerned about anything that was going on there. Rome's friend Massilia, however, was not so happy.[4] Massilia did much trade with the Spanish tribes, primarily through her trading colonies Emporiae, Rhode and Hemeroscopion; and she did not relish the prospect of Carthaginian competition. Massilia was of prime importance to Rome as a source of information about the Gauls in and around the valley of the Rhône; and we have seen that Rome was particularly worried about the Gauls in the years after 237. In the circumstances, Rome could not afford to offend Massilia, and Massilia may have encouraged Rome to inquire about Hamilcar's intentions in 231, if an isolated mention of a Roman embassy to him in that year is authentic.[5] A few years later, in 226, Massilia gave Rome advance warning about the Gauls assembling for their Italian invasion; and she probably took the opportunity of suggesting that Rome should make sure that Hasdrubal, who was in contact with the Spanish Celts, the Celtiberians, had no intention of helping them.

There is no reason, in fact, for believing that Hasdrubal had the slightest intention of joining or helping the Gauls; and the Roman Senate does not seem to have taken the suggested threat very seriously. However, not to offend Massilia, and just to make sure about Hasdrubal—Rome could not afford to leave any loophole open, however unlikely it seemed—Roman envoys made the long journey to New Carthage. The result was the so-called 'Ebro treaty', by which Hasdrubal undertook not to cross the river Ebro in arms. It contained no other provision about Spain.[6]

The Ebro, at its nearest point, is nearly 300 miles from New Carthage, and 200 from Alicante, the farthest generally assumed point of Carthaginian penetration by this date. Hasdrubal was not therefore conceding much to Rome by undertaking not to cross the river in arms. It costs little to agree not to go somewhere you have no intention of going! Nor did the Romans think that they were conceding much to Hasdrubal by implicitly allowing him the right to expand, even in arms, as far north as the Ebro, since they were

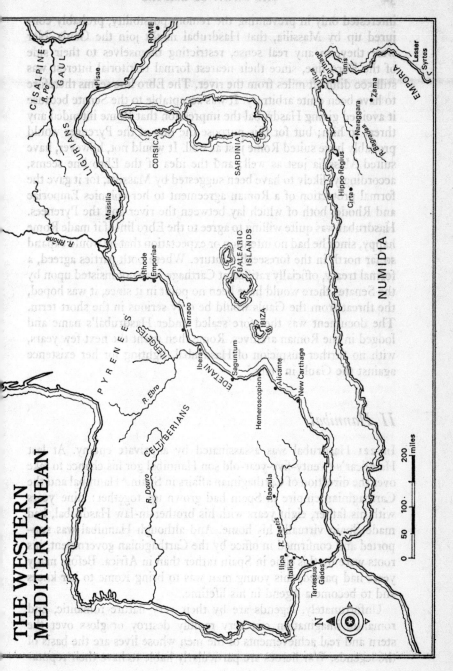

THE WESTERN MEDITERRANEAN

interested only in preventing the remote possibility, probably conjured up by Massilia, that Hasdrubal might join the Gauls. Nor
were they, in any real sense, restricting themselves to their side
of the Ebro line, since their nearest formal territorial interest was
still 500 difficult miles from the river. The Ebro line seems therefore
to have been quite arbitrary. It was acceptable to the Senate because
it avoided giving Hasdrubal the impression that Rome intended any
threat to him; but for this purpose the line of the Pyrenees would
probably have suited Rome just as well. It would not, however, have
suited Massilia just as well; and the idea of the Ebro line seems,
accordingly, likely to have been suggested by Massilia, for it gave the
formal protection of a Roman agreement to her colonies Emporiae
and Rhode, both of which lay between the river and the Pyrenees.
Hasdrubal was quite willing to agree to the Ebro line if it made Rome
happy, since he had no intention or expectation that he would expand
so far north in the foreseeable future. Where both parties agreed, a
formal treaty, officially ratified at Carthage, was not insisted upon by
the Senate: there would have been no point in it since, it was hoped,
the threat from the Gauls would be only serious in the short term.
The document was therefore sealed under Hasdrubal's name and
lodged in the Roman archives. Rome then spent the next few years,
with no further suspicion of Hasdrubal, fighting for her existence
against the Gauls in Italy.[7]

II Hannibal

In 221 Hasdrubal was assassinated by a private enemy. At last
Hamilcar's twenty-five-year-old son Hannibal got his chance to take
over the direction of Carthaginian affairs in Spain.[8] Hannibal and the
Carthaginian empire in Spain had grown up together: nine years
with his father, eight years with his brother-in-law Hasdrubal, had
made Spain virtually his home. And although Hannibal was supported and confirmed in office by the Carthaginian government, his
roots were by this time in Spain rather than in Africa. Before many
years had passed, this young man was to bring Rome to her knees
and to become a legend in his lifetime.

Unfortunately, legends are by their very nature romantic, and
romantic imagination can very rapidly destroy or gloss over the
stern and real achievements of the men whose lives are the basis of
the legends. War heroes are particularly liable to have their reputa-

tions distorted by subsequent romantic or propagandist reconstructions; for in the ancient world, as in the modern, wars and battles were constantly refought after the events by writers of memoirs, by historians 'official' or popularizing, by bar-room raconteurs. Much invaluable information is preserved and made available in these ways; but the search for sensation or—more insidious—for self-justification, whether national or personal, can obscure, sometimes irreparably, the real reasons for action, the real causes of wars.

So it was with Hannibal. Hannibal's war against Rome, because it was fought in Italy and because it was the gravest and longest immediate crisis which Rome had ever faced, ensured Hannibal a reputation as Rome's greatest enemy of all time. As a result, there was naturally much speculation about how and why Hannibal had been so incredibly persistent in his opposition to Rome. The view which met with the greatest favour in Rome and which accordingly had the greatest effect on the subsequent tradition, was that the whole confrontation stemmed from the wrath of the Barcid family, in particular of Hamilcar, Hasdrubal and Hannibal. After the war was over the Carthaginians were also apparently prepared to endorse this view, since to blame the Barcid family helped partially to absolve the Carthaginian government from responsibility.

Hamilcar, as we have seen, was personally undefeated in the First Punic War. Later Roman tradition made this the origin of the Barcids' implacable hatred for Rome: the peace of 241 and Rome's subsequent annexation of Sardinia were presented as the bitter Barcid disappointment which precipitated another war twenty-three years later. Hamilcar's exploitation of Spain is depicted by this tradition as having one sole purpose: to build up a power which could defeat Rome. Polybius' story—possibly authentic—that Hamilcar made Hannibal, when a child, swear never to be friends with Rome, was seized by this tradition in the second century B.C. and exaggerated: Hannibal is hereafter alleged to have sworn implacable hatred to Rome (which is by no means the same thing).[9] The war, when it came, is therefore alleged to have been long in preparation by the Barcids, and many consciences—particularly at Carthage—will have been disreputably soothed by this unhistorical explanation.

Yet all this does not amount to very much in practice. As far as we know, Carthage was not dilatory in paying off the indemnity for the first war. Indeed, the need to pay it without having the income from Sicily and Sardinia may have been the original stimulus (or part of it) to rebuild the empire in Spain.[10] It is one thing to say that

Hamilcar hated Rome after the First Punic War; his view will naturally have been shared by many Carthaginians of his generation. But it is another and an entirely different matter to develop this and to say that his hatred guided his policy to the extent that Carthaginian exploitation of Spain was aimed at destroying Rome, and that Hamilcar was prepared to risk all in another war. This is not the kind of strategy which had made Hamilcar so successful as to remain undefeated in Sicily; and nothing that we know of the man and his actions suggests that his hatred of Rome was of the short-sighted risk-all type. Similarly Hannibal's oath: it is one thing to swear never to be a friend of Rome—Rome's friends, after all, had a nasty habit of turning into Rome's subjects; but it is again an entirely different matter to swear to hate and (by implication) destroy. It is a very long step in the civilized world—and the Carthaginians had had centuries of civilization to condition their attitudes—from dislike and distrust, even from hatred, to open and implacable determination on war.

Nothing that Hamilcar did in Spain suggests that he was aiming at another confrontation with Rome. Nor did Rome do anything which suggests that the Senate thought he was aiming at this. If Massilia inspired Rome to send an embassy to him in 231, it was because Massilia felt her commerce threatened, not Rome her safety. In 226 the Ebro treaty with Hasdrubal was concluded with no sign of any suspicion or even hostility on either side. At this stage, certainly, Rome had not heard of the implacable hatred of the Barcids: if war with Rome was the avowed ultimate aim of Carthage's policy, no rumour of this leaked as far as the most interested party, the Roman Senate. Massilia seems to have done her best to arouse Roman suspicions, and may have been satisfied with the result; but Spain as such was still quite simply outside the sphere of Rome's active interest. As long as the Carthaginians did not join the Gauls—and, as we have seen, there is no indication that they had any intention of doing so—they could do what they liked in Spain so far as Rome was concerned.

Hannibal's actions as commander were equally irreproachable. They were no more than an active continuation of his predecessor's policy of extending and consolidating the Carthaginian sphere of operations in Spain. Hasdrubal had agreed not to fight beyond (north of) the river Ebro; Hannibal's activities, moving north from New Carthage, seem to have aimed at gaining control of a relatively narrow coastal strip up to the Ebro mouth. His two campaigns in

221 and 220 were very successful and, says Polybius, made a great impression on the native Iberians. The result was that nobody south of the Ebro would face him without thinking twice, except the people of Saguntum.[11] Hannibal was careful not to provoke Saguntum. This, however, does not necessarily mean that Hannibal had actually conquered the coastal strip as far north as the Ebro: it means rather that Saguntum was the strongest place left unconquered between him and the Ebro—Saguntum is about 100 miles south of the river—and that the other peoples were frightened of Hannibal's reputation.

This point is important in the sequel, for a few years before this Saguntum had become a friend of Rome. Perhaps on the advice of Massilia, the Saguntines had appealed for Roman arbitration in a civil war. Compliance cost Rome little and would please Massilia. The Roman arbitrators settled the civil war by recommending the execution of the leaders of one of the factions; and it seems that those executed may have favoured the Carthaginians. This, of course, does not mean that Rome was hostile to Carthage: the point is that those who appealed to Rome would become Roman clients, and would therefore expect to benefit from the rough and ready justice of the arbitration. This probably took place about 223.[12] The outcome of the arbitration seems to have given the Saguntines the false impression, which would doubtless be nurtured by Massiliot wishful thinking, that Rome was seriously interested in and opposed to Carthaginian advancement in Spain. Saguntum therefore considered herself a friend of Rome, and her claim seems to have been respected by Hannibal.[13] Despite Hannibal's care, Saguntum was worried at the implications of his advance towards the Ebro, and in 221 and 220 she bombarded Rome with requests to do something. For a long time the Senate turned a deaf ear, for Saguntum's claim to friendship, since it resulted solely from the arbitration, did not exert a very strong moral pressure on Rome. However, during the late summer of 220 the Senate at last gave way and sent envoys to investigate.

Their interview with Hannibal, at his winter quarters at New Carthage, was unfriendly. Hannibal and his predecessors had carefully avoided offending Rome. The result, it must now have seemed to the self-confident young Carthaginian, was Rome's unwarranted interference with Carthage's friends in Saguntum (who had been executed as a result of the Roman arbitration a few years before) and a claim stemming from this act, and thus doubly annoying to Carthage, of friendship with the city. The Roman envoys were on weak ground, since they knew that the Senate was not, in the last resort, particularly interested in Spanish affairs; but the Saguntines' constant requests for Roman intervention had been embarrassing; and the Senate had decided that they must be conciliated, if for no other reason than to ensure that Rome's friends everywhere would continue to trust the efficacy of Roman friendship. The attitude of the Roman envoys may therefore have seemed high-handed, but their words were as mild as was consistent with satisfying the Saguntines. They asked Hannibal to guarantee not to interfere with Saguntum, since the city was in Roman *fides* (in other words, Rome was committed to her friendship with Saguntum); and—perhaps to reassure Massilia—they reminded him of the existence of the Ebro treaty (to which Rome's *fides* was also committed).[14]

Hannibal's reaction was unexpected. He accused Rome of unjustly interfering at Saguntum in the arbitration—a reply to the Romans' mention of their *fides*—and declared that the Carthaginians never neglected the victims of injustice. He ignored their reference to the Ebro treaty.[15] Hannibal clearly regarded the Roman representation as an impertinence, and from his point of view with some justification. He had carefully avoided provoking Saguntum; he was as yet nowhere near the Ebro. There was no reason for Rome to have intervened, it must have seemed to him, unless the Senate had determined to use its friendship with Saguntum to establish a Roman protectorate in Spain. There were plenty of precedents for this interpretation. In Carthage's own experience Rome's conveniently adopted friendship with the Mamertines in 264 (which in the end destroyed Carthaginian Sicily) and with the Sardinian mercenaries in 237 (which destroyed Carthaginian Sardinia) was ominous. It will consequently have been only too easy for him to conclude that the Senate intended to use the Saguntines as a Spanish version of the Mamertines and the Sardinian mercenaries. It was a disastrous misapprehension.

He at once informed the Carthaginian Senate, adding (what may be substantially true) that Saguntum had relied on its friendship with Rome to attack some tribes subject to Carthage; he then asked for instructions. He doubtless also indicated his own interpretation of the Roman embassy, with which in any case the Carthaginian Senate will have sympathized. The Roman envoys also crossed to Carthage in accordance with their instructions, where they repeated their statements about Saguntum and the Ebro treaty before returning to Rome.[16] The Carthaginian Senate's reaction to Hannibal's information and to the message of the Roman envoys is not explicitly attested; but since the next thing we hear about is Hannibal's besieging Saguntum in spring 219,[17] we may reasonably conclude that the Carthaginian Senate had accepted Hannibal's view of Rome's purpose in giving diplomatic support to Saguntum. The fact that this view was wrong is irrelevant. What matters in the last resort is that the Carthaginians seem to have believed it. Hannibal's attack on Saguntum should therefore be seen as the first action of the war, an attempt to forestall Rome by removing the potential base before Rome could occupy it. At the start of the First Punic War, in just the same way, the Carthaginians and Hiero had desperately tried to capture Messana before the Romans arrived and began to use it as a bridgehead in Sicily.

Unfortunately for Saguntum the parallel ends there. The Mamertines in Messana were less than a mile from Roman territory, Saguntum was more than a thousand miles from Rome. The Romans had a formal relationship with the Mamertines based on surrender into Rome's *fides*, Saguntum relied on the much more tenuous claim of friendship, the practical interpretation of which was entirely in the hands of the Roman Senate. When news of Hannibal's attack on Saguntum reached Rome in summer 219, the consuls had already left for another campaign across the Adriatic in Illyria. Without them the Senate was reluctant to take a decision, and it did not think matters were serious enough to recall them. By the time the consuls returned it was already winter, when little could be done for Saguntum even if the Senate had wanted to; and when news finally arrived of the fall of Saguntum it was at the most only a few weeks before the Ides of March, when the new consuls would enter office (the exact date of the fall of Saguntum is not known). Discussion was therefore postponed until then, so that the men who would have to implement the Senate's decision could preside over the critical discussions.

The Senate's failure to send help to Saguntum, despite Saguntine appeals, suggests forcefully that the majority of the Senate was not yet convinced that Rome's interests were sufficiently deeply involved in Spain to merit recalling the consuls. With Saguntum Rome had no treaty, therefore no actual legal obligation to provide help. Some senators may even have been glad of the availability of a series of excuses which allowed them to postpone a decision with a fairly clear conscience until Saguntum had fallen, if it was going to fall, and the situation was clearer. Hannibal's attack, coming as it did immediately after his being reminded that Saguntum was a friend of Rome's, was of course a flagrant insult to the Roman Senate and could not in the last resort be totally ignored; but the character of the Roman response might be altered if Hannibal's attempt on Saguntum failed. The fall of the city, however, at once made the situation clear; and when the new consuls entered office shortly after the news arrived, the Senate acted quickly, at once backing up the moral commitment of its *fides* at Saguntum with the threat of force.

A committee of senior senators, perhaps including both the ex-consuls of 219, was chosen to travel to Carthage with the ultimatum.[18] Prestige was at stake. To impress the Carthaginians with Rome's seriousness, the envoys were armed with the ultimate sanction, a conditional declaration of war. Their ostensible purpose was to require the Carthaginian government to hand over to Rome the offender Hannibal and his war council. It could be claimed that it was a well-established Roman practice to surrender to the enemy their own commanders who had exceeded their instructions and outraged a third party; and they were apparently asking that the Carthaginians should honour the same principle and disown Hannibal.[19] But they can hardly have expected the Carthaginians to accept this way out: for Hannibal had not exceeded his instructions. He had captured Saguntum with the full approval of the Carthaginian Senate. His action had been officially sanctioned as Carthaginian policy.

Despite the unlikelihood of its acceptance, the Roman ultimatum was presented at Carthage with all solemnity appropriate to a possible declaration of war. But the Carthaginian Senate was labouring under the same misapprehension about Roman motives in Spain as Hannibal, and for the same reasons: Rome's apparently active interest in Saguntum in 220 was interpreted by Hannibal and by the Carthaginian government as tantamount to a declaration of war, in the same way as Rome's alliance with the Mamertines nearly fifty years before had been the prelude to a war. It was a tragic miscalculation, for in Spain the Roman Senate had no such intention.

Not surprisingly in the circumstances, the Carthaginian spokesman did not take the Roman offer very seriously, and evaded the issue. He tried to justify Hannibal's action by referring to the clause of Lutatius' treaty in 241 which secured the safety of the allies of each side from attack by the other: Saguntum was not a Roman ally in 241 and therefore, he argued, was not covered by the treaty. The point was a good one, for Lutatius' treaty had made no provision for future allies. But the Romans were not prepared to argue about legal rights and wrongs. The point which was clear was that the Carthaginian government was trying to defend Hannibal's action by justifying it. Fabius Buteo, the leader of the Roman envoys, made no verbal reply. The crisis had come. The Carthaginians were deliberately choosing to support Hannibal's action with the full authority of their government. In a dramatic gesture Fabius raised his arms across his chest and told the Carthaginians that the folds of his toga held both peace and war: he would shake out whichever they chose. On the Carthaginian chairman's indicating that he left the choice to Fabius, the old senator declared that he would shake out war. The Carthaginian Senate echoed with the cry, 'we accept', whereupon the Romans departed for their ships. At last the two sides understood each other.[20]

III The later tradition about the origins of the war

The immediate reasons for the war, being deep in mutual misapprehension, whereby neither side understood the other's point of view, were not surprisingly obscure to those who later came to write about the war. Indisputable facts were that the immediate preliminaries of the war concerned Spain; that the war was fought (partly) in Spain; and that one of its long-term results was a permanent Roman provincial administration in Spain. No one seems therefore to have been able to conceive that Rome's serious interest in Spain did not begin until Saguntum had been captured and Fabius shook war from his toga. One result of this failure was the large-scale invention of reasons and justifications for the war. The most obvious of these simplistic inventions, 'the wrath of the Barcids', we have already noticed. It was, of course, by far the easiest explanation for those who did not want to think very hard, for it allowed the comfortable belief both at Rome and at Carthage that the Barcids and nobody else were to blame. There is no need to re-examine the inadequacy of 'the wrath of the Barcids' as a cause of the war.

There were, however, more subtle and more partisan inventions. The Carthaginians, in replying to the Roman envoys' demand for Hannibal in March 218, tried to justify themselves, and Hannibal, by referring to the only relevant treaty they could think of which might help them, the treaty of Lutatius Catulus which had ended the First Punic War in 241. The point they tried to make about Saguntum was legally valid; but by then the Romans were playing power-politics. They were not prepared to argue, and they ignored the legal point as irrelevant. They did not, however, continue to ignore it. For Polybius records a later interpretation of Lutatius' treaty (which, incidentally, he agrees with) which argued that the Saguntines were Roman allies and therefore were protected under the clause of Lutatius' treaty which concerned the allies of each side—the very clause from which the Carthaginians had in 218 argued that the Saguntines were excluded.[21] In strict law there was much to be said for the Carthaginian view, for while the treaty contained a list of the allies at either side at the time, it made no provision for future allies (not to mention mere friends). It was, from the Roman point of view after the war, an important omission. But no amount of Roman argument could alter the fact that it was nevertheless an omission and that Lutatius' treaty simply could not help Rome.

Roman apologists also used the Ebro treaty. This had played no part in the discussions at Carthage—not surprisingly, since it was quite irrelevant.[22] Yet it subsequently became a key plank in the platform of Roman self-justification. Perhaps taking the cue from the Roman envoys' reminder about the treaty to Hannibal late in 220, and thinking, mistakenly, that it was immediately relevant to the complaints of the Saguntines, it became standard practice at Rome to justify Rome's action against Carthage by wildly distorting geography and alleging that to get to Saguntum from New Carthage Hannibal had crossed the Ebro.[23] This was grotesquely wrong, since Saguntum is some 100 miles south of the Ebro. But Roman wishful thinking, combined with a massive ignorance of and cavalier attitude towards the geographical facts, firmly blamed Hannibal for the outbreak of the war through this deliberate and disreputable distortion. Indeed, by Polybius' time, it had become such a frequent feature of the Roman case that, despite knowing quite well the relative geographical positions of Saguntum and the Ebro, he has absent-mindedly incorporated the error in one place in his own discussion.[24] There is no indication in Polybius' account, however, that this gross distortion was contemporary with the outbreak of the war: in 218 the Senates of Rome and Carthage rightly regarded the Ebro treaty as quite beside the point and did not argue about it at all.

What then were the real causes of the Second Punic War? Polybius himself favours 'the wrath of the Barcids', resharpened by Rome's seizure of Sardinia. But Polybius, despite all his excellent qualities as a historian, was a man of his time and, living in Rome, could not avoid adopting contemporary views and attitudes. The facts which his account provides tell a different story, as we have seen. Rome's lack of interest in Spanish affairs, until her slight obligation to Saguntum made her send the first critical embassy to Hannibal late in 220, is sufficiently well-attested to make it the most convincing interpretation of the evidence. Unfortunately, the purpose of the Roman embassy was completely misunderstood both by Hannibal and by the Carthaginian government, taking their lead from him. This misunderstanding led directly to the subsequent insult to Rome of the immediate attack on Saguntum in spring 219; the same misunderstanding made the Carthaginian Senate refuse to draw back when presented with the Roman ultimatum the following spring. The Carthaginians were no appeasers: to them there were worse evils than war, and Hannibal was a firm exponent of this attitude. But it was this attitude, reinforced by their disastrous—though comprehensible—misreading of the nature of Roman interest in Saguntum, which led to their enthusiastic but tragic acceptance of the war which Fabius Buteo shook from his toga in March 218.

CHAPTER V

THE WAR WITH HANNIBAL IN ITALY

I The Invasion

ROME'S declaration of war in March 218 confirmed the Carthaginian government and Hannibal, when he heard of it, in their view that Rome was concerned to prevent the extension of Carthaginian power and influence in Spain. In any military operation against Carthaginian Spain the Romans would need to bring their army south from the Pyrenees, either overland or by ship around the coast. Hannibal therefore determined to do all in his power to prevent the Romans from invading Spain by engaging them first in Italy. For Hannibal, the threatened Roman protection of Saguntum in winter 220/219 had been the sign that Rome had determined on war; so at about the time of his attack on Saguntum early in 219 he had sent messengers to the Gauls of the Po valley—who had only recently been quelled by Rome—in order to incite them to further active hostility towards Rome. And he promised Carthaginian assistance. By spring 218 his envoys had returned with favourable replies: the Gauls would support him.[1]

Hannibal was now ready for his great gamble of invading Italy. His plan was logical enough in its strategic conception, but it took little account of the immense practical difficulties. On the principle that the best form of defence is attack, he proposed to discourage further Roman intervention in Spain by forcing Rome to fight in Italy. What was the point of waiting for Rome to attack and of suffering the devastation of a war in Spain, when swift action could make Italy the scene of the devastation? The Roman government would be more effectively weakened if Hannibal succeeded in shattering the credibility of Rome's claim to be able to protect her Italian allies, on whose support Roman supremacy in Italy was founded. Such a policy might produce a swift Roman acknowledgement of Carthage's right to maintain her empire in Spain, and the war might be quickly over. There is no indication, except in the later tradition of a thoroughly frightened Rome, that Hannibal's initial aim was to destroy Rome. The war had started from an imagined challenge to Carthage's empire in Spain; and in its early stages at least, the Carthaginians would probably have been happy enough to have gained guarantees that Rome would stop interfering in Spain.

The Roman Senate's immediate reaction to the Carthaginians' acceptance of war similarly showed little inclination for a fight to the finish. The distribution of the consular provinces had probably been delayed until the envoys returned from Carthage with their answer to the Roman ultimatum; and even then the Senate did not know Hannibal's scheme of invading Italy—he probably had not left New Carthage when the Senate was considering its dispositions—and, as subsequent events show, had not thought it a serious possibility. The rejected Roman ultimatum had concerned Hannibal's activities in Spain; and to concentrate on Spain seems to have been the Senate's guiding principle. Hannibal and his advisers were in Spain, therefore one consul, Publius Cornelius Scipio, should take an army to Spain to put pressure on Hannibal. The Carthaginian Senate had fully supported Hannibal, therefore the other consul, Tiberius Sempronius Longus, should take his army to Africa and put pressure on Carthage. The normal consular armies of two legions and associated allied troops and cavalry—in all, around 20,000 men each—were assigned to the consuls.[2]

That they were not supported by larger-than-usual legionary forces was not because of lack of Roman manpower. It must indicate that, while the Senate regarded the war with all due seriousness, it considered the normal size of army to be adequate without exceptional reinforcements. This was immediately made even clearer when the Gallic tribe, the Boii, aroused by the recent establishment of Latin colonies at Placentia and Cremona and by the prospect of Carthaginian support, attacked the new Roman colonists, and the Senate sent the legions intended for Spain to deal with the Boii. Scipio was told to recruit more men for his own purpose, a procedure which delayed his departure until the end of July—and which is also a good indication that the Senate thought the rising of the Boii was more immediately important than the war with Hannibal.[3] Recruitment of legions was a slow process, though Roman manpower resources were very large. While discussing the Gallic wars in the 220's, Polybius estimated that Rome's potential manpower reserves were around three-quarters of a million men, of whom about ten per cent were cavalry. Of course these were not all Roman citizens: Polybius includes the Italian allies as about half his total. But by ancient standards, the potential power of Rome was massive.[4]

In contrast, the army with which Hannibal arrived in Italy was 26,000 strong (20,000 foot and 6,000 cavalry).[5] While he cannot have had any precise appreciation of Rome's enormous superiority in numbers, he must have been approximately aware of it. How, then, did he dare to think he had the remotest chance of exerting sufficient pressure on Rome to make the Senate contemplate capitulation? The answer seems to lie in his mistaken view of the character of Rome's control of Italy. The Gauls of the Po valley, he knew, were unruly and had only accepted Roman superiority unwillingly. They had promised in advance to support him, and it was on this support in the first stages that he was primarily relying. But Gallic aid would not be enough in itself. Hannibal's longer-term hopes—and it was here that his estimate proved to be crucially wrong—were aimed at encouraging the rebellion from Rome of her Italian allies. Had the Italian allies revolted in large numbers, of course, Rome would not only have been deprived at once of a large part of her potential manpower, but she would also have been confused in her efforts against Hannibal by the pressing need to operate at the same time against her rebellious allies. With this prospect in mind Hannibal announced after his arrival in Italy that he had come to bring freedom to Rome's allies; and to encourage general awareness of this he ostentatiously treated those of Rome's Italian allies whom he captured much better than he treated captured Roman citizens.[6] We shall soon see how ineffective this propaganda was in practice.

After making arrangements for the security of Africa and for Spain—where he left his brother Hasdrubal in command—Hannibal set off from New Carthage towards the end of April 218. Since the land north of the Ebro was not controlled by Carthage, Hannibal was forced to fight his way through to the Pyrenees; and by the time he reached the river Rhône it was already the middle of August. News of Hannibal's intentions will have been known to Massilia—at least as fearful speculation—as soon as he crossed the Ebro; and the Roman Senate would no doubt be quickly informed. Yet until Hannibal reached the Rhône, there seems to have been no suspicion at Rome that Italy was his ultimate objective: after all, to have crossed the Ebro, even to have passed the Pyrenees, was to have travelled less than half-way to Italy. And while Massilia might justifiably feel afraid—and the Roman Senate would, of course, do its best to help Rome's ally—there was as yet, it must have seemed, no reason for alarmist fears in Rome itself. It was therefore the end of July before Scipio set out from Pisa with his army for Spain. It took him five days to reach the neighbourhood of Massilia, where he stopped. He clearly intended to defend Massilia before proceeding to Spain, if this proved necessary. There was still no clear threat to Italy: this section of the war, even if the worst happened and Scipio were defeated, seemed likely to be fought out in the neighbourhood of Massilia.

But Scipio's information was bad. Hannibal had bought himself a quick and safe passage from the Pyrenees to the Rhône, and had already reached the river some miles upstream from Massilia when Scipio reached the area. By the time of Scipio's arrival, Hannibal had crossed the river and had a lead of three days, marching upstream. It was clearly pointless for Scipio to try to follow; for if Hannibal was well received by the Gallic tribes of the Rhône valley, they would join him against Scipio; and if they opposed him, Scipio would not need to involve himself. Hannibal's ultimate purpose had, however, at last dawned on the Roman consul. His fellow-consul was in Sicily, preparing to invade Africa; the only Roman army close enough and large enough to prevent Hannibal from seriously threatening Italy, if he did manage to cross the Alps, was Scipio's own. It was not the job of a Roman consul to obey his orders from the Senate to the point of abandoning Italy—even if the threat still seemed remote—to a potential invader. Scipio therefore divided his army. He sent his brother Gnaeus to Spain with one section, while with the other he himself returned to Italy with the intention of meeting Hannibal there, should he manage to cross the Alps.[7]

Much has been written about Hannibal's crossing of the Alps; particular interest has been shown in the ultimately insoluble problem of which pass he took.[8] His thirty-seven elephants—which were a much greater liability to him in the crossing than they were use when he arrived—caught the popular imagination in ancient times, as in modern; and as a result, Hannibal's Alpinism has become one of the best-known achievements of military logistics in the ancient world. Yet as early as the second century B.C. Polybius was protesting that writers were already exaggerating Hannibal's performance, and he points out that the mountains were by no means as desolate as they are often depicted: there was quite a sizeable population actually living in them, and large armies of Gauls regularly used the Alpine passes as routes from the Rhône to the Po valley.[9]

Hannibal's problems, as is quite clear from the accounts of Polybius and Livy, were caused not so much by the physical difficulties of the journey itself as by the hostility of the native population. At a crucial stage Hannibal's army was attacked by Gallic tribesmen; his guides proved disloyal; and from then on his passage over the mountains was a nightmare which almost ruined his imaginative enterprise before it had properly begun. But it is worth emphasizing that although Hannibal had great difficulties with the local Gauls and lost a large number of his troops and baggage animals as a result, Scipio's immediate decision to abandon the pursuit up the Rhône valley shows clearly that he knew very well—what Polybius later called attention to—that, given friendly inhabitants, the route over the Alps was a hard but short, quick and efficient way of reaching Italy from the Rhône valley.

Hannibal's route—probably over one of the Mt. Cenis group of passes—brought him by mid-September, five months after leaving New Carthage, into the upper Po valley near Turin, the territory of the large Gallic tribe, the Insubres. If Polybius' figure of 38,000 foot and 8,000 horse for Hannibal's army at the crossing of the Rhône is correct (it may have been exaggerated by the Roman tradition), Hannibal's opposed crossing of the Alps cost him no less than 18,000 foot and 2,000 cavalry; for the figure of 20,000 foot and 6,000 horse for his army after the crossing was taken by Polybius from the bronze plaque which Hannibal himself subsequently set up at the Lacinian promontory in southern Italy. Those who survived the journey were enfeebled by their efforts, but were nevertheless powerful enough to capture Turin, the chief city of the Taurini, with whom the Insubres were currently at war. The Insubres were impressed by this show of strength; and as the news spread, most of the other Gauls of the Po valley joined the Insubres in staying true to the offers of support they had given to Hannibal before he set out from Spain; and they joined him with their contingents as he travelled on.[10]

So far Hannibal's expectations of support—apart from the near-disaster in the Alps—had been fulfilled. With the support of the Gauls he could proceed to his next task, the provocation of a rising among Rome's Italian allies. In the meanwhile, once Scipio had appreciated that Hannibal intended to cross the Alps, he sent to his consular colleague Sempronius in Sicily and asked for support. Earlier in the year the Boii had been disaffected; the prospect of Carthaginian direction of another large-scale war with the Gauls was a threat which needed to be immediately trampled upon with as much strength as Rome could raise. But long before Sempronius' army could reach northern Italy, Scipio and Hannibal had clashed at the river Ticinus, north of the Po. It was not a large-scale battle; it was not even a particularly serious engagement; but it clearly indicated that the purely military threat from Hannibal was substantial, for Scipio was defeated and wounded, and was forced to withdraw across the Po. He pitched his camp near Placentia and determined to wait for Sempronius, but moved it to the river Trebia when the flat ground near Placentia began to seem dangerous; and he was still there when Sempronius joined him in December.

Scipio remained incapacitated by the wound he had received at the Ticinus, and Sempronius was therefore in command. Polybius knew personally many important members of the Scipionic family in his own day, and their family tradition has influenced his attitude towards Sempronius; for he depicts him as rash and over-eager for action. There may, of course, be some truth in this; but any Roman consul in normal circumstances, facing a projected invasion of Italy by a tired army and with winter at hand, would have thought he was neglecting his duty if he had not tried to bring about a decisive engagement. In detail, however, Sempronius can certainly be faulted; for he allowed his troops to join battle before they had had their breakfasts and on a cold snowy day. To attack the Carthaginians they had to wade across the river Trebia, which was swollen with floodwater from the December rain and snow; and by the time the battle was joined the Roman troops were already jaded. It was not long before it became obvious that Hannibal's travel-weary troops had won a substantial victory, though not without incurring losses. The Roman survivors made their way to Placentia, from where the distressing news was taken to Rome. Hannibal settled down to spend a more hopeful winter among his Gallic friends.[11]

II The Roman Reaction

If Hannibal's appearance in Cisalpine Gaul had made the consuls preoccupied with Italy's northern frontier, Sempronius' defeat at the Trebia made the Senate react on a wider front. On receiving the news of the battle, it immediately sent two legions to Sicily and one to Sardinia, to forestall any possible Carthaginian action there; and garrisons were installed at Tarentum and some other important places in Italy. Moreover, the Roman People seem, not altogether surprisingly, to have been unhappy with the way the war had so far been conducted; and their dissatisfaction was expressed by their

electing to the consulship of 217 their old champion Gaius Flaminius. It was his second consulship in six years, and like the first (in
223, when he had triumphed over the Gauls) he owed it in particular
to a continuing series of popular activities which gained him support
among the voters. Elected censor in 220, he had promptly let out contracts for a new circus, called after him the *Circus Flaminius*, and for a
new road across the Apennines to Ariminum, to which he also gave
his name, the *Via Flaminia*.[12] These measures were popular because,
apart from their practical value (in the case of the circus, entertainment
value), they inevitably created employment and the disbursement of
public funds in and around the city of Rome, where the voters lived.

Furthermore, Flaminius' popularity with the masses had been increased earlier in 218, the very year of his election to his second
consulship. The issue was this: Quintus Claudius, a tribune of the
plebs, had proposed a law which would prevent senators and their
sons from undertaking public transport contracts (which the Senate
let out) by limiting the size of the ships they were allowed to own.[13]
This was a popular measure outside the Senate because it would
prevent individual senators from making profits out of decisions of
state—and (what was probably more important), from letting their
hopes of private gain influence decisions of state. It was a law against
what we now call 'conflict of interest'. It was, however, very unpopular with the Senate, since trooping and supply contracts seemed
likely to become increasingly important and profitable with the
Senate's declared intention of taking armies to Spain and to Africa;
and Flaminius was in a minority of one in the Senate when he supported it. His support added further to his vilification at the hands
of the senators;[14] but the People passed the law, and Flaminius'
support of it will obviously have contributed substantially to his
being elected consul for the critical year 217.

Roman strategy for 217 was that Flaminius' colleague Gnaeus
Servilius Geminus should station himself at Ariminum with the
remains of Scipio's legions, in case Hannibal chose to cross the
Apennines along the route of Flaminius' new road. Flaminius was to
go to Arretium in case Hannibal should attempt a more northerly
route. The consuls would not be so far apart, it was thought, that
each could not reinforce the other as circumstances dictated. This,
at least, was the plan. But Hannibal's route over the Apennines and
his speed took the consuls of 217 by complete surprise.

Crossing the mountains into the valley of the upper Arno, riding
his sole surviving elephant, Hannibal cleverly avoided Flaminius'

army near Arretium. Flaminius was disconcerted at being so quickly outwitted; and, determined not to appear to be lacking in energy, he promptly packed up camp and followed him, so as not to leave Hannibal an undefended road to Rome. This, it turned out, was just what Hannibal wanted. Once the consul had been enticed into a precipitate and unprepared pursuit, he was at the adaptable Hannibal's mercy. The scene of the execution was lake Trasimene in Etruria, where Hannibal's ambush trapped Flaminius between the lake and the nearby hills and destroyed the greater part of his army. Polybius describes the dramatic scene as follows: 'It was an exceptionally misty day. And as soon as most of the Roman army had entered the narrows and when the head of the column had reached him, Hannibal gave the battle-signal, sent a message to those in the ambush, and attacked the Romans from all sides at once. Flaminius was taken completely by surprise at their sudden appearance; and since visibility was very bad due to the misty weather and since the Carthaginians were charging down from higher ground in so many places at once, the Roman centurions and tribunes not only could not take any effective counter-measures, but could not even understand what was happening. For they were attacked at the same time from the front, rear and flanks; and most of them were cut down while still in marching order, quite unable to protect themselves, betrayed, as it were, by their commander's imprudence; they were slaughtered without warning while still considering what to do. At the same time Flaminius himself, bewildered and depressed by everything that had happened, was attacked and killed by some of Hannibal's Gauls. Some 15,000 of the Romans fell in that valley, incapable of either yielding to circumstances or of effective resistance, but they clung to their traditional military principle of neither fleeing nor abandoning their ranks.'

And this was not all. For Hannibal shortly afterwards destroyed or captured 4,000 unsuspecting Roman cavalry, whom Servilius had sent as an advance guard to join Flaminius. There could be no concealing the seriousness of the situation for Rome: one consul and most of his army were dead; the Carthaginian victor was little more than three days' march from the city of Rome; and—worst of all—if he chose, he would be able to reach the city before the surviving Roman consul. In one of the most famous understatements of all time, the praetor Marcus Pomponius announced to the Roman People, 'We have lost a great battle.'[15]

To all appearances Hannibal was doing magnificently well. His military successes, fulfilling his wildest hopes, were outstanding. He had made very good use of the support of the Gauls; he might now expect that Rome's Italian allies would be sufficiently impressed at his success to follow the lead of the Gauls and begin to desert Rome. He had already taken steps to encourage this. Early in the year, he had freed without ransom those Italian allies whom he had taken prisoner at the Trebia—carefully distinguishing them from the Roman citizens, whom he did not release. The real purpose of the distinction he veiled with propaganda: he claimed that he was fighting on behalf of the Italian allies, that he had come to free them from the Roman yoke.[16] And on the credibility of this propaganda of 'liberation' his success ultimately depended; for while he could apparently inflict military blows on Rome with comparative ease, he had incurred losses of his own; and although he might in time receive reinforcements from Africa and Spain, Rome's potential forces would remain massively superior and more easily deployable as long as her Italian allies remained loyal. Therefore, after Trasimene, as after the Trebia, Hannibal hammered away at his propaganda. He again freed without ransom all prisoners taken from the Italian allies; and they returned to their homes with Hannibal's slogan drummed into them, that he had not come to fight the Italians, but to fight Rome on behalf of the Italians.[17]

Yet Hannibal needed to do much more than release prisoners and propagate slogans to bridge his credibility gap. For while he talked peace to the Italians, his actions were inconsistent with his words; and we do not know a single Italian community which defected to Hannibal as a result of Trasimene. Indeed, the Roman annalistic tradition—which may well be correct—makes Hannibal's first action after Trasimene an attack on the territory and city of Spoletium, which the inhabitants staunchly resisted. And Polybius agrees that Hannibal's subsequent activities involved the devastation and plunder of the areas through which he passed on his way to the Adriatic coast. He may, indeed, have been forced into this against his better judgment by his Gallic allies, who would expect to be allowed to plunder, although Polybius naïvely attributes it to his family's hatred of Rome.[18] Certainly it was, if deliberate, a foolish relaxation in view of his hope of gaining the support of the Italians; for the Italian communities would obviously continue to rest their hopes of survival on Rome—whose demands, apart from manpower, were quite light—as long as Hannibal allowed his troops and his widely-feared Gallic allies to loot and plunder. The plundering was an error of judgment which, despite Hannibal's military successes, augured very badly for the future of the crucial battle for the 'hearts and minds' of the Italians.

Roman reaction to the news of Trasimene paid due attention to its seriousness. The Senate obviously could not know that Hannibal did not intend to attack the city of Rome, and it had to take precautions. One consul was dead; the other was cut off by Hannibal. The situation clearly called for desperate remedies. A solution was found in activating the emergency office of dictator, to which a single man was appointed to supreme military authority (*imperium*) for a period of six months. But even here there was a difficulty, for a dictator was traditionally appointed by a consul, and no consul was available. For once the Senate was in no mood to quibble about constitutional technicalities. The emergency situation called for emergency action; and the appointment of the dictator was entrusted to the *comitia centuriata*, the assembly of the People which elected the senior magistrates; and, for this occasion only, the *comitia centuriata* also elected the dictator's second-in-command, the 'Master of the Horse' (*magister equitum*), although this appointment was tradition- ally the prerogative of the dictator himself. Not surprisingly, the men chosen reflected the unusual method of their appointment: the dictator was one of the highest Roman nobility, Quintus Fabius Maximus, who had already twice proved his capacity as consul (in 233 and in 228). His Master of the Horse, on the other hand, Marcus Minucius Rufus, while also an ex-consul (in 221), had been associated with Flaminius; and his appointment suggests that the Roman People were still prepared to back their own man, even after Flaminius' disaster—though, admittedly, there is no evidence that a large part of the Senate disapproved of Minucius' appointment at the time.

Two new legions were raised for Fabius; and taking over Ser- vilius' legions also, the dictator went after Hannibal, who was still plundering the Adriatic coastal plain, and still getting no support from the local inhabitants. Trasimene had clearly not shocked Italian loyalties so much as to make the Italians voluntarily exchange Rome's light rule for that of the rapacious Carthaginians and Gauls. Hannibal's only hope lay in forcing another and yet more serious defeat on Rome which might (he would hope) shatter the Italians' faith in Rome's ability to protect them. His policy of looting, of course, might conceivably do this: but it totally failed to make Hannibal's cause seem the more attractive. Hannibal must by now have realized that he had misjudged the temper of the Italians and the nature of

Roman rule in Italy: the Italians were not downtrodden and oppressed by Rome, as were Carthage's subjects in Africa and Spain; and as a result they showed no spontaneous enthusiasm for rebellion. It was clearly an impossible task for any propaganda to make out a convincing claim to be freeing people who did not regard themselves as subject!

Fabius' strategy was to deny Hannibal the chance of another major battle. It was eminently sensible in the circumstances, for a long war of attrition was the last thing Hannibal can have wanted, since it was now clear that he would gain little support in Italy by propaganda or by plunder. He needed another spectacular victory in a major battle, and, recognizing this, Fabius set out to prevent it. His tactics were to follow Hannibal closely and to skirmish with stragglers when the opportunity offered, tactics which earned him the nickname, '*Cunctator*', 'The Delayer'.[19] Fabius' strategy, of course, had its dangers: for it gave the impression that he was not concerned to stop Hannibal's depredations and that he was prepared virtually to abandon Italy to the invader rather than risk a battle. And indeed many did react unfavourably and regarded Fabius' caution as excessive. Trasimene, they would argue (wrongly, but sincerely, since contemporaries obviously could not enjoy the dispassionate hindsight of the historian), was an exceptional and unrepeatable accident, and not in itself a conclusive demonstration of Hannibal's real superiority in set-piece battles. But in practice these considerations seem to have had more serious effect on Fabius' relations with Minucius and with the Senate than on the Italians. For despite the unchecked devastation of Hannibal's invasion, which during the year spread into Campania, the richest farmland in Italy, and despite Fabius' failure to do much about stopping it, most Italians still saw little prospect of safety in changing their allegiance and joining the destroyer. By the end of the year, when Hannibal had retired to winter quarters at Geronium near the Adriatic coast, he had taken enormous quantities of booty and caused massive destruction; but not a single Italian community is recorded as having joined him voluntarily. In so far as Fabius had retained the loyalty of the southern Italian communities—though it was doubtless becoming strained—and in so far as he had avoided further military disaster, his guerrilla-type strategy could be said to have worked.

On the home front, however, impatient reaction to Fabius' careful strategy led directly to the following year's massive disaster at Cannae, a Roman defeat of such proportions that Hannibal harvested from it his first political break-through since gaining the support of the Gauls nearly two years before. Potential friction between Fabius and Minucius was inherent in the method of Minucius' appointment. He was not, we may reasonably believe, the man whom Fabius would have chosen had the appointment been left to him in the usual way. And while Fabius disciplined himself and refused to allow himself to be provoked into a battle by Hannibal's depredations, Minucius was not so easily convinced of the value of Fabius' caution—which he chose to interpret as timidity—and favoured the traditional grand-slam approach, of facing Hannibal in yet another general set-piece battle—exactly what Hannibal wanted.

Late in the year, while Fabius was busy with some religious ceremonies at Rome, Minucius was left in charge of the army and won some slight success against Hannibal. His supporters at Rome, when the news reached them, exaggerated this and used it as a political stick with which to beat Fabius' unspectacular, and therefore unpopular, policy; and they used it to such good effect that the tribune Metilius had Minucius appointed co-dictator with Fabius[20]—a division of responsibility which contradicted and made nonsense of the whole concept of the office of dictator. It is perhaps not surprising that only one more military dictator was appointed in this period of Roman history, in the crisis of 216.

The opponents of Fabius' strategy clearly had some political strength at Rome; and it does not seem to have been weakened even when Minucius put his legions at severe risk and was only saved from disaster by Fabius' intervention.[21] As a result, the elections for the consulships of 216 were held amidst great strategical controversy: the Fabians were accused of prolonging the war unnecessarily; and the plebeian consul elected by popular favour was one of Fabius' leading opponents, Gaius Terentius Varro. His colleague was Lucius Aemilius Paullus, an experienced senator who, as consul in 219, had won a triumph for a successful campaign in Illyria. The senatorial tradition recorded by Livy depicts the noble Aemilius as an opponent of the plebeian Varro, in order to blame Varro and excuse Aemilius for the subsequent disaster; but in fact Aemilius seems to have had no difficulty in co-operating with Varro.[22] Indeed, the strategy which the consuls jointly pursued—in sharp contrast with Fabius' method—of deliberately seeking battle with Hannibal, originated in the Senate;[23] and this suggests that the hostile reaction to Fabius' cautious and unspectacular guerrilla strategy in 217 was not only widespread among the mass of the people, but that it had also penetrated into the Senate.

Unfortunately for Rome, the senators soon wished they had continued to follow Fabius' ideas. The battle of Cannae, fought on the river Aufidus on August 2, 216, was the immediate result of their officially abandoning Fabius' strategy. It was the greatest military disaster that Rome had ever suffered. Its climax Polybius describes thus: 'Coming to the support of the Africans, Hasdrubal attacked the Roman legions in the rear, and making repeated charges with one squadron after another in many places at once, he encouraged the Africans and discouraged and dispirited the Romans. It was now that Lucius Aemilius Paullus fell mortally wounded in the thick of the fight, a man who was second to none in doing his patriotic duty even in his last moments. The encircled Romans held out as long as they could turn and offer a front to those pressing in on them; but as the outer ranks kept on falling, so the survivors were gradually shut into an ever smaller space, until finally all fell where they stood. Among them were Marcus [Atilius Regulus] and Gnaeus [Servilius Geminus], the consuls of the previous year, who had fought the battle bravely, as men worthy of Rome.' At a cost of some 6,000 of his own men (and these mostly Gauls,) Hannibal destroyed more than 50,000 Roman soldiers and captured another 10,000. Terentius Varro escaped with a small body of cavalry to nearby Venusia.[24] When he eventually reached Rome, no blame was publicly attached to him. Indeed, rather the opposite: it was no time for indulging in useless recriminations, and the Senate showed that it shared full responsibility for the disaster by publicly thanking the consul for 'not having despaired of the Republic'.[25]

III The Roman Recovery

The battle of Cannae shook Rome to the foundations. She was left with no effective army in the field except the two 'urban legions', whose job was to guard the city of Rome; and subsequent generations have followed the lead of frightened contemporaries by continuing to wonder why at this stage Hannibal failed to follow up his victory by marching on Rome. Later Romans in particular liked to regard this omission as Hannibal's decisive mistake, the mistake which saved Rome from complete annihilation and which eventually lost Hannibal the war. Livy, for instance, records and embellishes an apocryphal scene which originated in the historical work of the elder Cato in the mid-second century B.C. and which soon became a famous

feature of the Hannibal legend. According to Cato, Maharbal dramatically advised Hannibal that 'in five days you may dine on the
Capitol', a suggestion which Hannibal turned down. Had the suggestion in fact been made, Hannibal would have had ample justification for rejecting it. For Cannae was nearly 200 miles from Rome,
and the success or failure of an attack on the city—which was by no
means totally defenceless—would depend to a great extent on how
many Italians joined Hannibal. Immediately after the battle, it was
still too soon to know whether the effect of Cannae on the loyalty of
the Italians would be greater than the negligible effect of Trasimene:
if it were not, a ten-day forced march (no ancient army of foot-
soldiers could average more than twenty miles per day—particularly
through hostile territory—and Hannibal could not hope to take Rome
with cavalry alone) was an unhappy preliminary for an attack on a
desperately defended Rome. And if such an attack failed, as it easily
might, knowledge of the failure might largely negate the impression
on the Italians of the battle. Moreover, to abandon the area in which
the battle had been fought meant sacrificing the most immediate
prospect of exploiting its effect on the population of southern Italy.
An attack on Rome therefore—even supposing that at this stage
Hannibal wanted to destroy the city—would have been such a huge
military and political gamble that Hannibal can never have seriously
considered it.

It was, of course, some time before this became clear to the
frightened Romans, to whom the news of their shattering defeat
made no danger, however improbable, seem too remote. A dictator,
Marcus Junius Pera, was at once appointed and began to raise new
legions. But it was the calm Quintus Fabius Maximus, the ex-dicta-
tor, who managed to introduce a sense of proportion into the shaken
Senate by insisting that it should first ascertain the real facts—defeat-
ist rumour inevitably insisted that both consuls and all their troops
had been killed—before taking important decisions about the future
direction of the war. And when Varro's letter arrived with the more
hopeful news that he had himself survived, that he was now at
Canusium, and that something like 10,000 survivors had rallied round
him, the Senate also learnt that Hannibal was still at Cannae and was
more concerned about getting ransom for his prisoners than with
marching on Rome. Dispositions could now be made in a calmer
mood; and the Senate decided to send to Canusium the praetor
Marcus Claudius Marcellus (who had military experience against the
Gauls when consul in 222) to take command of the survivors. The

dictator raised four new legions; and 8,000 slaves were bought from their owners and trained as legionaries. But the city of Rome seemed to be in no immediate danger. Despite the massive defeat at Cannae, it seemed that the war would, as before, be fought out among Rome's allies in the south of Italy.

While Cannae had crippled Rome militarily only for a comparatively short time, it had at last—as Hannibal must have hoped—broken the widespread belief that Rome was willing and able to protect her Italian allies on any occasion. Hannibal's earlier victories at the Trebia and at Lake Trasimene, and the propaganda which had accompanied his release of Italian prisoners after them, had not induced any spontaneous uprising against Rome. The simple truth was that most Italians were reasonably satisfied with their relationship with Rome: and as long as Hannibal continued to plunder Italian territory, they would continue to see their ultimate safety lying in resisting Hannibal and remaining loyal to Rome. The lack of the expected spontaneous rebellion among the Italians put Hannibal in a vicious circle. If his propaganda of 'liberation' did not work, his only other available weapon was force. But the use of force tended to break confidence in his propaganda; and Fabius' tactics had prevented him from breaking the circle by defeating Rome in a pitched battle and thus shaking the Italians' confidence in the Romans' ultimate capacity to beat him. Cannae had changed all this, and he now began to break out from the circle. At last some Italian communities situated close to the war zone began to consider whether Rome would ever again be sufficiently strong to dominate the peninsula. Would their current suffering from resistance to Hannibal be worthwhile if Rome did not recover? It was this kind of doubt which Hannibal desperately needed to exploit.

After Cannae, as after his other battles, Hannibal freed Italian prisoners without ransom. By itself this gesture may have had no more effect than previously; but this time, as the news of Rome's defeat spread, scattered communities throughout southern Italy at last began to negotiate with Hannibal. Arpi in Apulia, no more than thirty miles from the battlefield, was the first to join Hannibal without suffering immediate pressure; and many other towns in the area followed suit: we know three of them, Aecae, Salapia and Herdonea. They clearly felt that they would get little support from Rome if they resisted. Some Campanians also made overtures; and with the lively prospect of encouraging widespread defections in rich Campania, Hannibal left Apulia. As he travelled across Italy, most of the

Samnites joined him; when his brother Mago visited Lucania and Bruttium with a small force, he won over nearly all the local communities. It seems clear that most southern Italians were at last convinced that Roman support was unlikely to be available to them and that resistance for its own sake was now futile. In the circumstances, to join Hannibal was the easiest thing to do: even Capua, the most important city in Campania and the second city of Italy, surrendered to Hannibal though not without some prior discussion.

These were undoubtedly great successes for Hannibal. Yet all was not straightforward for him. The Roman Senate had not shown the slightest inclination, even in the anxious and depressing weeks immediately after Cannae, to begin negotiations with the invader; and this must have distressed Hannibal. For since the Romans plainly refused to acknowledge the verdict of Cannae as decisive, it is difficult to see what more Hannibal could do to drive them into negotiations. Moreover, even in the tactics of the war Hannibal still had available only two ways of treating communities which refused to join him (and many, even in the south of Italy, did continue to resist): to destroy them, if he was prepared to waste time on a siege and to risk further damage to the credibility of his claim that he had come not to fight the Italians but to free them; or to ignore them, which meant in effect not punishing them for their insistence on remaining loyal to his enemy Rome.

Events in Campania nicely illustrate his difficulties. Capua, we have seen, quickly joined Hannibal. But two separate attacks on Naples were repulsed by the Neapolitans; and the important town of Nola, well-supported by Marcus Claudius Marcellus, survived frequent attacks despite the fact that some sections of the population favoured capitulation. Nuceria, on the other hand, Hannibal did capture: but only at great expense of time and after fierce resistance. Acerrae similarly refused to join Hannibal and, like Nuceria, was completely destroyed—a fate which did nothing to enhance Hannibal's image as the freedom-bringer! In the circumstances, given the Romans' total failure to consider any form of capitulation and the fact that the chief Roman commanders of the next few years, Quintus Fabius Maximus, Marcus Claudius Marcellus, and Tiberius Sempronius Gracchus, showed more than usual caution and competence, it is difficult to see how Hannibal, even in the long term, could ever have won sufficient success to end the war with the forces and techniques at his disposal.

As the Romans gradually recovered from the shock of Cannae,

their position with regard to their allies was much easier than Hannibal's; for voluntary defectors such as Capua could legitimately be punished for their failure to support Rome—indeed, those communities which (like Naples) stayed loyal, or those which (like Nuceria and Acerrae) only submitted to Hannibal under severe duress, might justly expect this. Those states which remained loyal would, of course, also deserve, where possible, Roman support (though in practice for the next few years Roman support was only effective in Campania). With the Italian situation thus more or less stabilized, and with Rome's position, through avoiding major battles, slowly but surely becoming stronger, the war could be actively pursued in other theatres: in Spain, where Gnaeus and Publius Cornelius Scipio had operated since 218, and in Sicily where the fleet carried out regular raids on Africa.[27] Progress again was slow. But it is worth emphasizing that it was not Rome and Italy which alone were suffering from the war: Carthaginian territories, even in Africa, were also under constant threat.

The full tedious details of the later years of the war in Italy are fortunately not central to this theme: we may therefore hope to avoid sharing the feeling of Livy who, after finishing his account of the war, remarked that he was as sick of it as if he had fought it himself![28] Rome's slow recovery after Cannae meant that Roman power would survive. Indeed, as early as the end of 216 it was already foreseeable that Hannibal had not the means to compel Roman capitulation (which is not at all the same thing as saying that Rome could easily get rid of him). Rome had certainly lost a good part of Campania and of the rest of southern Italy; but to set against these losses was the fact that none of the Latin towns and none of the colonies and communities in central and northern Italy had had their loyalty seriously and effectively shaken by Hannibal's passage (though there were some disturbances in Etruria which might have proved serious had Hannibal been able to exploit them).

In and after 215, when Rome's friend Hiero of Syracuse died, Carthaginian intervention in Sicily again threatened Italy; and for a few years thereafter Sicily was an important theatre of war and not just a safe base for the Roman fleet. But there too Rome prevailed, though Syracuse was sacked in the process (in 211). The chief event of Rome's recovery in Italy was the recapture of Capua in 211, after a year's siege, by Quintus Fulvius Flaccus whom Hannibal failed to distract from the siege even by a frightening but ineffective march on the city of Rome. The same year saw Tarentum, except for the citadel which remained in the hands of a Roman garrison, belatedly joining the Carthaginian side. But this was an isolated success for Hannibal. Rome's activities in Spain and the strength of her fleet had prevented more than occasional reinforcements from reaching him from Spain and Africa; and when in 210 Salapia fell to Rome's advance into Apulia, Hannibal lost the last 500 of his excellent Numidian cavalry. By then it was clear that unless he received reinforcements Hannibal had no real hope, barring miracles, of turning the tide.

Reinforcements were agonizingly slow to arrive; and without them in 209 Hannibal's situation deteriorated still further. He failed to hold his recent acquisition Tarentum against the veteran Quintus Fabius Maximus; and worse still, many of the Samnites and Lucanians who had joined him soon after Cannae now surrendered to Fabius. Without fresh troops Hannibal could not even keep what he now held; and since Rome controlled the seas by holding Sicily and Sardinia, reinforcements could only reach Hannibal overland from Spain. In 208 Hannibal's brother Hasdrubal tried to kill two birds with one stone: to draw away from Spain Publius Scipio, Rome's energetic and successful commander there, and to bring much-needed reinforcements to Hannibal. Avoiding Scipio's pursuit—which Scipio did not continue beyond the Pyrenees, thus frustrating one of Hasdrubal's aims—Hasdrubal set out on a repeat performance of Hannibal's own march to Italy. It was a last desperate effort to save Carthage's own war effort in Italy.

In spring 207 Hasdrubal crossed the Alps. One of the consuls, Marcus Livius Salinator, went to Cisalpine Gaul to deal with him while his colleague Gaius Claudius Nero watched Hannibal in the south. Claudius was fortunate enough to intercept messengers from Hasdrubal to Hannibal, and energetic enough to set out immediately to join his colleague with picked troops (6,000 foot and 1,000 cavalry). He found Livius camped opposite Hasdrubal at the river Metaurus in Umbria; and in the subsequent engagement the Roman consuls won a famous victory. Hannibal bitterly learned both of his brother's arrival in Italy and the result of the battle when Hasdrubal's head was thrown down before his outposts on Claudius' return to Canusium. Hannibal's last real hope of reinforcement was thus brutally shattered. He could, of course—and did—continue to maintain himself in Italy for some years more. But his hope of turning back the tide of Rome's advance was negligible. The irony was that his Italian campaign was shown to have no prospect of ultimate success by a battle in which he himself took no part.

CHAPTER VI

THE WAR WITH HANNIBAL IN SPAIN

I The Two Scipios

THE Senate's original intention, which Hannibal's sudden invasion of Italy had temporarily thwarted, had been to fight Carthage in Spain and in Africa; for the war had originated in Spain, and Africa was Carthage's home territory. For this reason Publius Cornelius Scipio, when consul in 218, had been given Spain as his sphere of duty. Hannibal's unexpected invasion of Italy had prevented any immediate Roman invasion of Africa and had stopped Scipio from reaching further west than the Rhône on his way to Spain.[1] As we have seen, the rest of his year as consul was fully occupied in facing Hannibal in Italy. Yet the series of Roman defeats of that year did not alter the Senate's original conception of where the war should ideally be fought. Despite the chilling threats to Rome's position in Italy, the Senate did not waver in its strategic conception: Spain remained crucial. The war had been begun because Roman prestige had been committed there: it would have meant losing sight of this fact and wholly abandoning Rome's Spanish friends if these operations had been suspended. Moreover, as the war in Italy continued, the Spanish sector took on the additional and highly important purpose of hindering the reinforcement of Hannibal in Italy.

Accordingly, throughout the Hannibalic War Roman operations against the Carthaginian empire in Spain continued alongside Hannibal's attacks on Rome's allies in Italy. When Publius Scipio turned back at the Rhône to meet Hannibal in Cisalpine Gaul, his brother Gnaeus, who was one of his lieutenants, took command of most of the navy and pressed on as planned to Spain, where he made his base at the friendly Massilian colony of Emporiae, and began operations against the Carthaginians. Rather belatedly, Rome was beginning to demonstrate to her few Spanish friends that she was prepared to protect them.[2]

Rome's purpose in sending an army to Spain was not at first to conquer the peninsula or to form a Roman empire there (though this was the ultimate result). Rather it was to prevent Carthage from enjoying her Spanish empire until the Carthaginian government came to terms with Rome and made Hannibal withdraw from Italy. The Roman method in Spain was not therefore simply to exert all available military power to defeat the enemy; but rather, by demonstrating to the Spanish tribes that Rome was prepared to support them against Carthage, to deprive Carthage of local Spanish support and willingness to co-operate with her, on which in the last resort her empire depended; and thus, by building a widespread network of Roman friends and allies among the Spaniards, to increase Roman influence and reduce Carthaginian. It was the same kind of strategy which Hannibal tried to employ in Italy.

Gnaeus Scipio began immediately by penetrating the coastal strip from Emporiae to the Ebro, and making friendly approaches to all communities en route. Those which accepted his advances he treated well and protected against possible Carthaginian reprisals; those which refused he reduced by siege. In this way he not only took control of the invaluable seaboard, but also gained a ready supply of local Spanish troops. With these he marched inland, defeated Hanno, Hannibal's commander in northern Spain, and took prisoner Hanno himself and Indibilis, the chief of the important Spanish tribe the Ilergetes. The main result was that much of Spain north of the Ebro—which had come under Carthaginian control for the first time earlier in that year—seized this chance to throw off whatever slight allegiance towards Carthage its people had had forced upon them in these few months. An attack on Gnaeus' ships was only a minor setback; and when he went into winter quarters at friendly Tarraco for winter 218/217 he had firmly fixed the pattern of Rome's method of operating in Spain.[3]

In 218 Gnaeus Scipio had not crossed the Ebro. He had not therefore operated in any territory in which Carthaginian rule was well entrenched, and accordingly had found little difficulty in obtaining Spanish allies. Carthage's chief commander in Spain was Hannibal's brother Hasdrubal; and he was determined to try, as far as possible, to prevent the forced and doubtful loyalty of his Spanish allies south of the Ebro from being tested. He consequently began his campaign of 217 by attacking the Roman fleet and army near the mouth of the Ebro. Unfortunately for Hasdrubal, he was badly beaten;[4] and when news of this encouraging success reached Rome, the Senate, despite Hannibal's dangerous proximity to the city, determined to follow up Gnaeus' victory. They therefore sent out his brother Publius, who as consul in 218 had originally been designated to the command in Spain, with reinforcements of twenty ships and 8,000 men. Polybius regards the Senate's chief aim in this exercise as being to prevent reinforcements from arriving for Hannibal from Spain;[5] but his view is probably anachronistic and may reflect the situation a few years later when this was certainly an immediate threat. There is no indication that it was so in 217—indeed, Hannibal was doing extraordinarily well on his own—or that the Senate had changed its mind about the purpose of the war in Spain from the previous year. As in 218, strategic reasons made Spain the obvious place for a major Roman expedition.

When the Scipio brothers joined together in summer 217, they immediately crossed the Ebro, hoping to exploit the effect on the Spaniards south of the river of Gnaeus' defeat of Hasdrubal. The Roman fleet ravaged the coast while the army advanced towards Saguntum, where the merest accident provided a useful opportunity of attracting more widespread Spanish support (though they did not in fact take the town). When Hannibal had captured Saguntum in 219 he had turned it into a garrison town in which he kept many of the hostages whom the Carthaginians were in the habit of taking from the Spaniards. Not unnaturally, this was a very unpopular practice; and when the Roman army approached, one of the local Spanish chiefs, Abilyx, decided he preferred Rome to Carthage: and in order to ingratiate himself with the Scipios, he tricked Bostar, the Carthaginian garrison commander, into putting the hostages into Roman hands. It was a glorious chance for the Scipios to demonstrate Roman magnanimity and to point a contrast with the Carthaginians' harshness; and they did not waste it. They repatriated all the hostages; and by sending Abilyx round with the returning prisoners, they made sure that the Spaniards were well instructed about the advantages of joining Rome. The result was a surge of Spanish hostility against Carthage and of support for Rome.[6]

The pattern of the Spanish war was further emphasized by events of 216. Hasdrubal began with rebellion among some of his western allies, the Tartesii; and he had to waste time in suppressing it. Before he could move against the Romans, who had again spent the winter in the comfortable safety of Tarraco, he received instructions from Carthage to march to Italy and join Hannibal. Once this order became widely known to the Spaniards, their inclination towards Rome became stronger, and Hasdrubal protested to his government that, if he left Spain in the present circumstances, Carthage's empire there would soon be lost. Nevertheless a new commander, Himilco, was sent out to Spain with reinforcements and Hasdrubal's orders to proceed to Italy were confirmed.

It was clearly the job of the Scipios to prevent this march: in 216 Hasdrubal's arrival in Italy in the aftermath of Cannae might have been disastrous for Rome. They accordingly met Hasdrubal and his army a little south of the Ebro near Ibera. The battle was violent, but the Scipios won decisively. Hasdrubal's army was cut to pieces; his march to Italy was frustrated; and the Scipios' success added impetus to those Spanish tribes which were prepared to be influenced by it to join the winners. Furthermore, the news of the battle, when it reached Rome, will have done something to relieve the depression of Cannae.[7]

One battle, however, did not win the war, as Hannibal also was currently finding out to his cost in Italy. Only the area north of the Ebro in easy reach of the coast was yet reasonably secure to Rome; Carthaginian influence was still pervasive throughout the south and west; and the Scipios could not, in the Italian crisis after Cannae, expect any reinforcements from Italy. The Carthaginians, on the other hand, were not so hard pressed. The Scipios accordingly had to rely increasingly on Spanish military support, and their advance after the battle of Ibera was correspondingly cautious. But they did gradually win over many Spaniards south of the Ebro; and in 213, by recovering Saguntum, they gained a strong base south of the river, the lack of which had hindered their progress.[8] Yet the reliance which circumstances forced them to place on local Spanish troops caused the greatest setback which the Scipios had yet received in Spain; for while their élite Italian troops were depleted, Carthage maintained three separate armies in Spain under Hasdrubal Barca, Hasdrubal son of Gisgo, and Mago. The Scipios faced a dilemma: to go on the defensive meant admitting their real weakness to the Spaniards, an admission which might have immeasurable implications in terms of reduced influence and prestige. Yet to attack was highly dangerous.

Characteristically, they chose the boldest, and most immediately dangerous, way out of their dilemma. Encouraged by reports of disagreements among Carthage's commanders, the Scipios, true to the dictum that Spain is a country where large armies starve and small armies get beaten, divided their forces for 211 and marched up-country against the Carthaginians. Large parts of their two armies were composed of Spaniards, the supposedly friendly Celtiberians. This, it turned out, was a fatal mistake. Gnaeus was first to suffer from Celtiberian desertions; and in his subsequent attempt to retreat he was cut off and killed by Hasdrubal Barca's army. Soon afterwards Publius was similarly killed in a clash with Indibilis, the chief of the Ilergetes who had actually been a Roman prisoner in 218; his army, except for a small remnant, was destroyed.[9]

So died the two Scipio brothers. Their importance in maintaining Rome's challenge to Carthage in Spain, where it hurt Carthage severely, cannot be overestimated. Their method of placating the Spaniards whenever possible by demonstrations of generosity and by making them true allies rather than, as the Carthaginians preferred, intimidated subjects, was still, despite their fatal misfortunes with the Celtiberians, likely to prove the most effective way of combatting entrenched Carthaginian influence. It was, undoubtedly, no accident that it was a repetition, in principle, of the method whereby Rome had built up her influence in Italy, which was even now proving its worth against Hannibal. It set the course for Roman policy in Spain for the remainder of the war; and subsequent Roman commanders followed precisely the same general technique. The two Scipios, just as much as Quintus Fabius Maximus, deserve high credit for keeping alive Roman prospects in the war as a whole in the weeks after Trasimene and Cannae. Their successful attempts to keep the Carthaginians occupied in Spain while Italy recovered from the early blows of Hannibal's invasion were crucial. The Senate at the beginning of the war had realized the vital importance of the Spanish front: the Scipios did not let Rome down.

II *The Younger Scipio*

The news of the deaths of the Scipios, as it spread through Spain, had a serious effect on many of the Spanish tribes which had recently joined Rome, for their loyalty seems to have been basically a personal relationship with the Scipios, not a public one with Rome. Thus while the men who took command of the remnants of the armies— Lucius Marcius, a tribune of the soldiers, and Tiberius Fonteius— managed to pull the armies together in the short term, they did not have much positive effect on the long-term outlook of the war (although the later Roman tradition, to compensate for the deaths of the Scipios, patriotically invented a striking victory over Hasdrubal for Marcius).[10] The unpleasant truth was that the deaths of the Scipios meant that Rome's position had to be withdrawn to the Ebro. Nothing south of the river was retained; indeed, the Carthaginians probably even managed to recover some territory to the north of it.

The Senate urgently needed to reinforce Rome's position in Spain. Fortunately the siege of Capua had ended in 211, and Gaius Claudius Nero, who had been involved with it, was now available. He was immediately sent out to Spain with some 6,000 troops as reinforcements. Nero was perhaps intended to be no more than a competent stop-gap, whose availability suggested his appointment. No decision would be taken about the longer-term commander until after the election of the magistrates in 210: Nero did not have sufficient troops to take the offensive—indeed, it is doubtful if he was intended to do more than try to stop the deterioration of the Roman position. But so far as propping up the wavering enthusiasm of the Spaniards was concerned, he seems to have been a failure; for although he carefully avoided a battle with Hasdrubal, Rome's position continued to worsen.[11]

When in due course the Senate came to consider a long-term appointment to the Spanish command, it deliberately adopted the unusual procedure of asking the People to elect a proconsul (the Senate usually appointed such officers itself). The man thus chosen was the twenty-six-year-old son of the late Publius Scipio, also called confusingly Publius Cornelius Scipio. His identity may give a clue to the reason for the unusual procedure of his appointment. For Scipio was very young for the post and comparatively inexperienced. He had held his only previous magistracy, the unimportant aedileship, as recently as 213. Yet he shared his father's name and fame, and was in his own right extremely popular with the mass of the people. He had served on his father's staff, as was the Roman custom, in 218 when the elder Publius, then consul, first met Hannibal at the Ticinus; and in that engagement Scipio saved his father's life, thereby winning a reputation for personal bravery which he never lost.[12]

A late Roman tradition, which Livy and some other writers mention, makes Scipio rally the Roman survivors after Cannae;[13] but Polybius, who got his information from Scipio's close friend Gaius Laelius, does not mention the incident, which must therefore be regarded as improbable. Perhaps more likely is that he continued on his father's staff when the elder Publius Scipio took up his command in Spain in 217. If so, he will have had first-hand experience of the methods of his father and uncle, and will have shared with them and learned their techniques of dealing with the Spanish tribes. This will of course have been in itself an excellent reason for his being appointed to the Spanish command after the elder Scipios' deaths, despite his youth and lack of formal experience as a magistrate. And, to compensate for this, the older and more mature Marcus Junius Silanus was given him as colleague.

Moreover, even if Scipio had not already been in Spain with his father and uncle, he was certainly the one man who could be expected to make the most of the personal connections with the Spaniards which they had forged. Gaius Claudius Nero was conspicuously failing to do this. Add that Hannibal was still in Italy, was still a formidable threat, and that experienced men to command the armies sent against him were in short supply, and it is reasonably easy to see how circumstances pointed firmly to Scipio as the most suitable candidate for the Spanish command. Yet the Senate could not itself make this virtually unprecedented appointment, because it involved giving the command of Roman troops to a private citizen—and a very young one, at that (though it was normal practice for the Senate to appoint the regularly elected ex-magistrates to proconsulships after their year of office). But by insisting that an election should be held, it drew attention to the unusual qualities both of the circumstances and of its choice for the command, and thereby it seems to have ensured that when the People came to vote there was only one candidate. The People had no alternative to appointing the man the Senate wanted (though the results will have made them happy enough).[14]

Scipio took up his command at once. After levying 10,000 new troops and 1,000 cavalry, he set out for Spain where he arrived at Emporiae in early autumn 210. At once the magic of his name began to affect Rome's wavering Spanish allies, and as he made his way to the Roman base at Tarraco, their representatives swarmed to meet him. His dead father's and uncle's prestige with the Spaniards was strongly reinforced by the strength of Scipio's own personality, and in his welcoming of the allies' delegates he exuded confidence and sincerity. By this time it was too late in the year for military operations; but while the troops stayed in winter quarters at Tarraco, Scipio did not waste his own time. He fully realized the importance of his exploiting the Spaniards' willingness to contract personal loyalties and obligations. His vigorous personality produced a pervasive impression of his sincerity and competence; and he took deliberate steps to spread this impression among the Spaniards by personally visiting the allied communities, strengthening and renewing the bonds they had formed with his father and uncle through first-hand connections of his own.[15]

By these means Scipio strengthened the resolve of Rome's Spanish allies north of the Ebro. But this in itself did not hurt the Carthaginians in the south; and accordingly it could have no appreciable effect on the war in Italy. What was ideally needed was to defeat the main forces of the enemy so decisively as to make it clear to the Spaniards, particularly to those in the south who remained under Carthaginian control, that Carthage was so badly beaten that she was unable to recover her power and influence in Spain without Rome's permission. In the meanwhile, to stimulate widespread Spanish awareness of Rome's vitality and continuing involvement in Spain, Scipio conceived the need for a quick but spectacular success; and he saw this in nothing less than the capture of Carthage's Spanish capital, New Carthage, where her Spanish treasure, baggage and hostages were kept. As it happened, the Carthaginian commanders had found it convenient to split up their army and to winter in three separate places, all a considerable distance from New Carthage. The absence of an energetic Roman commander since the deaths of the elder Scipios had made this seem safe enough. But when Scipio discovered not only this, but also that in spring 209 each Carthaginian division was at first operating separately near its winter quarters, he determined to put into effect at once the imaginative plan that he had conceived during the winter.

Scipio's forced march over the 300 miles from the Ebro to New Carthage, the surprise of the small Carthaginian garrison, the convenient wind which made shallower than usual the protecting lagoon and which allowed Scipio to claim to his troops that the sea-god Neptune was on their side, the bravery and spirit of the Roman troops stimulated by Scipio's attractive and flamboyant character, these are all detailed by Polybius and Livy and can easily be found in their books.[16] Here it is sufficient to notice that by nightfall on the day of the assault the garrison had surrendered and the city had fallen. Scipio's extravagant gamble had come off. Both the power and, perhaps more important in the long term, the prestige of the Carthaginians in this area of southern Spain, where their influence had for a generation been paramount, had suffered a blow as devastating as it was sudden. And Scipio intended to exploit his spectacular success by spreading the news of it over a wider area of southern Spain than the immediate environs of New Carthage.

His means were conveniently to hand. A large number of citizens had been taken prisoner and hostages captured during the attack. The citizens of New Carthage were easily dealt with: they were simply dismissed to their homes after Scipio had made sure that they knew to whom they owed their freedom. Artisans he employed as slaves in manufacturing war materials for his army and navy, but with the encouraging promise of freedom if Rome won the war— which was probably more than they could have expected from Carthage in the event of her success. Some of the prisoners he even employed as oarsmen in the fleet, again with the stimulating promise of freedom if Rome won. But his chief hope of fully exploiting his success lay in the 300 or so noble Spanish hostages whom the Carthaginians, according to their normal unpopular practice, had taken from the Spanish tribes under their control and had kept at New Carthage. To them Scipio promised freedom if their tribes would join Rome; and as an earnest of his generous intentions he distributed presents to them and took especial care to prevent the women from being violated.

Scipio's capture of New Carthage and his method of exploiting his success bore immediate fruits, both in Rome and in Spain. Towards the end of the year Gaius Laelius carried the news of Scipio's success to Rome, and the Senate decreed a day of public thanksgiving. There could clearly be no question of recalling Scipio and Silanus: Scipio's adventurous appointment had paid off handsomely. Indeed, when the Senate came to consider its appointments for 208, instead of extending their commands in Spain for the usual single year, Scipio and Silanus were confirmed indefinitely, 'until such time as the Senate might recall them'.[17] In Spain Scipio's friendly treatment of the captured Spanish hostages began to produce results as soon as he returned to his winter base at Tarraco and was widely received as a 'new deal' by men who were already finding irksome the Carthaginian rule of fear.[18]

The first Spanish chief to accept Scipio's invitation was Edeco, whose tribe, the Edetani, lived between the Ebro and Saguntum. He asked, in a way which the Romans will have regarded as unconditional surrender (*deditio*), to be a friend and ally of Rome. Scipio, as was his nature and his technique, received Edeco as a personal friend, granted all his requests and restored his hostages. Edeco's kind treatment thereafter brought a stream of Spanish chiefs to

Tarraco, who bound themselves to Scipio and to Rome, and grate-fully received the restoration of their hostages. The most important of these chiefs were the brothers Indibilis and Mandonius of the Ilergetes who, despite living north of the Ebro, had in the past been enthusiastic supporters of the Carthaginian cause—indeed, Indibilis was responsible for killing Scipio's father—but who had, for this very reason, begun to resent the fact that they were not trusted and still had to supply Hasdrubal with hostages as guarantees of their good behaviour. Scipio's capture of their hostages was the crucial turning point for them. Early in 208 Indibilis led a mutiny of the Spaniards in Hasdrubal's army, who deserted in large numbers and began negotiations with Scipio. The result—though Scipio may have retained some doubts, later shown to be justified, about the sincerity of these Spaniards—was a formal written treaty in which the main clause declared that Indibilis would subordinate himself to the Roman generals; he will no doubt also have been required to provide supplies.[19]

Scipio's capture of New Carthage had had very largely the result he had hoped for. The Carthaginians were severely embarrassed by the Spanish defections and by the strength of the support which Scipio seemed to be attracting from the Spaniards; yet Hannibal was still committed to the war in Italy, committed, it must by now have seemed to the Romans, to an extent where he was apparently pre-pared to lose Spain altogether rather than abandon his Italian enter-prise and admit that he had failed. But since Hannibal was, despite all Rome's efforts, still entrenched in Italy, Scipio had no immediate alternative but to penetrate still further into Carthaginian Spain. And his method, of forming personal contacts with the Spaniards—turning them, in effect, into his clients—made it seem progressively less likely, the longer he operated in Spain, that Rome would ever be able to shrug off the web of mutual obligations which Scipio was spinning between Rome and the Spaniards. The Spanish war had been begun in order to hurt Carthage as deeply as possible at the least risk and expense to Rome. It had certainly hurt Carthage; but not to the extent that she was prepared to give up the war in Italy. The further Roman armies advanced into southern Spain, the more likely it began to seem that the result might be to drive the Carthaginians from Spain altogether. Yet by now it must have been reasonably clear to the more percipient of the Romans that even this extremity would probably make little impression on Hannibal's tenacity in Italy (or, apparently, on that of the Carthaginian government). It was, in fact, fast becoming evident that the only way Carthage could be vitally damaged and Hannibal driven from Italy was—as the Senate had, indeed, planned from the beginning of the war—by striking firmly and directly at Carthage's position in Africa.

Since 218 the Roman fleet, based on Sicily, had nearly every year attacked the coast of Carthaginian Africa, though it had never stayed long enough to do more than superficial damage. The elder Scipios had tried to make these efforts more effective in 212 by contracting an agreement with a dissident African neighbour of Carthage's, the Numidian sheikh Syphax; but this had come to nothing because Syphax was badly beaten by Massinissa, another Numidian sheikh who continued to support Carthage, and because the Scipios were killed the very next year.[20] But the elder Scipios' contact with Syphax was a stimulating example for the younger Scipio, who soon realized that Carthage could only be ultimately beaten in Africa. And events of 208 must have made this realization even clearer. For although Scipio won a major battle against Hasdrubal at Baecula, in the Baetis valley, the rich heartland of Carthaginian Spain, Hasdrubal still made no attempt to come to terms, despite heavy losses in men and prestige. Scipio again made his characteristic generous demonstration of freeing all Spanish prisoners without ransom and restoring them to their homes. The contrast between his success with this policy in Spain and Hannibal's failure with it in Italy is a measure of the difference of the character of the rule of Rome and Carthage over their respective allies. On this occasion Scipio paid particular attention to freeing his prisoner Massiva, since he realized the ultimate importance of Africa in the war. For Massiva was the nephew of Syphax's Numidian opponent Massinissa, who was currently one of Carthage's strongest African allies. This was Scipio's first attempt to follow the example of the elder Scipios and obtain for Rome a personal connection with a powerful African chief, and to put into practice in Africa the policy of seducing Carthage's local allies, which had been so successful in Spain.[21]

But the continuation of this policy was still some distance away. Spain remained to be dealt with. It did not take Scipio long. After the battle at Baecula Hasdrubal withdrew to the north with his remaining 10,000 men. His intention, it soon became clear, was to march to Italy and join Hannibal, who badly needed reinforcements, but the circumstances in which Hasdrubal set out—virtually abandoning Spain to Scipio—suggest that it can only have been an act of desperation, an attempt to trick Scipio into following him, as the elder Publius Scipio had followed Hannibal from the Rhône in 218, and thus to relieve pressure on Carthaginian Spain. The ploy failed, as Hasdrubal must have suspected. Scipio merely detached a small force to ensure that Hasdrubal did indeed cross the Pyrenees, so that he could send advance warning to Rome of Hasdrubal's approach. When Hasdrubal arrived in Italy, as we have seen, the Romans were quite capable of dealing with him. Scipio has often been blamed for letting Hasdrubal get away: but if he had followed, he would have done exactly what Hasdrubal wanted, for such an action would have left Spain denuded of Roman troops and free to be recovered by the other two Carthaginian commanders, in the absence of Scipio's formidable personal abilities. The threat of Hasdrubal's arrival in Italy, though serious enough if it had been unexpected or unchecked, was much exaggerated by the later patriotic Roman tradition which liked to see him, wrongly but understandably, as another Hannibal. Hasdrubal was not another Hannibal, and Rome in 207 was by no means as ill-prepared for invasion as was Rome in 218. Hasdrubal's march, it seems clear, was a gambler's last throw, a final desperate attempt to panic the Roman Senate into making peace in order to save Italy: for only such a quick peace in Italy could now save Carthaginian Spain.[22]

Hasdrubal had misjudged his man. Scipio stayed firmly in Spain and Hasdrubal's desperate march ended in the Carthaginian fiasco of the battle on the Metaurus. The chief immediate result was felt not in Italy but in Spain, where the balance of power and influence now tipped dramatically in Rome's favour. 207 saw no major battle in Spain; but early in 206 Hasdrubal son of Gisgo was heavily defeated at Ilipa, near Seville. Carthage's remaining influence with the Spaniards now quickly collapsed. By the end of 206 only Gades remained from Carthage's Spanish empire; and it survived only until the next year.[23] Spain was conquered from Carthage; Scipio was victorious. Yet Rome's success, disappointingly, did not bring about the ending of the whole war which the Senate had hoped it might. Carthage did not surrender; Hannibal remained entrenched as firmly as ever in southern Italy, a lingering threat to the security of Italy which even now the Senate could not afford to underestimate. Thus even after Scipio's outstanding success in Spain, Rome faced a pair of difficult problems, one old, one new: how, now that Rome's success in Spain had not ousted Hannibal from Italy, was Hannibal to be finally defeated? and how, now that Rome's victory over Carthage in Spain was complete, was the Senate going to deal with Spain? The first question required an immediate answer; the second was not so pressing, and we, like the Roman Senate, may defer answering it until later.[24]

To the first question Scipio had his own answer ready. It was clear to him that Carthage could only be brought to make peace by a Roman invasion of Africa—some initial preparations for which, in the form of further personal contacts with the two Numidian sheikhs, Syphax and Massinissa, he had made even before leaving Spain.[25] To put his strategic answer into practice, however, he would have to convince the Senate that he was right, and to do this most effectively he needed the consulship. His arrival in Rome was, conveniently, shortly before the consular elections for 205; and though his reasonable hope for a triumph was dashed when jealous members of the Senate produced a very dubious trumped-up technical objection, the Senate did not elect the consuls and it could not prevent his election. Together with another distinguished young noble, Publius Licinius Crassus, he was elected to the supreme magistracy for 205.[26] The final and decisive phase of the war was about to begin.

CHAPTER VII

THE WAR WITH HANNIBAL
IN AFRICA

I Why Africa?

WHEN Rome declared war on Carthage in 218, the Senate's first intention had been to send armies to Spain and Africa. This plan was upset by the unexpected appearance of Hannibal in Italy, but although both consuls had been forced to abandon their first intentions and unite to defend Italy, part of the Roman expeditionary force to Spain had continued as planned. It was, however, less easy to carry out the projected invasion of Africa with the reduced manpower and other resources which were available after Hannibal's invasion; and it had perforce to be indefinitely postponed. This did not mean that Carthaginian Africa escaped scot-free. Throughout the war a Roman fleet was stationed at Lilybaeum in western Sicily, and part of its duty was to carry out guerrilla raids on the coast of Carthaginian North Africa: from 217 to 207 inclusive, with the possible exceptions of 214–212 (when Rome's forces in Sicily were fully occupied with the defection of Syracuse) and 209, the fleet mounted some kind of raid on Africa each year. These forays obviously could have nothing like the military effect of a serious invasion, but they served as a sharp and constant reminder to the Carthaginians that the Roman Senate had not lost sight of its first objective.[1]

Raids on the African coast, however regular or successful, were only one small aspect of Rome's overall strategy. They could never do sufficient damage to be more than a token gesture of Rome's total involvement in the war. Another series of incidents led more directly to the invasion of 204. In 213 the elder Scipios, while operating in Spain, had contacted the powerful Numidian sheikh Syphax who had agreed to co-operate with them. Nothing had come of this agreement, since in 211 the Scipios were both killed; and in Africa Carthage kept Syphax occupied by encouraging against him Gala, another Numidian sheikh, whose son Massinissa quickly ended

Syphax's immediate threat to Carthage.[2] Syphax nevertheless valued his Roman connection; and when in 210 his position improved, he asked the Senate for Roman friendship. The Senate gave him no active help, but sent him gifts: such friends clearly deserved encouragement.[3]

This example was followed by the younger Scipio in his ostentatiously friendly treatment of Massinissa's nephew Massiva;[4] but it was another two years, after Hasdrubal's death at the Metaurus and after Scipio's victory at Ilipa, before Massinissa was sufficiently convinced of Rome's superiority to follow up Scipio's flattering advance and to approach Silanus. Influenced by his friendly reception, Massinissa returned to Africa to try to persuade his tribe that their future lay with Rome.[5] Scipio also hoped to persuade Syphax who, though encouraged both by his earlier contacts with the elder Scipios and by his recent presents from the Roman Senate, had nevertheless returned to his alliance with Carthage; for there was no obvious sign of a firm Roman commitment to fight in Africa. After Ilipa and the defection of Massinissa, Scipio decided to re-open negotiations with Syphax: for, Scipio hoped, he would soon be able to provide proof of Rome's seriousness to his African friends, in the form of firm plans for a large-scale Roman expedition. Syphax might therefore now find Scipio's proposition more attractive.

He first sent Gaius Laelius across to Syphax with gifts, to make the initial approach; but although Syphax seemed to give Laelius a friendly reception, he refused to conclude any formal agreement before discussing it with Scipio in person. This awkward stipulation may have been designed to deter Scipio, but if so Syphax had chosen the wrong man; and he was duly impressed with Scipio's seriousness when his challenge was accepted and Scipio crossed to Africa. Although Scipio was nearly captured en route by Hasdrubal son of Gisgo, who was also travelling to visit Syphax—a fact which, taken together with Syphax's subsequent vacillation, suggests that he had not expected Scipio to come—he arrived safely and was entertained to a diplomatic dinner-party at which Hasdrubal was also a guest. Syphax, though Livy depicts him as proud to be courted by the two most powerful nations of the world, can in practice only have been embarrassed at the potentially disastrous choice before him, of inevitably offending one or the other. The result was that Scipio and Syphax agreed to co-operate; but in view of Syphax's wavering loyalty to Carthage and indecisive toying with friendship with Rome over the past few years, Scipio can have placed little real faith in his reliability so long as no Roman army was in Africa. But he clearly felt that he could not afford to throw away untried any chance, however slight, of securing so potentially valuable a friend.[6] On his return to Spain and before leaving for Italy, Scipio also had his first meeting with Massinissa—Silanus had conducted the earlier negotiations—and formed a personal friendship with him which, in time, like Scipio's personal friendships with the Spanish chiefs, produced enormous benefits for Rome and for Massinissa.[7]

It is clear from all this that when Scipio returned to Rome at the end of 206 he was determined to conduct the long-postponed Roman invasion of Africa, originally scheduled for 218. He had himself done no recent fighting in Italy; and his success in Spain had convinced him that Hannibal could be winkled out of his Italian shell only by a Roman attack on Carthage in Africa which might sap the will of the Carthaginian people to resist. The sincerity of Scipio's convictions, however, did not mean that he would necessarily find it easy to convince the conservative Roman Senate that he was right. Most of the distinguished senior senators had been actively fighting Hannibal in Italy for thirteen weary years. The Senate as a body thus contained emotional vested interests in the conventional strategy of directing Rome's main war effort against Hannibal himself; and in the circumstances, many members might well have resented the implications of the young Scipio's suggestion, that there was no longer any point in continuing the Italian campaign on the traditional large scale and that the Senate's aim—to get rid of Hannibal—could more easily be achieved by another dangerous and expensive overseas venture. And the conservative senators may have seen some confirmation of their doubts in the fact that Hannibal had been prepared to see Carthaginian Spain lost rather than abandon his position in Italy.[8]

Furthermore, Scipio's difficulties were compounded by the personal and political jealousy of many senators at his successes in Spain —jealousy which had been sufficiently powerful to persuade the Senate as a whole to think up some dubious legalistic objections to its awarding him a triumph.[9] Scipio's opponents in the Senate, however, were not strong enough to stop the People electing him consul for 205. After the election, the real struggle, personal, political and strategic, on which the outcome of the whole war might depend, came when the Senate allocated provinces to the new consuls; for it was now that it had to decide whether to confirm or reject Scipio's view of the way the war should henceforward be conducted.[10]

Before the crucial debate in the Senate Scipio had offended some senators by unwisely trying to forestall discussions, through letting it be widely known among the People that he expected Africa as his province. Had he had more experience of practical politics, he would have realized that such tactics would not stampede the Roman Senate. For the view that Hannibal, being in Italy, could only be defeated in Italy, was an entrenched part of the strategic thinking of many older senators; and their view was expressed by its most distinguished proponent, Quintus Fabius Maximus, the veteran dictator of 217. The general theme of his speech was to emphasize the crucial importance of the war in Italy—in effect, amounting to the assertion of the patriotic slogan, 'no negotiation while the enemy remains on Italian soil'—and to attack Scipio's personal ambition.[11] His views were conservative, but they were no less honourable, authoritative or sincere for that reason.

But Scipio was consul. He was one of the men who would have to carry out the Senate's decision, whatever it was; and his views obviously must have carried great weight. In the end, a majority of the Senate seems to have been reluctantly convinced—according to Livy, only after Scipio had threatened to appeal directly to the Roman People—and Fabius and his supporters were effectively beaten. But even then Scipio had to be satisfied with a less enthusiastic senatorial commitment than he had hoped for—in effect, a compromise which saved the face of the conservatives: one consul should have Sicily, thirty ships and permission to cross to Africa if he thought this in the public interest; the other should have the war against Hannibal in Italy. Since Scipio's consular colleague was the chief state priest (*pontifex maximus*), whose religious duties made it difficult for him to leave Italy, Scipio had clearly won, though less decisively than he would ideally have liked. For even at this stage, his opponents managed to persuade the Senate to refuse him permission to levy the new troops which he asked for. But despite the Senate's grudging support, the last phase of the war, in essence a return to the long-postponed plan of 218, was about to begin.[12]

II 'Scipio Africanus'

There was a great difference in strategic conception and in practical difficulty between mounting small-scale guerrilla attacks on the north African coast—the recent Roman practice—and mounting a large-scale expedition. For the latter needed the capacity to fend for itself while living indefinitely in Africa, and, when necessary, to confront and defeat whatever forces Carthage might raise. The most recent precedent—and that more than fifty years ago—was the expedition of Marcus Atilius Regulus in the First Punic War. It was scarcely encouraging. But Scipio had certain advantages which Regulus had not possessed. Perhaps most important in the short term was Scipio's confidence in his own ability—a confidence which, unlike Regulus', turned out to be fully justified. But this did not lead him to neglect essential military preparations—despite the difficulties which his senatorial opponents created for him—which went ahead on a massive scale in Sicily throughout 205 and which impressed a senatorial investigation committee when it arrived to examine mischievous charges of negligence and laxity brought by his opponents. Secondly, and perhaps most importantly in the long term, Scipio had, when he was in Spain, already equipped himself with African allies in Syphax and Massinissa, whose Numidian cavalry had been up to now one of the most effective weapons of the Carthaginian war machine.

Syphax, as it turned out—and as Scipio may have suspected— proved unreliable; but Massinissa remained a staunch friend of Rome until his death more than fifty years later, and his help and advice were immediately crucial. In 205, however, Scipio was too busy with his preparations for the major invasion to mount more than a conventional raid on the African coast, near Hippo Regius. It was conducted by his friend Gaius Laelius, and it had more immediate effect on Carthage than any earlier Roman raid, since the Carthaginians at first thought it was the expedition of Scipio himself; but they quickly learned the truth, and although Laelius collected rich booty, the raid was militarily unimportant. But politically it had some consequence. For Massinissa came to see Laelius, alleging that Syphax—a bitter enemy, past and present, of Massinissa—was unreliable, and complaining that Scipio's delay was losing the potential advantages of Carthage's unpreparedness. Scipio would no doubt take these warnings cautiously, even if he was already doubtful about Syphax; for Syphax's hostility had recently made Massinissa an exile, whose only hope of recovering control of his own tribe lay in the Roman invasion. Hence his attempt to discredit Syphax and to urge Scipio to act quickly. But, in any case, by then it was too late in the year for Scipio to do anything, and he held firm to his intention of beginning the invasion in 204. Massinissa would have to support himself over the winter as best he could.[13]

Scipio, however, soon learned that Massinissa had not simply been venting his personal hostility towards Syphax. During winter 205/204 Hasdrubal son of Gisgo—Scipio's fellow dinner-guest when he had visited Syphax in 206—persuaded Syphax to repudiate the alliance which he had made with Scipio in 206 and instead to rejoin the Carthaginians. Hasdrubal's immediate bait was his nubile daughter Sophonisba, and the amorous Syphax was easily induced to let his lust direct his foreign policy. Before Massinissa could be persuaded to defect by any similar Carthaginian diplomatic pandering to his equally volatile lust, Scipio took his first opportunity in spring 204 to cross to Africa, where he was soon joined by Massinissa with 200 Numidian cavalry.[14]

Massinissa's local knowledge and excellent cavalry were major factors in Scipio's subsequent success; and he was well rewarded in the final settlement, in full recognition of his value. The military details of the African campaigns, however, need only be dealt with briefly.[15] It is sufficient to note that in 204 and 203 Scipio and Massinissa were so successful in ravaging Carthaginian north Africa, in defeating Carthage's armies, and finally in capturing Syphax and restoring Massinissa to his sheikhdom in Numidia, that the Carthaginians were forced to admit that they did not have the resources to repel Scipio. This was, of course, exactly the admission that Scipio had hoped for: by forcing it, his strategy for ending the war in Italy by attacking Carthage in Africa had been completely vindicated by the end of 203. For in the late summer the Carthaginians reluctantly took the momentous step of finally acknowledging that Carthage's attack on Rome had failed: Hannibal was recalled to defend his home.[16]

The safety of Italy was now assured. Whether Scipio won or lost the final battle which, it seemed, any campaign in 202 must produce, Italy was safe. A victory for Hannibal on African soil would of course affect the terms on which peace was eventually agreed, and therefore Carthage's prospects of post-war recovery: but it was now inconceivable that it would persuade the Carthaginian Senate that any advantage could be gained from Hannibal's returning to Italy. The war was not yet over; but its most dangerous sector (for Rome) had been firmly closed.

While Hannibal was being recalled, the Carthaginians began for the first time 'talks about talks' about peace. They do not seem to have been very serious about them, however, since, almost as soon as Hannibal had returned safely, they contrived an incident which broke the truce arranged for the discussions. But this gives us no reason for believing that Scipio and the Roman Senate were also merely playing with words, for Rome now had little to gain from delaying a settlement. The proposed terms therefore give us some idea of the kind of settlement which would satisfy the Romans. They stipulated that Carthage should hand over all Roman prisoners of war and deserters; that she should withdraw her armies from Italy and Gaul (where a small Carthaginian army under Hannibal's brother Mago was desperately trying to incite another Gallic insurrection); that she should keep out of Spain and withdraw from all islands between Italy and Africa; that she should retain only twenty warships, supply Rome with half a million measures of wheat and 300,000 of barley, pay an indemnity of 5,000 talents, and recruit no more mercenaries; that she should restrict her territories to the area marked out by the 'Phoenician Trenches' (we do not know exactly where this line ran); and that Massinissa should have his traditional kingdom of the Massyli and as much of Syphax's kingdom as he could get for himself.[17]

These proposals would have reduced Carthage to a mere African power. And since they would consequently have severely circumscribed her activities in the Mediterranean world as a whole, they were severe enough to be unacceptable. For Carthage, particularly after Hannibal's return, still had the strength to fight on. Nevertheless, the terms indicate clearly enough that Rome had no intention of capitalizing on her strength and taking over direct control of any African territory. Carthage was to be left with her activities watched over by Rome's friends, but not directly by Rome herself. Rome had no territorial aspirations in Africa. The Carthaginians, however, did not see the proposals quite like this, for, not unnaturally, they were chiefly aware of what they would lose. And although Carthaginian envoys travelled to Rome and Scipio's proposed terms were approved by the Senate, Hannibal's arrival in Africa encouraged the Carthaginians to attack some Roman supply ships which were stranded just outside the harbour of Carthage. They thus broke the truce. When Roman protests were ignored, the war recommenced.[18]

It did not last much longer. After making all necessary preparations the two armies met at Naraggara in the decisive engagement conventionally known as 'the battle of Zama'.[19] Hannibal, directing his first major battle since Cannae, was heavily defeated, largely because of the ineffectiveness of his elephants which panicked and did as much damage to their own army as to the Romans, and to energetic cavalry actions by Laelius and Massinissa, the final one of which Livy regards as decisive for the whole battle: 'Just at the right moment, Laelius and Massinissa, returning from pursuing the defeated cavalry for some distance, charged the enemy's line in the rear. This cavalry charge finally shattered the Carthaginians: many were surrounded and cut down, still in their ranks; many perished as they scattered in flight over the whole open plain, where the Roman cavalry were in complete control.'[20] Recorded Carthaginian casualties vary from 20,000 killed and the same number taken prisoner, to 25,000 killed and 8,500 taken prisoner. The combined losses of Rome and Massinissa were about 5,000.[21] But whichever figures are correct (if either!), the disparity shows the depth of Hannibal's defeat. Hannibal himself was one of the first to recognize it; and after the battle his was the most insistent among Carthaginian voices recommending capitulation. Nothing, it seemed, could now be gained from fighting on. Carthage's breach of the truce the previous winter already ensured that Rome's terms would be harsher than those proposed then: no sensible Carthaginian could want to continue the war and by doing so to drive the Roman Senate into a position where the total destruction of Carthage began to seem the only way of forcing her to capitulate. Fortunately for Carthage, good sense prevailed, though there were die-hards who, ostrich-like, ignored reality and even now advised fighting on.[22]

The terms of the final settlement do not show any change in Rome's basic attitude towards Carthage and north Africa from the previous winter. But since in the meanwhile Carthage had broken a truce and had fought on for another year, thus costing Rome much money and many lives, they were more severe in detail. Carthage was, as in the draft proposals, territorially restricted to the area within the 'Phoenician Trenches', but within these she was allowed to keep all her property; no Roman garrison was imposed nor any change made in Carthage's traditional practices of government. These, as Polybius points out, were mild conditions; and they show clearly the complete absence of any Roman territorial ambition. Nor do the penal clauses of the treaty suggest otherwise: Roman prisoners of war and deserters were, as in the draft, to be handed over to the Romans; Carthage's war fleet was to be restricted to ten triremes (the rejected draft had allowed twenty); all war elephants were to be surrendered and no more trained; Carthage must not make war at all outside Africa and within Africa only in self-defence and within her own territories—a firm enough protection for Massinissa, as long as he continued to be a friend of Rome. Massinissa also benefited from a refinement of the draft proposal, no doubt in recognition of his value in the final battle, by being granted, in an imprecise phrase whose vagueness contained ominous repercussions for Carthage's future, 'all houses, lands, cities, and other property which had belonged to him or to his ancestors'. The indemnity proposed in the draft was now doubled, from 5,000 to 10,000 talents, but it was to be paid at the rate of 200 talents per year for fifty years; and a hundred hostages were to be given. Certain other clauses concerned the immediate welfare of the Roman army.[23]

The terms were finally approved in Rome early in 201. Their acceptance there and at Carthage was followed by the evacuation of the Roman army and the celebration of a splendid triumph by Scipio, an honour which his opponents could no longer deny him. The war, which had absorbed the major energies of both participants for half a generation, was ended; and in recognition of Scipio's supreme achievement in bringing this about he was henceforth universally known as 'Scipio Africanus'.

CHAPTER VIII

EAST OF THE ADRIATIC

I Illyria

WE return to Illyria at this point because the foundations of Rome's eventual control over the Balkan peninsula were being laid at the same time as she was struggling against Hannibal in Italy and against the Carthaginian empire in Spain. And while the 'Second Illyrian War' did not itself bring about an immediate increase in Rome's formal control east of the Adriatic, it contained the seeds from which grew the commitment of Philip V of Macedon to oppose Rome, from which in turn developed Rome's long-standing intervention in the Balkans. The Roman settlement after the 'First Illyrian War' had not been enforced by the permanent establishment of Roman garrisons. Rome's interest was not sufficiently great. The Senate had been content to rely on Rome's friendship with Demetrius of Pharos and various communities—the Atintanes, the Parthini, Apollonia, Epidamnus, Issa and Corcyra—who had supported Rome during the war against queen Teuta. The 'Second Illyrian War' had its origin in this settlement.

The facts are straightforward in outline. The war took place in 219, on the eve of the war with Hannibal—indeed, while Hannibal was actually besieging Saguntum. It was conducted by both consuls of the year, Lucius Aemilius Paullus and Marcus Livius Salinator, both of whom won triumphs. Their success consisted of defeating Rome's recent friend Demetrius of Pharos, destroying his base town Pharos, his castle Dimallum, and his control over that part of Illyria which had been assured him as Rome's friend in the settlement after the 'First Illyrian War'. They also drove him into exile with the new king of Macedon, nineteen-year-old Philip V. As Demetrius' influence with Philip increased over the next few years, Philip began to envisage a grand alliance with Hannibal against Rome. Since this development was a critical turning point in Roman policy towards the east, we must first examine how Demetrius had changed in less than eight years, from being Rome's ally and friend to being an enemy who required the deployment of two consular armies, and whose defeat merited the award of two triumphs.

The surviving sources are poor, but a reasonably coherent picture can be assembled. Polybius says that the Senate's reason for acting in 219 was its awareness that war with Carthage might soon be necessary; and, as we have seen, this will have been based on the report of the Roman envoys who had visited Hannibal and Carthage late in 220. Polybius then goes on to explain why the war in Illyria was necessary at all: 'It happened that at this time Demetrius of Pharos had chosen to ignore the benefits which the Romans had conferred on him, since he had come to despise Rome for two reasons, firstly because of her difficulties in dealing with the Gauls, and secondly because of the danger which currently threatened Rome from Carthage. Demetrius now placed all his hopes in the Macedonian royal house because he had fought alongside Antigonus (Philip's predecessor) and taken part with him in the battles against Cleomenes. He was now ravaging and destroying the Illyrian cities subject to Rome; and he had sailed beyond Lissus, contrary to the treaty, with fifty light ships (*lemboi*), and had pillaged many of the islands of the Cyclades. When the Romans looked at these events and, moreover, saw that the Macedonian royal house was flourishing, they were anxious to secure the eastern flank of Italy and believed that they had time to do it, in this way correcting the misconceptions of the Illyrians and censuring and punishing the ingratitude and fickleness of Demetrius.'[1]

How much of this motivation can we regard as authentic?[2] Polybius' source was probably the Roman senator Fabius Pictor, which means that his picture is likely to be slanted, at the very least, in favour of Rome. Moreover, it was written up later when, in the light of subsequent events, these Illyrian affairs assumed more significance than they seemed to possess at the time. In particular, Polybius' double emphasis on the danger of Macedon is likely to be a subsequent interpretation; for in 219 Rome had never shown the slightest interest in Macedonian affairs. Furthermore, it is simply not true that the affairs of the Macedonian royal house were flourishing at this time. For the new king, Philip V, had only recently come to the throne, and he was currently involved in a war with the Aetolian League in which he had so far come off worse. Only a later interpreter who knew how powerful Philip ultimately became could have thought that Macedon was flourishing in 219. We can therefore reject fear of Macedon as the Senate's motive.

THE BALKANS
AND ASIA MINOR

DARDANIA

Lissus

Epidamnus

MACEDONIA

Abdera

Pella

Amphipolis

ORESTIS

Thessalonica

Apollonia

Oricum

R. Aoüs

Pydna

PERRHAEBIA

Tempe

Phoenice

Phaloria   Atrax   Larisa

THESSALY

Cynoscephalae

CORCYRA

EPIRUS

Pindus Mts.

ATHAMANIA

Phthiotic   Demetrias

Pharsalus   Thebes

Ambracia

DOLOPIA

Larisa
Cremaste

ADRIATIC

ACARNANIA

Lamia

Heraclea

Oreus

EUBOEA

Thermopylae   Nicaea

AETOLIA   PHOCIS

Coronea   Haliartus   Chalcis

SEA

Amphissa

Eretria

Naupactus   LOCRIS   Delphi   Thebes   Delium

Aegium   BOEOTIA   Oropus

Leontium   Thisbe

Sicyon   Eleusis   Athens

Carystus

Corinth

ELIS   ACHAEA

Argos   Aegina

Megalopolis

Messene

Sparta

Pylos

N

0   20   100
miles

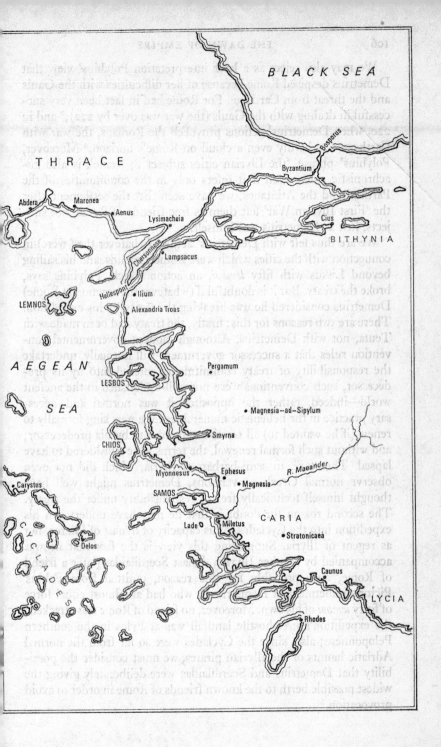

We may also reject as a later interpretation Polybius' view that Demetrius despised Rome because of her difficulties with the Gauls and the threat from Carthage. For Rome had in fact been very successful in dealing with the Gauls (the war was over by 222);[3] and in 220, when Demetrius' actions provoked the Romans, the war with Carthage was hardly even a cloud on Rome's horizon.[4] Moreover, Polybius' phrase, 'the Illyrian cities subject to Rome', is also anachronistic since, even if it refers only to the communities of the Parthini and the Atintanes, we have seen that the settlement after the 'First Illyrian War' left them as free friends of Rome, not subjects, just as Demetrius was himself.

We are thus left with Demetrius' actions (whatever they were) in connection with the cities which were Rome's friends, and his sailing beyond Lissus with fifty *lemboi*, an action which, Polybius says, broke the treaty. But it is doubtful if (whatever the reaction at Rome) Demetrius considered he was breaking the treaty by his expedition. There are two reasons for this: firstly, the treaty had been made with Teuta, not with Demetrius. Although modern governmental convention rules that a successor government will normally undertake the responsibility of treaty commitments entered into by its predecessor, such conventions were not well-established in the ancient world—indeed, rather the opposite: it was normal and necessary practice in the hellenistic monarchies for a new king formally to renew (if he wanted to) all treaties entered into by his predecessor; and without such formal renewal, the terms were considered to have lapsed. Therefore, in semi-barbarous Illyria, which did not even observe normal Greek conventions, Demetrius might well have thought himself technically free of responsibility under the treaty. The second reason for doubt is that he may have undertaken his expedition into the Cyclades in his capacity of dynast of Pharos, not as regent of Illyria. Supporting this view is the fact that he was accompanied by another Illyrian dynast Scerdilaidas (later a friend of Rome, and, probably for this reason, omitted from Fabius Pictor's indictment of Demetrius!), who had an almost equal force of forty *lemboi* of his own. Moreover, no friend of Rome was attacked: the expedition's first hostile landfall was at Pylos in the southern Peloponnese; also, since the Cyclades were so far from the normal Adriatic haunts of the Illyrian pirates, we must consider the possibility that Demetrius and Scerdilaidas were deliberately giving the widest possible berth to the known friends of Rome in order to avoid provocation.[5]

Why, then, was Rome provoked? Even if the Senate thought Demetrius had broken the treaty, he had not damaged any friend of Rome by it. A verbal protest ought therefore to have been a sufficient reminder of Rome's interest in him. It is thus clear that the Senate did not go to war for any of the superficially plausible reasons that we have looked at so far (at least, not in the way that Polybius presents them). We are thus left with the activities which Polybius describes as 'ravaging and destroying the Illyrian cities subject to Rome'. What did this amount to in practice? When the Roman consuls were about to land in Illyria in early summer 219, Demetrius expelled his political opponents in all the cities and installed his friends in power.[6] He clearly had not *already destroyed* the cities, despite the phrase which Fabius Pictor, followed by Polybius, found it convenient to use to describe his activities. But if he was able in 219 to provoke widespread *coups d'état* at such short notice, it is reasonable to assume that he must have been discreetly extending his own influence within the communities of Rome's friends over the last few years, perhaps from the time of his assuming the guardianship of Pinnes. And he will no doubt have been encouraged to do this by Rome's failure to show any obvious interest in events east of the Adriatic after 228. In 228 Rome had left her friends in Illyria, including Demetrius, free: her subsequent lack of active involvement will have encouraged Demetrius to believe in the absolute validity of that freedom.

But his belief was based on a misconception. For Rome, in fact, regarded Demetrius as a Roman client, just as she regarded all her free friends as Roman clients, wherever they might be and for however long they might seem to have been neglected by the Senate; and the obligation to do the Senate's will was the moral duty of all Roman clients. Polybius says explicitly that Demetrius had ignored the benefits conferred on him by Rome and had to be punished for his ingratitude. What this means is that in Roman eyes he had not fulfilled the moral obligation attendant on his clientship. Demetrius thus had the doubtful privilege of being the first non-Italian—but not the last—to misunderstand the nature of his free relationship with Rome. *Clientela* was not part of his Greek political vocabulary. Left legally free and, apparently, actually free also, he had acted without regard to the interests of the source of his freedom. He had, it is clear, set out discreetly to extend his influence among Rome's friends; he may even have seduced the Atintanes before the threat from Rome appeared.[7] But the Senate discovered and proved suspicious of his ultimate intentions, for if he gained control of Rome's free friends, he might thereby destroy the effective weakness of the Illyrians, a weakness which had been the main safeguard built into the settlement of 228. By expanding his influence, Demetrius was becoming that very factor which had first involved Rome in Illyria in 229, a sizeable independent maritime power on Rome's eastern flank. With war threatening in the west (by spring 219, when war with Demetrius was decided on, this must have been clear), the Senate could not afford the luxury of neglecting Demetrius' aspirations and giving him the benefit of the doubt. He had forgotten his status as client, forgotten, as Polybius puts it, the benefits conferred on him by Rome.

Demetrius was attacked because the Senate, judging from what it regarded as his past faithlessness, was afraid not so much of what he was but of what he might become. Points of detail might be raised against him (though it seems unlikely that explicit charges were brought at the time), but these would be mere pretexts.[8] Later patriotic historians, looking only for plausible pretexts for the Senate's action which concealed the real reason, 'discovered' the 'attacks' on Rome's friends and the breach of the treaty, which Polybius in turn took over from Fabius Pictor. Some even invented support by Demetrius for Rome's enemies of the moment, the Histri, in 221 (a fable perhaps originating in some independent action by Illyrian corsairs).[9] Further apologetic distortion introduced the anachronistic fear of a flourishing Macedon. It seems that anything would do for these later writers as long as it avoided the morally damaging admission that Rome might have fought a war in which two triumphs were won with insufficient *legal* right on her side.

The war, once begun, was quickly over.[10] Demetrius' inland castle Dimallum collapsed after a week's siege by the Roman consular army, and with its fall Demetrius' local support melted away.[11] The Roman fleet sailed to Pharos, where the town was razed and Demetrius' friends taken into Roman custody. Demetrius himself fled to neighbouring Macedon, where he found asylum. Rome's settlement, like that after the 'First Illyrian War', again shows clearly that, as yet, the Senate had no interest in taking long-term direct control of any territory east of the Adriatic. The Roman consuls took no action against Scerdilaidas, the other powerful Illyrian dynast. Yet Scerdilaidas, just as much as Demetrius, had (in Roman eyes) allegedly broken the treaty with Teuta by sailing south of Lissus in 220, and he also had just allied himself with Philip of Macedon—thus, inci-

dentally, proving conclusively that Macedon was not yet on Ro
political map. Rome's old friends and the two places captured in t.
war, Dimallum and Pharos, were restored to their previous free
status—though Demetrius' experience will have made them more
fully aware of its implications. Pinnes was left on the Illyrian throne,
though he was apparently ordered to pay an indemnity—the Senate's
way of recouping Rome's costs. But the whole settlement amounted
to no more than the restoration of the status quo. Thus Rome had
taught the first overseas lesson in the meaning of *clientela*. But when
Demetrius was suppressed, the consuls considered their job done.
All Roman troops were withdrawn; Aemilius and Livius returned to
Rome to celebrate their easily won triumphs.

II War with Macedon

When Demetrius of Pharos found asylum with Philip V of Macedon
in 219, Philip was deeply imbroiled in a war with the Aetolian League.
In itself this did not concern Rome at all; but this time the Senate
took care to keep an eye open for developments in Illyria which
might affect Rome. Demetrius' fellow-dynast Scerdilaidas, whose
base was probably Scodra, was the immediate cause of Rome's next
intervention east of the Adriatic. Scerdilaidas had had an alliance
with Philip; and until 218 he had duly provided the Macedonian
king with all aid. But Scerdilaidas had gained little advantage from his
alliance, since Philip's resources were too heavily strained to be able
to reward his Illyrian ally as Scerdilaidas had expected. The by-now
traditional Illyrian road to riches was through piracy; and since his
alliance with Philip had not produced the expected profits, in 217
Scerdilaidas turned to piracy. No place was immune from piratical
raids: the weak were always fair game. Macedon, despite being
Scerdilaidas' ally, was currently weakened by the war. Scerdilaidas
therefore, in addition to freebooting in the Adriatic, invaded Pela-
gonia and Dassaretia, the areas of Macedonia closest to Illyria, and
even captured a few towns. He could expect little mercy from Philip
when he extracted himself from the Aetolian war.[12]

This happened much sooner than Scerdilaidas—or anybody—had
foreseen. Philip was keeping himself informed of Hannibal's progress in Italy, perhaps on the advice of Demetrius, who hoped to use
Philip to regain his Illyrian possessions for him. While Philip was
celebrating the Nemean festival at Argos in July 217, his latest

Italy brought news of Rome's defeat at Lake Trasi-
' immediate reaction was to urge him to end the
oon as possible and to devote himself to gaining
, since this was a necessary preliminary to any
. Demetrius' self-interest in urging the importance
Illyria is evident: his encouragement of the young
o play a major role in world affairs had as primary
objective his own restoration to his Illyrian kingdom.[13]

Philip, however, took the bait. He began negotiations with the
Aetolians at once, and completed them in the autumn at a peace
conference at Naupactus. But there were those who, while desiring
peace, thought Philip was doing the right thing for the wrong reason,
and saw grave danger in his reason. Polybius records at length a
speech by the Aetolian leader Agelaus in which he took a very
gloomy view—which eventually turned out to be fully justified—of
the future of the Greeks as a whole if Philip developed his anti-
Roman project: 'If Philip once waited for the clouds looming in the
west to settle over Greece,' said Agelaus, 'I am very much afraid
that the truces and wars and other games which we currently play
with each other will be torn from our control with such violence that
we shall find ourselves praying to the gods for the power to make
war and peace with each other whenever we wish, and in general to
be masters in settling our own disputes.'[14]

But Philip was not inclined to take such unexciting advice from a
recent enemy. Demetrius' constant presence was a more potent
stimulus; and since Scerdilaidas' defection, Philip had good reason
on his own account for planning an expedition to Illyria. He had
time before winter 217/216 for a *Blitzkrieg* recovery of the areas of
Macedon which only that spring Scerdilaidas had occupied, and for
a similarly rapid attack and conquest of southern Illyria. After that,
Scerdilaidas can have had little doubt of what the next campaigning
season would bring; and a report from him to the Roman Senate
may have been responsible for its sending to Philip, either late in 217
or early in 216, asking him to surrender Demetrius. This was a clear
indication that the Senate, despite its Italian and Spanish preoccupa-
tions, was still keeping an eye on Illyria, as was the request which the
envoys made in Illyria (if Livy's record is authentic) for arrears of
Pinnes' indemnity or hostages in lieu.[15] Needless to say, Philip did
not surrender Demetrius nor did he change his plans in any way as a
result of the Roman request. The Senate had doubtless not expected
that he would. But Scerdilaidas might feel comforted to know that

Rome retained an interest in Illyria, despite the seriousness of contemporary events in Italy.

It is not therefore altogether surprising that when Philip invaded Adriatic coastal waters in 216 with a recently built fleet of 100 *lemboi*, Scerdilaidas asked Rome for help, perhaps exaggerating Philip's threat to Rome's other friends in Illyria by suggesting that Philip intended to attack Apollonia. The Senate, in the year of Cannae, was not easily moved into opening another front of the war, and reacted cautiously by detaching an exploratory squadron of only ten ships from the fleet stationed in Sicily. The news of this squadron's approach—which Philip, with a ridiculously inflated sense of his own importance, interpreted as the forerunner of the main Roman fleet—caused panic in Philip's fleet. He at once abandoned his expedition, losing nothing, says Polybius scathingly, except prestige.[16]

Not surprisingly, the Romans were not very impressed at the danger from Philip which Scerdilaidas had conjured for them, and the Senate saw no immediate need to interfere further in the eastern Adriatic. Italy would be sufficiently protected against the remote chance of a lightning raid by Philip by twenty-five ships stationed to guard the most vulnerable part of the coast of southern Italy, between Brundisium and Tarentum.[17] But by the end of summer 215 the Roman commitment had been increased by a further thirty ships, which were now put under the direct command of the praetor Marcus Valerius Laevinus. Laevinus was further instructed to cross the Adriatic and to do anything necessary to ensure that Philip did not sail to Italy.[18]

The reason for the Senate's suddenly higher evaluation of the possibility of danger from Philip was the incompetence of a messenger whom Philip sent to Hannibal, an Athenian called Xenophanes. Xenophanes was unfortunate enough to be caught by the Roman fleet while accompanied by three Carthaginian officers and while in possession of a signed treaty of alliance between Philip and Hannibal. The terms of co-operation recorded in the treaty, as copied by Polybius from the captured document, are expressed in very general terms and do not in themselves necessarily mean that Philip intended an immediate invasion of Italy—although this was how some later Roman writers liked to see them, thus dramatically darkening still further Rome's darkest hour in order to exaggerate by contrast the achievement of Rome's recovery.[19] But a general agreement to cooperate (which is what the treaty actually was) *might* mean an invasion, and the Senate could not in 215, the year after Cannae, afford to ignore that risk, now that it had solid evidence in black and white that it really existed. Hence its immediate reinforcement of the Adriatic fleet and revision of its orders. Yet there is no good indication that Hannibal would have welcomed Philip's presence in Italy to share the spoils and the glory after the chief fighting (so he will have hoped) was over; or indeed, that Philip was in a sufficiently strong position at home to leave Macedon for adventure in Italy. What Hannibal wanted was a diversion. He clearly hoped to dissipate Rome's strength by making her fight on yet another front; and to achieve this he was prepared to acknowledge Philip as an ally. It cost him nothing to agree that in any settlement he reached with Rome, Rome's current friends in Illyria should be removed from her sphere of influence, and that Demetrius of Pharos' friends, captured in 219 when Pharos fell and since then incarcerated at Rome, should be freed.

For Philip—and for the whole of Greece, as Agelaus of Naupactus had foreseen—his willingness to begin unprovoked war with Rome, made common knowledge by the premature disclosure of his treaty with Hannibal, was eventually disastrous. The immediate consequence, however—the reinforced Roman fleet—was merely an inconvenience so long as it was not permanently stationed in Illyrian waters. Yet the campaign of only one more year brought the Roman fleet to a permanent station in Illyria. The events which produced this escalation were, if anything, even more tragi-comical than those of the previous two years. In 214 Philip's enlarged fleet of 120 *lemboi* sailed to Oricum on the straits of Otranto, seized the important harbour town, and moved against Rome's friend Apollonia. Although Hannibal's contemporary attack on Tarentum may have been designed to distract Roman attention, Laevinus, who was still in Italy, coolly split his forces and crossed the Adriatic in accordance with his standing orders. Apollonia was relieved, Oricum retaken; and Philip, whose light *lemboi* were no match for the Roman quinqueremes if it came to a naval battle, was ignominiously forced to burn his fleet at the mouth of the river Aous and to retreat overland to Macedon. Philip had certainly avoided a direct confrontation with Rome by this action, but his operations of the year had nevertheless produced a substantial escalation in the Roman commitment. For the chief result of his fruitless campaign was that the Roman fleet was henceforth and until the end of the war permanently stationed in Illyrian waters.[20]

Yet the task of the Roman fleet, despite its new advanced base, was still no more extensive than to prevent Philip's threat to Italy from developing. And in accordance with this limited purpose Laevinus seems to have been content not to interfere with Philip's activities very much as long as they were confined to the interior. As a result, Rome's inland friends began to suffer; in particular, Philip seems to have managed to take control of the Parthini, Dimallum and the Atintanes through expeditions directed primarily against Scerdilaidas. His efforts were crowned in 213 or 212 with his capture of the strong fortress city of Lissus, which may have been part of Scerdilaidas' territory. By doing so, Philip both regained access to the Adriatic and cut off Scerdilaidas by land from the Roman base at Oricum further south. In the meanwhile, Demetrius of Pharos had died, so that although Philip had lost his stimulating Illyrian adviser, he now felt no moral pressure to hand over to him his newly conquered Illyrian coastal lands.[21]

III Greek Allies

Laevinus had only his fleet and enough marines to count as a single legion, and was thus ill-equipped to counteract Philip's landward attacks on Rome's friends. And although his chief purpose remained what it always had been, to ensure that Philip stayed in the Balkans, Rome's position in Illyria was rapidly deteriorating, as her inland friends were gradually absorbed by Philip's advances. The developments were potentially serious; and the Senate accordingly authorized Laevinus to take a further step in escalating the war—though it did not have the effect of increasing the direct Roman commitment—by seeking a strong ally in the Balkans who might complement Rome's naval strength and take an active part in fighting Philip on land. Only in this way, it seemed, could landward pressure on Scerdilaidas and on Rome's other friends in Illyria be relieved. In 217 Philip had broken off his war with the Aetolian League in order to fight Rome. It had been a war in which the Aetolians had had sufficient taste both of success and of bitter suffering to ensure that the peace was an unstable contrivance; and it seemed possible that the Aetolians might by now have recovered sufficiently to be willing, given sufficient guarantees of profit, to begin another war with Philip.

Laevinus' estimate of the Aetolians was correct; and with his bargaining position fortified by news of Rome's recapture of Capua and Syracuse in 211, he approached them probably in late summer 211. He found immediate encouragement in the fact that the energetic militarist Scopas had just been elected as chief Aetolian magistrate (*strategos*) for the following year. And his initial encouragement was not disappointed. He made a speech in which he pointed out to the Aetolians Rome's recent successes at Capua and Syracuse, and he was fully supported by Scopas. A written treaty was then drawn up, part of the Aetolian copy of which, seized in a raid by Philip on the Aetolian shrine at Thermum later in the war, has recently been found at Thyrreum in Acarnania.[22]

Laevinus had no Roman territorial aspirations to compromise, and could afford to be generous in the negotiations. The main terms— the ruthlessness of which, incidentally, shocked Greek public opinion, which already regarded the Aetolians as unprincipled robbers— were that the Aetolians should immediately declare war on Philip by land and receive the support of at least twenty-five Roman quinqueremes, half the Roman fleet; that Aetolia should keep all towns captured as far north as Corcyra (the limitation was presumably to protect Rome's friends who had already succumbed to Philip's advance, and who were all situated north of Corcyra), while all moveable booty—including people—should belong to the Romans. In particular, neighbouring Acarnania, whose independence and support for Philip had long irked the Aetolians, should be Aetolian if captured. Additional clauses provided safeguards for either state if the other made peace with Philip—a clause which eventually became crucial—and stipulated that certain specified Roman and Aetolian allies might, if they wished, opt into the treaty.

Such was Rome's first formal alliance with a Greek state. It seems clear both from the circumstances in which it was negotiated and from its terms that it was concerned solely with improving the prosecution of the war with Philip and not at all with Roman territorial expansion. And despite a delay of more than a year before the Senate ratified the terms, joint operations began at once, at the beginning of 210. The Senate's delay clearly did not affect Scopas' eagerness for the war, or seem to him to cast doubts on Roman sincerity. And indeed, there is no reason why it should have, since the delay seems to have been quite accidental and in no way concerned with the Senate's doubting the usefulness or desirability of the treaty. The Senate customarily dealt with such matters early in the official year (which began on March 15), when it was presided over by the new consuls. In 210 Laevinus was himself one of the new consuls, having been elected in his absence. But on March 15, 210 he was still in the Balkans, and therefore was unable to give the Senate a detailed personal exposition of the terms of the treaty, as was usual. Furthermore, he fell ill and was very late in reaching Rome; and probably after attending to only the most urgent business, he rushed off to Sicily. There was no chance for the Senate to ratify the treaty, if it was to take account of Laevinus' personal explanation, until (probably) the next new consuls took office in March 209.[23] But this did not matter much. The technical delay had no effect at all on the Balkan war. Indeed, the appointment of Laevinus' successor, Publius Sulpicius Galba, probably indicates, if anything, an increasing awareness in the Senate of the importance of the Balkan war, for Sulpicius was a proconsul, and therefore was superior in status to Laevinus, who had been only propraetor.

The effectiveness of Laevinus' treaty was soon increased when other friends of Aetolia opted in (the most important of them was Attalus, king of Pergamum in Asia Minor), and this ensured that the Senate need no longer worry that Philip might join Hannibal in Italy. Rome's military commitment east of the Adriatic was not increased; but Laevinus' treaty ensured its maximum effectiveness. Subsequent events of the war need not concern us in detail:[24] it is sufficient to notice that it dragged on for four more years with no significant military advantage to either side—though the Romans, who now had no difficulty in achieving their limited objective of keeping Philip tied down in the Balkans, would be quite satisfied with this. The Aetolians, however, soon began to feel, not without good reason, that Rome was merely using them, since the Senate stuck to the terms of the treaty and supplied only naval support. But since most of the fighting was on land, the Aetolians bore the brunt of it. The crisis of Aetolian confidence came in 206. For the Senate had for the last two years been so heavily occupied with events in Italy and in Spain that the Balkan war, once it was clear that Philip would not be able to join Hannibal, had been starved of Roman support; and Attalus of Pergamum had suddenly been forced to return to Asia Minor to defend his own kingdom against his neighbour, the Bithynian king Prusias, whom Philip had made his ally for this very purpose. The Aetolians thus had some justification for feeling isolated and neglected. Philip astutely tried to take advantage of their war-weariness and suggested that they make peace; and despite the fact that to do so without safeguards for Rome would break their treaty, they nevertheless welcomed his approach and accepted his terms, in the process ignoring Sulpicius' efforts to prevent them.[25]

Superficially it seemed that Rome's position in the Balkans had reverted to that of five years before. But in practice, conditions in 206 were very different from what they had been in 211 when Laevinus first sought the Aetolians' alliance. Firstly, 206 saw the virtual end of Carthage's empire in Spain; secondly, Hasdrubal's desperate attempt to reinforce Hannibal, which had put Carthaginian Spain into Roman hands, had also shown that Hannibal could not be effectively reinforced, and that he was therefore a declining threat; thirdly, despite Philip's success in persuading the Aetolians to break their treaty and conclude a separate peace without safeguards for Rome, the ineffectiveness of his alliance with Hannibal during the past nine years gave the Senate little cause for fearing that he might still cross to Italy. Nevertheless, Rome still had friends in the Balkans; and the jaundiced Aetolian view of Rome's attitude—that Rome would, in effect, fight to the last Aetolian—could not be allowed to prevail unchallenged. The Senate also faced the additional complication of deciding what it should do about the treaty-breaking Aetolians: to take effective action against them would cost much effort and would indicate a positive Roman interest in the Balkans which her other friends might find alarming; but to do nothing, to ignore them without demonstrating that, just as Rome kept faith with her friends, so she expected them to keep faith with her, might also have dangerous consequences.

Yet circumstances were not favourable to continuing the war in Greece for long. Scipio was consul in 205, and Scipio's intention, if he could win the Senate's support, was to invade Africa—a plan for which all available Roman troops and transport would be required. In view of this, the Senate decided to make a final military demonstration in the Balkans: for the present, at least, Rome would take the risk of ignoring the Aetolians' breach of faith, and would concentrate on protecting her other friends. Publius Sempronius Tuditanus was therefore sent out in 205 to replace Sulpicius Galba. He took with him 10,000 infantry, 1,000 cavalry, and thirty-five ships, as reinforcements. Ignoring the treaty-breaking Aetolians, Sempronius supported Rome's old friends, the Parthini, who immediately rebelled against Philip with their neighbours; he then laid siege to Dimallum. But the Epirotes, perhaps anticipating that Rome's commitment was not as great as this surge of new activity seemed to indicate, began negotiations, possibly on Philip's suggestion, which brought Philip and Sempronius to a peace conference. They met during the summer at Phoenice, the Epirote capital, which gave its name to the peace which they agreed.[26] The terms largely confirmed the status quo: that the Parthini, Dimallum, and two unknown towns or forts, Bargullum and Eugenium, should all be Rome's;[27] her only concession was to cede the Atintanes to Philip. No mention was made of any of the Aetolians' operations, nor of the Aetolians themselves. The 'Peace of Phoenice' concerned solely the Illyrian territories and places which Rome had regarded as her friends since 228 and over which Philip had challenged Roman good faith by attacking them in 216.

Territorially Rome had gained nothing from the war: but she had not fought it because she wanted to gain territory. By keeping Philip out of Italy, the war had achieved everything the Senate had expected of it. Territorially, indeed, Rome might have seemed to be less influential as a result of the war (by the cession of her old friends in Atintania to Philip). But despite this appearance, Rome's position east of the Adriatic was in practice much more complicated after the war than it had ever been before it. With the exception of Atintania, she had ultimately protected her friends in Illyria: here the situation was much as it had been before. But the war had produced for Rome new associates, who by virtue of their wartime alliance had also, by Roman convention, become Rome's peacetime friends and clients. Scerdilaidas' friendship (though he was now dead and had been succeeded by his son Pleuratus) had simply extended Rome's interest in Illyria; but further afield, Rome now had friends in the Peloponnese, where Nabis (the king of Sparta), Elis and Messenia had all appended their names to the treaty of peace as friends of Rome (Livy calles them *adscripti*); in central Greece Athens, though she had not apparently taken much, if any, part in the war, was similarly included; but perhaps most pregnant with long-term implications were the friendship of the Asian Greeks, Attalus of Pergamum and his satellite city Ilium, who were also *adscripti* to the peace treaty as friends of Rome, and the ominously ambiguous status of the Aetolians, who were not mentioned in the peace terms at all.[28]

Rome's friendship with the cities and tribes of Illyria had made her suspicious of Demetrius of Pharos and of Philip of Macedon in turn, when she faced major involvement elsewhere and Roman self-interest seemed temporarily to coincide with that of her friends. But Rome now had a much more numerous and much wider range of friends in the east. And the pattern of the past, if it repeated itself, might have far-reaching future implications. In face of what new threat, real or imaginary, might the Senate find itself again intervening east of the Adriatic, when it was persuaded that Rome's interests coincided with those of one of her new and even more distant friends? The web of friendship and clientship and its accompanying obligation which the war established could not so easily be undone after it. And as Rome's friendship became even more widely extended so might her commitments (if the Senate chose to honour Rome's moral obligations) and her view of Roman interests similarly extend.

In 205 such extension was far from the minds of the peacemakers. The long-term implications of the First Macedonian War and of the Peace of Phoenice were not the Senate's immediate concern, and in any case nothing much could now be done about them. In 205 Rome left the Balkans superficially as she had come to them in 214, empty of territories directly ruled or exploited by Rome. The Senate's immediate concern was with Hannibal and with Scipio's projected African expedition: the lands east of the Adriatic were therefore left, as before, to look after themselves. In 205 it must have seemed to the more sanguine of the Greeks that the cloud in the west which Agelaus of Naupactus had imaginitively detected in 217 had blackened only to dissipate itself in the blue sky of the Roman evacuation.

CHAPTER IX

THE EFFECTS OF THE
WAR WITH HANNIBAL

I Rome's Friends

THE seventeen years of the Second Punic War which led to the defeat of Carthage was the most decisive single phase of Rome's rise to world power. Before the war Rome had been no more than an Italian power with directly controlled provinces only in the offshore islands of Sicily, Sardinia and Corsica; after it she was the unchallenged supreme power in the western Mediterranean, and in the east she had extended her friendship into Asia Minor. She did not at once take any greater territory under direct control, for the acquisition of territory had not been the object of the war; but there was no longer any power in the western Mediterranean which the Roman Senate could regard as representing a major threat to Rome's security or vital interests.

The effective power of Carthage had been shattered by the war and by the terms of the peace which Scipio had dictated: her influence was now restricted to north Africa; and even there Rome's friendship with Massinissa and the explicit provisions of the peace-treaty in his favour ensured that Carthage would be closely watched if she made any attempt to contravene the spirit of the treaty. As a result, Carthage was content to work quietly and peaceably towards restoring, as far as possible, the commercial prosperity which her citizens had traditionally enjoyed. From Carthage, it seemed, Rome had no more to fear.

Yet the time was long past when Rome could return to a narrow internal Italian outlook. The Roman Senate, though as a body conservative in attitude and inevitably Italian-oriented, had never been deliberately isolationist. If it had been, Rome would never have been able to build up her power even in Italy. And from the time of the First Punic War, when the People had accepted the appeal of the Mamertines and Appius Claudius had crossed to Messana to defend them, the Senate had shown an increasing awareness of the value of overseas friends. King Hiero at Syracuse had enjoyed Rome's friendship until his death in 215, and had made it unnecessary for Rome to undertake the labour of administering directly more than a portion of Sicily after the war. In Gaul, Massilia had long been of incomparable value to Rome in providing information about the movements and dispositions of the Gauls; and if she had exaggerated the extent and the implications of Carthage's ambitions in Spain in the 220's and had encouraged Saguntum also to cultivate Rome's friendship, this was unlikely to be held against her now, even if the Senate realized it: for reflection on the course of the war, coloured by propaganda and by wishful thinking, will have readily produced both the impression and the desire to believe that Massilia's early forecast of the implications for Rome of Hasdrubal's activities in Spain, far from being mischievous, had been inspiredly correct.

East of the Adriatic Rome's friends in Illyria had been less useful to her only because their geographical position in regard to Rome's current strategic interests made them less intrinsically important. Nevertheless, they had proved their value when they had made it easy for the Senate to intervene in Illyrian waters when Philip of Macedon allied with Hannibal. By the end of the war with Hannibal, it was becoming clear (though there were still many who did not recognize this) that the future belonged to the faithful friends of Rome. For while the Senate had found Rome's first overseas friends useful, it had nevertheless proved in practice impossible to intervene anywhere in support of any one of them without at the same time forming still more friendships with still more kings, cities, or tribes. Indeed, the systematic seeking for friends, which was the natural political technique of a Roman aristocrat while operating in his own political milieu, had been, when translated to the field of foreign policy, perhaps the most important feature of the politico-military technique of the three Scipios in Spain and of Africanus in Africa. Even in the small holding operation east of the Adriatic, the 'First Macedonian War', it had in the end proved impossible for Rome to fight without seeking new local friends and allies.

The first effect of this technique of fighting the war had been that Rome won. This was undeniable. Yet wartime friendships, once formed, could not, by the Senate's long-standing code of conduct which originated in the deep-seated Roman social institution of the client-patron relationship, be simply shrugged off and abandoned. Once a friend of Rome—even if a short-term emergency caused the initial contact—always a friend of Rome. And friendship, as Rome understood it, had *mutual* obligations attached to it. Demetrius of Pharos had the doubtful distinction of being the first overseas friend of Rome to have this fact brought forcibly to his notice: it had required a war to make the Senate's point sufficiently firmly. Demetrius lost his kingdom through his misinterpretation of his freedom granted by Rome, a misinterpretation which the Senate had regarded as ungrateful behaviour. The free and friendly kingdom of Syracuse had been next to learn the meaning of its freedom. When Rome's long-standing friend Hiero died in 215, his successor Hieronymus and his advisers and supporters chose an embarrassing moment for Rome to offer open encouragement to Hannibal. In Sicily, as with Demetrius in Illyria, the result was a war which had equally disastrous results for the ungrateful client: the destruction of Syracuse in 211 and the subsequent union of the hitherto free kingdom of Syracuse with the Roman province of Sicily. Rome's free friends, it was now clear to all with eyes to see, were regarded as free and friendly only as long as they continued to act in the interests of the Roman Senate and People *as interpreted by the Roman Senate*: that is, as long as they faithfully maintained the standards of loyal behaviour expected of a Roman client.

If the misinterpretation of the freedom granted by the Roman Senate and People could bring disaster, the corollary was also true, that unwavering attention to the requirements of the client-patron relationship could bring enormous benefits. The prime instance to date—we shall see more as we move into the second century—is Massinissa (though Hiero at Syracuse had set the trend); for until Massinissa had gained the support of Scipio and had, in effect, become his client, his supremacy even within his own Numidian tribe, the Massyli, was decidedly precarious. Yet with Roman support, he had made this secure, with Roman encouragement he had extended the bounds of his kingdom, through a Roman treaty he had secured the commitment of the Roman Senate and People to his supremacy in Numidia (and, depending on the interpretation of the treaty, perhaps in Africa). Massinissa had been made what he was and what he remained for more than fifty years by his friendship with the Roman Senate and People.[1]

It is clear therefore that the war with Carthage had not only extended the range and number of Rome's friends: it had also made clearer to those who would take notice what was implied by being a friend of Rome and what benefits and moral obligations attached to such friendship, even if a treaty formally regulated the relationship.

By the end of the war Rome possessed free friends in Africa, Spain, Illyria, the Greek mainland and Asia Minor. Even Rome's earlier slight contact with Egypt had been strengthened when in 209 the Senate asked Ptolemy IV if he could send some grain to Italy to supplement the war-ravaged supplies of Italy, Sicily and Sardinia.[2] Thus the war produced new friendships of varying degrees of warmth not only in the western Mediterranean where the war had been primarily fought, but also in the east. The future alone would show whether Rome's friends in the east would prove the stimulus to more direct control east of the Adriatic, in the way in which her friendship with the Mamertines had led to Rome's acquiring her first province in Sicily, and in which her friendship with Massilia and Saguntum, by bringing about the war with Hannibal, led to direct Roman control of Spain.

II Spain and Gaul

Spain was a major problem for the Roman Senate after Scipio had expelled the Carthaginians; for at that time the war with Carthage was still continuing and Spain, after being fought over for so long, could not be simply abandoned, since the Carthaginians might march straight back. For the rest of the war, therefore, it was necessary to maintain a Roman military presence in the peninsula. This was no more than prudent commonsense. But it had certain implications. It meant, for instance, that when in 205 Indibilis and Mandonius withdrew their loyalty from Rome, their revolt had to be quelled, since it might be exploited by Carthaginian sympathizers; and it meant that the proconsular military commands in Spain which the successors of Scipio and Silanus, Lucius Cornelius Lentulus and Lucius Manlius Acidinus, held after their departure, were continued until 200, when the war with Carthage was finally over.[3]

When the treaty with Carthage was agreed, the Senate still had not decided what to do with Spain. Could Spain simply be abandoned now, together with Rome's friends of the war years? Were her Spanish friends—in particular Saguntum, Rhode and Emporiae— sufficiently powerful to deal with any potentially dangerous development without Roman aid? Might it again be possible for Carthage— or for any other power—discreetly to gain a foothold in southern Spain which Rome might again underestimate until it was too late? The only way to take care of all possible contingencies was to take over

Spain as one or more formally administered Roman province, just as after the First Punic War parts of Sicily had been acquired formally because the Senate could think of no better way of dealing with the situation.

While the Senate was making up its mind, two Roman proconsuls continued to hold Spain for Rome, as they had throughout the war. This temporary arrangement had by then continued for so long that, for practical reasons, by 199 their spheres of duty had been roughly divided up into 'Nearer' and 'Further' Spain (*Hispania Citerior* and *Hispania Ulterior*). This convenient division was, whether consciously or not, the first step towards the organization of Spain as two provinces; and it was followed only two years later, in 197, by an administrative measure which indicated that the Senate had at last made up its mind: two extra annual praetorships were created, whose holders were charged with governing the new Spanish provinces, the exact boundaries of which the first holders of the new magistracies were to draw up. Pacification (in the sense of a widespread willingness to accept the formal rule of Rome) was still far away; many years and many wars were needed to secure it. But in 197 the Roman Senate had decided that the formal government of Spain as two provinces, together with the imposition of a permanent annual tribute to make the administration pay for itself (as far as possible), was the only way that it could be certain of the security of the peninsula. The decision had, no doubt, been made easier by the need to keep armies in Spain on a war footing even after the Carthaginians had been expelled; it may have been slightly influenced by Scipio's settlement of some of his sick and wounded Italian veterans in the rich Baetis valley, in a community which he appropriately called Italica.[4] But the chief influence was probably the recognition that this was the easiest long-term solution—on a by-now well-tried pattern—of the problem of what to do to prevent a resurgence of hostile influence (whether Carthaginian or other) in the much fought-over territory, when local friends, however loyal and reliable, were not themselves strong enough to do this.

Spain was not the only military problem involving Rome's long-term security which was left unsolved at the end of the war with Hannibal. Much closer to Rome, Hannibal had found uncomfortably large support among the Gallic tribes of the Po valley who, a mere seven years before Hannibal invaded Italy, had been defeated in what Rome must at that time have regarded as a decisive battle. The Gauls had fought throughout the war at Hannibal's side, both in his army in southern Italy and against whatever Roman armies were sent into the Po valley; even in the last phase of the war, while Scipio was already operating in Africa, Hannibal's brother Mago and other Carthaginian agents were trying to provoke a rising against Rome among the Gauls and their neighbours, the Ligurians. Once the war with Carthage was over, this kind of insecurity on the borders of Italy could no longer be tolerated, and Rome now had time to deal with the problem. Liguria controlled the coastal route, both by land and by sea, to Massilia and Spain; and now that Rome had a continuing commitment in Spain, this route was an essential artery of communications. The post-war operation in the Gallic area began while the war with Carthage in Africa was still going on, in operations against Mago, who was expelled late in 203. Mago's defeat in no way reduced the Roman commitment to gaining control of the self-confessedly hostile population of Liguria and Cisalpine Gaul. Now that Rome and Italy were, for security purposes, effectively synonymous, the northern borders of Italy had to be secured. It took fifty years, and it is unnecessary to go into the military details here:[5] but what we must notice is that the stimulus which finally precipitated the Senate into a systematic conquest of Liguria and Cisalpine Gaul was the war with Hannibal, in particular Hannibal's success in gaining support from Rome's longest-standing enemy, the Gallic tribes on Italy's northern border.

III Rome and Italy

Outside Italy we have seen that the war with Hannibal, while making Rome a power unequalled in the western Mediterranean, had also produced in its wake a large series of moral commitments and obligations, actual and potential, in an area stretching from the Atlantic to the Aegean, from the Alps to Africa. Before we follow through into the second century B.C. the implications of the much wider potential involvements in every part of the Mediterranean, particularly in the east, which the war had brought to Rome, it will be appropriate to look briefly at the effect of the war on Rome herself and on the character of Rome's rule within Italy. For in Italy also the war produced changes which substantially affected the response which Rome was to make to the challenges from the east, and the kind of rule which Rome, within the next fifty years or so, was to extend to every part of the coastlands of the Mediterranean.

All wars bring enormous losses and disruption to their participants, particularly to the areas where the actual fighting occurs. In this respect the war with Hannibal was no exception; and although the physical devastation of the countryside does not bear comparison with the effect of modern explosives and chemicals, the losses in manpower were still enormous. Thus while it is a mistake to envisage the physical destructive effect of Hannibal's invasion of Italy as being anything like the effect of, say, the First World War on the towns and fields of Flanders—after all, Hannibal had to feed his army from what could be grown in the areas under his control—the numbers of men killed in battle and by disease, in conditions in which any serious wound (and many minor ones) was likely to prove fatal in the absence of medical attention and at a time when malaria was endemic, was very large indeed. The social disruption of a war lasting, in Italy, for fifteen years, and involving in varying degrees the whole population, was similarly enormous. Unfortunately, any attempt to fix overall casualty figures cannot hope to be realistic, since the figures for troop numbers which have come down to us do not allow scholars even to agree on the number of legions in the field in some years, still less on the casualties which patriotic Roman writers liked to minimize (even if we suppose that accurate casualty figures were ever collected) and which, even if accurate, would not account for the 'walking wounded', many of whom will have soon died from their wounds off the battlefield. All we can safely say, therefore, is that the manpower losses will (probably) have to be counted in tens, perhaps hundreds of thousands, rather than in millions.

The physical effects of the war on Italy, therefore, while immediately considerable, were nevertheless comparatively short-term. Manpower losses could be largely repaired within a generation; burnt cornfields could be ploughed and resown at once; destroyed orchards and vineyards would take longer to repair, but within twenty years recovery will have been substantial, if not complete: for even in Flanders after the First World War agriculture was substantially back to normal within twenty years, and there is no reason to assume that Italy was worse affected after the Hannibalic War. The only major long-term effect will have been on those areas where trees had been felled on a large scale for ship-building. Such deforestation creates conditions which are ripe for erosion. But this process will obviously have begun in the First Punic War, when Rome first began to operate a large navy, and was not just a consequence of the war with Hannibal. Physical effects of the invasion were therefore almost all essentially short term; and certainly they did not affect in any traceable way Rome's subsequent policies overseas.[6]

The chief long-term effect on Italy was on Rome's political position within the peninsula, particularly within that complicated web of mutual alliances on which her power was based and which modern scholars have called 'the Italian Confederacy'. Most of Rome's Italian allies had remained loyal. Only in the south had any appreciable number of communities joined Hannibal, some through force, some through hopeful anticipation of Hannibal's success. By doing so and by denying their support to Rome, they broke their treaties; and since the treaties did not lay down any procedure to be followed in the event of a breach, Rome, as the offended partner, felt legally and morally free to take what action she regarded as appropriate. The standard penalty for collaboration with the enemy was the confiscation of the whole or part of the land belonging to the offending community—the amount in each case no doubt depended on Rome's view of the willingness of the collaboration—which was then added to the territory of the Roman People as public land (*ager publicus*), which could be disposed of at the will of the Roman People.[7]

But Rome's effective dominance in the partnership with each of her Italian allies was extended in the course of the war not only at the expense of those communities which broke their treaties and collaborated with Hannibal, though it is naturally most obvious in these cases. Minor delinquents were also reminded of Rome's dominance in power which enabled the Senate to enforce its interpretation of the relationship between Rome and any Italian state. So even among the Latins. Twelve Latin colonies in 209 had refused to send their contingent to the Roman army. They were brought to book in 204, when not only was a double levy exacted from them, but Rome also interfered in their internal affairs to the extent of insisting that in future the recalcitrant colonies should use the Roman census procedure (whereby the lists of soldiers liable to the levy were compiled), and of stipulating that such lists, when drawn up, were to be filed at Rome for the use of the Roman government. To pay these potential troops, Rome also insisted on a special tax (*tributum*) being levied on the delinquent Latin colonies.[8] They would not again be able to plead lack of manpower without good justification. Similar interference in Etruria and in Umbria during the war, where collaboration had only been threatened (or, if carried out, ineffective), and investigations of collaborators throughout Italy after it, similarly served to emphasize that Rome was firmly in a position to impose her interpretation of what the treaties or conventions with the Italian states meant to her.[9]

Even communities which had remained loyal beyond suspicion came more firmly under Roman control as a result of the war. This came about informally and imperceptibly through constant co-operation during more than fifteen years of non-stop warfare, through constantly fulfilling the clause in their treaties by which Rome could require troops, through constantly sharing the danger from Hannibal. The soldiers provided by the allied communities were just as much under the command of Roman magistrates as were Roman citizens; they shared the same military discipline and conditions of military service; their future life and the safety of themselves and their families were just as dependent on Roman success as those of the Roman citizen troops. Not surprisingly, therefore, Rome's success, following the many years of shared danger, produced in Italy a widespread awareness and a voluntary acceptance of Roman supremacy and leadership, which was quite independent of legal responsibilities and obligations enshrined in the treaties. The loyal Italians felt they had what is now called a 'special relationship' with Rome. They had acquired the habit of looking to Rome as leader, and they were correspondingly prepared to put up with such intervention as Rome from time to time thought necessary to maintain her interpretation of their relationship. The war with Hannibal, far from shattering Rome's hold over her Italian allies as Hannibal had hoped it would do, resulted by reaction in both a much tighter actual Roman control over Italy and a greatly increased willingness to accept this control and to see their future depending on Rome on the part of many of the Italians. Thus, paradoxically, thanks to Hannibal Rome could face the challenges of the second century with a virtually united Italy at her back.[10]

On Rome itself the war had also inevitably had its effect. As its seriousness increased, so the Senate had increasingly taken upon itself the responsibility for running it. After the disasters of Trasimene and Cannae, both brought about by consuls who seem to have had a large popular backing, the Senate was left in virtually unchallenged control of the war. That meant, among other more strictly military matters, control of foreign policy and of finance. With this senatorial control the war had been won. After the war the 'establishment' in the Senate which had run the war was reluctant to give up the powers which it had corporately taken upon itself; and as a result, Rome now entered on what was perhaps the narrowest based and most authoritarian period of her government since the popular agitations of the fourth century. It was not unchallenged; but challenges until the end of the second century were resisted with comparative ease and success. As a body, though it was by no means always united within itself, the Roman Senate in the second century was prepared, in the last resort, to stand united against attack from outside. In the end this attitude produced corruption, brutality, inefficiency and neglect, which eventually stimulated challenges which destroyed the system. Hannibal can hardly be blamed for the way the Roman senatorial class reacted to his invasion and, after it, consolidated their political gains. But it is true to say that it was the war with Hannibal which gave the Roman Senate the influence and authority within Rome itself which produced the firm government, which in turn conditioned and directed the Roman response to the complex overseas situations which began to emerge as soon as Hannibal had admitted defeat.

PART III

THE EAST BEFORE PYDNA

PART III

THE EAST BEFORE PYDNA

CHAPTER X

THE RETURN TO THE EAST

I *The Origins of the Second Macedonian War*

SINCE the withdrawal of Roman troops from Greece in 205 after the Peace of Phoenice, Rome's chief interest had centred on Africa and on the decisive events of the struggle with Carthage. This did not, however, mean that the Senate lost all interest in events in the Balkans: ever since the First Illyrian War twenty-five years before, the Senate had regularly taken notice of significant developments across the Adriatic. Moreover, the Peace of Phoenice had been made chiefly because Rome had exhausted her most useful allies in the Balkans and was not prepared to continue the war alone in view of the impending invasion of Africa. Its terms, therefore, while acceptable in the circumstances, were not, we may imagine, what the Senate would ideally have wished for. In view of this and of the fact that as long as Hannibal remained in Italy Philip could not in the last resort be trusted, the Senate retained an interest in Balkan affairs. Rome's friends in Illyria and Greece would expect it, and there were also, it seems, good strategic reasons for doing so.

In these circumstances it is not very surprising to find that three Roman envoys were dispatched to Greece in 203 with three quinqueremes at their disposal. Livy says that they were sent in response to appeals by ally cities in Greece (which he does not name) which had failed to obtain satisfaction from Philip for alleged ravagings of their territory.[1] They also alleged, almost certainly without justification—perhaps to incite the Senate to take action—that Philip had sent 4,000 soldiers to Africa to help Carthage.[2] In addition, we know that in breach of the Peace of Phoenice Philip had invaded certain Illyrian territories, no doubt trusting that Roman warweariness and the Senate's preoccupation with events in Africa would cause it to ignore his obscure marginal violations of the treaty.[3] But he had reckoned without Rome's friends. It seems likely that these raids on Illyria are what the Greek cities complained of to the

Senate in 203 and which brought about the mission of the Roman envoys.

In one sense Philip had gambled correctly when he thought Rome would not start another war in the Balkans at this time simply because of a few pieces of Illyrian territory; but in another sense he was very wrong indeed, for the mission of the Roman envoys indicated clearly that the Senate still did not trust him and, even at this critical stage of the African war, was prepared to take at least diplomatic action to protect its friends. Indeed, the envoys may have done more than simply offer diplomatic support, for one of them, Marcus Aurelius Cotta, stayed behind and was still there two years later, perhaps as 'military adviser', in summer 201.[4] Philip saw the danger and confined his subsequent infiltration to less easily detectable political methods. His military attention he turned elsewhere, to expansion in the Aegean, which immediately produced hostilities with Rhodes and with Rome's single friend in Asia Minor, king Attalus of Pergamum.

But it was already too late to escape Roman suspicion. The Senate's interest in Illyria and its distrust of Philip had already revived. The mission of the envoys, the continued presence of Cotta, and the reports he sent to the Senate will have made this clear, although the Senate refused to increase its commitment when the insensitive Aetolians asked it to, perhaps in 202.[5] The Senate's anger at the Aetolians was doubtless caused by their lack of faith in making a separate peace with Philip in 206: it clearly does not reflect lack of Roman interest in the Balkans. Indeed, even before the peace was made with Carthage (though after the final battle), when in spring 201 new appeals from some of Rome's Balkan friends reached Rome—doubtless again those in Illyria, perhaps urged to travel by Cotta and reinforced by a report from him—the Senate reacted by detaching part of the fleet from Sicily under its most experienced Balkan expert, Marcus Valerius Laevinus, and sent him to watch Macedon.[6] The Senate clearly could not afford, in this of all years, to risk an invasion of Italy by Philip which might give the Carthaginian die-hards the hope of fighting on in Africa.

It does not matter that with hindsight we know there was really no risk of such an expedition by Philip: the important thing is what the Roman Senate thought. At Rome it must have seemed that on the surface developments in the east seemed to be shaping towards a possible repetition of the events of 216/215 when, as now, Philip had sought influence and territory in Illyria and when, also as now, he was operating a naval policy. There were, of course, major differences: Philip's current naval policy seemed to be concerned solely with the Aegean; it was not at present being used to support his fifth-column infiltration in Illyria. But how could the Roman Senate be sure that this would continue? How could it be certain that a sudden change of policy by Philip—he was famous for such mercurial behaviour—would not again bring the Macedonian fleet into the Adriatic and once more present a threat to Italy? It was clear from his recent aggression and infiltration in Illyria that the treaty of Phoenice would not stop him if he saw advantage there and thought he could take it without provoking Rome. Moreover, early in 201 the Senate did not yet know for certain that the war with Carthage would be finally settled within a few months. Even after the battle of Zama there were people at Carthage who favoured fighting on—though Hannibal was not one of them—and after sixteen years of war it must have seemed to many senators that such men might yet cause the war to drag on for some years. In the circumstances, therefore, it was only sensible for the Senate to re-erect the safeguards of 215 and to station a fleet in Illyrian waters to prevent the worst from happening; and no one was more appropriate to command it than the experienced veteran, Marcus Valerius Laevinus, the man who had performed exactly the same role in 215.

When Valerius arrived he met Aurelius Cotta and learned the results of Cotta's investigations into Philip's fifth-column activities among Rome's Illyrian friends. In due course they decided to inform the Senate of the facts which Cotta had collected. Meanwhile Philip's operations in the Aegean were achieving some success. He had begun a vigorous new offensive against Pergamum and Rhodes during which he fought two sea-battles, at Chios and Lade. At Chios he was beaten by their allied fleet, a defeat which, with characteristic resilience, he followed up by landing in Pergamene territory and ravaging it, right up to the suburbs of the city of Pergamum itself. And although his advance on land was then checked, his victory over the Rhodians in the subsequent sea-battle at Lade showed that the threat from his Aegean activities to Rhodes and Pergamum—particularly since Philip's ally Prusias of Bithynia was a hostile neighbour of Pergamum—was still substantial. And this was further emphasized when he also began to attack Rhodes' mainland territories in Caria.[7]

Pergamum and Rhodes were not the only Greek states to suffer from Philip's Aegean activities in 201. Athens also was affected, perhaps chiefly through having her grain supplies disrupted—a trade in which Rhodes had a particularly large stake. Even before this, it seems, Athens' relations with Philip had deteriorated to such an extent by early 201 (though we do not know the details) that two Athenian voting units which, more than a century before, had been named Antigonis and Demetrias, to honour two of Philip's ancestors, were then abolished.[8] It was clearly time for Athens to seek allies, and Cephisodorus, the leading Athenian statesman of the time, looked first to Philip's immediate enemies, Attalus of Pergamum and Rhodes; and, among others, help was also sought from Egypt, Crete and Aetolia.[9] Attalus and Rhodes did their best for Athens, but they were themselves hard-pressed and could not in practice contribute very much. Moreover, Athens' position was not improved when the Athenians summarily executed two Acarnanians who had accidentally committed sacrilege by straying among the crowds into the solemn religious celebration of the Eleusinian mysteries in early autumn 201, without having been previously initiated. Their punishment was excessively brutal; and it was quite so uncivilized, we may suspect, only because the Acarnanians were allies of Philip. The Acarnanian reaction, however, was equally severe, for an appeal to Philip brought him (or perhaps one of his generals) into Attica on a ravaging expedition, the excuse for which was to take revenge for the two victims at Eleusis.[10]

Attalus, the Rhodians, and Athens' other allies could do little to help physically, since they were all fully occupied in defending their own territories. But diplomatically Attalus and Rhodes were not so impotent. Knowing that the Senate had already shown renewed interest in Philip's Illyrian activities—Roman ships had been stationed in Illyria throughout 201—they determined to try to exploit Roman fears and to draw the Senate into protecting them against Rome's old enemy Philip. Attalus had been a useful Roman ally during the First Macedonian War; Rhodes had at various times during that war attempted to negotiate a peace, and had in any case been a distant friend of Rome for a hundred years. If, as recent developments in Illyria seemed to indicate, the Roman Senate needed little stimulus to push it into a further Balkan involvement, Rome's ties of friendship with Attalus and Rhodes might prove sufficiently strong to secure them Roman protection against Philip. And they cannot have believed that they had much to fear from Roman intervention, since Rome must by now have been famous for not wanting territorial acquisitions (201 was the year of the final treaty with Carthage, by

which Rome took over no part of Africa); the benefits which Massilia, for instance, had received from Rome's friendship, in protection
of her colonies in Spain, would be good omens for Pergamene and
Rhodian benefits from similar Roman intervention in the east.
When the Athenians learned the intention of Attalus and Rhodes,
they determined to join them and exploit their friendship with Rome,
which dated from their reception of the Roman envoys at the end of
the First Illyrian War: they accordingly sent Cephisodorus.[11]

The Greek envoys arrived at Rome in late autumn or early winter
201/200, while the consuls of 201 were still in their provinces and
shortly before the election of the following year's consuls. The
Senate, however, decided at once to send three envoys to Greece to
investigate Philip's activities, no doubt in the hope that the mere
threat of Roman intervention would make him desist. They were also
to go on to Egypt to announce Hannibal's defeat. The men chosen
were two distinguished ex-consuls, Gaius Claudius Nero (the victor
of the battle of the Metaurus) and Publius Sempronius Tuditanus
(the peacemaker at Phoenice), and a younger man from the prominent Aemilian family, Marcus Aemilius Lepidus.[12] Perhaps even more
indicative of the attitude of an important section of the Senate was
the election of Publius Sulpicius Galba and Gaius Aurelius Cotta
as consuls for 200. They were clearly a 'hawkish' pair as far as
Philip was concerned, for Galba was a Balkan expert (during the first
war with Philip, he had succeeded Laevinus in 210 and retained his
command until 206), and Aurelius was a relation of the Aurelius
Cotta who was already in Illyria and whose report, when it arrived
shortly before the allotment of the consular provinces (along with
another Athenian embassy), was very unfavourable to Philip. When
in due course the Senate allotted the consuls their spheres of duty for
200, Macedon was one of them, and the lot gave it to Galba.[13]

It is clear that although the war with Carthage was now over, the
Balkan experts urged upon the Senate the view—now reinforced by
Philip's activities, particularly in Illyria, since the Peace of Phoenice
—that Philip was a quite unreliable neighbour and constituted a
clear threat to Italy. Those who had doubts about the reality of this
threat, now that the war with Carthage was over, will have been con-
soled by the reflection that Philip, quite unprovoked, had stabbed
Rome in the back when he allied with Hannibal in 215, and that
revenge was sweet. The long war with Hannibal had certainly produced a brutalization and directness in the Roman attitude: the
Senate seems to have reached the degree of suspicion at which it was

no longer simply prepared to take Philip's actions at their face value and to wait to see what, if anything, developed. The appeals of Rome's Illyrian and Greek friends provided a comfortable excuse for Roman action, even for those senators (if there were any) who sympathized neither with the strategic appreciation of the Balkan experts nor with the emotional reaction of the revenge-seekers. The envoys were therefore sent off to the Balkans early in 200, a fact which in itself suggests that the Senate had already virtually made up its mind to ask the *comitia centuriata* to declare war. The formal decision, however, was not taken until the new consuls entered office on the Ides of March. It was taken, as we have seen, for a variety of reasons; but the most important of them seems to have been that an influential section of the Senate now distrusted Philip so deeply that it could not rest content until he too was reduced, like Carthage, to the status of a Roman client, with all that that implied.[14]

By the Ides of March 200 the Senate had decided. The Roman People still had to be persuaded formally to declare war, of course, but the Senate anticipated no difficulty in this constitutional formality, since the years of the war with Carthage had accustomed the *comitia centuriata* to accept the Senate's recommendations; and the fact that only a short time before it had elected as consuls the two Balkan 'hawks' suggested that the *comitia* would not obstruct the declaration of war. It was therefore a complete surprise when one of the tribunes of the plebs, Quintus Baebius, spoke at a preliminary meeting before the *comitia* voted on the war motion, and persuaded the plebs that the war was unnecessary. In due course, nearly all the centuries voted against the war. Despite the Senate's surprise, it is not too difficult to understand why this happened: for the seventeen years of war with Carthage had just ended, and the threat to Rome from Philip, which the Balkan experts were conjuring, now seemed remote. Baebius expressed for the People their long-standing desire for peace, and they accordingly voted against the Senate's recommendation and against the war.[15]

The Senate, however, had already made its decision, and it was not so easily to be thwarted. Senatorial envoys were already in the east and no doubt—though they could not issue a declaration of war until the *comitia centuriata* had formally sanctioned it—their message, that they had come to ask Philip to stop making war on the Greeks and to make reparations to Attalus, was interpreted by all the Greeks who heard it as an indication that the Senate was prepared to go to war, if this was necessary to secure a satisfactory peace.[16] The consul

Galba was therefore instructed to ask the *comitia centuriata* again to declare war on Philip. But this time he did not rely on the prestige of the Senate's recommendation alone to carry the bill, but made sure in advance that Baebius would not object by promising that he would levy no veteran troops for the new war. He then emphasized to the People the potential (though, by now, highly exaggerated) danger from Philip; and with this preliminary conditioning and with Baebius' objections silenced, the *comitia* did not this time refuse the consul his war. Some time, however, had been lost in all this politicking. The final decision of the *comitia* can hardly have been taken before May; and it was therefore towards the end of summer 200 before Galba had levied his new troops, trained them, and transported them across the Adriatic.[17]

II *The Preliminaries to the War in Greece*

Despite the delay in the *comitia*'s formally declaring war, the Roman commitment was clear once the Senate had made its decision. Philip must be made to accept that where his interests seemed to the Senate to clash with those of Rome, Rome's were the more important. What this meant in practice was that Philip must be turned into a Roman client. As later events show clearly, the Senate was not concerned to destroy Philip or even the appearance of Macedonian power, but only to ensure that he did not interfere with Rome's interests. Indeed, this limited purpose was evident in the activities of the Roman envoys early in 200, even before the *comitia* had declared war and Galba had taken his army across the Adriatic to Apollonia. While travelling to Athens, they called on various Greek states, Epirus, Athamania (where king Amynander would be a useful friend), Aetolia, and Philip's Peloponnesian ally, the Achaean League. They announced in each place—clearly looking for support for Rome if there should be a war—that they intended to ask Philip, in the name of the Roman Senate and People, to make war on none of the Greeks, to submit his dispute with Attalus to arbitration, and if necessary to pay him compensation.[18]

When they reached Athens they met Attalus and representatives of Rhodes. They no doubt repeated to them the substance of what they had told the states they had visited on their journey, and they may have explained the implications in greater detail. The Athenians chose this occasion to honour the Rhodians and Attalus, presumably principally for having helped to repel recent Macedonian raids, but perhaps also for having successfully provoked Roman intervention. Moreover, Attalus also influenced the Athenians to declare war on Philip, probably as a further attempt to exert moral pressure on the Romans (though if so, it was based on a misunderstanding of Roman motives, for the Senate was not contemplating war with Philip primarily to defend Rome's Greek friends: it only gave the impression of being moved by moral obligations because this was convenient). Athens' declaration of war was therefore, strictly speaking, unnecessary, as the sequel showed; for although the Roman envoys had not yet received authorization from Rome to precipitate war if Philip refused their 'request', they clearly expected to receive it at any time. Thus when Nicanor, one of Philip's officers, led another Macedonian attack on Attica, this time ravaging the countryside up to the Academy, just outside the walls of the city, he was surprised to find Romans present, who demanded an interview.[19]

The Roman envoys then announced to Nicanor, for delivery to Philip, the statement which they had made to the Greek states. This was obviously not yet a declaration of war. But it was an ultimatum, though the alternative was not spelled out: if Philip did not yield to the Roman 'request' (and it is clear from events in Rome before any reply could possibly have been received from Philip, that the Senate had no expectation that Philip would accept the ultimatum), it was implied that war would follow. But the envoys were temporarily hamstrung; they could not state these implications unambiguously because they had not yet heard from Rome the result of the vote of the *comitia centuriata*. It may have been an effect of this slightly ambiguous position that doubt arose in the minds of the Greeks about Roman intentions; for an Egyptian embassy travelled to Rome in spring 200 with an offer to send help to Athens if Rome was not prepared to. This embassy had no practical effect, since when it arrived the *comitia* had already voted for war. But it is possible that when it was sent, it was intended as a further attempt to exert moral pressure on the Roman Senate and People.[20]

Once the *comitia* had voted and the envoys in Greece had heard the result, their position became obviously much stronger. We do not know exactly when they received the news, since there is no precise record of when the decisive vote was taken, but it cannot have been before June, and it may have been much later. Meanwhile, however, Philip showed clearly that he did not intend to yield to Roman pressure without a fight, despite the fact that his acceptance

of the ultimatum which Nicanor had received from the envoys
at Athens would have left him, to all appearances, still a major
power. The truth, however, was that since the Romans had already
publicized the terms of the ultimatum within the Balkans, Philip's
acceptance would immediately make it obvious to the Greeks that in
an important sense Macedon had become dependent on Rome. Rome
would thus achieve recognition as protectress of the Greeks, thereby
usurping the traditional political attitude of Philip's family. In
Philip's view, Rome had no legal or even traditional right to interfere
on behalf of her Greek friends: Philip did not therefore intend to
capitulate to Roman demands, even if they were politely phrased as
requests, and to allow his prestige to be massively diminished without striking a blow. The ultimatum was quite unacceptable. And his
reply came in the form of another attack on Athens (this time conducted by his general Philocles) and the active continuation of his
conquests at the expense of the Greek towns in Thrace and on the
Hellespont.[21] By this implicit rejection of the Roman ultimatum
Philip had, in effect, declared war on Rome. Yet he had, by doing so,
played into Roman hands; for his action allowed the Romans to
manoeuvre themselves even more firmly into the comfortable moral
position of being able to represent themselves as fighting a defensive
war on behalf of their Greek friends and allies. We shall see later
how this attitude was subsequently developed and exploited.

After the Roman envoys had delivered their ultimatum to Nicanor
at Athens, they called at Rhodes on their way to Egypt and Syria,
where they hoped to meet king Antiochus III, 'the Great'. They
may even have been in Rhodes when they received news of the war
vote in the *comitia centuriata*. But since Philip had, in effect, already
declared war on Rome, and since a Roman army was even now being
prepared for crossing the Adriatic, the commander of which, Sulpicius Galba, could announce Rome's formal declaration of war on
Philip when he arrived, the envoys had no immediate need to do
more than make sure that Rhodes would continue to support Rome;
for the powerful Rhodian navy would doubtless prove a useful
weapon in the coming conflict.[22]

It is perhaps in this Rhodian context that we should consider the
final mission of these envoys in the Aegean. By perhaps August
200, Philip's conquests in Thrace included the Egyptian possessions
Aenus and Maronea, and some other small towns. He then turned
his attention to the important city of Abydus, which could control
the passage of shipping through the narrows of the Hellespont. The

potential consequences of his action immediately affected Rhodes, since much of her sea-borne trade was with the Black Sea region, and therefore passed through the Hellespont. Twenty years before, when in 220 Byzantium—which controlled the Bosphorus, as Abydus controlled the Hellespont—had tried to levy tolls on shipping passing through her strait, Rhodes had objected so strongly that she had conducted a full-scale war against Byzantium. Philip's possession of Abydus might obviously have an even more disastrous effect on Rhodian trade with the Black Sea; and there was no army in the area which could even try to prevent him.

Diplomacy, however, was worth the attempt; and the Roman envoys, who now knew that they could support their 'request' with the threat of war, were prepared to try to stop Philip at Abydus, no doubt chiefly as a public-relations exercise to please the friendly Rhodians. The fact that only the youngest of the three envoys, Marcus Aemilius Lepidus, travelled to Abydus suggests that the Romans did not have much hope that the meeting might produce any substantial result. However, in case Philip had changed his mind and preferred, even at this eleventh hour, to negotiate, Aemilius repeated the terms of the earlier ultimatum, with some minor variations: that Philip should make war on none of the Greeks; that he should submit to arbitration his dispute with Attalus and Rhodes; and that he should not lay hands on Ptolemy's possessions (a reference to his recent capture of the Ptolemaic towns in Thrace, Aenus and Maronea). Failing acceptance, Aemilius made it clear that war would result. Philip chose to argue; Aemilius became arrogant; and the interview ended. Philip had made his choice. Three days later he took Abydus;[23] and shortly after returning to Macedonia, he heard news that the consul Sulpicius Galba had arrived at Apollonia with Roman troops. The war had begun.

CHAPTER XI

THE SECOND WAR WITH MACEDON

I Publius Sulpicius Galba

ROME had decided to go to war with Philip again because the Senate felt that it could not trust him. It had used the opportunity offered by the appeals of Rome's friends in the east, particularly those of Attalus and the Rhodians, to provide, on a now-traditional pattern of working, the excuse for intervention. As a result, the excuse, when translated into practice, became propaganda: hence the 'requests' of the Roman envoys in 200 that Philip should not make war on the Greeks. Rome, in accordance with the pattern which had successfully operated in Italy, in Sicily, in Illyria and in Spain, was now depicting herself as the protector of the Greeks.

This picture was, of course, presented primarily for consumption by the Greeks themselves, among whom it had long been recognized that the proclamation of protection by a powerful third party was often merely a convenient cloak for imperialism. The reason why they seem, at first, to have been favourably impressed by the Roman proclamation, despite their past experience of similar announcements, seems likely to be the widespread recognition that Rome was not interested in territorial expansion, but only in increasing her influence; and this appeared to have been demonstrated by Rome's evacuation of her armies after her three previous trans-Adriatic adventures. Many of the Greek states were therefore prepared to believe that the same result would end Rome's new military involvement in the Balkans, and were accordingly prepared to support Rome against Philip. The chief believers were, of course, Attalus, Rhodes and Athens.

But even those Balkan states which believed that Rome's intentions were no different from those which the Hellenistic great powers had pursued for more than a century were prepared to be impressed by sheer power and to bow to the inevitable when the Roman army and fleet reached Apollonia in autumn 200. This time, it seemed clear, the Romans intended to humble Philip; the period of narrowly defensive wars was long past. In the last resort, success or failure would depend to a great extent on how many Greek and other Balkan states chose to fight alongside Rome. Her friends of the earlier wars were, of course, certain: the Greek cities of the Illyrian coast, Pleuratus of Illyria (Scerdilaidas' son and successor as dynast at Scodra), Attalus, Rhodes and Athens were at once prepared to co-operate; so also were Macedon's traditional non-Greek northern enemies, the Dardanians, and those who felt they had not the power to resist and therefore preferred to collaborate, such as Amynander, king of the small mountain principality of Athamania.[1]

All, however, were not immediately convinced. The most important of the doubters was Rome's treaty-breaking ally of the First Macedonian War, the Aetolian League. Despite Rome's disenchantment with Aetolia, the League was too powerful and too strategically important to be ignored. The envoys in 200 had called on the Aetolian government; and in spring 199 Sulpicius sent his new ally Amynander to the general assembly of the Aetolian League. His purpose was to persuade the Aetolians to join Rome, as they had in the earlier war against Philip. But Amynander did not succeed. Philip had also sent representatives to the Aetolians; and, no doubt by reminding the League of its dissatisfaction with its earlier relationship with Rome, persuaded the Aetolians to remain neutral. The Aetolians' dilatoriness in joining Rome, when added to their defection in the first war, was to have important consequences for the treatment of their League after the war.[2]

Philip also spent time in trying to encourage his allies. Constant attacks on Athens warned what might happen to his enemies; his garrisons at Demetrias and Chalcis (which, with the Acrocorinth, the citadel of Corinth, he called the 'Fetters of Greece') served to keep open a safe route to the south through Euboea. His chief ally in the Peloponnese, the Achaean League, had supported him for most of his first war with Rome; and the Achaeans' continuing loyalty, since their League controlled most of the Peloponnese and, most importantly, all the vital Peloponnesian coastline of the Gulf of Corinth, was crucial to his control of southern Greece, since he maintained this only with a small string of garrisons, the chief of which was on the Acrocorinth. Yet despite the Macedonian garrisons, Philip could not be certain of Achaean support. The Roman envoys had visited the League in 200 and been received encouragingly by Philopoemen, who was then chief magistrate (*strategos*), and by his friend Aristaenus; and although Philip's chief Achaean supporter Cycliadas was elected *strategos* for 200/199, he was much less effective militarily than Philopoemen. This was important because Achaea's southern enemy, Nabis of Sparta, immediately began attacks on Achaea which Cycliadas could not prevent. In late autumn 200 Philip came to Achaea and offered to fight Nabis for the Achaeans. Superficially, the offer was very attractive; but it had strings attached which strangled its usefulness. For Philip also asked the Achaeans to supply reinforcements for his own garrisons at Oreus and Chalcis, in Euboea, and on the Acrocorinth. Cycliadas, despite his Macedonian sympathies, did not find this double-edged offer tempting: for by asking for Achaean troops, Philip was clearly trying to commit the Achaeans to war with Rome and at the same time to secure hostages for Achaean good behaviour. Achaea's immediate danger from Nabis was not so great that Cycliadas was prepared to risk his popularity (and with it, incidentally, the Macedonian cause) by supporting such an obvious ploy. He therefore ruled Philip's proposal out of order on a constitutional technicality. Thereupon Philip abandoned his offer to fight Nabis and left Achaea, having failed to commit his old ally to his new war.[3]

Despite his failure in Achaea, events of 199 did not suggest that Philip's cause was altogether hopeless. Sulpicius invaded Macedonia and raised such tempting prospects of massive booty that the Aetolian League no longer saw profit in remaining neutral; and late in the summer it joined the Romans. Ironically, it was the Aetolians who then gave Philip his chief military encouragement of the year, which otherwise passed without a major engagement. Late in the year they attacked parts of Thessaly; but their troops acted so unprofessionally, concerning themselves solely with plunder, that they were badly beaten by Philip and only saved from complete disaster by the good sense of Amynander of Athamania. Nor were the Aetolians Rome's only allies to be disappointed by the fierceness of Philip's resistance: the Dardanians too, when they invaded Macedonia in concert with the Romans, were surprised at Philip's energy and were driven back without much difficulty. The Roman and Pergamene fleets operated throughout the year in the Aegean against Philip's possessions and sympathizers; but nobody on either side thought the war could be decided by naval operations, and their only substantial effect was to relieve pressure on Athens. Thus at the end of the first year of the war Philip not only survived, but he might reasonably think that the inconclusiveness of the events of the year provided him with a basis for hope that he might soon bring the Romans to the conference table.[4]

II Titus Quinctius Flamininus

Late in 199 Sulpicius was replaced by his successor in the consul-ship, Publius Villius Tappulus. Since Villius could begin no military activity during the winter, he began his period of effective command with enforced military idleness. He chose to winter in the friendly comfort of Corcyra, though the troops, as in the previous year, win-tered farther north, on the mainland near Apollonia; and he seems to have exploited his closeness to Epirus (on the mainland) to con-tact those Epirots who were willing to abandon Epirus' traditionally close relationship with Macedon and to bend before the wind of Rome's advance. Thus it was Charops, one of these Epirots, who in early spring brought Villius the information that Philip was taking up a position in the narrow gorge of the river Aous, the main river-valley route from the region around Apollonia into Thessaly and western Macedonia. He clearly intended to block any Roman attempt to repeat the previous year's invasion of Macedonia.

Villius' immediate inclination was to investigate the feasibility of dislodging Philip from the vital valley by bringing him to battle. He therefore collected his troops from their winter quarters and led them to within five miles of Philip's position. But Villius' hope of a decisive action was immediately dashed, not by any military con-tingency but by the news that Titus Quinctius Flamininus, his successor in the consulship, had already reached Corcyra and was about to relieve him. We do not know how Flamininus managed to arrange his arrival in the Balkans so soon after his inauguration on March 15. Villius himself had not taken over his command until the previous autumn. But the result was that Flamininus could expect at least a whole year in command (and more if he could persuade the Senate to extend his magistracy). Villius had no alternative but to return to Rome. He had accomplished nothing except to make a useful contact with Charops in Epirus.[5]

Flamininus was a remarkable young man in more than the fact of his unprecedentedly quick arrival in the Balkans—though the way he seized this opportunity was typical. Not yet thirty, he had held only the quaestorship of the offices customarily filled before a Roman gained the consulship; yet considering his age, his career in the war with Hannibal had been distinguished: a mere junior officer (tribune of the soldiers) in 208 under Marcellus, in 205, though he may have held no magistracy at all, he was given the *imperium* of a praetor and the command of Tarentum, which he held for two years. In 201 he became a member of the senatorial commission which allotted lands to Scipio's African veterans; and again in 200 he served on a colonizing committee. He was clearly, despite his youth and lack of formal experience as a magistrate, already accepted by the Roman 'establishment'. Perhaps between 204 and 199 he held his one and only preliminary magistracy, the humble quaestorship.[6]

It was an outstanding achievement for Flamininus to have himself elected consul for 198. Unfortunately, we cannot discover with any certainty which senators supported him.[7] It has often been thought that Scipio Africanus' influence was most important; and while this cannot be proved, it seems likely that the precedent set by the success of Scipio's own precocious and unorthodox appointment to his Spanish command will have influenced those who supported Flamininus, whether or not Scipio himself was one of them. However Flamininus was by no means unopposed. Indeed, two tribunes of the plebs tried to have him prevented from standing for election at all on the ground that he had previously held only the quaestorship and that his worth had therefore not yet been satisfactorily proven. But there was, at this time, no law which prevented Flamininus from standing; and when the Senate turned the tables of the tribunes by enunciating the principle on which the tribunes' own power was based, that the Assembly of the People was sovereign and might elect whom it wished, the votes were cast and counted, and Flamininus, with Sextus Aelius Paetus as his colleague, was duly elected.[8]

When the consuls were appointed to their provinces, Flamininus, whether by accident or by arrangement, received Macedonia. His appointment had enormous implications for the future of Graeco-Roman relations; for he subtly managed to impose his own shape on Roman policy in the Balkans, a shape which conditioned attitudes for the crucial generation in which Rome achieved dominance in the eastern Mediterranean. For Flamininus, through his service among the Greeks of southern Italy and his command during the war in the Greek city of Tarentum, had acquired not only a fluent knowledge of the Greek language, but also a sympathetic awareness of the most important features of Greek life and attitudes. It is not therefore surprising that under Flamininus Roman policy in Greece became more closely attuned to Greek ways of thought, and exploited Greek political weaknesses and Greek public opinion to achieve the ends of Roman policy. In this sense Flamininus' policy may reasonably be described as 'philhellenic'.

His immediate problem on his arrival in spring 198 was to make the Roman war-effort effective; and Flamininus started well by reaching Corcyra in time to command the first operation of the year. This in itself was an important indication to the Greeks and to Philip of the seriousness of Rome's commitment. But Flamininus brought more than new energy to bear on the war: he also brought a new policy, which was particularly adapted to appeal to Greek sensibilities. In the form in which it had been worked out at Rome, this new policy made its appearance when Flamininus met Philip soon after his arrival. When Flamininus took over from Villius, the Roman army was camped facing Philip's position near the narrowest part of the Aous gorge; and Philip immediately asked for negotiations in the hope of being able to exploit his strong military position to exact concessions. He was by now deeply impressed by the obvious seriousness of the Roman commitment, and offered to accept (in effect) the terms which Aemilius Lepidus had offered him at Abydus two years before: that he would give up places he had himself captured and submit to arbitration on the allegations of war damage.

At Abydus in 200 such an offer might have prevented war. In 200 the Roman Senate might have been satisfied with it. But in 198, with a Roman army in the Balkans and Greek allies committed to the war, it was no longer enough. Flamininus presented the Senate's new policy when he denied the need for arbitration and asserted that Philip was palpably guilty of aggression; and when they came to detailed discussions as to which peoples Philip might free in order to produce a solution acceptable to Rome, Flamininus began by naming the Thessalians—who had been virtually assimilated with Macedon for nearly 150 years. It was rather as if at Munich in 1938 Adolf Hitler had demanded the 'liberation' of Scotland. This, then, was the Senate's new policy:[9] Philip was not only to be humbled, but he was to be universally seen to be humbled. If he had accepted the Roman ultimatum in 200, he would have retained the appearance of power and influence in his traditional spheres (such as in Thessaly), though as a Roman client. But the terms demanded in 198 implied that this appearance also was to be shattered. Philip obviously could not negotiate on these terms while he was still militarily undefeated; and preliminary skirmishing began the next day.

Philip did not get much satisfaction from the campaign of 198. Flamininus soon outflanked his apparently impregnable position in the Aous gorge, thanks to information sent by the Epirot Charops about a mountain sheep-track. Philip was forced to retreat to Thessaly to avoid a massacre. Even so, he lost some 2,000 men. After pursuing an ill-advised scorched-earth policy in Thessaly, which reduced his popularity there to an unprecedentedly low level (which he could scarcely afford, while Flamininus was at the same time claiming the intention of 'liberating' the Thessalians), he returned to Macedon, where the Aetolians, encouraged by the Aous battle, had again invaded. Amynander also took the opportunity of attacking those areas of Thessaly which abutted on his kingdom of Athamania.

Flamininus delayed his pursuit of Philip because of supply difficulties. If ships were to land supplies in the most convenient places on the west coast of the Balkans, Epirus, through which the supplies would need to be transported, must be pro-Roman (or, at least, not positively hostile); and so far only Charops had shown enthusiasm for the Roman cause. Flamininus therefore spent some time on diplomacy in Epirus; and it proved well worthwhile, for he persuaded the Epirots to join the Roman allies before he followed Philip into Thessaly. Thus another of Philip's sympathizers was lost to him. In Thessaly, however, Flamininus had no swift success. Philip had left garrisons in the most important places, and Phaloria and Atrax in particular offered vigorous resistance. Phaloria was captured and the whole town burnt down after a siege—a brutal success which led some nearby communities to surrender 'voluntarily'—but Atrax held out for so long that Flamininus abandoned the siege to make preparations for his winter quarters. For these he wanted access to the sea and a less difficult approach to Thessaly and Macedonia than was possible from Epirus. He therefore resolved to conquer Phocis, a neighbour of the Aetolian League, chiefly because it had useful harbours on the Corinthian Gulf. The rest of the campaigning season was spent on capturing the Phocian cities. While Flamininus was operating in Thessaly and Phocis, his brother Lucius was in command of the Roman fleet. Enlarged by ships from Attalus and from Rhodes, the fleet again attacked Philip's possessions in Euboea, and captured Eretria and Carystus.[10]

These were undoubted successes; and the superiority of Roman determination and of Roman arms had gained widespread recognition by autumn 198. Nowhere was this recognition more embarrassing to Philip than in the Achaean League, which perforce played host to one of his 'Fetters', the Acrocorinth. During the First Macedonian War the League had honoured its alliance with Philip because Philip had had the good sense to try to protect it against its enemies, Aetolia and Sparta, which were both Roman allies. But attitudes were changing in Achaea. The Achaean army had been so much improved by Philopoemen that the threat from Sparta was ended for the time being in a major battle fought at Mantinea in 207 without Philip's help. And when, after the war with Rome, Philip had turned his attention to the Aegean, the League had been left to fend for itself against the new Spartan ruler Nabis.

For a few years it had managed very well. But in the last resort Achaea could not remain neutral in this new war with Rome; and Rome could not be successfully opposed by the techniques which had kept Sparta reasonably quiet. The Roman envoys had visited Achaea in 200 before the declaration of war, and had had a friendly reception from Philopoemen; and although the pro-Macedonian leader Cycliadas was elected *strategos* for the following year, even he, as we have seen, was unwilling to commit the League to active hostilities against Rome.[11] Yet neutrality, however firmly enunciated, was unlikely to be respected by the Romans when the Achaeans harboured one of Philip's most important garrisons. In the circumstances, the maintenance of the alliance with Philip would clearly ensure Roman attacks, particularly since the Roman naval base was on Attalus' island of Aegina, only a short distance from the Achaean coastline. The Achaeans seem to have realized their vulnerability when they elected Philopoemen's friend Aristaenus *strategos* for 198 and exiled Cycliadas. This latter act was a positive demonstration which might compensate, it was hoped, for the embarrassing presence of the Macedonian garrison on the Acrocorinth—about which neither Aristaenus nor any other Achaean could do anything.

By late summer 198 Aristaenus thought the time ripe for persuading the Achaeans to ally with Rome. To add force to the arguments of the delegates from the Romans, Attalus, Rhodes and Athens, who assembled for the crucial meeting of the League's general assembly at Sicyon, the allied fleet approached the nearby Corinthian port of Cenchreae and began to besiege Corinth. The carrot which the allies dangled before the Achaeans was the restoration of Corinth to the League as a city free from Macedonian interference; but the real issue was safety or destruction in the short term, and of friendship or enmity in the long term. These immediate issues were quite clear. But despite their clarity, the Achaean alliance with Macedon retained a large traditional support in Achaea; for the League had certainly benefited from it in the past, and it was argued that both gratitude and self-interest suggested that the Achaeans should abide by it now. For some time the outcome of the debate was doubtful, and a decision of any kind was almost prevented by a constitutional technicality. In the end, however, Aristaenus won; the Achaeans voted to repudiate their alliance with Philip and to join Rome. The Romans thus won their greatest advantage of the year; Philip's chief means of exerting political influence in the Peloponnese was destroyed. It no longer mattered so much that the allies' attack on Corinth was unsuccessful.[12]

Although the defection of the Achaean League meant that Philip's prospect of recovery in southern Greece was very slight, he did not immediately give up. He still kept his garrison at Corinth, now commanded by the experienced Philocles; and Philocles soon managed to occupy the Achaean city of Argos, where Philip had long-standing personal connections and where a significant section of the population handed their city to Philocles because they were dissatisfied with the League's decision to join Rome. But it was a demonstration of loyalty which, however gratifying in itself, was in practice embarrassing to Philip: for with Achaea's changed attitude, he simply could not adequately defend Argos, however much he wanted to. Philip soon saw his solution in Achaea's enemy, Nabis of Sparta (though the Argives were justifiably not enthusiastic about it). Late in the winter Philocles was instructed to approach Nabis with an offer of a marriage alliance with Philip, if Nabis would protect Argos against the Roman allies. Nabis agreed. But no sooner had he occupied Argos than he too began negotiations with Flamininus, which ended in his joining Rome and suspending hostilities against Achaea.[13]

Meanwhile Philip had again tried to stave off the impending Macedonian disaster by re-opening negotiations with Flamininus in early winter 198/7. The meeting took place at Nicaea, near Thermopylae; and this time Philip was clearly prepared to make whatever reasonable concessions Flamininus required. While military operations were suspended for the winter, Flamininus had no objection to spending time on negotiations, particularly since he was as yet unsure whether the Senate would extend his command into 197. If it did not, the negotiations might even be advantageous to him, since in that case he would doubtless have liked to end the war by negotiation and get the credit for it before his successor arrived; if it did, he would easily be able to find some excuse for breaking off the negotiations and reverting to his plan of humbling Philip for all to see.[14]

Flamininus was accompanied at the negotiations by representatives of all his Greek allies. He opened by repeating his demand of the spring conference at the Aous gorge, that Philip should evacuate the whole of Greece. Additionally, all deserters and prisoners were now to be released, the area in Illyria which Philip had occupied since the Peace of Phoenice should be restored to Rome, and all places taken from Ptolemy V should be returned to him. When the allies spoke, each listed the particular places and conditions which Philip must give up to satisfy them. Much pointless bickering passed between Philip and the Aetolian representatives, in which Flamininus discreetly took no part. But since the conference seemed to be getting nowhere, Philip asked for the demands of each party in writing so that he might study them.

He made his reply the next day in closed session with Flamininus alone. According to Flamininus' report, it amounted to the partial satisfaction of the detailed requirements of each group of allied representatives. Flamininus' allies were quick to assert that partial satisfaction of their demands was not enough, since it did not amount to the evacuation of the whole of Greece—the slogan under which they were all fighting and to which they were all committed—and they therefore regarded Philip's concessions as inadequate. Again Flamininus expressed no opinion, since he wanted to keep his options open, of either ending the war by negotiation if his command were terminated, or continuing it if his command were extended. Thus when Philip suggested that he was willing to send an embassy to the Senate to negotiate disputed points, Flamininus was eager to agree, since the timing was such that his friends in Rome would be able to decide whether to advise the Senate to accept or reject Philip's terms, depending on whether or not Flamininus' command were extended.[15] The conference broke up after agreeing to two months' truce. Embassies from all parties then travelled to Rome to present all points of view to the Senate.

Shortly after these embassies arrived, the Senate, doubtless advised by Flamininus' senatorial friends, decided that neither of the new consuls of 197 should take over the war against Philip. Accordingly, Flamininus' friends no longer needed to advise accepting an unsatisfactory negotiated peace which would leave Philip undefeated and inadequately humbled. The Senate heard the Greek allies first. They chose to emphasize that Philip's proposals did not mention his evacuation of the 'Fetters'—Demetrias, Chalcis and the Acrocorinth—though he had offered the town of Corinth to the Achaeans; and they argued that the abandonment of these strongpoints was a prerequisite for a satisfactory settlement with Philip. They made this point so emphatically that the Senate seized on it as soon as Philip's envoys entered the chamber: their prepared defence of Philip's proposals was ruled out of order and they were simply asked if Philip was prepared to abandon Chalcis, the Acrocorinth and Demetrias. The Macedonians were taken aback at the directness of the demand, and their surprise suggests that Flamininus had either avoided talking to Philip about the 'Fetters', or had explicitly indicated that they would not be an issue. In either case Philip had been cynically misled; and his envoys could only reply that they had no instructions about the 'Fetters'. The Senate was not satisfied. It immediately voted to continue the war, and confirmed the extension of Flamininus' command.[16]

III The Freedom of the Greeks

By spring 197, when Flamininus left his winter quarters to seek a decisive battle with Philip, almost the whole of southern and central Greece was allied with Rome. Flamininus' military task was thus made appreciably easier. After some manoeuvring, the armies met about the end of May at Cynoscephalae in Thessaly. The battle was accidentally begun on ground unsuited to the Macedonians; but it was wholly decisive. Philip's army was destroyed as an effective fighting force.[17] Military recovery was now beyond his power. The actual conflict was over; but serious problems remained. The crucial question was, how would Rome use her victory? For there was no doubt that Philip could now be made to evacuate the whole of Greece, as the allies' slogan had demanded. What would Rome put in his place?

The Aetolians were particularly exercised by this. They had participated in the final battle; in their own view they had made a major contribution to the victory; and they now expected the traditional reward of the victor, their share of the spoils. Indeed, so eager were they for booty that they even seized the chief immediate spoils of the campaign by plundering Philip's camp before the Roman troops arrived. This incident did not improve Flamininus' opinion of the Aetolians; and as soon as the battle was over, his attitude towards them became noticeably cool. Nor was the situation improved when the Aetolians began to realize that they had fought the war under ambiguous political conditions. For it seems that they had been misleadingly encouraged to believe that Rome was letting them fight on the same generous terms of alliance applicable during the first war with Philip—the terms of the treaty of 211—although this agreement had never been formally re-negotiated. Sulpicius Galba must have deliberately misled them, though he had good military reasons for doing so: for until Philip was defeated it was crucially important that the large block of territory which the Aetolians controlled should be firmly committed to Rome. Sulpicius also had a personal grudge against the Aetolians, since it was during his command in the Balkans in 206 that the Aetolians had ignored his personal protests and broken their treaty with Rome. After Philip's defeat, however, the strategic argument lost much of its importance. The Romans could again afford to regard the Aetolians as ungrateful treaty-breakers: hence Flamininus' sudden coolness.

Rome's cynical exploitation of the Aetolians began to emerge as soon as Philip was defeated, when the allies met to discuss their individual demands after the battle; but since the Aetolians were very unpopular throughout Greece because of their notoriously predatory habits, Flamininus' treatment of them actually won him approval: it was classic 'divide and conquer' technique. Alexander, the Aetolian spokesman, began the conference by suggesting that, now that Philip was defeated, he should also be deposed—a suggestion which Flamininus immediately squashed by moralistically asserting that this was not the Roman way; moreover, Flamininus also argued, it was important that Philip should retain a certain minimum power in view of the constant danger which Greece as a whole ran from invasion from the north. This was reasonable enough; but he left unspoken his major consideration, that he intended to preserve Philip's Macedon (though substantially weakened) essentially as a political counterweight to the Aetolians themselves. His idea was to establish a balance of power in northern and central Greece in case any future development in the area turned out to appear dangerous to the suspicious Romans. Accordingly, Flamininus proposed to recommend that the Senate accept peace on the terms which the allies had required at the Nicaea conference, that Philip should evacuate the whole of Greece.

When Philip arrived at the conference he offered these very terms. Again the Aetolians could not restrain themselves and asked, why then did he not hand over to them three towns, Larisa Cremaste, Pharsalus and Phthiotic Thebes, which had once been members of their League? Philip's attitude was that they could have them if they wanted them; but Flamininus quickly intervened. He said they might have only Phthiotic Thebes, because it alone had refused to submit voluntarily to Rome. The other towns had submitted voluntarily and were now in Rome's protection. When the Aetolian Phaeneas argued that the treaty of 211 gave all these towns to Aetolia, he was bluntly informed that the Romans did not regard the treaty of 211 as still being operative. The other Greeks enjoyed the Aetolians' discomfiture and approved Flamininus' attitude; for although the exact terms of the final settlement were still uncertain, Flamininus was making it quite clear that he had no intention of allowing Philip's domination of the cities of central Greece to be straightforwardly exchanged for Aetolian dominance.[18]

An armistice was then agreed and envoys were sent to Rome. After considerable discussion, the Senate agreed to accept Philip's offer of the terms it had demanded the previous winter, and a peace treaty was drawn up on that basis. The Senate also appointed a commission of ten senators to help Flamininus decide the details of how Greece was to be dealt with and 'to secure freedom for the Greeks'. The Senate's decree, when in due course it was made known in Greece, announced that 'all the Greeks of Asia and Europe are to be free and live by their own laws; those ruled by Philip and those cities garrisoned by Philip, Philip shall hand over to the Romans before the Isthmian festival' (this was held about July 196). The decree continued to stipulate that the more distant towns, mostly in Asia Minor, still held by Philip, were to be left free; and even Cius, which Philip had captured in 200 for his ally Prusias of Bithynia, was the subject of a 'freedom letter' from Flamininus to Prusias; Philip was to give up all his warships except for five light ships and one state galley, and to pay 1,000 talents indemnity to Rome and to give hostages.[19]

The Greeks could have no doubt that Philip's acceptance of these terms prevented him from ever again being a threat to Greek freedom; and the firm inclusion of all the Greeks of Asia Minor—not just those ruled by Philip—was also an advance warning of Rome's interest in Asia Minor to the Seleucid king, Antiochus III, who was currently operating in that area and re-asserting the long-standing territorial claims of his dynasty. But what was this freedom which the Romans claimed they were bringing to the Greeks? The Aetolians had no doubt that, as with previous Hellenistic campaigns waged under the same banner of liberation, the freedom was illusory and the Roman claim fraudulent, that they had, in effect, simply exchanged one master for another. They saw conclusive proof of their view in the fact that the peace terms laid down that Philip's possessions in Greece, including the three 'Fetters', Demetrias, Chalcis and the Acrocorinth, were to be handed over to the Romans. What else, they argued, could this mean? To the Aetolians it seemed immediately obvious that the Roman liberation was just as much a confidence trick as the 'liberations' of the earlier Hellenistic kings.[20]

The Aetolian interpretation hurt because it had a superficial ring of truth about it. For although Flamininus knew what he wanted to do—to build the security of Roman interests in the Balkans firmly on a foundation of Greek goodwill—he had not yet convinced the majority of the ten senators who formed the settlement commission that this was how Roman interests could best be protected. The reason for this was very largely the fault of the Greeks themselves, particularly of the Aetolians: for the commissioners were much impressed by the importance which the Greek envoys had laid in Rome, and were still laying in Greece, on the 'Fetters'. And since Antiochus III had moved from Syria into Asia Minor during Rome's war with Philip, and since his ultimate objectives were obscure (though the Romans pessimistically suspected, as they had always suspected strong neighbours, that he intended to cross into Europe and that he therefore threatened Roman interests in the Balkans), many of the commissioners were inclined to accept the Greek estimate of the importance of the 'Fetters' and to keep them for Rome.

Flamininus' view was different, and it ultimately prevailed. By now he had spent long enough in Greece to realize that if once a large majority of the Greeks could be made to believe that Rome had no more than a friendly interest in their welfare, that, in effect, their freedom was genuine, their liberation unfettered (except for the obvious moral obligations that gratitude would impose), then whatever Antiochus did or claimed, the Greeks on the whole would support Rome. And the more suspicion the Aetolian trouble-makers threw on Roman motives, the more important it became that the rest of the Greeks should be convincingly shown that the Aetolians' allegations were utterly wrong. In Flamininus' view, this could now only be done by physically evacuating *all* Greek possessions given up by Philip to Rome—including the 'Fetters'.[21]

Flamininus eventually convinced the commissioners of the importance of these considerations. He was then ready to shatter the suspicion of Roman motives which the Aetolians had aroused. And he carefully chose the Isthmian festival as the most effective occasion for his demonstration of Roman sincerity, for this was a religious and athletic ceremony at which representatives from all Greek states would normally be present; in addition, it was the date fixed by the Senate's decree by which Philip was to have evacuated all his Greek possessions. A major speech to the General Assembly of the United Nations would even today win no greater effective publicity than a proclamation at the Isthmian festival. When the crowd had collected in the stadium to watch the games, the herald trumpeted for silence and announced Flamininus' dramatic and unexpected proclamation: 'The Roman Senate and Titus Quinctius the proconsul, having defeated king Philip and the Macedonians, leave free, ungarrisoned, without tribute, subject only to their own traditional laws, the following peoples: the Corinthians, Phocians, Locrians, Euboeans, Phthiotic Achaeans, Magnesians, Thessalians and Perrhaebians.'[22] These were all the territories which Philip had directly controlled in the Balkans (and the 'Fetters' were included in them), and Flamininus' announcement made it clear and explicit that they were to be treated just like the other Greeks.

The general euphoria created by this theatrical proclamation swept away all suspicions that the Aetolians' allegations were well-founded: they were now firmly branded before the nations of Greece with their traditional reputation of being ungrateful troublemakers. It was now, it seemed, only a matter of time before the Romans would again evacuate Greece and this time would leave the Greeks freer than they had felt themselves as a whole for more than 150 years. Gratitude to Rome was poured out on all sides; statues of Flamininus and dedications to him were set up in every important place throughout Greece. The work of the commissioners was not yet completed in every respect, but Flamininus' proclamation made certain that their assurances, their arbitrations, and their adjustments would now be accepted everywhere, except in Aetolia, as given in good faith. If Antiochus crossed to Europe now, he would find the Greeks, with only one major exception, united behind the firm barricades of freedom erected by the Isthmian proclamation.

Flamininus' triumphantly publicized diplomatic good sense both exploited the Greeks' yearning for long-lost freedom and welded it to the Roman concept of the free client state, which the Senate had first experimented with in Sicily nearly fifty years before. In the Balkans complications and misunderstandings eventually arose, and the welding of the two concepts proved in time to be imperfect. But in the short term it worked. And Flamininus' policy and his Isthmian proclamation have been justly regarded, both in ancient and modern times, as one of the most sensible and effective pieces of diplomacy in the whole course of Rome's rise to world power.

CHAPTER XII

ANTIOCHUS THE GREAT

I Rome's Evacuation of Greece

THE Roman settlement of Greece after the second war with Philip was conditioned, as we have seen, by the Senate's suspicion of Antiochus III of Syria. As a result of Philip's defeat and of Rome's acquiring a firmer commitment within the Balkans, Antiochus had had thrust upon him the invidious role of Rome's most powerful eastern neighbour. Rome had always been suspicious of strong neighbours, and time and time again had acted on her suspicions, both in Italy and overseas. Antiochus III's activities in Asia Minor, therefore, made him an automatic candidate for Roman mistrust. Moreover, although Rome's only immediate interests in Asia Minor were her friendship with Pergamum, Rhodes, and a few smaller places, Antiochus' activities in Asia Minor nevertheless had their ominous aspect. Fortunately for Rome, however, this did not fully emerge until her war with Philip was almost over.

Indeed, during the initial stages of the war with Philip the Senate chose to regard Antiochus as a friend of the Roman People. This relationship seems to have begun with an exchange of ambassadors with one of Antiochus' ancestors, and it may have been resumed by the envoys of 200 who, after leaving Rhodes, went on to Egypt and Syria, where they met Antiochus.[1] They no doubt received satisfactory assurances that Antiochus did not intend to join Philip. The next attested contact was in 198, by which time Antiochus had penetrated into Asia Minor and invaded the territory of Rome's friend Attalus of Pergamum. Attalus was, of course, an important Roman ally, particularly in that crucial year; and when he asked the Senate for permission to pull his forces out of Greece to deal with Antiochus in Asia Minor, the Senate not only allowed him to do so but also sent Roman envoys to Antiochus who politely asked him to withdraw from Attalus' kingdom. The Senate's message was that friends of the Roman People should be friendly towards each other; and after receiving it Antiochus seems to have withdrawn at once. He even sent envoys to Rome to tell the Senate that he was complying with its envoys' request. The Senate was favourably impressed and voted complimentary decrees for Antiochus.[2]

Unfortunately, Antiochus drew the wrong conclusion from the Senate's friendly reaction; and as soon as his envoys had returned, he began the expedition which he had long been planning, to re-conquer the empire in Asia Minor which had been held by his family for a large part of the third century B.C. During 197 therefore, while Flamininus was defeating Philip in the campaign of Cynoscephalae, Antiochus penetrated into southern Asia Minor. There he clashed with Rome's friend and ally Rhodes, who had important possessions on the Asiatic mainland in Caria (the 'Rhodian Peraea') which only a few years before had been severely threatened by Philip. Afraid of a possible coalition between Antiochus and Philip—Antiochus' lieutenant in Asia Minor, Zeuxis, had helped Philip in 200 during his attack on Rhodes' possessions in Caria—Rhodes demanded that Antiochus should withdraw. But when the news of Cynoscephalae removed the Rhodians' fears, they dropped their bold pose of opposition to Antiochus: they might now reasonably expect to be able to persuade the Romans to deal with him, as Attalus had done when Antiochus invaded Pergamum the previous year.[3]

The Rhodians were not disappointed. Antiochus' steady advance into Asia Minor during 197 at once aroused Roman suspicions. The Senate will almost certainly have felt that Antiochus' ambassadors had misled them in 198 and that the king was taking advantage of Rome's preoccupation with Philip. And while the senators obviously could not know Antiochus' real intentions, it was evidently safest to take the precaution of making certain of peace with Philip as quickly as possible. Fortunately, by then Cynoscephalae had been fought and Flamininus was able to persuade Philip to accept terms which the Senate had previously approved. Polybius makes it clear that the circumstances in Asia stressed the urgency of ending the war in the Balkans as soon as possible;[4] and it is clear that the Senate's suspicions of Antiochus' intentions caused Flamininus to develop his idea of achieving a balance of power in central Greece through preserving sufficient authority for Philip to counterbalance the unreliable Aetolians. For the Aetolians seemed likely to prove disaffected as soon as they learnt that Flamininus fully intended to implement 'the freedom of the Greeks' after Philip's defeat; for it implied a fragmentation of powers which would deprive them of their expected territorial gains. We have seen how Flamininus achieved his balance of power in practice: by humbling Philip but not entirely destroying his strength. For what Rome *might* have done with him, compare, for instance, how the Carthaginians' power had been destroyed by their peace settlement. The additional safeguard in Greece was that Flamininus refused to allow the Aetolians to benefit territorially from occupying the places which Philip had evacuated.

At the same time as these developments in the Balkans, Antiochus was quickly—though not as quickly as he would have liked—recovering control of Asia Minor. He may have hoped to cross to Europe and, by exploiting Philip's weakness, to re-establish the full extent of the empire of Seleucus I, the founder of his dynasty; he may have been trying to seize as much territory as he could before Rome stopped him; or he may simply have been trying to forestall Rome in gaining firm control of the area, since he naturally could not know Rome's ultimate intentions. In any case, he kept diplomatic silence during his campaign in Asia Minor and did not even immediately send the customary formal congratulations to Flamininus on his defeat of Philip. Instead, he pressed on to the Hellespont; and though he failed to win over the important cities of Smyrna and Lampsacus, in spring 196 he crossed to Europe in the Thracian Chersonnese and began to rebuild the abandoned city of Lysimacheia. Only then, when he had secured this bridgehead in Europe and when Lampsacus had appealed to the Senate against him, could Antiochus no longer afford to delay. At last he sent his belated congratulations to Flamininus on his victory over Philip, though by then he must have known about it for nearly a year. The instructions of his envoys, Hegesianax and Lysias, were doubtless to congratulate Flamininus and to assure him that Antiochus' intentions were peaceful. But the contrast between what Antiochus was doing and what his envoys said, the long interval without diplomatic communication, and the appeals of Rome's friends in Asia Minor, merely stimulated Roman suspicion.

That Antiochus was in the minds of the Roman commissioners is clear from the way in which they dealt with Greece in 196: Flamininus' insistence that the support of the Greeks was vital, and that this could only be secured by ostentatiously liberating them, finally won over those of the commissioners who would have preferred a more old-fashioned approach and would have retained Rome's hold on the 'Fetters'. Because of Antiochus' active presence in Asia Minor, the terms of the Roman decree stated explicitly that the Greeks of Asia,

as well as those of Europe, should be free—an obvious claim to the
support of the Asiatic Greeks against Antiochus (should it prove
necessary), just as the European Greeks had risen to the same bait
and supported Rome against Philip. Thus when Hegesianax and
Lysias arrived at Corinth, the Roman reply to Antiochus' congratulations and pacific assertions was in some respects similar to the
message delivered by the Roman envoys to Philip, through Nicanor,
at Athens in spring 200: Antiochus was asked to evacuate the cities
of Asia Minor which he had recently captured and which had previously belonged to Ptolemy or Philip, to withdraw from all the
free Greek cities that he had occupied or was currently attacking
(this had particular reference to Lampsacus which, like Athens,
Rhodes and Pergamum in 200, had now appealed to Rome), and not
to cross into Europe; for he must not bring war and enslavement
to those just freed by Rome.[5]

What was missing from this statement—though its propagandist
intention is clear enough—marks the chief difference between the
Roman's ultimatum to Philip in 200 and their present message to
Antiochus. For to Antiochus they implied no threat of war: the
Roman reply was not yet an ultimatum. The Senate clearly had no
intention of fighting Antiochus unless such action was forced upon
it: and Flamininus had no intention of wrecking his settlement of
Greece, if he could possibly avoid it: the technique which Flamininus
and the commissioners chose to employ was that of the 'cold war'. In
accordance with the unwritten rules of the game, Antiochus protested
his pacific assertions, while the Romans expressed their readiness
to talk to anybody anywhere. Accordingly, later in 196 some of the
commissioners duly travelled to confer with Antiochus. They found
him already in Europe, at Lysimacheia, which he had begun to rebuild. The discussions, in the familiar technique of the 'cold war',
were conducted by each party with as much a view to convincing
outside public opinion of the rectitude of their stance as to for-
warding the negotiations themselves. The Romans made three
demands: that Antiochus should evacuate the cities belonging to
Rome's friend Ptolemy; that he should urgently evacuate those which
had been Philip's, since it was ludicrous, they claimed, that Antiochus
should take the prizes which were Rome's by right of conquest; and
they urged him to keep his hands off those cities which were free (a
statement which was not wholly compatible with either of the first
two demands, but was made chiefly for its propagandist effect). They
left to the end the point which actually bothered the Senate most,

Antiochus' presence in Europe, and they asked for an explanation of this.

If the Romans had hoped for a propagandist success from these demands—the 'cold war' equivalent of a military victory—they were disappointed, for this kind of open diplomacy was a familiar technique to Antiochus who, along with other Hellenistic kings, had always paid due regard to the influence of Greek public opinion. He therefore had appropriate answers ready. He denied to Rome any right to intervene in Asia Minor on any pretext whatever, just as he himself would never consider intervening in Italy; he had crossed to Europe because, he claimed, he had a historical right to do so, stemming from the claim of Seleucus I to Thrace (established by Seleucus' defeat of Lysimachus in 281, now eighty-five years ago, and never exercised in practice!). Moreover, he could hardly be said to be 'enslaving' Lysimacheia, since he was actually rebuilding the abandoned city and protecting and subsidizing its inhabitants; and he firmly intended it to be a residence for his son Seleucus. The crowning glory of his reply Antiochus saved until last: that his disputes with Ptolemy had already been settled in such a friendly way that the young Ptolemy was about to marry Antiochus' daughter; and, as for the free cities of Asia Minor, he was perfectly willing that they should be free as long as they recognized that Antiochus, not Rome, had granted their freedom. And when the Romans played their trump card in the explicit complaints of Lampsacus and Smyrna against Antiochus, Antiochus mildly offered arbitration and chose Rhodes, not Rome, as his preferred arbitrator. The offer was so obviously fair and reasonable that the Romans could not hope for widespread Greek sympathy if they openly rejected it: for that would have immediately branded Rome as the unreasonable warmonger.[6]

Antiochus had clearly won a sweeping propaganda victory; and he followed it up by asking Flamininus for a treaty of alliance with Rome (though he cannot have been very serious about this, since his envoys did not bother to go on to Rome when Flamininus referred them to the Senate). Yet the Roman Senate was not convinced that at present Antiochus represented a threat great enough to make it worth Rome's while to take any far-reaching action against him. Asia was, after all, a long way from Italy. On the other hand, the future of the Roman army in Greece had not yet been finally settled: should it be withdrawn, as Flamininus' policy of liberation required, or should Greek public opinion be ignored and the army kept in

Greece as a warning to Antiochus? It was an awkward decision; and for the moment, at the end of 196, even Flamininus could see the virtue of delaying its withdrawal to see whether Antiochus' attitude might become clearer over the next year.

Fortunately, a convenient excuse for delaying the evacuation of the troops was at hand in the Peloponnese, where Nabis of Sparta, a last-minute ally of Rome in the war with Philip, was patently supporting an oppressively autocratic and unpopular régime at Argos, which Philip had handed over to him in the winter before Cynoscephalae. The Achaean League, of which Argos had been an important and distinguished member, was easily convinced that the freedom of Argos was worth fighting for, particularly since the enemy was the unpopular and dangerous Nabis and since Roman troops would bear the brunt of the campaign. And Rome's other allies, with the exception of the disaffected Aetolians, were equally eager to join Flamininus in the glorious task of continuing the liberation of Greece by freeing the famous Peloponnesian city.

The campaign began in spring 195 after an assembly of all the Roman allies had democratically voted for it. But while the liberation of Argos was the proclaimed object of the campaign, Flamininus also had other aims. When he suggested that the best way of liberating Argos was to defeat Nabis, his proposal met little opposition, for this was exactly what the Achaeans, at least, had been hoping for —so that Nabis might never again threaten Achaean security and that Sparta might even be incorporated in their League. As it turned out, this was not what Flamininus had in mind, though to keep the Achaeans happy during the war he encouraged them to hope for it. What he actually intended to do was to repeat in the Peloponnese the pattern of his settlement of central and northern Greece: there he had maintained Philip with a modicum of power in order to counterbalance the Aetolians; in the Peloponnese, Nabis, when defeated and enfeebled, was to be maintained to counterbalance the Achaeans, in case either Nabis or the Achaeans should consider becoming friendly with Antiochus. This he achieved. Nabis was defeated, humbled and weakened, but not destroyed. But Flamininus had misjudged the Achaeans. There was never any danger that they might support Antiochus; and the chief result of Flamininus' defeating Nabis but insisting that he remained in control at Sparta, though much weakened, was the growth in Achaea of a deep mistrust of Flamininus' motives—the very thing he had hoped to prevent. In Achaea, however, this distrust did not become serious until the crisis with

Antiochus was passed, and it did not affect, in the short term, the overall success of Flamininus' policy.[7]

During 195 Antiochus made no new move. And since by the end of the year Nabis was duly defeated and Argos restored to the Achaean League, the Senate had run out of excuses for keeping the Roman army in Greece, and had at last to take a decision about the future direction of Roman policy in the Balkans. The question of the evacuation came up for discussion early in 194, in a nervous atmosphere; for the widespread suspicion of Antiochus was now compounded by the fact that in 195 Hannibal had sought asylum at his court; and the resulting tension had won Scipio Africanus a second consulship.[8] Nevertheless, Flamininus' friends, who were now doubtless supported by those other experts on Greek affairs, the senatorial commissioners—who had themselves eventually been convinced of the correctness of Flamininus' judgment—carried the decision to evacuate Greece.[9] It was a critical move; for it meant that the Senate had at last been brought to accept that Greek public opinion was an immensely potent weapon in the hands of a skilful operator, and that, paradoxically, the goodwill won by an immediate Roman evacuation of the Balkans might, if war with Antiochus eventually became necessary, be the decisive factor in Rome's favour. Flamininus duly carried out the evacuation, characteristically making the most of its propagandist potential. In the process he confirmed in power with the weight of his patronage those groups of people—predominantly middle-class—in the various cities of Greece whose commercial and property-owning interests were most firmly on the side of peace and stability—and who therefore favoured the Roman settlement.[10]

II Rome's Return to Greece

Flamininus intended the Roman evacuation of Greece to be interpreted by the Greeks as the final proof of the reality of their liberation by Rome. Most of them believed it. Even Antiochus seems at first to have been convinced, to the extent that he thought he could reach a settlement with Rome which would allow him to keep Lysimacheia. Accordingly, he sent envoys to Rome in 194/3. They were Menippus and Hegesianax (the same man who had visited Flamininus at Corinth in 196), and their visit coincided with the presence of envoys from all parts of the Greek world who were trying to influence the details of the Senate's final ratification of Flamininus' settlement of Greece. Antiochus hoped he might obtain some kind of treaty.

But Antiochus had again misinterpreted Roman intentions. For he seems to have thought that Roman military withdrawal from the Balkans implied loss of interest in Balkan affairs. He was not allowed to entertain his misinterpretation very long. Menippus and Hegesianax were first interviewed by a senatorial committee composed of Flamininus and the ten commissioners who had worked out the Balkan settlement. The meeting was held *in camera*, and Flamininus was therefore able to make the Roman position quite clear without constantly having to bear in mind the propagandist implications of what he was saying. The issue was cynically stated: if Antiochus evacuated Europe, Rome would drop her interest in the freedom of the Greeks of Asia Minor; if Antiochus stayed in Europe, Rome would insist on retaining this interest. Antiochus had confidently expected that Flamininus would, as before, be concerned to save Roman face by reaching some kind of compromise agreement. Accordingly Menippus and Hegesianax had no instructions on how to deal with this totally unexpected development, and could only ask that negotiations should not be broken off.

Having failed to obtain satisfaction by power-politics, Flamininus returned to propagandizing, and proceeded to make the best use of the numerous Greeks who had come to Rome as envoys. They were all present, by invitation, at the meeting of the Senate when Flamininus reported the result of his secret negotiations with Menippus and Hegesianax. He said nothing (hardly surprising) of the power-politics which had dominated their discussion. Instead, all heard Flamininus proclaim the new corollary to his Isthmian proclamation, that the Roman People would liberate the Greeks from Antiochus with the same good faith they had shown in liberating them from Philip. Menippus and Hegesianax did not dare to expose Flamininus' trickery for fear of starting a war on the spot—which they had explicit instructions to avoid. They could not therefore prevent Antiochus from being branded publicly, in the hearing of the Roman Senate and of all the Greek envoys, as an enemy of Greek freedom.[11]

The Roman position was at last clear to Antiochus: on the freedom of the Asiatic Greeks the Senate was prepared to strike a cynical bargain; but to Antiochus' presence in Europe the Senate was quite firmly opposed; and moreover, it was prepared to use every available propaganda weapon, however disreputable, to oppose it.

On their return journey to Antiochus, Menippus and Hegesianax stopped off at Delphi.[12] They presumably did this because they wanted to contact the council of the Aetolian League, the one Greek power which might sympathize with Antiochus' point of view, as it was the one Greek power which, like Antiochus, had lost all faith in the sincerity of Roman motives for the liberation of Greece. We have noticed the great importance which both Rome and Antiochus attached to Greek public opinion: the Aetolians could not therefore be ignored. Yet this meeting with the Aetolians proved to be a major blunder, for the League jumped at the prospect of Antiochus' support in a war against the Roman settlement of the Balkans. And the consequential pressures exerted on Antiochus by Aetolian eagerness for war turned out to be the catalyst which, reacting on the already delicate balance of mutual fear and suspicion between Rome and Antiochus, in a short time produced a war which neither of the major contestants in it wanted. Much encouraged by their conversations with Menippus and Hegesianax, the Aetolians decided in spring 193 to send envoys to Antiochus, Philip and Nabis with a view to setting up an alliance against Rome. And although Antiochus and Philip were not immediately influenced by this premature approach, Nabis was rash enough to react. The Achaean League took measures to suppress him; and Flamininus' balance of power in the Peloponnese seemed to be working very smoothly.[13]

The Aetolian League, however, was not the only minor power which deliberately set out to stir up a war for what it thought were its own interests. One of Rome's friends also exerted similar pressure on her. Attalus of Pergamum had died in 197; and Eumenes II, his son and successor, now wanted Rome to intervene in Asia Minor to stop the threat to his kingdom from Antiochus, just as Attalus had persuaded Rome to intervene in 200 to protect him against Philip. Eumenes fully expected that if this happened, he would be the chief beneficiary from Rome's success, for since Rome was obviously not interested in territorial aggrandisement in European Greece (and despite the Aetolians' perverse propaganda, most Greeks still believed this), she could hardly be suspected of desiring territory in Asia Minor. Moreover, Hannibal was still in exile at Antiochus' court and, like political exiles everywhere, he was intriguing with anti-Roman elements at Carthage and trying to persuade Antiochus to support him in another invasion of Italy.

None of this intrigue and persuasion need have had any effect on relations between Rome and Antiochus, had they not already been fearful and suspicious of each other's intentions. But another group of Roman envoys who travelled to Antiochus in summer 193 will only have confirmed mutual suspicions, since they neither offered nor gained further concessions.[14] In the circumstances, Antiochus did not think it wise to ignore his only potential Greek allies, the Aetolians; and he therefore gave a more favourable reception, later in 193, to Thoas, the leader of the Aetolian anti-Roman party, than he had to the previous envoy. Indeed, he sent Menippus back with Thoas early in 192 with the promise that Antiochus would restore the Aetolians' freedom which, he claimed, the Romans had in practice destroyed. The Aetolians then passed a decree inviting Antiochus to free the Greeks and to arbitrate between them and Rome.[15]

This was not in itself a declaration of war. No doubt the moderating advice of Menippus had ensured that. But neither Antiochus nor Menippus can have realized how firm was the Aetolians' determination to precipitate war. By this time Flamininus was again in the Balkans. The Senate had sent him in 192, together with three senatorial colleagues, to re-assert Roman influence and to counteract Aetolian hostility in the face of Antiochus' continuing ambiguity. When Flamininus politely asked the Aetolian *strategos* Damocritus for the contents of the decree which the Aetolians had passed, Damocritus rudely refused and said he would soon tell him when he was camped on the banks of the Tiber. The obvious immediate interpretation of that reply was that the Aetolians had decided on war and, since Antiochus' representative Menippus had been present at the meeting, that Antiochus had agreed to support them. It was not true. But Damocritus deliberately encouraged the Romans to believe that it was. And by doing so he had obviously taken a large step closer to the Aetolian goal of driving Antiochus to war with Rome.

The Aetolians pressed home their advantage before Flamininus could learn the truth. They determined to seize Demetrias and Chalcis (two of Philip's 'Fetters' on which the Aetolians, as we have seen, had always laid great importance) and Sparta, where the weakened Nabis had been unable to make much advance against the now militant Achaeans, led once again by Philopoemen. At Sparta and Chalcis they failed. But their success at Demetrias was a critical development. Earlier in the year Flamininus had tried to strengthen the pro-Roman party at Demetrias, which was wavering in the face of a rumour that Rome intended to restore Demetrias to Philip as the price of his alliance against Antiochus. The truth of the rumour we do not know; but in any case, Flamininus gave it substance by failing explicitly to deny it. His reason was that he did not want to dash Philip's hopes of regaining Demetrias; but, not surprisingly, such equivocation failed to convince the people of Demetrias of Rome's sincerity; and when the Aetolians arrived with their announcement that Antiochus had promised freedom, they had little difficulty in gaining the town.[16]

Thoas at once returned to Antiochus with the good news.[17] He found him at last on the point of sending out Hannibal with a small naval force to stir up diversionary trouble for Rome in the west. Antiochus had ready only a small army and navy, certainly not sufficient to suggest that he had resolved on an invasion of Greece. Yet the Aetolians' capture of Demetrias was a wasting asset if it were not quickly consolidated, in view of Rome's publicized intention of recovering the ungrateful town; and Demetrias was an important strategic possession if war eventually broke out. By capturing it, the Aetolians had committed themselves to war with Rome: the crucial question was, had they also committed Antiochus? Could he now stand aside, let them fight unsupported, and inevitably be destroyed?

Antiochus decided that they had committed him. And his decision seems in the last resort to have been based on the pessimistic assumption that, in the light of recent diplomatic exchanges, his relations with Rome could only deteriorate, that in effect war had become ultimately inevitable. Far better, clearly, that if so it should be fought in the Balkans than in Antiochus' own territory in Asia Minor. In any war in the Balkans, as the Romans had early discovered, local allies were essential; and since the majority of the Greeks—including, it now seemed, Philip—appeared to be firmly under Roman influence, Antiochus could not afford to allow his only Balkan ally, the Aetolian League, to be defeated before he arrived, and thereby to earn himself the unhappy reputation of being ready to fight to the last Aetolian. Since at present the Aetolians held the important strategic garrison town of Demetrias, now—if ever—was the time to cross to Greece.

Militarily, Antiochus was not ready. To conserve his resources for the crossing he even withdrew his slight support from Hannibal's diversionary expedition to the west. Even so, his army was quite inadequate to fight a major war: only 10,000 infantry, 500 cavalry, and a mere six elephants.[18] The only consolation was that Rome was equally unprepared: a small fleet and a propaganda mission of four senior senators was the extent of Rome's active presence in the

Balkans. Time, it seemed, might yet be on Antiochus' side, if he could drum up allies and reinforcements before a full Roman consular army were transported to Greece. About one thing, however, there could be no doubt: Antiochus' precipitate decision to cross to Demetrias in the autumn of 192 finally resolved the 'cold war' situation. The 'cold war' monster of suspicion and propaganda had finally induced Antiochus to believe, rightly or wrongly, that in the last resort he could not avoid a real war. If war was in any case inevitable, Antiochus preferred to take the initiative and to strike the first blow.

CHAPTER XIII
INTO ASIA

I Antiochus in Greece

ANTIOCHUS' crossing to the Balkans was a disappointment to everyone concerned: to the Romans and their Greek friends, who had hoped it would not happen; to the Aetolians, who had anticipated a larger and more effective army; to Antiochus himself who had been led to expect a more enthusiastic reception from the Greeks for whose liberation he claimed to have come. Only at Demetrias was he unequivocally welcomed. Elsewhere all was doubtful. When with Aetolian support he invited the people of Chalcis to allow themselves to be liberated by him, he received a firm refusal: the aristocratic government of Chalcis expressed itself satisfied with the freedom it already enjoyed by the gift of Rome.[1] On Aetolian advice, Antiochus then tried the Boeotians, who were democratically (and, therefore, less stably) governed, and who had not been over-happy about Flamininus' earlier interference in their affairs; but even here he received only the cautious reply that they would consider their position if Antiochus came to them in person.

Ever sanguine, the Aetolians had also advised Antiochus to attempt to seduce the Achaean League; but the Achaeans, in the presence of Flamininus, were not content simply with rejecting Antiochus' overtures, but crowned their rejection by formally declaring war on Antiochus—a demonstration of gratitude to Rome which the Senate rewarded with the grant of a formal treaty of alliance which technically recognized Achaea as an equal ally of Rome.[2] Antiochus' only success from these initial diplomatic exchanges was in remote Athamania, where king Amynander chose this unhappy moment to abandon his earlier friendship with Rome and to float a wild scheme to put his brother-in-law on the throne of Macedon with Antiochus' help.[3]

Thus by late autumn 192 it must have been clear to Antiochus that the Greeks, where not positively hostile (as was the Achaean

League) were singularly unenthusiastic about greeting their new liberator. The Roman propaganda of liberation had worked effectively against Philip; Flamininus' insistence that its sincerity should be demonstrated was now shown to have been fully justified by the widespread lack of support with which Antiochus was received. But Greek public opinion would not be sufficient in itself to defeat Antiochus' army; Greek apathy towards him was only a helpful climate in which the Romans could work. Accordingly, when the news of Antiochus' crossing arrived at Rome, the Senate, which had already envisaged that war might prove necessary against Antiochus in 191, entrusted its conduct to one of the consuls, Manius Acilius Glabrio, who in spring 191 made immediate preparations for crossing to the Balkans.[4] The immediate excuse for the war, with which the Romans salved their elastic religious scruples about always fighting 'just wars', seems to have been a sharp conflict in early winter 192/1 at the sanctuary of Apollo at Delium in Boeotia, between Antiochus' general Menippus and a small Roman detachment, probably from the fleet, which had been sent to aid Chalcis. The Romans were massacred in the sanctuary, though war had not been formally declared; and the offence was sufficient to allow the Romans to believe (or, at least, to claim) that they were holding true to their tradition of fighting only 'just wars', though there is no legal substance to the Roman view, which Livy records, that the asylum of the sanctuary should have protected the Roman troops.[5] Sanctuaries gave no protection to military personnel.

Antiochus' operation against Chalcis was, in fact, just one of a series which he carried out in the early winter, in which he forced 'liberation' on several reluctant communities in Euboea and Thessaly. His military successes, slight though they were, caused other states not in the front line of his advance to hedge their bets in the absence of a strong Roman army. In the Peloponnese, for instance, Achaea's western neighbour Elis, traditionally a friend of the Aetolians, but hitherto uncommitted in the present crisis, sent to Antiochus asking for a garrison. In the north-west, the Epirots, who had been inactive in Rome's first war with Philip and reluctant allies of Rome in the second, sent Charops—who in 199 had been Rome's first friend in Epirus—to Antiochus with the message that if he came and could demonstrate that he was physically capable of protecting the Epirots, he would get a friendly reception; but if he could not guarantee their protection, they asked not to be involved in the war. The Epirots clearly did not care much either way as long as their safety was assured. Even in Boeotia, Antiochus found less than whole-hearted enthusiasm when he appeared in person, as he had been in-vited to do, before the Boeotian council. For their safety's sake the Boeotians passed a decree friendly to Antiochus; but it was im-precisely worded and did not bind them to any action.[6]

Antiochus' subsequent brief campaign in Thessaly similarly won no willing adherent and offended many by his continual insistence on imposing 'liberation' on those who regarded themselves as being already free; and—perhaps most damaging to his long-term pros-pects—it ensured that Philip of Macedon would never join him, for Antiochus now made clear that he supported Amynander of Atha-mania's brother-in-law as pretender to Philip's throne. Indeed, Philip dutifully expressed his clientship to Rome by offering the Senate money and grain for the war without being asked for them. After a short campaign, Antiochus abandoned his ungrateful task and returned to Chalcis, where he spent the rest of the winter en-joying the early months of his recent marriage with a Euboean girl.[7]

Antiochus' fortunes did not revive with the return of spring. In May the Roman consular army under Acilius Glabrio arrived and marched straight across the Pindus mountains into Thessaly. This march put a quick end to Antiochus' attempt to persuade the Acar-nanians to join him, and he returned to Chalcis where he began to fortify the nearby narrow pass of Thermopylae; this was where the Roman army would have to face him if Glabrio wanted to avoid a massive detour. While Glabrio marched south through Thessaly, capturing the towns which Antiochus had taken only a few months before, another of Antiochus' allies, Amynander, was being knocked out by Philip who, hardly surprisingly, did not relish Amynander's scheme to replace him. Nor did the Aetolians prove to be much help to Antiochus for, having lured him to Greece, they ungratefully seemed content to let him do most of the fighting while they pursued their own interests in central and western Greece. As a result, they supplied only 4,000 men for the defence of Thermopylae, and they insisted on using 2,000 of them to garrison their nearby town of Heraclea. The last straw was the fact that Antiochus' recruiting officers had not yet had time to raise and deliver to Greece many reinforcements from his unwieldy Asian empire.[8]

Massively outnumbered, Antiochus had nevertheless no alterna-tive but to face Glabrio in the position he had prepared in the narrows of the northern 'gate' of the pass of Thermopylae. The battle was fierce; but in a repetition of a more famous march over the mountains behind the pass nearly 300 years before, by the Persian invaders of Greece in 480 B.C., Glabrio's distinguished lieutenant, the ex-consul Marcus Porcius Cato, drove off the Aetolian defenders of the mountain path and took Antiochus' position in the rear. By then the battle was effectively over; and gathering the scattered remnants of his army, Antiochus hastily abandoned Europe and took ship immediately for the luxurious safety of Ephesus, a strategically convenient city from which to plan his future operations. Travelling in the opposite direction, Marcus Cato bore the news of the victory to Rome.[9]

II Aetolia

The fact that Glabrio refrained from at once pursuing Antiochus to Asia did not mean that the Roman Senate was satisfied that a final settlement with Antiochus would result from the battle of Thermopylae. But the first urgency, now that Antiochus had so readily returned to Asia Minor, was to complete the new settlement of the Balkans, where the Aetolians remained in arms and undefeated by the battle in which they had played only a minor part. The Boeotians, who had been foolish enough to entertain Antiochus (though they had not actively co-operated with him), suffered some ravaging from Glabrio's army as it passed through their country; but the Aetolians remained the real enemy, and it was against them that the Roman campaign in Greece was now directed.

Their city of Heraclea which, lying near Thermopylae, they had insisted on garrisoning, was the object of the first major Roman offensive. The town was enthusiastically attacked and desperately defended; but after a month's siege, it could withstand the Roman attack no longer. The Aetolians were foolishly dismayed at Roman thoroughness in following up Antiochus' defeat; and in desperation they sent Thoas on another mission to Antiochus to persuade him to return to Greece. But Antiochus was now wary. He had seen sufficient during his short stay in Greece to know that the Balkans could not so easily be won from Roman control; and he must by then have been aware that his ill-advised invasion had created the lively probability that the Romans would not be satisfied merely with having driven him back from Greece, but would be inclined to repay his invasion in kind by themselves crossing to Asia. If there was one thing that could be guaranteed to turn probability into certainty, it was a second attempt to cross to Greece. The Aetolians therefore can have had no real hope of getting Antiochus' renewed support; and they were lucky to receive not only a reasonably friendly reception but also some money, supported by vague promises of future support which might bolster their morale.[10]

Meanwhile Heraclea had fallen and the Aetolians gave way to their discouragement so far as to ask for negotiations. Their experience during them proved a salutary lesson, not only to the Aetolians themselves but to the whole Greek world, of how the Romans might use their superiority in power if they chose to. The Greeks had so far been lucky in the Romans they had dealt with. Flamininus, in particular, had been sensitive to Greek feelings and traditions, which he had been able to manipulate for his own purpose. It was the Aetolians' unpleasant experience to discover how an unsympathetic Roman might regard ungrateful ex-allies. At first Glabrio claimed he was too busy even to talk to their envoys, and delegated the initial hearings to one of his officers, Lucius Valerius Flaccus. The rebuff had its effect, for the Aetolians proved ready to accept Flaccus' advice. They had wanted to plead their case by pointing out their past services to Rome, but Flaccus stopped them by saying that these were now irrelevant in view of their recent hostility: their best chance of a satisfactory outcome was to surrender themselves into the good faith of Rome.

This they agreed to do. But it quickly transpired that they had no understanding of the implication of their action. Relying on the apparent meaning of 'good faith', they assumed that their action meant that they would automatically receive merciful treatment from Glabrio. They were therefore harshly disillusioned when they realized that the Roman interpretation of their action was that they had surrendered unconditionally, that they had completely abandoned all their legal rights, and that there was no necessary implication of merciful or even just treatment. Glabrio's initial stipulations were not in themselves sufficient to make the point clearly enough to the uncomprehending Aetolian envoys: that no Aetolian should cross to Asia, and that the two Epirots who were aiding Aetolia, and Amynander and his Athamanian supporters, should be handed over. Phaeneas, the chief Aetolian negotiator, chose to remonstrate—an unwise intervention, which Glabrio interpreted as insolence from those who had voluntarily and unconditionally surrendered all their legal rights. In a brutally dramatic demonstration of the full implications of what surrender into Roman good faith might mean, the envoys were

chained together with iron collars, the humiliating treatment given
to recalcitrant slaves and prisoners of war.

Not surprisingly, the envoys were shocked at their savage and unexpected treatment. When they realized its full significance, they
made the excuse that a general assembly of all the Aetolians was
needed to ratify any decision reached by the negotiators; and they
were released to obtain this ratification. When they returned to
Aetolia it soon became clear that Glabrio's proposed treatment of an
undefeated Aetolia was not acceptable to the general mass of the
Aetolians. Indeed, it proved in practice impossible to get an assembly
together even to discuss the terms. Moreover, it was just at this time
that the Aetolian envoys returned from Antiochus with money and
the (vain) hope that Antiochus might again cross to help them. As
Antiochus had hoped, this news made the Aetolians decide to fight
on. They would thus keep Glabrio occupied and give Antiochus more
time to prepare to meet any Roman invasion of Asia Minor. But not
even he could have anticipated that Glabrio's unprecedentedly
brutal treatment of the Aetolian negotiators would have ensured
that they would fight on even without his money and promises.[11]

Where Flamininus might have been firm but conciliatory (and
certainly polite), Glabrio had been offensively assertive of Roman
supremacy. Flamininus might have secured a peace on the spot
which would have allowed the Romans quickly to take what further
action the Senate thought necessary against Antiochus; by standing
on his Roman dignity, Glabrio had ensured that his army would be
wastefully tied down in the Aetolian mountains. The Aetolians now
took refuge in Naupactus, where Glabrio had no alternative but to
begin yet another lengthy and time-wasting siege. In the autumn,
after the siege had been going on for two months, Flamininus, who
was still in Greece, came to Naupactus and patched up a truce,
during which the Aetolians were to send envoys to Rome. In this way
the year ended. Glabrio's insensitive treatment of the Aetolians'
attempt to negotiate had ensured that Antiochus had a whole year
in which to prepare for future developments. The only Roman action
against him in 191 after Thermopylae was a naval engagement in
which the Roman praetor Gaius Livius Salinator beat Antiochus'
admiral Polyxenidas; but the greatest importance of this engagement
was not the defeat itself but the fact that it confirmed Antiochus'
suspicions that Rome had not yet finished with him.[12]

The events of the winter in Rome, when he knew of them, will
have certainly confirmed Antiochus' view: for the consuls elected

for 190 were none other than Scipio Africanus' brother Lucius and his friend Gaius Laelius. And when the Senate came to discuss where the consuls should serve, Africanus' offer to act as lieutenant (*legatus*) to his brother ensured that Lucius Scipio obtained the command in the Balkans. The most ominous aspect for Antiochus of this appointment was the additional provision that Lucius might take his army over into Asia if he thought it in the interest of the state. The Senate was still clearly afraid of what Antiochus might do, and still worried at the fact that Hannibal continued as *persona grata* at Antiochus' court. For the Senate to feel completely safe, Antiochus must be curbed even further; if possible he must be made to withdraw altogether from the Aegean coastline where his insidious and disruptive influence was too close to mainland Greece for Roman comfort.[13]

The winter also showed that Glabrio's policy towards the Aetolians had important adherents in the Senate. The Aetolians' treatment, when they appeared before the Senate, formed a sharp contrast with that given to the Epirots, who were pardoned for their wavering, and to Rome's ex-enemy Philip, who was rewarded for his recent support by having his younger son Demetrius, who had been a hostage at Rome since 197, restored to him. Epirus and Macedon, it seemed, were now Rome's friends. The Aetolians, despite being represented in the Senate by the conciliatory Flamininus, had it made perfectly clear to them that they had forfeited Rome's friendship by their recent actions, and therefore had no moral or legal claim on her clemency beyond that of any other defeated enemy. They were offered a harsh choice: either to entrust themselves to the free discretion of the Senate; or to pay 1,000 talents and to have the same friends and enemies as Rome. The envoys obviously could not themselves make the invidious choice; but after their experience with Glabrio and their earlier surrender to Roman good faith, they were more cautious, and asked what the first alternative meant (though it was, of course, expressed in different words, it was simply another demand for unconditional surrender). The second alternative was clear enough and at present unacceptable: an impossibly large fine and the complete subordination of their foreign policy to the will of Rome. However, the Senate remained ambiguous on the matter of the surrender and did not clarify the issue, though to judge by the terms of the eventual settlement, it would in practice have been much the same as the second alternative, even if the indemnity might have been smaller. The Aetolians returned home quite unsatisfied.[14]

The Senate as a whole, like Glabrio earlier, had made the mistake of letting its anger at Aetolian pride and ingratitude govern its policy. Thus once again, in spring 190, the Roman army in Greece had to be diverted to Aetolia and to waste time there, when it would have been better employed in cutting short the time Antiochus had available for preparations. Fortunately for Rome, the delay did not in practice make very much difference, though Eumenes and the Pergamenes would have been spared some suffering if the Roman army had reached Asia rather earlier.

When Lucius Scipio, accompanied by his brother Africanus, arrived in the Balkans with reinforcements and orders to take over Glabrio's army, they found him engaged in the siege of another Aetolian city, this time Amphissa. Fortunately, Africanus had his priorities right and wanted to get rid of the Aetolian war as soon as possible. He immediately began new negotiations with the Aetolians and encouraged them to be hopeful for peace. The talks proceeded smoothly until his brother Lucius, who as consul was formally responsible for the results of the negotiations, clumsily sabotaged the delicate negotiations by quoting at the Aetolians the harsh terms of the Senate's reply to their envoys at Rome. The Aetolians were thoroughly perturbed by this apparent conflict between the ideas of the two brothers, and their fears of personal violence if they surrendered to the 'free discretion' of the Senate seemed well founded when they remembered the treatment which Phaeneas and his fellow-negotiators had received from Glabrio. Nevertheless they eventually decided to ask for a six-month armistice so that envoys might again be sent to Rome; and since they had the good sense to approach first the sympathetic Africanus—who wanted to end the Aetolian war and come to terms with Antiochus in Asia—he was able to ensure that this time Lucius said nothing tactless which might prevent the armistice.[15]

III *Asia*

The six-month armistice in practice gave the Scipios almost a year free of the Aetolian war; for six months from its agreement (perhaps about July) carried the truce into winter 190/189 when military operations were not normally undertaken. They could therefore firmly direct their attention to Antiochus. Much time had nevertheless been wasted; and since the joint Roman, Pergamene and

Rhodian fleet had not yet managed to obtain naval supremacy in the eastern Aegean, it would obviously be highly dangerous to attempt to transport troops across the open sea. The alternative was a march of several weeks through northern Greece and across Thrace to the Hellespont which, being less than a mile wide, could more easily be crossed without complete naval supremacy, as long as both shores were friendly. Not surprisingly, therefore, it was already late summer when the Roman army reached the Hellespont and crossed where no Roman consular army had crossed before, into the continent of Asia.

Before the Roman army arrived in Asia Minor, Antiochus had spent the summer in intense naval activity, which had the chief aim of trying to prevent the Scipios from being able to cross. The Roman fleet, commanded by the praetor Lucius Aemilius Regillus, was supplemented by the fleets of Eumenes and of Rhodes; and though, as with so much of the naval activity of the ancient world, the events were fairly unspectacular, they were still crucial: for if Antiochus' fleet came out on top, it might be able to prevent the Roman army from being transported even across the narrow Hellespont. In the event, Rome and her allies became dominant. The decisive engagement took place at Myonnesus, near Samos, where Regillus and the Rhodians shattered Antiochus' fleet by capturing or sinking forty-two of his eighty-nine ships. In panic and fear that he would no longer even be able to defend his European city Lysimacheia, he immediately withdrew his garrison from it.[16]

If the result of the naval war was disappointing for Antiochus, his diplomatic initiatives also gave him little encouragement. Eumenes of Pergamum he had no real hope of seducing from Rome though, ignoring no possibility, however slight, he had tried to make a truce with him before the Scipios arrived and before the decisive battle was fought, in order to gain yet more time and (perhaps) to stir up the Aetolians to further resistance and divert the Roman army back to Aetolia. But his offer was, not unexpectedly, refused. He had better hopes of Prusias of Bithynia, who ruled the strategically vital area on the southern shore of the Sea of Marmora. Prusias had been an ally of Philip of Macedon, and even now he had personal reason for hostility to the interfering Romans: in 196 Flamininus had written to him requiring that his Greek city Cius should be freed, since it was Philip who had captured it for him. Prusias, therefore, had no reason to believe that he had anything to gain from the Roman presence in Asia—and he might have much to lose if the

Romans insisted on freeing his Greek cities. But Africanus, just as much as Antiochus, had realized the crucial importance of Bithynia to any army crossing the Hellespont. And using the diplomatic technique of personal initiative and contact which had served him so well against the Carthaginians in Spain, he and his brother wrote a long letter to Prusias, giving, in effect, assurances that if he joined Rome he would run no danger of losing his kingdom. The letter was decisive, and Antiochus had lost another potential ally.[17]

Antiochus' naval defeat, the loss of his hoped-for alliance with Prusias, and his failure to prevent the Roman army from crossing the Hellespont all combined to influence him towards opening negotiations with the Scipios. The fact that winter was approaching might make the Romans more willing to talk. Accordingly, he sent one Heracleides of Byzantium to find out on what terms the Romans would consider making peace. Heracleides was given permission to offer to Rome the cession of Lampsacus, Smyrna and Alexandria Troas (the cities which Rome had first used, as long ago as 196 when Lampsacus appealed to her, as an excuse for showing interest in Antiochus' activities), and any other cities of Asia Minor which had supported Rome in the naval war. Antiochus also offered to meet half the Roman expenses of the war. Had he made this offer six months before, when his navy appeared strong enough to hinder the Roman crossing and when the Aetolian war was still in progress, there might have been some chance that his offer would be considered, at least as a basis for negotiations. Now, however, the situation was enormously altered. It was a slight concession to offer to vacate cities which, in the last resort, he could not hope to defend; and the Romans saw no reason why they should contemplate settling for less than wholly satisfactory terms now that their army was safely in Asia. Accordingly, their reply was that they thought Antiochus should pay *all* Rome's expenses for the war, and that he should retire from all territory north and west of the Taurus mountains. The effect of this latter provision would have been to remove Antiochus from all influence in Asia Minor and from all effective contact with the states of the Aegean coastland. Not surprisingly, Heracleides had not been briefed to deal with such harsh demands; and he therefore ended the official negotiations. He did, however, approach Africanus in private. Africanus' son had been captured by Antiochus in Greece. Heracleides offered his free release and a sum of money as a bribe if Scipio would use his influence to have the proposed terms accepted. Bribery was a normal technique of diplomacy in the Hellenistic east; it often worked; and some Romans might have succumbed to it. But not Scipio. Heracleides returned to Antiochus with not even the hope of a compromise to offer.[18]

The decisive battle—which Scipio had warned Antiochus, through Heracleides, to avoid—was fought four weeks later, perhaps about December, at Magnesia-ad-Sipylum, not very far from Smyrna. It was joined in the absence through illness of the great Africanus, but in the event this made little difference. Scipio discovered, as has many another great man, that nobody is indispensable. Antiochus' huge army consisted of some 70,000 men, and was gathered from all parts of his enormous empire, which stretched from the Aegean to the foothills of the Himalayas. But it was decisively defeated by the 30,000 Romans and allies. The Romans claimed to have killed 53,000. There could be no question of further immediate resistance; and when Antiochus had recovered his family and his wits, he opened negotiations which eventually led to a peace settlement.[19]

IV The Settlement

Africanus had recovered from his illness when Antiochus' negotiators arrived. They had little doubt about the terms which might be agreed, since a basis for an agreement acceptable to the Romans had, in effect, been spelled out to Heracleides in the abortive earlier negotiations. The chief point of doubt was whether their success in battle would encourage the Romans to ask for more, or whether they would remain satisfied to receive acceptance of the earlier terms. In fact, since the Senate had agreed on the Scipios' crossing to Asia Minor because it believed that Rome's security in the Balkans could only be achieved by that means, there was never any danger that Roman demands would step beyond the point which met this view of Roman security. Thus the provisional terms for peace which the Scipios agreed with Antiochus—provisional because they needed to be ratified by the Roman Senate and People—were essentially the same as those demanded from Heracleides: Antiochus must give up all his possessions in Europe and in Asia beyond the Taurus mountains; he must pay 15,000 talents indemnity (to cover the cost of the war to Rome); an additional 400 talents, which had for some reason been agreed with Attalus of Pergamum but had never been paid, were now to be paid to Eumenes; Hannibal, Thoas and some other enemies of Rome were to be handed over; twenty hostages, chosen by the Romans, were to be given.[20]

Since the battle of Magnesia was fought during the winter, the Senate had already decided its dispositions for the following year (189) before the news of it arrived at Rome. The chief consideration had been the Aetolians' renewed failure to conduct themselves sufficiently humbly before the Senate, when they took advantage of their truce with Scipio to send envoys again to Rome. In the circumstances, Greece and the Aetolian war clearly had to be the province of one of the consuls. Also, since the news of Magnesia had not reached Rome by the time of the provincial distribution, and since the Scipios' supporters in Rome were not influential enough to get Lucius Scipio's command extended without it, their opponents in the Senate insisted that Asia obviously had to be the province of the other consul. In the allotment, Gnaeus Manlius Vulso received Asia and Marcus Fulvius Nobilior got Aetolia.[21]

By the time the consuls set out, however, the news of Antiochus' defeat had at last reached Rome; and it was soon followed by envoys from Antiochus, by king Eumenes in person, and by representatives of the Rhodian republic and of other Greek communities in Asia Minor. There was obviously no longer much to be gained militarily by Manlius' going to Asia; but the Senate had decided, and did not want to disappoint Manlius of his command. They accordingly concocted a military task for him: to deal with the Celtic Galatians of central Asia Minor, who had allied with Antiochus and who were ethnically related to Rome's long-standing enemies, the Gauls of the Po valley and the sub-Alpine regions. Manlius set off happily enough to his consolation-prize campaign, and travelled throughout central and southern Asia Minor, subdued the Galatians and other ex-adherents of Antiochus, and collected an enormous quantity of plunder.

But more was involved in Manlius' campaign than simple military activity. When he set out, the Senate had not finally decided how it should deal with Asia Minor when Antiochus vacated it; and the prevailing mood of the Senate, even after the news of Magnesia, was hostile to the Scipios. Their recall and replacement by Manlius meant that they and their lieutenants, the only Romans with first-hand military experience in Asia Minor, would not be able to attend to the details of the final settlement. This, it now seemed, would fall to Manlius, who at first had no knowledge of Asiatic conditions. But not for long; for the new consul's apparently unsystematic travels throughout central and southern Asia Minor—nominally directed against the Galatians, but in practice having a much wider scope—had the effect of turning Manlius and his team into the most experienced and knowledgeable Asiatic experts the Senate had available.

While Manlius was acquiring his Asiatic experience and rich booty in his side-show campaign against the Galatians, Rome's real business was still with Antiochus, and this was done in Rome in the consuls' absence. The big question was not whether the Senate would ratify (in principle) the preliminary terms negotiated by the Scipios; for the general kind of settlement which would satisfy the Senate must have been discussed and settled even before the Scipios set out. So it was not particularly surprising that the broad terms agreed in the preliminary talks were duly ratified, though the Senate added some important details which restricted Antiochus' right to wage war in Europe and Asia Minor, which limited his navy, and which forbade him to keep war elephants. The final drawing up of the detailed terms of the treaty, including the stipulation of precise geographical limitations and the drafting of clauses to deal with the interests of Rome's friends in Asia Minor, seems to have been left to Manlius and the ten senators sent out as settlement commissioners to help him.[22] But while the terms imposed on Antiochus were fairly predictable, what the Senate would decide to do about the parts of Asia Minor to be evacuated by Antiochus was by no means so certain. Rome had fought the war allegedly to free the Greeks of Asia: was the Senate now going to insist on this, as Flamininus had insisted on the Greeks of Europe being freed from Philip?

In Greece in 196, as we have seen, Flamininus had insisted, against all opposition, that in view of the developing threat from Antiochus, the interests of Rome required the Greeks to believe that their freedom was real. On the whole his policy had been successful, even though the Greek island of Aegina, which the kingdom of Pergamum had held since 210, was tacitly allowed to remain in Eumenes' control. For Eumenes was the last man the Romans could afford to offend if they thought war with Antiochus was a possibility. But with the Greeks of Asia Roman support of their 'liberation' had from the beginning been more opportunist. Flamininus, at his secret conference with Menippus and Hegesianax at Rome in 193, had bluntly stated that the Senate was prepared to give up championing the Greeks of Asia if Antiochus would undertake not to interfere in Europe. The reason for Rome's different attitude towards the Greeks of Europe and those of Asia was primarily a matter of geography: the

Balkan peninsula was much closer to Italy than was Asia Minor, and therefore was more vital to the Senate's conception of Rome's security. Moreover, effective freedom for Greek city-states implied a fragmentation of power from which inter-city squabbles and potential anarchy might emerge. In the Balkans, within Rome's sphere of effective power, this might even be advantageous, for the Senate could have more immediate control in this way; but in Asia Minor, outside the range of Rome's effective power of control, the potential anarchy which freedom would bring about was a real threat in itself, for instability carried with it the possibility of interference by interested third parties. Thus from the point of view of Roman security, the freedom of the Greeks of Asia could most conveniently be simply abandoned, so long as the Balkans remained subject to Roman influence.

Now the war was over, did the Senate intend to maintain its view that Asia Minor was not an essential area for Roman security and did not need to be particularly carefully controlled? Did it now matter any longer if Rome's propaganda of 'liberation'—not, in fact, very much in evidence once the 'cold war' had flared into military activity—was not seen in Asia to have been justified by its result? The freedom of the European Greeks had had a purpose: it had helped to defeat Antiochus. But what advantage, now that Antiochus was defeated, would be gained by a similar demonstration of sincerity in Asia Minor? Would the temporary enthusiasm of cities, many of which had supported Antiochus, be adequate compensation to Rome for the grave offense which would be given to Rome's good and long-suffering friend, Eumenes of Pergamum? The kingdom of Pergamum already controlled the interests of a number of Greek cities in its vicinity; and in a speech to the Senate Eumenes himself emphasized that if Rome did not intend to administer Asia Minor herself, he expected substantial rewards for his own and his father's unwavering loyalty to Rome over more than twenty years of warfare in Greece and Asia Minor. The Senate made it clear at once that it appreciated Eumenes' aspirations, and it even asked his advice about how to treat Asia Minor, which to most senators was completely unknown territory; and this sympathetic reaction to Eumenes' ambitions should not be surprising, for even at the height of Flamininus' liberation campaign in European Greece Eumenes had been quietly allowed to keep Aegina.[23]

Eumenes' friendly reception made it clear that the Senate had in fact no intention of pressing in Asia Minor the widespread policy of 'liberation' which it had followed in European Greece and which its initial propaganda had encouraged people to believe would follow a Roman victory in Asia. What Eumenes had been chiefly afraid of, if the Greek cities were in fact individually liberated, was that Rhodes, Rome's other major ally in the war, would scoop the pool of influence in Asia Minor: for Rhodes was a Greek republic, and free Greek states would probably prefer the protection of Rhodes (if any protection became necessary) to that of the monarchy of Pergamum, the founder of which, it was said, had not even been a Greek. And when the Rhodians' turn to address the Senate came, they argued that the liberation of the Greek cities, which Roman propaganda had led them to expect, should now be put into effect, for this would prevent Eumenes' aggrandisement at the expense of the prosperous Greeks. They tried to suggest a solution to the problem of Eumenes' legitimate territorial ambitions by arguing that there were plenty of non-Greek communities in Asia Minor which could be given to Eumenes to satisfy his imperialistic urge (though they did not say that these non-Greek communities were for the most part much less wealthy and desirable than the Greek cities!). The Rhodians were no doubt supported by the representatives of the other Greek states present, many of whom, such as Smyrna and Lampsacus, had supported Rome in the war.[24]

How was the Senate to compromise these legitimate but conflicting expectations of Rome's Asiatic friends? The one thing which it particularly wished to avoid was the propagation of instability in the area vacated by Antiochus; the inevitable result was a compromise, the minutiae of which were to be worked out in the areas concerned, as in Greece after the war with Philip, by the committee of ten senators who would travel to Asia Minor. They were to decide, in consultation with Manlius, the details both of the final terms of the treaty with Antiochus and of the settlement of the Asiatic territory vacated by him. The principles on which they should work, however, were firmly stated by the Senate. It made clear that, to all intents and purposes, it was abandoning the Roman claim to be freeing the Asiatic Greeks: all Asia Minor which had been subject to Antiochus was divided into two unequal parts, of which the southern and smaller part—Lycia and Caria as far north as the river Maeander, with certain specified exceptions—was given to Rhodes as reward for her support in the war and the price of her scruples about the freedom of the Asiatic Greeks; the rest went to Eumenes with the stipulation —a last lip-service to the freedom of the Asiatic Greeks—that those

Greek cities which had been free before the battle should remain so, and that Eumenes should not exact tribute from those which had paid tribute to Antiochus, unless they had previously paid it to Attalus. The precise communities concerned and the other details of the settlement were then left to the commissioners.[25]

In fact, when the commissioners fixed the details of the settlement, they modified this last provision in Eumenes' favour, and exempted from tribute to him only those cities which they had good reason to believe had been genuinely sympathetic to the Roman cause. Additionally, Eumenes was now allowed to occupy Antiochus' possessions in Europe, in the neighbourhood of the Thracian Chersonnese, including Lysimacheia.[26] The effect of the Roman settlement was to create two major states in Asia Minor, Pergamum and Rhodes, both of which owed their pre-eminent power and status solely to their support of Rome and to Rome's gratitude. The final detailed peace treaty was agreed at Apamea in 188. It ended any possible danger to Rome from Antiochus. The Senate's grant of new strength to Pergamum and Rhodes was therefore not so much designed to keep Antiochus in check—though they would obviously keep a wary eye on him and his successors—as to save Rome the trouble of having to administer Asia Minor herself. For similar reasons in Africa Massinissa had been raised to prominence as a client king; and in the Balkans Philip of Macedon had (it was hoped) been turned into a dutiful client who would faithfully govern his allotted territories in independence, but according to Roman principles.

The overseas 'client kingdom' was as old a technique in Roman diplomacy as Rome's first adventure outside Italy: in Sicily Hiero of Syracuse had been given exactly this status (though he had also had a treaty with Rome while the war with Carthage lasted). Hiero had understood well the implications of his clientship, though disaster had come to Syracuse when his successor tried to exploit, at Rome's expense, his illusion of complete independence. We have yet to see how Rome's crop of new client states in the east would understand the peacetime implications of their clientship. The present generation of rulers might, indeed, prove to be, for the most part, complaisant clients. But the real test would come, and the real trouble (if ever)— as had already happened at Syracuse—when new and less experienced persons came to power. In the meanwhile, however, all was peace, and Roman troops were withdrawn from Asia.

CHAPTER XIV

PEACE IN THE EAST

I Aetolia

IT OFTEN happens that firm alliances built by the pressures of war are splintered or made unworkable by the less powerful but more subtly debilitating pressures of peace, and by the ambitions of the peacemakers. So it had been with the Aetolian League's friendship with Rome when peace was made with Philip in 196; the result was that the League dragged Antiochus, all-unprepared, into war with its ex-ally Rome and, ironically, remained at war with Rome even after Antiochus was defeated at Magnesia in winter 190/189. The Aetolians were granted their truce by Scipio Africanus and his brother Lucius in the summer of 190. The Scipios' purpose was clear enough: that they should be free to cross to Asia Minor to deal with Antiochus. The Aetolians, however, despite their earlier rebuff at Rome, were serious about wanting an honourable peace; and to obtain his truce Scipio had felt it necessary to encourage their hopes. There, unfortunately for the Aetolians, lay the rub; for Glabrio's treatment of their negotiators in 191—demonstrating that unconditional surrender to Rome's *fides* meant the total surrender of all their legal rights—had represented the Senate's policy, and therefore had been supported by the Senate's firm refusal to consider any offer short of unconditional surrender in winter 191/190. This should have made it clear to the wiser among the Aetolians that the Senate had no intention of allowing Rome's ungrateful and unfaithful ex-friends to extract any honour from peace. Nevertheless, Scipio Africanus' friendly attitude when he negotiated the truce misleadingly encouraged an unfounded hope.

When the Aetolians' envoys appeared before the Senate they were quickly disillusioned. Choosing to regard themselves as equals, they inappropriately recited the League's past services to Rome and now demanded 'fair' treatment in compensation for these. Not surprisingly, the Senate was aggrieved that the Aetolians seemed even

now to have learnt nothing from the failure of their earlier negotiations. It therefore simply repeated its earlier demand: that the
Aetolians should unconditionally surrender both themselves and
their right to operate an independent foreign policy. The Aetolians
made no reply; and when they had left the Senate House, their old
opponent, the ex-consul Manius Acilius Glabrio, took the lead in
proposing that they should be ordered to leave the city within
fifteen days, and that no Aetolian negotiators should again be allowed
to come to Rome without the express permission of the Roman
commander in Aetolia and unless accompanied by a Roman com-
missioner.[1]

   This brusque dismissal of the ungrateful clients meant not only
that peace with honour was impossible for the Aetolians, but that
peace of any kind was unobtainable without more fighting. The
Senate duly sent against Aetolia Manlius Vulso's colleague as
consul in 189, Marcus Fulvius Nobilior. Fulvius immediately began
operations in spring 189; and the chief event of the year was his
attempt, on the advice of the Epirots and on the pattern of Glabrio's
policy, to take by siege the Aetolian city of Ambracia.[2] The fall of
Ambracia turned out to be decisive. At last the Aetolians acknowledged that they had suffered too much and were prepared to swallow
their distrust of Roman good faith; at last they realized that in the end
they would have no alternative to submitting to whatever conditions
the Senate might impose. But they took the sensible precaution of
asking negotiators from Athens and Rhodes to represent Aetolian
interests in the initial talks with Fulvius, for experience suggested that
the Aetolians were not the best proponents of their own interests.

   The terms which Fulvius eventually agreed were much more
favourable than the Aetolians' fear and mistrust had led them to
expect—though once the Senate had broken the Aetolians' pride
and their will to resist, it would gain nothing from postponing a
settlement. Fulvius therefore exercised his discretion in imposing
terms, and trusted that his supporters in the Senate would ensure
that the essential elements of his settlement were in due course
ratified. His agreement stipulated that the Aetolians should pay,
over six years, an indemnity of 500 talents, and that Roman deserters
and prisoners should be restored without ransom; it denied the
Aetolians the right to incorporate in their League for the future any
cities which, after spring 190 (the crossing of the Scipios), had been
captured by or had allied with Rome; and the whole island of
Cephallenia was excluded from the treaty.[3]

These were the preliminary terms, and when the Senate drew up a formal treaty, it made no substantial change, though it altered some details. But two additions were made, which amounted to delarations of principle: one, which had been implicit or explicit throughout all the negotiations with Aetolia since Antiochus' defeat at Thermopylae—and which may, indeed, have been included in Fulvius' draft, though Polybius does not mention it—was that the Aetolians should have the same friends and enemies as Rome. The effect of this, as we have already noticed, was to deny to the Aetolians any right to an independent foreign policy. Chiefly by this clause Rome would control the future of her defeated ex-ally; and by agreeing to it, the Aetolians accepted both a legal restriction on their right to control their own foreign policy and an obligation to help the Romans to carry out theirs.

The Senate's other major addition to Fulvius' draft was a clause which stipulated that the Aetolians 'shall preserve the empire and sovereignty of the Roman People without fraud'.[4] This is the first known instance of a formulation which later became almost standard practice in Roman treaty-making. Its purpose was to formulate in words the nature of the unwritten moral obligations which the Romans expected their overseas clients to feel—obligations which the Aetolians had so dismally ignored. Since they had failed so completely to comprehend the importance of unwritten extra-legal obligations, which were the essence of *clientela*, the Senate decided to enshrine them, with all their convenient looseness, in a legal treaty, which no one could possibly misunderstand in principle. The Aetolian League was thus the first Balkan state to have its moral obligation to Rome spelled out in explicit detail. It is not surprising that, although Aetolia never recaptured her importance in Balkan politics, she never again, as a state, failed to understand what Rome required. Further serious provocation was left to others.

II The Achaean League

The Aetolian League was not the only major Greek state which misunderstood what the Romans required from the unwritten rules of *clientela*. The Aetolian League had made itself an enemy of Rome by its involvement with Antiochus; the Senate had accordingly had no compunction about treating it quite brutally or about finally spelling out in the peace-treaty exactly how it expected the Aetolians to behave in the future. To a defeated enemy like the Aetolian League, this could easily be done, particularly once Antiochus was defeated and the Senate no longer felt any urgent need to preserve Greek goodwill by sparing the Aetolians' feelings. But it was a different question when Rome's friends, of whose loyalty on the major issues of the wars with Philip, Antiochus and the Aetolians, there had never been any real doubt, failed to grasp fully their moral obligations. In these cases the Senate was impotent, tied in the moral strait-jacket of Rome's patronal obligations in the *clientela* relationship; and this restriction was actually reinforced by the propaganda of Greek freedom which had been put out with such success during the wars with Philip and Antiochus.

The chief state in question—and the only one about which we have sufficient information to be able to trace developments—was the Achaean League. The League had joined Rome at a crucial time during the war with Philip, had remained loyal for the rest of that war, and had benefited from Flamininus' proclamation of 'the freedom of the Greeks' by having Corinth and Argos restored to her and by seeing her Spartan enemy Nabis defeated and seriously weakened. Thereafter, the League had been an essential part of Flamininus' scheme for a balance of power in the Peloponnese in the face of Antiochus' ambiguous behaviour. With Achaea Flamininus' scheme had worked well. When Nabis, aroused by the Aetolians, started to attack Achaean territory in 193, the Achaeans under Philopoemen dutifully informed Rome, and in 192 campaigned independently against him. Moreover, later in 192, to demonstrate their loyalty to Rome and their gratitude for the freedom which Rome had brought them, they anticipated the Roman declaration of war on Antiochus by themselves being the first to declare war on him as soon as he arrived at Demetrias. For this, the Achaeans were rewarded by a grateful Senate with the granting of a treaty on equal terms with Rome (a *foedus aequum*) which formally recognized them as free and equal allies of the Roman People.[5]

This equal treaty was the Senate's reward for the Achaeans' conspicuous loyalty over the past six years. By it the Senate did not wish to alter the close relationship between the two states in any way, and certainly did not intend to weaken the moral obligations which it expected the Achaeans to continue to feel towards Rome, however the treaty was phrased. This intention became clear in the sequel. But Greek states were accustomed to having treaties which meant what they said and which said what they meant. So when the

Achaeans received their 'equal treaty' which recognized them as free and equal allies of Rome, they were, not unreasonably, immediately ready to take its terms at face value and at face value only. This meant that they would resent any attempt by the Senate to interfere, for instance, in Achaean internal affairs; for, they would have argued, if Rome required the right of internal interference, the Senate should have said so explicitly when it drafted the treaty: now it was too late. The written agreement must rule.

The first clash between the two interpretations of the treaty occurred in autumn 191, the very year of the treaty, when Flamininus and Glabrio attended an Achaean assembly to deal with some matters of mutual concern. Intending to settle matters in the usual Roman paternalistic way, by extending patronage and receiving gratitude, the Romans were quickly awakened to the new situation which the treaty had created: their request that exiles from Sparta should be restored—Nabis was now dead and Sparta had become a member-state of the Achaean League in 192—was turned down flat by Philopoemen, who was again chief magistrate. He said that he had no objection to restoring the exiles (which was not strictly true), but he wanted the Achaean government and himself, not Rome and Flamininus, to get the credit for it. And Flamininus incurred a similar defeat on the question of Elis, an ally of Antiochus in the war, which now wanted to join the Achaean League, but asked explicitly that it should be allowed to do so without Roman interference. Philopoemen agreed, and the Romans were snubbed.[6] How the situation had changed since the treaty! For, only a few months before, Flamininus' open interference had prevented the previous Achaean *strategos*, Diophanes, from enforcing the entry of Messene into the League; he had then promptly engineered this union himself. It was a heavy-handed exercise in patronage which, he hoped, would earn him gratitude; but in practice it and other similar manoeuvres annoyed the Achaeans so much that for more than ten years they insisted on interpreting literally the terms of their treaty with Rome, even after their leaders had realized that this had not been the Senate's intention in granting it.

The main issue which kept relations between Achaea and Rome unpleasantly simmering was the problem of Sparta; the men who insisted on their legal right of internal independence under the treaty were Philopoemen and his party, which included Lycortas, the father of Polybius the historian, and Polybius himself. The Spartan problem was particularly intractable. It was chiefly concerned with the existence of a large number of exiles who had been made homeless by the various revolutionary Spartan régimes of the past forty years, but whom the Romans now insisted should be restored. This insistence would have seemed reasonable enough but for one thing: the exiles, almost to a man, were hostile to the Achaean League and to Spartan membership of it; and, Philopoemen anticipated, they would quickly create internal trouble for the League if they were restored. However, once the war with Antiochus was over and the Balkans were again peaceful and out of danger, the Senate had no objection to creating some niggling internal difficulties for the Achaeans, just to keep reminding them that despite their treaty— which Roman gratitude had granted them—the Senate considered the Achaeans should act as Rome thought best, even in controversial internal matters. The Spartan dispute dragged on throughout the 180's. But as various brutal and partisan—and, in practice, useless —solutions were effected under increasing Roman pressure, so Philopoemen gradually stirred up opposition to himself in Achaea, chiefly among those political opponents who were wearied by the anarchic chaos and disruption in southern Achaea and by the constant giving of offence to Rome, which Philopoemen's hard-line policy entailed.

The most prominent of these men was Diophanes of Megalopolis, a fellow-citizen of Philopoemen who had once supported him and who had at times had his own reasons for being annoyed at Flamininus' methods. His chief claim to influence in the League stemmed from the fact that he was the *strategos* who in 191 had finally secured the unity of the whole Peloponnese under the Achaean League.[7] As early as 191, however, he had quarrelled with Philopoemen on the Spartan question (though at the time he had lost the argument and much influence with it); and by 185 he had become sickened by Philopoemen's unrealistic insistence that the question should be solved by the Achaeans themselves, without Roman interference. For by then it seemed clear that Philopoemen was merely using the argument as a cloak under which he imposed his own partisan settlements on Sparta, and that he had no intention of trying to solve Sparta's problems fairly. And Diophanes was, not unreasonably, afraid that the resulting Spartan dissatisfaction with Philopoemen's policy would wreck the unity of the Peloponnese which he himself had struggled to create. When the Roman envoy Quintus Caecilius Metellus visited Achaea in 185, Diophanes launched a scathing personal attack on Philopoemen, his party and his policy. But Diophanes' verbal assault did not have the immediate effect that he had anticipated; for when Metellus supported him by asking Philopoemen for an audience with the general assembly of the League—which he had no *legal* right to do—Philopoemen refused point-blank, and thus provoked a crisis in Achaean relations with Rome in which the immediate problem of Sparta temporarily assumed second place.[8] The crisis therefore passed without a solution to the Spartan question emerging. But events of the next few years showed that Diophanes' dissenting voice had been heard in Achaea as well as at Rome. When Philopoemen died in 182 while conducting an expedition against Messene—which had also seceded from the League—Polybius' father Lycortas became leader of his party. He tried to assume Philopoemen's partisan and obstructive role when the perennial Spartan problem again came up for discussion; but Diophanes' opposition constituted a stronger challenge now that the authoritative and influential Philopoemen was dead. And he bluntly suggested that all remaining Spartan exiles should now be restored—an exact echo of Flamininus' policy, which the Senate had by now been unsuccessfully urging for ten years.

It is clear from the fact that Lycortas partially yielded to Diophanes and actually restored some of the Spartan exiles, that control of Achaean affairs by Philopoemen's group was less complete than it had once been.[9] And it was this crack in the fabric of Philopoemen's 'no surrender' policy towards Sparta which a younger sympathizer with Diophanes, Callicrates of Leontium, managed to exploit. Callicrates had himself appointed as Achaean envoy to Rome in 180/179; and his visit proved to be epoch-making in Roman-Greek relations. For Callicrates forcefully told the Senate that it should stop relying on the Greeks' consciousness of moral obligation to achieve the peaceful aims of its policy in Greece, because this method simply was not working. If the Senate really wanted to control the legalistically-minded Greeks with the minimum of trouble to itself, if it wanted to avoid repeating elsewhere its damaging experiences with Philopoemen's party in Achaea, it should issue orders rather than requests, take sides in disputes rather than try to please everybody by appearing paternalistically neutral, and generally to make quite clear what it wanted. Some unpopularity would inevitably result. But this was the necessary price to be paid if chaos and universal dissatisfaction were to be avoided.[10]

The success of Flamininus' propagandist slogan, 'the freedom of the Greeks', during the war with Antiochus—which relied for its effectiveness on the Greeks' awareness of their moral obligation to

Rome from Rome's granting their freedom—had led the Senate to believe that its requests would in peacetime also be treated with the compliant respect which it expected from clients, that the ties of gratitude which bound the Greeks to Rome would be as effective a means of directing policy in peace as in war. The senators were wrong. And they were wrong because their explanation of why the Greeks had co-operated with Rome during the war was also partly wrong: for even in the war with Antiochus those Greeks who had supported Rome had done so chiefly because they thought that Rome was the more powerful and that Rome would win, not because they felt any strong moral obligation to support Rome in all circumstances. The Senate's post-war experience with the Achaean League showed this clearly enough; and, for all we know, similar disputes may have also been simmering elsewhere in Greece, though Achaea's 'equal treaty' (a rare concession), and the Achaean interpretation of it, made Rome's dealings with the League particularly intractable. Callicrates' speech to the Senate, however, ended all the dithering. Roman policy again became firm; the internal government of the Greek states gradually fell, with Roman encouragement, into the hands of men like Callicrates, who realized that in the last resort the Senate simply wanted the Greeks to bother Rome as little as was compatible with Roman security.

Polybius, himself a political heir of Philopoemen and a personal opponent of Callicrates, regarded such men as traitors, chiefly because they chose to abandon the legalistic pretence of regarding their states as equals of Rome; and doubtless some of them from the beginning indulged in internal party monopolies, and in discrimination and violence against political opponents. But Callicrates was, at first, one of them only in the matter of relations with Rome: for the first thing Callicrates did, when he was elected *strategos* of the League on his return from Rome, was to restore the long-suffering Spartan exiles; and the period of peace at Sparta and in Achaea as a whole which followed was enough to prove groundless Philopoemen's fear that chaos and anarchy would result from their wholesale restoration. Indeed, anarchy had come much closer to Achaea through Philopoemen's resistance to their restoration than from the restoration itself![11]

The Achaeans now had available an influential man who understood that their 'equal treaty' with Rome was not exactly what it seemed to be, was not a complete definition of the relationship which the Senate wanted. Moreover, Callicrates not only understood the moral obligations of *clientela* but was also prepared to comply with them. He still, at times, had to struggle to assert his influence in Achaea; Lycortas and his group still retained some support for their attempt to operate a rather watered-down version of Philopoemen's 'independent' foreign policy, as the treaty with Rome seemed to allow. But after Callicrates' visit to Rome and his enthusiastic reception by the Senate, all Achaeans of all parties recognized that their treaty-given equality and independence were largely illusory, and that they were vitally conditioned—and, if necessary, completely controlled—by the Roman Senate's view of Roman interests.

III Rhodes

Although the Senate's settlement of Asia Minor in 188 abandoned almost all pretence of Rome's being the freedom-bringer to the Greeks of Asia, this did not mean that the Senate lost interest in Asiatic affairs. The first major sufferer from a dispute about the settlement was Rhodes, which had shared with Eumenes of Pergamum the territorial spoils of Antiochus' defeat. When the Roman commissioners were discussing the details of the settlement, Rhodes had conveniently forgotten her insistence that the Greeks of Asia should be freed, and had asked for Caria and Lycia—Hellenized territories on the Asiatic mainland which contained some purely Greek communities. But at the same time two envoys from Eumenes' satellite city Ilium—which claimed a mythical kinship with Rome—asked the commissioners that the Lycians should be pardoned for having supported Antiochus. The commissioners did not regard the two requests as incompatible, and therefore, to please the Ilians (and Eumenes, if he had prompted their request), no recriminatory measures were imposed on the Lycians; but to please the Rhodians, Lycia, along with parts of Caria, was duly 'granted' to them as they had requested.

In this superficially straightforward decision lay seeds of trouble for Rhodes, which germinated and took root almost immediately; for the Ilians at once travelled to Lycia and, proudly exaggerating their influence with Rome, said they had obtained freedom for the Lycians. The Rhodian envoys, on the other hand, returned to Rhodes and, interpreting as a gift the Romans' 'grant' of Caria and Lycia to Rhodes—the exact terms on which the 'grant' was made were probably never thoroughly thought out by the Romans—announced this interpretation as the Romans' decision. The Rhodian and Lycian interpretations obviously conflicted; and the next development came almost immediately. The Lycians, proudly asserting their new freedom (or so they thought), sent to their important neighbour Rhodes and proposed that the two free states should form an alliance. They found to their shock that the Rhodians had already appointed governors for their newly 'granted' territories of Caria and Lycia; and not only did the Rhodians refuse to discuss an alliance with Lycia, but they made it quite clear that they regarded the Lycians as subject to Rhodian rule as a result of the Roman decision. Not surprisingly, the Lycians decided to resist, and war soon broke out.[12]

About the course of the war we have no information except that as late as 180 the Rhodians still regarded it sufficiently seriously to ask Eumenes for help;[13] and that by 178 it was effectively over, in the Rhodians' favour.[14] Meanwhile, the Senate, so far as we know, had limited its interest in Asia Minor to lending Eumenes diplomatic support against his two northern neighbours, Prusias of Bithynia and Pharnaces of Pontus. It had not interfered at all in the Rhodians' struggle in Lycia, no doubt thinking (if it was seriously aware of the matter at all) that any situation which kept Rhodes occupied, which prevented her from becoming too strong and from upsetting the Asiatic balance of power, and which did not threaten Rome's security, was a satisfactory state of affairs. In 178/7, however, the Senate was forced to take notice of the Lycians, for their envoys, now that it seemed that Lycia had finally been crushed by Rhodes, came to Rome as a last resort and appealed against Rhodes' oppression.[15]

Their complaints fell on receptive ears, as it happened. For the Achaean Callicrates had recently made his critical visit to Rome, and Roman policy towards the east was, as a result, becoming firmer. Moreover, Rhodes had recently refurbished her fleet with generous Macedonian assistance, and Rhodian ships had escorted Laodice, Perseus of Macedon's new Seleucid wife, from Syria to Macedon. These activities had aroused unfounded suspicion at Rome that Rhodes might be a party to some Macedonian-Syrian-Rhodian alliance which might at some time affect Roman security in the east. Thus, when the Lycians appealed to Rome, some influential sections of the Senate were already predisposed to regard Rhodes as a potentially ungrateful client, and were glad of an opportunity to clip her wings. The Senate therefore agreed to send envoys to Rhodes.

They now found it convenient to accept in full the Lycians' interpretation of the original Roman settlement—which the commissioners
had left imprecise—and carried the message to Rhodes that 'the
Lycians had not been granted to Rhodes as a gift, but rather as
friends and allies'.

That the Romans probably meant more by 'friends and allies'
than did the Lycians does not much matter, for the new interpretation of the settlement was never put to the test. The official Rhodian
view was that the Senate had been bamboozled by the Lycians
(though many Rhodians seem to have soon realized that the Senate
was deliberately seeking to exhaust Rhodes' new-found naval strength
and that a new war in Lycia was a convenient way to do it—for
nobody, neither at Rhodes nor in Lycia, believed that the Senate
would bother to intervene physically in the dispute). The Rhodian
government, therefore, at once sent envoys to Rome to state their
case, thinking that the Senate would favour them when it knew all
the facts; but their reply merely confirmed the suspicions of those
who thought Rome was becoming unfriendly towards Rhodes. For
while the Lycians had received a positive and friendly answer to their
request, the Senate merely listened to the Rhodians and postponed
giving a positive answer.[16] This Roman attitude was fuel for the
flames of anti-Roman feeling which was already building up at
Rhodes; for opponents of the friends of Rome (who were the current governing party) could now point to the fact, no doubt exaggerating it, that Rome seemed no longer to be a true friend of
Rhodes. The result was a great increase in the influence of Rome's
Rhodian opponents who, after a few more years, were able to gain
control of the government during the crucial years of the Third
Macedonian War. When that war was over, the Rhodians would
have given much to have found their Callicrates before they had
offended Rome beyond repair. We shall return to this later. Suffice it
to say here that the years of peace showed that the Roman settlement
of Asia Minor had its flaws (from the Roman point of view), just as
much as the settlement of the Balkans. It differed only in so far as
Asia Minor was physically further away from Rome than the Balkans, and might therefore be regarded as less important for Roman
security.

IV Macedon

Even after Philip's defeat at Cynoscephalae Macedon remained the greatest power in the Balkans: Rome had conquered Philip but had not crushed him. Preserved by Flamininus to create a balance of power with the Aetolians in northern and central Greece, Philip remained important to Rome, though reduced to the status of a Roman client. When Antiochus invaded Greece on the Aetolians' invitation, Flamininus' balance of power swung smoothly into action, and Philip dutifully co-operated with Rome, fighting against the Aetolians and facilitating the Scipios' overland march to the Hellespont through Macedonia and Thrace. From subsequent events it seems reasonably clear that during the war with Antiochus Philip had been encouraged to believe that Macedon would receive some gains from a Roman victory; yet as soon as the war was over in Asia and in Europe, it became obvious that the Senate had no intention of allowing Philip to capitalize on his co-operation which, they thought, was due to Rome from the gratitude which Philip owed for being allowed to keep a viable kingdom after Cynoscephalae.

Not surprisingly, Philip could not sympathize with the Senate's view. Especially troubling for him were two areas, of which he had had great hopes: south-west of his kingdom, he had hoped to recover Orestis, an integral part of Macedon which had broken away from him in 197; and in the south he had hoped for some of the Thessalian towns, in particular for the strategically important city of Lamia, which was essential if he was ever again going to be able to operate an effective Greek policy. These were explicitly refused him. In the east, in Thrace, where his services to the Scipios had been crucially important, he was galled to see his enemy Eumenes of Pergamum given control of Antiochus' possessions in the Thracian Chersonnese; and even the small towns of Aenus and Maronea, in which Antiochus had kept garrisons, were not granted to Philip but were left free—a status which, in this dangerous area, meant that the neighbouring Thracians would constantly threaten their very existence. Here also Philip gained nothing.[17]

With some justification, Philip felt that he had been cheated, though he had received no specific promises. Only confirming his view of what was likely to happen to the free towns of Aenus and Maronea was the difficult journey which Manlius Vulso had made in that very area when he brought his army back from Asia late in 188. He had neglected to contact Philip and to obtain his help and advice

before beginning his dangerous march (as the Scipios had been careful to do); the result was that attacks from the Thracian tribes deprived him of much of the booty which he had assiduously collected in
Asia. Unwilling to blame his own incompetence, Manlius hinted that
his disastrous march must have been caused by Philip's treachery.[18]
But in fact it was Philip who first saw the lesson of Manlius' disaster:
if a victorious Roman army could survive only with difficulty against
Thracian hostility, what hope of survival was there for the little free
towns of Aenus and Maronea? Moreover, if the Thracians once got a
firm foothold on the coast there, Philip might soon find his own
coastal possessions in eastern Macedonia under Thracian threat.

We have no more information for the two years after Manlius'
disaster. But in winter 186/5 envoys from all parts of Greece were in
Rome. One group was from Eumenes; and they were supported by
exiles from Maronea who alleged that Philip had by now taken
possession of both Aenus and Maronea. It appears that both towns
had been split politically between supporters of Philip and of
Eumenes—though both groups no doubt recognized, what the
Senate had apparently failed to appreciate, that real independence
meant in practice submission to or destruction by the Thracians.
While Eumenes had been careful not to encourage his supporters,
in order to avoid antagonizing the Senate by seeming to challenge
its settlement, Philip felt aggrieved at Roman bad faith and had
exploited the party dissension to gain control of both towns. He then
installed Macedonian garrisons. The Senate could not afford to
ignore this direct challenge to its settlement, even if Philip had
technically acted on the invitation of the Peoples of Aenus and Maronea; and since the Thessalians had also brought a complicated series
of complaints which required Roman decisions, a commission of
three senators, led by Quintus Caecilius Metellus, was sent to the
Balkans to hear any grievances against Philip.[19]

Metellus and his colleagues went first to Tempe. Here the Thessalians presented an enormous ragbag of complaints, many of which
they seem to have thought up chiefly because they expected that
Rome would favour them against Philip, however unjust their demands. They were not disappointed. After listening to all the complaints in detail and to Philip's defence, the Roman commissioners
decided against Philip in every single case—quite arbitrarily, it
seems, since many of the Thessalians' claims were trivial or invented
for the occasion. The commissioners were offended at Philip's
attitude when he hinted that he did not really expect a fair deal, and

when he blustered in terms which the Romans regarded as threats. Moreover, there was no doubt that Philip had been trying to resuscitate some vestiges of Macedon's old power and prosperity; for he had re-opened mines and issued new coinage, had raised harbourage dues, had tried to stimulate the birth-rate, and had imported new population from Thrace into eastern Macedonia. In practice all this amounted merely to consolidating Macedon against the constant threats from the tribes of the northern Balkans. But the Roman commissioners chose to interpret it, along with Philip's claims to places in Thessaly, as the groundwork for new Macedonian expansion into Greece. Accordingly, they decided that Philip must withdraw 'within the ancient boundaries of Macedonia', an imprecise formulation which was intended merely to satisfy the excessive demands of the Thessalians.[20]

This decision was neither fair nor reasonable, for Philip had longstanding and, by the standards of the times, legitimate claims in Thessaly. But worse was yet to come. When the Roman commissioners arrived at Thessalonica to reconsider the status of Aenus and Maronea, they found that Eumenes was now laying discreet claim to the towns. This was more than Philip felt he could stand, and his frustration impressed the Romans, who had no mandate for provoking him into war. They accordingly asked merely that he should withdraw his garrisons from the towns until the Senate should decide. During the following winter the Senate duly decided, and again—while it did not grant the towns to Eumenes—the decision went against Philip: he was to withdraw completely not only from Aenus and Maronea but from the whole Thracian coast outside Macedonia. Moreover, as an insultingly provocative indication that the Senate did not trust Philip to comply with its decision without direct Roman supervision, another Roman commission was sent out to the Balkans in 184, this time led by the ex-consul Appius Claudius Pulcher. Its purpose was to make sure that both in Thessaly and in Thrace Philip did as he was told.[21]

It says much for Philip's peaceful intentions that even now he did not consider opposing the decisions of the Senate in principle, however unjust he regarded them. But over Maronea, at least, he yielded to his frustration. Suspecting that although the Senate had reiterated its decision that Aenus and Maronea should be free, this was only a first step towards giving them to Eumenes, Philip determined to prevent this sell-out. If the towns were left free, Thracian raids would quickly threaten them. To kill three birds with one stone—to frustrate Eumenes, to show that Philip's assessment of the unviability of the freedom of Aenus and Maronea had always been right, and to work off his own frustration at the Senate's decision— he anticipated the inevitable by arranging that Thracians should be introduced into Maronea. A massacre of the Maroneans then followed.

Philip's satisfaction at his demonstration of how weak Aenus and Maronea were against the Thracians was short-lived. Appius Claudius ignored Philip's insincere protestations that he had not been responsible for the massacre, and demanded that Cassander, Philip's governor of Maronea, and Onomastus the governor of his Thracian province, should go to Rome and explain to the Senate what had actually happened. Onomastus Philip managed to beg off; Cassander's journey he was forced to agree to, but Cassander conveniently died *en route*. It was bound to be said, whatever the truth, that Philip had poisoned him; and moreover, the suspicion of his complicity in Cassander's death led the Romans (and the Greeks) to believe that Philip had indeed arranged the massacre at Maronea— facts which he had wanted to conceal. The morass of mutual suspicion and bad faith in which Romano-Macedonian relations were foundering seemed to be deepening.[22]

It must have seemed to Philip, viewing events through the bitterness of his disappointment at Rome's treatment of him since Antiochus' defeat, that whatever he did was wrong, that the Senate was merely seeking an excuse to destroy him. He probably erred in this: for the Senate's chief aim seems to have been merely to keep all its friends happy—particularly the Thessalians and Eumenes—as far as was consistent with Rome's security in the Balkans; and if interests conflicted, then Philip's, being those of the most powerful state and a defeated enemy (though he was now technically a friend and ally), were most easily expendable. Philip, however, not unnaturally, did not take this view; and as a last-ditch attempt to restore stability to his relations with Rome he decided to send his younger son Demetrius to represent his interests to the Senate. Demetrius ought to have been a good choice for this mission, since he had already lived at Rome for six years when he had been a hostage for Philip after Cynoscephalae. And Demetrius was indeed well received by the Senate.

The trouble for Philip was that Demetrius was too well received. Despite the multiplicity of charges levelled against Philip by Eumenes and by the Thessalians (who, it seemed, would never be satisfied with their good fortune, but who would doubtless have been deeply offended if the Senate had told them to slacken their demands), Demetrius was not required to answer any of them. He simply read out Philip's private notes of justification, and the Senate expressed itself satisfied. It seemed to be a complete change of front. But it was not. Demetrius' presence in Rome had merely given the Senate a new idea about how Macedon might be controlled. Demetrius was tractable and unsubtle: his naïve reading out of Philip's notes clearly showed this. The Senate thought it could use such a simple man. Accordingly, the formal reply which Philip received from the Senate stated explicitly that he owed the acceptance of his defence solely to the favour with which the Senate viewed Demetrius (and, by insulting implication, not to the force of his arguments or to the inherent justice of Philip's position); and they would send another group of Roman commissioners whose task was to check that everything was being done according to the Senate's wish and to emphasize that Philip owed his good fortune to Demetrius.

Nor was this all. For Flamininus, who was still one of Rome's most influential eastern experts, encouraged Demetrius to hope that he might, with Roman support, succeed or even supplant his father on the Macedonian throne, although he was not even first in the line of succession; and he wrote to Philip, asking that Demetrius and as many as possible of his Macedonian noble friends should be sent to Rome as soon as possible.[23] While Philip will doubtless have been pleased enough at the Senate's acceptance of Demetrius' representations, he was clearly disconcerted by the manner of the Roman reply. Demetrius was not his eldest son. Perseus was first in line of succession—for which Philip had long been training him—and Philip was naturally offended that Demetrius seemed to be about to become the 'Roman candidate' for the Macedonian throne. And as the awareness of Roman favour for Demetrius and of Demetrius' gullible acceptance of Roman approaches became widely known in Macedon, the court seems to have been split into two factions. This was Rome's first, but by no means last, attempt to weaken a client kingdom by interfering in its internal dynastic affairs; and it seemed to be working well.

But the Senate had reckoned without Perseus' determination. Philip's own reaction to Demetrius' new-found favour at Rome was at first uncertain. He did not want to offend the Senate; that was clear from his compliance, when it was insisted upon, with the Senate's decision that he must evacuate coastal Thrace.[24] But he could not easily accept the mutual alienation of his sons. On this issue Philip soon showed where he stood. In 183, soon after Demetrius' return from Rome, he made an expedition on his northern frontier, the only region where the Romans had not yet objected to his activities, against the non-Greek Dardanians. During this expedition he founded a city which he called Perseis, after his eldest son.[25] But when he tried to consolidate his position on this frontier still further, by forcibly transporting Macedonian settlers from the more prosperous cities of the Aegean coast, Philip made himself so unpopular within Macedon that there seems to have been a conspiracy against him which he quelled only by taking large-scale reprisals.[26]

It was in the midst of this trouble and uncertainty that the dissension between Demetrius and Perseus came to a head. A drunken party produced the accusation from Perseus that Demetrius had tried to kill him; and though Philip took no immediate action, the situation was obviously dangerous. If he was to make a clear judgement, Philip had to know the facts about Demetrius' activities at Rome; so during winter 182/1 he sent two of his friends to Rome to find out what, if anything, Demetrius was planning. But to be on the safe side, even before their return, Philip refused to take Demetrius with him on an expedition in 181 into Thrace.[27] The crisis came soon afterwards. Demetrius' escort Didas soon discovered that Demetrius intended to flee to Rome from the climate of fear and suspicion in Macedon; and he promptly informed Philip. Such a flight, it seemed, could have only one purpose: to obtain Roman support for his dynastic aspirations. If true, the intention was clearly treasonable. Yet even now Philip did not act decisively until his friends returned from Rome bearing a letter purporting to be from Flamininus, which confirmed that when Demetrius was in Rome he had had conversations with Flamininus about the Macedonian succession; but the letter denied that Flamininus had encouraged him. Livy, who preserves the letter, says it was a forgery; and the truth we cannot ultimately tell. But forgery or not, Demetrius' conversation with Flamininus about the succession was fact, and the letter may have been authentic.[28] Philip delayed no longer, Demetrius was clearly guilty of treason: if Macedon was to survive, Demetrius must go. The poison was administered soon afterwards.[29]

The Roman scheme of supplanting Perseus with an obedient puppet had clearly failed. Indeed, if Flamininus' letter to Philip was authentic, it seems likely that Flamininus had realized, as soon as

Philip's friends began making enquiries at Rome about Demetrius' activities, that the scheme could not work and, by callously incriminating Demetrius, had tried to destroy the evidence for Roman complicity. However this may be, the execution of Rome's favourite, Demetrius—which the Romans and the Roman tradition chose to regard as murder—was yet another nail in the coffin of harmonious relations between Rome and Macedon. For Philip died soon afterwards, in 179, still full of schemes for regenerating Macedon through a viable Balkan policy which, he hoped, would not offend too heavily against Roman sensibilities. Perseus duly succeeded his father. But he inherited not only the by now traditional Roman suspicion of all Macedonian activities, but he was additionally branded by the reputation he had gained as the man who had procured his accession by murdering Rome's friend Demetrius. The Senate had been suspicious of Philip, though since 196 he had given it no good reason to be: it was to prove doubly suspicious of Perseus.[30]

CHAPTER XV

PERSEUS

I The First Years

PERSEUS came to the Macedonian throne in 179. His opposition to Rome's friend, his brother Demetrius, and his close relationship with his father Philip during the previous ten troubled years, had ensured that the Senate's view of his activities would be coloured from the moment of his accession. Nevertheless, diplomatic courtesies were at first preserved: on his accession Perseus sent to Rome, asking for the renewal of Philip's 'friendship' with the Roman People, and for assurances that the Senate recognized him as Macedonian king. The Senate was pleased to give its gracious assent. At this time it would have gained nothing from refusing.[1]

But Perseus' subsequent activities, though in practice harmless enough, did nothing to destroy his reputation for being hostile to Rome. In the Greek states Rome had tended on the whole to see her interests best represented by the conservative, property-owning classes. Perseus began his reign, after the formal renewal of 'friendship' with Rome, by declaring an amnesty for Macedonian debtors, many of whom had fled from Macedon to Greece from where they continually threatened Macedonian stability. His aim seems to have been to eradicate these nests of discontented exiles who might prove dangerous to his throne, but one unexpected effect of his amnesty was that the poor in many of the Greek states began to regard Perseus as the champion of the under-privileged, wherever they might be; and the corollary was that Rome's property-owning supporters became in their turn suspicious of Perseus' intentions.[2]

Nor was the amnesty Perseus' only action which aroused Roman suspicion. In 178 or 177 he married the Seleucid princess Laodice, the daughter of Seleucus IV, grand-daughter of Rome's old enemy Antiochus III.[3] Such dynastic marriages had in the past nearly always implied some political connection. Was Perseus, his enemies—particularly Eumenes of Pergamum—immediately asked, hoping by this marriage to erect a new power-grouping in the east which might again provide effective opposition to Rome? Were the successors of Philip V of Macedon and of Antiochus III of Syria hoping to unite their kingdoms as they had united their families? There was no sign of this, beyond the bare fact of the marriage; but, for those who were already hostile, the marriage itself was sufficient indication. Even Rhodes, as we have seen, was tarred with suspicion merely for having provided ships in which to transport Laodice and for having received rich rewards from Perseus for doing so. Nor was this Perseus' only newly-made dynastic connection at this time; for soon afterwards his sister Apame married Prusias II of Bithynia, the son of Philip's old ally Prusias I and no lover of his powerful neighbour, Eumenes of Pergamum, Macedon's chief opponent and Rome's chief friend in the east.[4] There is no good indication that these marriages were intended to bring about a political or military alliance hostile to Rome: but it was clearly in Eumenes' interest to argue that they were.

While Roman suspicions were being activated by Perseus' marriage contracts, they were also strengthened by formal complaints against him made in Rome by the Dardanians and Thessalians. We have seen how Thessalian complaints had hounded Philip out of all his possessions in Greece during the 180's, and had made him look to the north for any future Macedonian consolidation. On Macedon's northern border the Dardanians and the Thracians had always threatened Macedonian security; and one of Philip's last schemes had been to encourage the friendly Germanic tribe of the Bastarnae, whose home area was near the Black Sea, to challenge the Dardanians for the territory which they had long held on Macedon's northern border. Roman historians added—almost certainly following a tradition established by the hostile interpretation of Eumenes of Pergamum—the false and fantastic notion that Philip intended also to encourage the Bastarnae to attack Italy.[5]

When Philip died the Bastarnae were already on the move; and it did not take the Dardanians long to realize that they and their territory were the prime objective. They naturally assumed that Perseus was responsible, and followed the by now well established Balkan practice of appealing to Rome. Their envoys were at Rome during the winter of 177/6; and Thessalian envoys were there to confirm their complaint. The Senate, nothing loath to send some of its members to discover what, if anything, was going on in Macedon, dispatched Aulus Postumius Albinus, who had been consul in 180,

as head of the commission.[6] When Postumius returned, he reported
that war was in progress between the Dardanians and the Bastarnae,
but he tacitly allowed that he and his colleagues had found no indication that Perseus was implicated. Envoys from Perseus explicitly
denied that he had encouraged the Bastarnae (though they said
nothing about Philip's contacts with them). But despite Perseus'
denials and despite the negative findings of Postumius' commission,
the Senate was not wholly convinced: its reply to Perseus' envoys
was that he should take redoubled care not only to respect his treaty
with Rome but to ensure that he was seen to be respecting it.[7]

It was an ominous beginning to the renewed flood of diplomatic
activity between Rome and the Balkans. And Perseus' comparative
youth and diplomatic inexperience made him far less careful than
Philip had been to avoid offending the Senate and far less ready to
make concessions to Rome. It was perhaps simply unfortunate
for Perseus that a probably innocent exchange of envoys with
Carthage in 174 should have coincided with the renewal of Roman
suspicions of Carthage's intentions, and have resulted in the Senate's
sending another Roman investigation commission to Macedon.[8] But
it was clearly a provocative action (even if not, strictly speaking, contrary to his treaty with Rome) when in the same year Perseus intervened in Dolopia and restored it firmly to Macedonian control by
military action; for although the exact status of Dolopia may not
have been precisely defined in the treaty with Rome which confined
Macedon to her 'traditional boundaries', his intention was clearly
aggressive and as such was likely to arouse the Senate's suspicions.

And this was not all, for from Dolopia Perseus visited Delphi, still
accompanied by his army, and returned to Macedon through central
Greece and Thessaly. Again, strictly speaking, his march was not
contrary to his treaty with Rome, which was merely concerned to
prevent Macedon from acquiring any territory outside its 'traditional
boundaries': after leaving Dolopia Perseus did not acquire any
territory or do any damage to any of the areas he passed through.[9]
Indeed, from the Roman point of view, this was part of the trouble:
for Perseus was actually well received in many places, and the one
obvious and indisputable result of his march was an increase of
genuine enthusiasm for Perseus in many Greek communities. That
it was Perseus' deliberate policy to acquire friends and influence in
Greece was clear also from his sending out envoys and letters to a
wider range of Greek states than those which lay on his direct route.
His theme was reconciliation: that disputes which had upset rela-

tions between the Greeks and Philip in the past should not now be continued *vis-à-vis* Perseus. The message was loud and clear, that Perseus hoped to be widely accepted as a friend of the Greeks. Those others—Eumenes and Rome—who also regarded themselves as friends of the Greeks again began to be alarmed at the implications. Indeed, the Roman envoys who had been sent to Macedon in 174 were unable even to have an interview with Perseus, since he was so busy; and, putting the worst construction on what they saw and what they heard from Rome's middle-class Greek friends, reported bluntly that preparations for war were clearly being made and that war was not far off.[10]

This was a great exaggeration; and although the Senate had no doubt noted the conviction of its envoys, their report produced no immediate Roman reaction beyond the dispatch of yet another group of senators, instructed to visit Macedon on their way to Alexandria. Envoys from the Aetolians—among whom civil war had now broken out—gained the appointment of the experienced ex-consul Marcus Claudius Marcellus to sort out their differences; and when a little later news arrived that Thessaly and neighbouring Perrhaebia were also virtually in a state of civil war as a result of a massive debt problem, another ex-consul with Greek experience, Appius Claudius Pulcher, was sent out to settle matters there. In addition to dealing with their immediate tasks—which both men seem to have done reasonably efficiently—they were obviously in a good position for assessing at first hand the extent to which Perseus' activities presented a serious threat to peace in the Balkans, and to take measures to strengthen the resolve of those parties in each state which supported Rome.[11]

Marcellus, for instance, after finishing his business in Aetolia, visited the Achaean League. His purpose, it soon became clear, was to strengthen the position of Callicrates, Rome's chief friend in the League. The previous year, the Achaeans, along with other states, had received a letter from Perseus asking for reconciliation. The particular point at issue was that the Achaeans had some years before passed a rigorous law which excluded any Macedonian from setting foot on Achaean soil, and Perseus now wanted them to repeal it. So also did a group of Achaean slave-owners; for many slaves had taken advantage of the effective suspension of diplomatic contacts to escape from their Achaean masters and seek refuge in Macedonia, from where they could not be recovered. Callicrates' opponents—Lycortas and other followers of Philopoemen—viewed these slave-owners as potential supporters; and in any case they saw no Roman interest threatened if Achaea re-opened friendly relations with the new Macedonian king. They therefore welcomed Perseus' overture. Callicrates then had great difficulty in persuading the Achaean assembly that this might be dangerous, that the Romans, despite superficial friendship with Macedon, already suspected Perseus' intentions, and that to repeal their restrictive law at that particular time would be regarded by the Senate as tantamount to hostility to Rome.

Callicrates won in the end, but only after a major effort. Rome had always tried to support her friends when her own interests were not damaged by doing so; and when Marcellus addressed the Achaeans in 174, he made it clear that the Senate's view was that the Achaeans' decision to maintain their law against the Macedonians had been quite right. By doing so he tacitly administered praise to Callicrates and a rebuke to Lycortas' party; and moreover, his speech made the Achaeans (and others who learnt of it) aware that Rome was hostile to and suspicious of Perseus' activities. The Achaeans could thank Callicrates' sharp appreciation of the true state of affairs for having saved them from the danger of Roman displeasure. But even so, all did not escape. By flirting with Perseus' proposals, Lycortas' party merely confirmed the reputation which Philopoemen's earlier legalistic activities had gained for it, of being basically unfriendly towards Rome. It was not true: but it was not long before they paid the price of their reputation.[12]

II The Outbreak of War

When Marcellus had completed his mission in Greece, Roman suspicion of Perseus had not yet turned into readiness for war, though a few senators, including the glory-seeking consuls of 172, were openly in favour and tried to persuade the Senate to make Macedonia a consular province for that year. Their attempt failed, since the unwillingness of the Senate's majority to declare war so precipitately was compounded by political differences with the consul Gaius Popillius Laenas.[13] Yet despite this initial reluctance, 172 proved to be a crucial year. By the end of it war had been decided on, a propaganda campaign had been launched, and an advance contingent of the Roman army had crossed the Adriatic.

The chief cause of this change of attitude was the personal visit

which Eumenes of Pergamum made to Rome in spring 172. Eumenes
was by now Rome's most powerful friend in the east; and—what was
to prove more important at the present time—he was also Perseus'
most powerful enemy. The combination proved disastrous for
Perseus. Impressed that the king of Pergamum should regard the
Macedonian situation as worthy of his personal intervention, the
Senate, which was already predisposed to be suspicious of Perseus,
gave Eumenes careful attention when he addressed it. He propounded
at length the theory that Philip had been planning war with Rome
when he died, and that Perseus had simply inherited his blue-
print; as evidence he cited the death of Demetrius and the movements of the Bastarnae which, he claimed, were directed ultimately
against Rome.

Having made this dubious major assumption, Eumenes proceeded
to interpret every ambiguous action of Perseus' in the light of it. His
present consolidation of Macedonian economic and manpower resources; his marriage connections with the Seleucids and with
Prusias; an alliance which he had made with the Boeotian League;
his negotiations with the Achaeans; his march to Dolopia and to
Delphi; even his border defence against a Thracian prince Abru-
polis, who subsequently found it convenient to claim to be a friend of
Rome; various unexplained disappearances of Greek political leaders;
and his popularity with the lower classes in many of the Greek
states: all these matters and some others were lumped together and
interpreted by Eumenes as being part of Perseus' determination to
take Macedon to war with Rome yet again. On nothing was Perseus
given the benefit of the doubt: indeed, Eumenes, if challenged,
would doubtless have denied that there was any doubt.[14]

But Eumenes was not challenged, since his indictment suited only
too well the Senate's prevalent suspicious attitude towards Perseus.
For the present, strict secrecy was observed about the content of
Eumenes' speech: only later did its contents leak out; but by then
Eumenes' catalogue of charges had already become the standard
Roman justification for the war, a justification which appeared in
much subsequent diplomacy and propaganda both during and after
the war, and which became enshrined in the Roman historical tradition. Even Polybius took over Eumenes' partisan viewpoint when he
attributed the causes of the war not to Perseus himself, but to
Philip's schemes; and Livy's and Polybius' accounts of Philip's
activities in the 180's—particularly over the affair of Demetrius—
have been retrospectively distorted by their acceptance of the

Roman tradition, which originated in nothing but Eumenes' partisan exposition of the intentions of Philip and of Perseus.[15]

There might reasonably have been doubt both about the details and about the underlying assumption of Eumenes' interpretation of Macedonian affairs. But the Senate found in it merely the confirmation of its own suspicions, which had already been aroused and sharpened by the reports of its envoys to Macedon over the last few years. Where existing suspicion and the military aspirations of those who looked for commands were supported by the firmly expressed view of Rome's strongest and most influential friend in the area—to refuse whose interpretation would in any case have been a major insult— Perseus had no chance of staving off war. His naïvely open actions during the seven years since he had become king had played into Eumenes' unscrupulous hands, which had in turn found no difficulty in manipulating the compliant Senate. When Perseus' over-arrogant envoy Harpalus protested to the Senate a few days later that Perseus had neither said nor done anything hostile to Rome, the Senate heard him with exasperated impatience, which provoked Harpalus indiscreetly to bluster that Perseus would nevertheless defend himself if Rome was determined to fight. The drift to war had suddenly become a landslide.

Harpalus' reply to Perseus on his return to Macedon was, not surprisingly, that Rome was manifestly eager for war, though no actual preparations were yet being made. These were not long delayed. For soon after Eumenes had left Rome, a report arrived that he had been set upon at Delphi by assassins hired by Perseus, and had been in danger of his life. What actually seems to have happened is that Eumenes was caught in an avalanche and badly hurt. Determined to reap advantage from his accident, political expediency led to the facile, but quite unsubstantiated, claim that Perseus was behind it all. The lack of evidence did not deter Eumenes, nor did it bother the Roman Senate, which was at much the same time provided with a 'confession' from one Rammius of Brundisium that Perseus had tried to hire him to poison certain persons, who conveniently remained unnamed. On the level of propaganda, at least, it was clear that the war was going to be fought with no holds barred.[17]

At about the same time, Eumenes' father-in-law, Ariarathes of Cappadocia, made his own disposition clear (doubtless on Eumenes' advice) by sending his young son to Rome with instructions that he was to be educated there. Some other states also felt a similar necessity to demonstrate their goodwill towards Rome: even three

Thracian tribes sent asking for Roman friendship and alliance; some
Thessalians and Aetolians put in an appearance; and one of Rome's
old friends in Illyria, the island of Issa, complained about the activities of the current Illyrian king Genthius, and alleged that he was in
touch with Perseus. This latter 'information' was enough to provoke
Roman action, and senatorial envoys were sent to investigate. Other
envoys were also dispatched to tour the Aegean and Asia Minor, and
to call on Antiochus IV of Syria and on the current Ptolemaic administration in Alexandria. The diplomatic war had immediately
swung into action.[18]

By late summer 172 the Senate had decided in principle on war
with Perseus; and although it did not yet formally ask the Roman
People to declare war—leaving this to the consuls of 171, one of
whom would conduct it—it decided to send an advance force as soon
as possible into the western Balkans to prevent Perseus from seizing
the routes across the Pindus mountains from Epirus and Illyria into
Thessaly and Macedonia. This action effectively committed Rome
and ensured that the Roman People would feel that it had no alternative to declaring war when the new consuls made their formal
proposal after their entry to office. This advance force, under the
praetor Gnaeus Sicinius, was not ready to leave until October or
November. But the Senate also decided to send a propaganda mission to Greece and appointed the ex-consul, Quintus Marcius
Philippus, one of its Macedonian experts, to lead it. Philippus' job
was to ensure that the Greeks, particularly those in the areas which
seemed to contain groups sympathetic to Perseus, knew what was
expected of them as Roman clients in the approaching conflict. He
naturally did not take as long as Sicinius to prepare for his journey,
since his was not primarily a military mission; and by September he
had crossed to Corcyra. It was probably November before Sicinius'
force reached Illyria.[19]

Marcius Philippus and his four colleagues began work at once.
The most important areas of central Greece—those closest to
Macedon itself—Philippus himself and the next senior envoy,
Aulus Atilius Serranus (who also had previous experience of Greek
conditions), undertook to visit personally. Philippus soon satisfied
himself that Epirus, Aetolia and Thessaly were as secure to Rome as
his presence and propaganda could make them (although every
region by now contained numbers of Macedonian sympathizers).
Boeotia, where the Boeotian League had formed some kind of
alliance with Perseus and whose internal struggles had created a

delicate balance of party power, was a more complicated problem which Philippus chose to leave until last.[20] For since his arrival in the Balkans the possibility had offered itself of using his diplomatic expertise to hamper Perseus' military preparations over the winter.

While Philippus was still at Corcyra Perseus wrote to him asking why Roman troops were crossing to Greece. Philippus did not directly answer this; but he did reply by claiming that Rome was, as always, acting for the protection of the Greeks. A few weeks later, while he was in Thessaly, new envoys arrived from Perseus. This time they asked for a conference, and Philippus agreed to meet Perseus near the pass of Tempe. Philippus began the talks by repeating the charges which Eumenes had made against Perseus in the Senate; but he encouraged Perseus to defend himself. After Perseus had done so, Philippus proposed that Perseus should yet again send envoys to Rome. A truce was agreed for the winter to enable this to be done. Perseus, now eagerly hoping for 'peace in our time', and apparently at last prepared, at this critical moment, to imitate his father's appeasement of Rome during the 180's, was misled by Philippus' apparent reasonableness into believing that his truce was an earnest of the Senate's sincere willingness to negotiate.[21]

He could not have been more wrong. His truce was agreed to by Philippus for one reason and for one reason only: to gain time for the main Roman army to reach the Balkans before Perseus realized what was happening and used the winter to prepare his defences. As a serious indication of the Senate's desire to settle matters peaceably, it was not worth the paper it was written on. Philippus' truce was as disreputable a piece of Roman diplomatic duplicity as many senators had ever witnessed; and some older senators, when they learnt of it, expressed their firm disapproval of this 'new wisdom'. But by then it was already too late. Perseus naïvely respected the truce throughout the winter until his envoys—who were deliberately delayed by the Senate so that Rome might achieve the maximum advantage from Philippus' bad faith—returned with their bad news, that the Roman People had seen fit to declare war on Perseus even before the Senate had received them.[22]

Philippus' conference with Perseus did not mark the end of his mission. The Boeotian League remained to be dealt with, and he chose nearby Chalcis in Euboea as his base. His arrival there caused a tremendous upsurge of political activity both in the League itself and in its constituent city-states. The Boeotian League had always been something of an unconventional thorn in the flesh of Rome's settlement of Greece, for many of the constituent cities were reluctant members, and the federal organization was held together only by the pressure of the majority; moreover, Boeotia had retained a 'democratic' (and thus, almost by definition, unstable) form of government, rather than the conservative and stable property-owning oligarchies which Rome preferred. The League's unfortunate alliance with Perseus was the excuse Philippus now used to solve both of these long-standing Boeotian problems, for he exploited genuine existing dissatisfaction with the conduct of the central government of the League to cause it to be broken up. His method was brutally simple: he refused to accept the representatives of the central federal government of the League, and insisted that Rome would deal only with each separate constituent city. If Rome refused to negotiate with the League, it was obviously no longer a viable political unit. The dissolution of the League was a harshly open demonstration of what the Roman patron might require from an unsatisfactory foreign client state which had only irritated, but not damaged, Rome. There could be no effective resistance by the League's central administration. Only three cities—Thisbe, Haliartus and Coronea—remained loyal as individual cities to the League's alliance with Perseus. Their unworthy reward was to be told that because of his truce with Rome Perseus could send them no help.[23]

On the level of immediate political effectiveness Philippus' mission was a great success. So also, it seemed, was that of another group of Roman envoys, led by Tiberius Claudius Nero, which visited Asia and the Aegean islands and paid particular attention to Rhodes. We have seen how Rhodes' dispute with Lycia and how Rome's failure to decide it in Rhodes' favour had led to a worsening of relations between Rhodes and Rome and to the growth of an anti-Roman party at Rhodes. These developments were also accentuated by Rhodes' suspicion of and hostility towards her Asiatic neighbour, Rome's good friend Eumenes of Pergamum. Rhodes, however, still had a strong navy; and the Senate had no wish to precipitate a crisis with Rhodes just at this critical time. The Roman envoys were therefore conciliatory and they received the satisfactory assurance from the current leaders of the Rhodian government that Rhodes would, as before, give Rome all necessary support. It was fortunate that the envoys had visited Rhodes and boosted the morale and internal support of the pro-Roman party; for during the winter Perseus circulated widely his version of the specific points which seemed to be at issue in his dispute with Rome, and he made a major effort to gain

Rhodian sympathy and support. For the present, however, Rhodes remained under the control of the pro-Roman party and refused to give Perseus any assurance of help or even of mediation.[24]

By winter 172/1 Roman diplomacy had achieved all it could. The foundations had been laid for the formal declaration of war, which was brought before the Roman People in the *comitia centuriata* by the new consuls of 171 after the return of the various diplomatic missions.[25] Roman determination to go to war with Perseus had been fixed since shortly after Eumenes' visit to Rome the previous winter. Yet this war, as so many before it, was not simply a war of conquest, a war which would indulge a desire for territorial expansion. Even after it Rome still took no direct control of any territory in the Balkans. The real trouble with Perseus, from Rome's point of view, was that he was behaving like an equal of Rome, not like a dutiful client. The Senate regarded this as culpable and dangerous. But it was in fact basically once more a failure of the Greek mind to understand the full implications of the *clientela* of a free state. This had never been spelled out to Macedon; and Perseus had accordingly offended against Rome's paternalistic view that her clients should not cause Rome any bother.

Whatever the rights or wrongs of individual issues, Perseus from the beginning of his reign—and, indeed, even before it—had caused bother for Rome by creating tension among those who were suspicious of him or openly hostile to him. The stream of querulous eastern embassies to Rome, culminating in Eumenes' personal appearance, all of which poured out complaints against Perseus, led the Senate—already itself suspicious of Macedon's recovery and of Perseus' personal intentions—to believe that so many of its friends could not all be wrong; and this impression was confirmed by Roman envoys who were not treated with the deference they expected from a client, and who found plenty of Greeks willing to tell them what they wanted to hear. Thus even if the troubles and complaints were none of them Perseus' fault—and few Romans will have believed that— the easiest way to put an end to them seemed to be to eradicate their common denominator, the Macedonian monarchy. It was not a fair or a just solution to the problem: but it certainly seemed the easiest. Thus, it seems that after Eumenes' visit to Rome the Senate no longer wished to live at peace with Perseus on the traditional terms, though war was not declared immediately: Perseus' truce with Philippus at Tempe in autumn 172 was Macedon's Munich.

CHAPTER XVI

THE END OF THE MACEDONIAN MONARCHY

I The Third Macedonian War

THE Senate's decision to go to war with Perseus finally ended its policy of trying to co-exist peacefully with the Macedonian monarchy and to control it merely by exercising its moral rights under the client-patron relationship. The vote for war indicated that a majority thought this policy had failed, and that a more direct and efficient method of controlling the Balkans was needed. To achieve this, the Macedonian monarchy, now proven, it seemed, to be an unstable influence throughout the Greek east, needed to be abolished. It was a more brutal and direct view of Balkan affairs than the Senate had ever before officially advocated, still less committed itself to; and the political ruthlessness of the policy-makers was mirrored in the brutal actions in the field of many of the Senate's commanders. Quintus Marcius Philippus might in 172 proclaim a pale shadow of Flamininus' 'freedom of the Greeks' when he alleged that Roman arms would protect the Greeks against Perseus.[1] But this time nobody was convinced: Rome was so obviously fighting for purely Roman interests that even the Roman commanders subsequently made little attempt to conceal the truth by traditional forms of propaganda.

Against such Roman determination Perseus never stood a chance, though the incompetence of some of the first Roman commanders made this dangerously unclear not only to Perseus himself but to other Greek states and parties which, in the course of the war, in-advisedly chose to join him. The first Roman consular army left Italy in spring 171 under the command of the consul Publius Licinius Crassus.[2] Before Crassus' arrival at Apollonia Perseus had learnt the news of Rome's declaration of war from his returning envoys. He had then collected his army together, and marched it into Thessaly, where he immediately captured some cities, though he found no great enthusiasm for his cause. This was hardly surprising since the Thessalian cities had been among the chief traducers of Philip and Perseus to Rome. Nevertheless, Perseus established himself in northern Thessaly and prepared to meet Crassus when he crossed the mountains.[3]

Perseus soon persuaded Crassus and his Greek allies to meet him in battle. The conflict was dominated by cavalry, and it resulted in a resounding victory for Perseus, who claimed to have killed more than 2,000 Roman troops.[4] But the chief effect of the battle was merely to harden Crassus' attitude—the very opposite of what Perseus believed should have happened. Indeed, Perseus so underestimated Rome's determination as to try to start negotiations with Crassus, offering to accept the same terms as Philip had received from Flamininus in 197/6. His ingenuousness was ludicrous and his offer was scorned. Far from admitting that his defeat had made any difference, Crassus not only did not take Perseus' offer as serious bargaining, but demanded that Perseus should offer unconditional surrender. Perseus abandoned his attempt to negotiate.[5]

Though Perseus' victory had no important effect on Crassus, it changed many attitudes throughout Greece, where Perseus' military prospects seemed to have been enhanced by it. They had not been. Yet the Romans' reaction inadvertently encouraged this trend, for their setback seems to have stimulated a wave of Roman brutality towards Greeks who opposed them (or seemed to oppose them), and this in turn provoked an unfavourable reaction among the Greeks. For the Roman defeat an immediate scapegoat had to be found: no Roman consul would admit incurring defeat through his own incompetence, if he could avoid doing so. And a scapegoat was indeed readily available, among Crassus' Aetolian allied troops. Alleging misconduct, Crassus summarily arrested five of the Aetolians' leaders and sent them to Rome.[6]

There was, however, more substance to this incident than Livy's short account suggests; for these five Aetolians were unenthusiastic about the new Roman military intervention in Greece—though, it seems, they were not active supporters of Perseus. Unfortunately for them, mere lukewarmness towards Rome was liable to be interpreted as tantamount to treason in the current political climate: war has no time for political subtleties. They opposed Lyciscus, the pro-Roman leader in Aetolia, and that in itself was, it turned out, sufficient to condemn them to deportation. Their extradition had repercussions in neighbouring Epirus, where a similar internal politi-

cal balance was delicately preserved in favour of Cephalus, the leader
of the 'neutralists'. His chief pro-Roman opponent was Charops
(grandson of the Charops who had helped Flamininus in 198), who
had already spent some years in Rome learning Latin, forming contacts and gaining influence. Cephalus, if he had been forced to choose
a sovereign power, would have chosen Macedon, whose language he
knew and whose methods he understood, rather than Rome; and it
seemed to him that the unhappy experience of the five deported
Aetolians suggested that a mere hint of his attitude dropped by
Charops to Crassus would ensure that Cephalus also was deported to
Rome as 'unreliable'. Rather than suffer this, Cephalus preferred to
support Perseus openly, for Perseus, even if successful, was unlikely
to purge the undecided or unenthusiastic. And with him Cephalus
carried the loyalties of his tribe, the important Molossians.[7]

Contemporary events in Boeotia, however, were an ominous warning to those like Cephalus who chose openly to oppose Rome. Of
the Boeotian cities, only Coronea, Thisbe and Haliartus had retained their alliance with Perseus after Marcius Philippus' visit to
Boeotia in 172. They soon suffered for choosing the wrong side. At
Haliartus, the campaigning season of 171 began with a siege. The
praetor, Gaius Lucretius Gallus, who took command of the be-
siegers on his arrival, had been ill during his journey from Rome.
But whether his illness contributed to the ill-disciplined brutality
which he encouraged his troops to perpetrate throughout the year,
or whether he was simply following what he thought was the current
mood of the Senate, we cannot tell. Certainly, the Boeotian cities,
friend and foe alike, suffered from his furious activity. Haliartus,
first to be attacked, was first to fall. Many citizens were slaughtered
in the capture; those who surrendered were sold into slavery; all
valuables were collected and the whole city was razed to the ground.
Perhaps sated with this destruction, Lucretius treated Thisbe rather
better, though the estates of Rome's political opponents were sold
by auction and the city put into the hand of Rome's friends. Later
in the year Coronea fell to a similar assault by the consul Crassus.
Even friendly Chalcis, which had by now remained a loyal friend of
Rome for nearly twenty-five years, and which was the indispensable
base of the Roman fleet, was looted and plundered by Lucretius'
undisciplined troops; Athens also suffered from extortionate re-
quisitions of grain.[8]

There could be no doubt that in 171 the Romans in the field had a
quite different attitude to the Greeks in general from that of earlier

Roman generals in the Balkans. But at Rome, many senators were receptive to Greek complaints; and in 170 they acted firmly when Chalcis continued to be ravaged by Lucretius' successor Lucius Hortensius. The Chalcidians had dramatized their situation by sending their crippled pro-Roman leader, Micythion, to Rome to complain about the activities of Lucretius and Hortensius; and their objections were well-received, for even before their return from Greece, Lucretius and Crassus had been attacked for their unnecessary brutality by tribunes of the plebs. In summer 170 the evidence against them began to pile up, as envoys from the offended Greek states flocked to Rome. Among them were the chief victims of Hortensius' campaign of 170, the people of Abdera. They, like the Chalcidians, were old friends of Rome; but this had not prevented them from being plundered or from seeing many of their leading men summarily executed or sold into slavery.[9]

It was clear that Rome would not for long retain the goodwill of her Greek friends if Roman commanders continued to encourage or allow their troops to behave in this ill-disciplined and uncivilized way; and so long as the war with Perseus continued, the Senate simply could not afford to offend the Greeks. For their support, even their neutrality, were important factors in Rome's favour. Already in Epirus Cephalus had joined Perseus in anticipation of Roman injustice; in Illyria, king Genthius was reputed to be mildly hostile to Rome, though he had not yet joined Perseus; and most Greek cities contained a group, sometimes quite large, of men who favoured Perseus and whose support would inevitably increase so long as Roman commanders acted like Crassus, Lucretius and Hortensius. Already the previous winter, when the Senate had drafted its decree of settlement for Coronea, which had been captured and abused by Crassus, it had checked the consul's short-sighted excesses by firmly asserting that those who had been Rome's friends at Coronea before Crassus' attack might retain their land, houses and other property. This stipulation probably meant not only that pro-Roman exiles from Coronea would get their property back, but also that Crassus would have to restore some, at least, of his loot. It was a sensible gesture to Greek public opinion, and a delicate reproach to Crassus, which partially saved the face of the high-ranking consul.[10]

There was not the same need—or possibility—to save the face of the praetors Lucretius and Hortensius. Hortensius was still in Greece, and he was firmly reprimanded for his activities at Abdera and Chalcis; he was also instructed to restore to freedom all Abderites

whom he had sold into slavery (though those whom he had irresponsibly executed obviously could not be brought back to life).
Lucretius was in Rome; and though the Senate tried to close ranks
and restrict the hearing of complaints against him to its own members, two tribunes of the plebs would not allow this apparently
obstructionist attitude to prevail, and accused Lucretius before the
Roman People. At his trial Lucretius was unanimously condemned
by all thirty-five tribes, and heavily fined the sum of one million
asses. Nor were these the only Roman actions of 170 which aimed
to impress upon its friends in Greece that Rome had their interests
at heart. When the Senate considered the fate of Thisbe, the Boeotian city which had surrendered to Lucretius, a complicated series
of issues was firmly settled in favour of the pro-Roman party at
Thisbe. Their chief gains were that they received control of the
city's public land (which Lucretius had confiscated for Rome);
and they were not only granted the exclusive right to hold magistracies at Thisbe for the next ten years, but were allowed to fortify
the city's acropolis and live there themselves, while the rest of the
city remained unfortified. The general pattern of the settlement was
similar to that already drawn up for Coronea; and its purpose was
clearly to strengthen the resolve of pro-Roman parties everywhere,
even where they were not in control of their communities (as they
had not been at Thisbe and Coronea). The Senate also relieved the
Greeks of the extortionate and haphazard exactions of supplies by
Roman commanders, of which many of them had complained, by
ruling that nobody should make any war contribution to any
Roman magistrate unless the Senate had explicitly authorized it.[11]

So in 170 the drama was all at Rome. In the Balkans the year
passed without the commanding consul, Aulus Hostilius Mancinus,
gaining any major advantage. Indeed, the Senate was so irritated by
the ineffective continuance of the war that it sent out two of its members to investigate what was happening: it will have caused little
surprise, after the activities of Crassus and Lucretius the previous
year, when they reported that poor discipline was the cause of the
Roman army's mediocre performance.[12] But by then the campaigning season was over, and nothing could be done but to replace
the commander. Before Hostilius was relieved, however, he showed
he had learnt something about the importance of conciliating Rome's
Greek friends from the way the Senate had treated the Greeks' complaints during the year. When he heard of the Senate's attitude, in
the autumn he sent Gaius Popillius Laenas (who had himself been an

undisciplined consul in 172, though not in the Balkans) and Gnaeus Octavius on a tour of central and southern Greece. Their job was to publicize the Senate's decision to stop the casual requisitioning of supplies by Roman commanders. It was essentially a public relations exercise, an attempt to undo some of the damage which the first two years of the war had done to the Roman image; for the longer the war lasted, the more important this became.

Their first stop was at Thebes in Boeotia. Here they simply encouraged the Thebans to remain loyal to Rome. This was straightforward enough. But when they went on to Achaea, their problem was more difficult, since Achaea contained a substantial party, led by Lycortas and Polybius, which (though it had once, under Philopoemen, advocated wholly independent action for Achaea) now saw Achaean interest lying wholly in benevolent neutrality. The Romans suspected Lycortas' party for its traditions as much as for its current lack of enthusiasm for Rome's cause—though some Achaean troops were fighting in the consul's army—and they let the news leak out that they intended to accuse Lycortas, Polybius and Archon, of being opponents of Rome. The leak itself was enough to keep Lycortas' party quiet; and in the event the Romans made no accusation and treated the Achaeans with all friendliness. But it was a discreet warning that neutrality, however benevolent, was no longer enough, that in some circumstances it might even be interpreted as actual hostility to Rome. Thoughtful Achaeans will doubtless have noticed the parallel between Lycortas' party and the five Aetolians who had already been summarily interned at Rome and with the neutralist Cephalus in Epirus, who under similar pressure had chosen to join Perseus.

When they reached Aetolia, Popillius and Octavius immediately became involved in the lingering civil war. For when they commended the friends of Rome, trouble at once broke out. They had initially asked for hostages, but they quickly dropped this request when rioting occurred, and made a hurried departure to neighbouring Acarnania. Aetolia was suffering yet again for its chronic instability. In Acarnania, Chremas, the leader of the pro-Roman party, asked for Roman garrisons to prevent the cities from going over to Perseus. But here the Romans accepted the view of the neutralist Diogenes, who argued that garrisons were for enemies, not for friends. In any case, Rome had no troops available for garrison duty in Acarnania, and it soon became clear that Chremas represented only a minority of the population.[13]

Despite this propaganda activity in the closing months, 170 was a bad year for Rome's war effort; and Perseus was encouraged by her failure to defeat him. He had strong hopes of attracting support from Genthius in Illyria, since Genthius had already incurred Roman hostility because of his Adriatic piracy. But Genthius, true to his freebooter origin and technique, demanded money; Perseus was reluctant to pay; and the negotiations came to nothing. At the end of the winter the new Roman commander, the consul Quintus Marcius Philippus, arrived; and the new campaign began without Perseus' winter diplomacy having achieved anything. Philippus was very experienced, and was one of the Senate's Balkan experts; he had already been consul as long ago as 186; and we have seen how he had 'negotiated' with Perseus before the present war began. Both his knowledge of the importance of Greek public opinion and pressure from the Senate ensured that his campaign was more active than those of his predecessors. But although he managed to take the offensive by invading Macedonia (with some difficulty), when the end of his year came he too had failed to bring Perseus to a decisive battle.[14]

Philippus had at least avoided a major defeat, had avoided giving the potentially disastrous impression to the Greeks that Rome was on the defensive. The Achaeans were soon impressed. Lycortas' party, which controlled the government at this time, was determined to prove groundless any suspicion of their loyalty. They therefore sent Polybius and some others to the consul, offering the whole Achaean levy. Philippus thanked them for the offer, though he rejected it since he already had sufficient troops. But it was clearly a welcome gesture; and Polybius stayed with the Roman army, in effect a voluntary hostage, while it invaded Macedonia. Philippus could have no serious doubt about the loyalty of the Achaean 'neutralists'.[15]

Although Philippus had not ended the war, by invading Macedonia he had brought the end significantly closer. Perseus could not now afford any long delay before he faced the Roman legions; and a battle fought in Macedonia was bound to be decisive if he lost. There can have been few who seriously doubted the ultimate outcome. But there were those who were sufficiently remote from the scene of action or too deeply entrenched in their traditional attitudes to realize that Perseus' end was already near. During the winter of 169/168 Perseus at last promised Genthius the money he had demanded, and Genthius, belatedly and ineffectually, joined the opponents of Rome. By this time the Rhodians had also been impressed by Rome's failure to defeat Perseus, even after three consular campaigns; and the pro-Macedonian party led by Polyaratus at last gained power. Thus when Perseus' envoys arrived at Rhodes during the winter, they had a friendly reception from Polyaratus and his friends, and were promised that Rhodes would try to open negotiations for peace. Even the usually hard-headed Eumenes of Pergamum toyed with the idea of a negotiated peace, and offered to represent Perseus' interests in negotiations if Perseus paid him 1,500 talents. Perseus was parsimonious and, hardly surprisingly, did not trust Eumenes; and the projected deal fell through. But to all three—Genthius, Rhodes and Eumenes—their belated flirtation with Perseus proved disastrous, in varying degrees, when the war was over and their secret dealings came to light.[16]

The speed with which the end came in 168 surprised everyone except the Roman commanders concerned. The praetor Lucius Anicius Gallus first destroyed Genthius' fleet, besieged him in Scodra, and received his surrender, all in the space of a month. The campaign was unique in Roman history in that its successful conclusion was announced at Rome before its beginning! So much for Genthius who, with his family and other leading Illyrians, was immediately shipped out to Rome, following the precedent set by Crassus in 171 when he had deported the five Aetolians. Had the Greeks had the time to realize it, this result was an ominous beginning to a crucial year.[17]

Meanwhile all attention was on Macedonia, where the new consul, Lucius Aemilius Paullus (a very distinguished man, who had already held a consulship in 182), arrived in the spring. His first efforts were directed towards improving the army's still lax discipline; and after this he began manoeuvring against Perseus, who now based his operations on his port of Pydna. By mid-June Paullus had encamped opposite him. The decisive battle was fought near Pydna (from which town it took its name) on June 22; and its result was an overwhelming victory for Paullus. Livy summarizes it thus: 'It is easily agreed that the Romans had never killed so many Macedonians in one set-piece battle, for some 20,000 men were killed, and some 6,000 who had taken refuge from the battlefield in the town of Pydna were taken prisoner, as well as another 5,000 whose flight was haphazard. The victors lost no more than 100 men killed, most of them being Paeligni [Italian allies]; rather more were wounded. If the battle had begun earlier in the day so that there had been daylight for a full pursuit, the whole Macedonian army would have been annihilated; but as it was, the approach of darkness both hid the refugees and made the Romans reluctant to pursue, since they did not know the ground.' Perseus himself was among those who escaped from the battlefield, but by the end of the year he had been induced to offer unconditional surrender to Paullus. The last king of Macedon thus placed his kingdom and his person at the free disposal of the Roman People.[18]

II The Settlement of Europe

The Senate had fought the war without compromise so that it could impose its final solution on the recurring Macedonian problem. For this reason its commanders had refused to negotiate and had refused any offer from Perseus except unconditional surrender. We have seen that this political ruthlessness was interpreted by many Roman commanders early in the war as being equally applicable to the whole of Greece. It was an interpretation which the Senate as a whole was not prepared to tolerate during the war itself, but once the fighting was over, the Senate's velvet glove could be removed: after Pydna the whole of Greece waited to discover whether it had clothed a mailed fist or the open hand of friendship.

Concerning the fate of Macedon and its monarchy there could be little real doubt. The only questions could concern details, not principles. Three times now Rome had fought wars with the Macedonian monarchy; for the first time the result had been unconditional surrender. The Senate now intended to take steps to ensure that no Macedonian king would cause Rome to fight a Fourth Macedonian War. When the Senate had digested the good news from Macedon and Illyria at the end of 168, it re-appointed the successful commanders, Paullus and Anicius, to their respective posts until the customary senatorial commissioners had arrived in the Balkans to discuss with them the details of the final settlements. But it also took the inevitable major policy decision, that the conquered territories were from now onwards to have non-monarchical constitutions—though the Senate was not yet prepared to undertake direct rule and to turn them into formal Roman provinces.[19] This was a momentous decision, momentous none the less for having been foreseeable from the beginning of the war. For it meant that the Senate was in practice abandoning its pretence of treating defeated enemies (at least in the Balkans) as individuals with rights and traditions which would normally be respected. From now on, Rome was not only the acknowledged mistress of the Mediterranean world, but she was also prepared to act the part. The war had been fought largely because the Senate was tired of argumentative and unco-operative opposition, which insisted on its legal rights to the exclusion of its moral obligations to Rome. The decision to abolish the Macedonian monarchy, to make a settlement, the effectiveness of which would no longer depend on an individual's interpretation of his moral obligation, was a major decision of principle which had far-reaching implications for every overseas state, whether friend, enemy or neutral. Rome was no longer prepared to argue and compromise: the Senate now intended to rule.

The Third Macedonian War and the decisive battle of Pydna which ended it therefore mark more than the end of Macedon as a major independent power: they mark also a decisive change, a turning point, in Rome's whole attitude to her numerous overseas clients and in the development of the empire.[20] Yet Rome still undertook no more direct formal supervision of the conquered areas. The Senate's experience with the two Spanish provinces, where it had been found necessary to wage major wars almost from their establishment in 197, made it extremely reluctant to form any new provinces, if there seemed to be a viable alternative. And in Macedon and Illyria all expedients were not yet exhausted. The Senate did, however, at last establish a direct financial interest in the administration of the defeated territories, for it decided that it would continue to collect the taxes which the kings had levied (though their rate was halved). Yet even this was no innovation in principle: the closest parallel is Sicily, where Rome had found a people accustomed to paying taxes and had simply continued to collect them. So in Macedon. The difference was that Sicily was closer to Italy and had also had some formal supervision by a Roman magistrate from the beginning.

The absence of direct Roman supervision of Macedon made it easier for the Senate to expect to be believed when the same decree revived the old propagandist chestnut that the defeated peoples— this time the Illyrians and Macedonians—were to be free (though, in fact, Cato's argument that Rome simply could not defend the Macedonians was probably the decisive motive). The Senate was, no doubt, serious as far as strict law was concerned. In the sense that it imposed no direct Roman rule, Macedonia and Illyria were free. But it made sure that they were so weak that no exploitation of their legal freedom might lead them to forget their moral obligations to Rome, as Perseus and Genthius had done. In Macedon the metal mines, the chief source of the monarchy's wealth, were closed down; Macedon itself was to be divided up into four self-governing republics which, when the details were worked out by the Senate's commissioners, were refused permission to co-operate economically, socially, or militarily. The intention of the new administrative structure, it seems clear, was not primarily to create viable political units, but rather to destroy the sense of Macedonian unity which the monarchy had created and which the kings had exploited. For similar reasons and in a similar way, Illyria was broken up into three parts.[21]

These principles of settlement constituted as ruthless a piece of political demolition as Rome had ever perpetrated. Its immediate precedent (though on a much smaller scale) seems to have been the dissolution of the Boeotian League by Marcius Philippus in 172— and Philippus, with his large experience of contemporary Greek affairs and as recent ex-consul, was doubtless prominent in the Senate during the discussions on the Macedonian and Illyrian settlement.[22] When the commissioners for Macedon arrived at Amphipolis, where Paullus had established his headquarters, they worked out the details of the settlement, including the boundaries of each of the four new Macedonian republics. The Senate's regulation regarding the mines they relaxed in order to allow the continued exploitation of iron and copper; but additional restrictions were announced on trade in salt, on the right to own landed property and to marry outside an individual's home republic, and on cutting timber for ship-building. The stranglehold on Macedonian unity which the Senate had decreed was thus drawn even tighter by these acts of its commissioners.[23]

The regulations for Macedon and Illyria were cruel, but they were comprehensible as the exercise of victor's rights over defeated enemies. But the Greeks also soon learned that, as far as they were concerned, Rome's hastily adopted velvet glove had indeed concealed a mailed fist, despite the enthusiasm for Greek culture which Aemilius Paullus showed when he played the tourist during the winter of 168/7 at the most famous classical sites in central and southern Greece.[24] Unfortunately for the Greeks, Paullus' cultural enthusiasm did not necessarily mean that they enjoyed Rome's political sympathy—particularly since the chief political decisions were taken at Rome, in Paullus' absence. The arrival of the commissioners bearing the Senate's instructions marked the beginning of the change. Yet even before their arrival, the pro-Roman party of Lyciscus and Tisippus in Aetolia had jumped the gun and carried out a massacre

of their political opponents, in which more than 500 leading Aetolians were killed and many more driven into exile with the loss of all
their property. Lyciscus and Tisippus fully expected to have Roman
approval for this bloody purge since Aulus Baebius, the Roman
garrison commander at Demetrias, allowed Roman soldiers to help
them. And they were not disappointed; for although Paullus postponed passing an opinion on the massacre until the commissioners
had arrived from Rome, thereafter, in full knowledge of the Senate's
new hard-line attitude towards Balkan affairs, he acquitted the per-
petrators of the massacre, confirmed the exile of those expelled,
and merely censured Baebius for having allowed Roman troops
to take part in it.[25]

This decision must clearly, in principle, have had the backing
of the Roman Senate; and in practice it amounted to the declaration
of a field day for Rome's partisans in the cities and states of Greece
to purge their opponents. Eagerly anticipating the Senate's rigorous
new attitude after Perseus' defeat, the leaders of the pro-Roman
parties throughout Greece had soon hurried to Amphipolis to
congratulate Paullus on his victory and to try to influence the
commissioners. From Achaea came Callicrates and some friends,
from Aetolia Lyciscus and Tisippus fresh from their successful
purge, from Boeotia Mnasippus, Chremas from Acarnania and the
scheming Charops from Epirus. The commissioners were impressed
at the unanimity of the advice they received from these leading
Romanophiles; and—no doubt again following the general precepts
of the Senate—they invited these partisans to provide them with
lists of 'unreliable elements' in each community, who were then
required to travel to Rome without trial.[26]

It was an invitation which few Greek politicians of any age could
have resisted: Polybius condemns Callicrates and Lyciscus in particular for having been responsible for many names—first and foremost, of course, 1,000 politically prominent Achaeans among whom
was Polybius himself—but there is room for doubting whether
Polybius' party would itself have acted much differently had the
roles been reversed. The result, however, was such wholesale in-
forming by the pro-Roman partisans that it amounted to a ruthless
political purge of their opponents, quite as drastic in its effects as
anything twentieth-century totalitarianism has perpetrated. Neutrals
and open opponents of Rome alike were listed, together with anyone who had obstructed or for any reason objected to the régimes
of the pro-Roman groups during their climb to power. It was in

Achaea that the full force of Rome's changed attitude was felt, for no evidence was ever found that any leading Achaean had actively sympathized with Perseus: the 1,000 Achaean deportees, most of them supporters of Lycortas and Polybius, were removed not for loving Macedon too much (which they had not done), but merely for loving Rome too little. Ten years before, Callicrates had been responsible for hardening Roman policy towards Greece: he now received his reward when, alone of the pro-Roman leaders, his purge of his Achaean opponents was supported by the presence of the two senior Roman commissioners.[27] There could be no doubting that Callicrates was Rome's Greek friend *par excellence*. Elsewhere, the lists provided by Rome's partisan friends were also accepted in full and without question; and the purge even spread to the Aegean and Asia Minor. At Amphipolis, two men, an Aetolian and a Theban, whom Paullus judged guilty of favouring Perseus, were executed on the spot.[28] But such summary execution was rare: Italian prison camps were both less objectionable morally and a more effective means of keeping control of the friends and relations of the detainees who were left behind.

After celebrating his success with a splendid festival at Amphipolis, Paullus had the plunder looted from Macedon loaded for transport to Rome. But he had not yet finished with the Balkans. The embarkation point for his army was Oricum, on the Adriatic coast; and to reach there from Amphipolis, the troops had to march through Macedon and Epirus. Parts of Epirus, under the unfortunate lead of Cephalus, had, as we have noticed, joined Perseus—though in practice, only some of Cephalus' own tribe, the Molossians, had actually done much against Rome. When Anicius settled Illyria, he had had little difficulty in forcing the surrender of Epirus, including the defecting cities of the Molossians. Cephalus and the few other Epirot leaders who had committed themselves and their peoples to Perseus were lucky to be killed in the little fighting there was, and they incidentally earned Polybius' praise for their honourable death in struggling for their principles.[29]

The settlement of Epirus, however, the Senate kept for Paullus. More particularly, it seems, it explicitly reserved the booty of the places which had opposed Rome for Paullus' army. In practice 'opposition' was widely interpreted—probably on the partisan advice of Charops—to include (at least) all the cities and communities of Cephalus' Molossians. The plundering was a fine example of Roman efficient organization: no less than seventy separate Molossian communities, which were adjudged to be Rome's opponents (though only four of them had offered serious resistance to Anicius), were looted on the same day; even the population was seized and 150,000 persons were sold into slavery. The brutality was excessive, and to some extent self-defeating: for since the markets were all flooded with goods and slaves, the soldiers may have received less for their plunder than they had expected.[30] It is difficult to find any justification for Paullus' barbarous interpretation of the Senate's decree granting him booty from Rome's opponents in Epirus. While at Amphipolis he and the commissioners had accepted the black-lists provided by their partisans of the 'unreliable elements' in each state. Epirus and neighbouring Acarnania were no exception to this, and from here also leading men, who survived the looting of the Molossians, were deported to Rome. Since Paullus must have taken Charops' advice about this general purge in Epirus, he probably also took it on the matter of the Molossian 'collaborators' with Perseus; and the prospect of large booty from the Molossians—doubtless exaggerated by Charops—would allow Paullus to indulge the plunder-lust of his troops while retaining for his triumph all the rich spoils of Macedon. If Charops was responsible for sowing this appalling idea in Paullus' mind, he well deserves Polybius' description of him as the most savage and crooked man of all time. Paullus, however, cannot escape responsibility simply by blaming Charops or by citing the Senate's decree, for even the most brutal order needs to be interpreted in detail by the man on the spot. This latter justification is emphasized by our sources; but we must remember that it will probably have begun with Polybius, whose good friend, Scipio Aemilianus, was Paullus' son![31]

From Oricum Paullus, accompanied by his army, his booty, and his gaggle of miserable Macedonian and Greek political prisoners, crossed back to Italy where in due course he celebrated the richest and most magnificent triumph Rome had ever witnessed—though not without some opposition from those who thought he had been insufficiently generous to his troops. The booty was so massive that the Senate was able to cancel the land-tax hitherto paid by the Roman People. Macedon's power was destroyed; Greece rested firmly in the hands of men who owed everything to Rome. The war and the settlement had changed the whole ethos of the relationship between Rome and her free clients overseas. After the battle of Pydna, there can have been few who seriously doubted that Rome had risen to world power.

PART IV

WORLD POWER

CHAPTER XVII

EUROPE AFTER PYDNA

I Macedon

AEMILIUS PAULLUS' settlement left Macedon shattered and broken. The monarchic system of government, which had made Macedon one of the most powerful nations of the Mediterranean world for nearly 200 years, was suddenly destroyed. Perseus, his family and his most important friends were taken to Italy to grace Paullus' triumph, to be interned, and to die. Macedon, which had been powerful through its unity, was irreparably damaged by Rome's insistence that it should no longer have any central government, and that each of its four new republics should, as far as possible, be economically, politically and socially separate. This was what Rome now meant by 'freedom', a concept which was clearly capable of being divorced in Roman practice from 'immunity' (freedom from taxation)—as it had long been in the Hellenistic kingdoms—since the Macedonians paid tax to Rome as they had to Perseus (though at a lower rate, since additional taxation for local matters would still be required). In this, at least, the Romans were influenced by long-established Hellenistic convention.

After drawing up these rules, Paullus and his army withdrew, as every Roman army which had ever crossed the Adriatic had withdrawn, and left the Balkan states, as before, to look after themselves within the administrative and constitutional framework which he and the commissioners had constructed. Unfortunately, we hear little of how the Macedonians adapted themselves to their new conditions; but what we do hear suggests that there were substantial difficulties. Macedon had, in historical times, always been ruled centrally by kings, and only its cities had had separate local administrations. Now each of the four new republics was expected to operate under the government of a representative council—we do not know how these were appointed—and it is perhaps not surprising that problems arose. In 163 Roman envoys who were being sent to

Syria were also instructed to investigate what was going on in Macedon. 'For,' says Polybius, 'the Macedonians were not used to their republican form of government by representative councils, and were in a state of civil war.'[1] Polybius does not explain further at this point, but a year later he mentions a certain Damasippus, 'who had assassinated the councillors at Phacus'—Phacus was the citadel of the old royal capital city, Pella, which was also the capital of one of the new republics—'and fled with his wife and children from Macedon'.[2] The reason for the disturbances is unknown, but it seems likely that Damasippus' exploit at Phacus was one of the incidents which the Roman envoys were instructed to investigate in 163.

In 158 permission was granted to the Macedonians to open the gold and silver mines, a dispensation which would help at least two of the four republics, although the Roman motive may have been purely economic, since Rome insisted on taking a share of the profits. But the two republics which had mines in their territory (numbers One and Two—the republics were never given other than numerical names) began to issue quite substantial numbers of silver coins which, apart from anything else, would facilitate the payment of their tribute to Rome.[3] However, we do not know whether the chief cause of the trouble in the 160's was economic. Certainly in the 150's, the re-opening of the mines did not end political troubles in Macedon, though again we have no details. In 151 Publius Cornelius Scipio Aemilianus, son of Aemilius Paullus and friend of Polybius, was specifically requested by the Macedonians to come to sort out their problems. His friendship with Polybius was doubtless well known, and he had in any case been in Macedon with his father in 168 and 167, and therefore knew the country. In the event he did not go; and since we hear of no replacement conciliators being sent out by the Senate, the details of the Macedonian trouble remain obscure. All we can be sure about from this incident is that there was still a good deal of internal discontent in Macedon.[4]

But the unrest in Macedon was not serious enough to trouble Rome very much at a time when Carthage had again begun to seem difficult and when Roman attention was primarily concentrated on Africa. Macedon was weak and would obviously remain so. Its internal squabbles were comparatively unimportant for Rome; for in essence the Roman settlement of Macedon in 167 seemed to have worked. Roman satisfaction with it and consequent lack of real interest in Macedonian affairs was largely responsible for the comic-opera series of events which again brought a Roman army to the Balkans and which, this time, ended in the Senate's deciding to keep a permanent eye on Macedon by making it a formal 'province' with a regular Roman governor responsible directly to the Senate in Rome.

The man who began this chain of events was one Andriscus, who first turned up in Syria among the mercenaries of king Demetrius I. When he started to pass himself off as Perseus' son Philip (hence earning the name Pseudo-Philippus from Greek contemporaries), to whom he bore a physical resemblance—but who had, in fact, died in Italy a couple of years after Perseus himself—Demetrius thought him not worth bothering about. But when Andriscus collected trouble-making supporters who began to agitate against Demetrius himself, Demetrius conveniently reminded himself that Rome might be interested in anyone claiming to be a son of Perseus, and accordingly shipped Andriscus out to Italy. The Senate was not much exercised by Andriscus, as it happened, and did not take him at all seriously; for although he was initially interned in Italy, the Senate did not act when he escaped and made his way to Miletus in Asia Minor. The Milesians, as Demetrius had been, were more alarmed at Andriscus' claim than the Romans were—particularly now that he was a refugee from Rome—and they in turn imprisoned him, only to have their fears taken lightheartedly by some Roman envoys who happened to be passing through Miletus, and who cavalierly suggested that Andriscus might as well be freed.[5]

This was a mistake, as it turned out, though it is difficult to blame the Romans for it, since they can have had no suspicion that Andriscus would find such support as would soon require the intervention of Roman legions to suppress him. Putting about a story that he had been brought up in Crete—Perseus had tried to escape to Crete—and that he possessed wax tablets which, he claimed, showed the exact hiding place of some of Perseus' concealed treasure at Amphipolis and Thessalonica, Andriscus made his way successfully through Asia Minor via Byzantium to Thrace, attracting support as he went. In Thrace Teres, one of the Thracian chiefs, had married a daughter of Philip V, and accordingly gave Andriscus a friendly reception; for whether or not Teres believed his claims, all Thracians had always been eager to encourage disturbances in neighbouring Macedon. Teres and others therefore gave him some troops with which he invaded Macedon, probably in 150. Since Aemilius Paullus' settlement had been more concerned to break up and weaken Macedon as a threat to Rome than to make it effective

as a buffer for the southern Balkans against its non-Greek neighbours
—though the three republics which had external borders were each
allowed to keep a small militia—Andriscus and his Thracians had
no difficulty in defeating the small forces raised against them.

Even then, when Macedon had effectively fallen to Andriscus—in
sharp contrast to the eagerness with which the Senate had decided
on war against Perseus twenty years before—the Senate merely
sent an envoy to investigate and to produce, if possible, a peaceful
solution. The man they sent was senior enough, Publius Cornelius
Scipio Nasica, who had already been censor and twice consul;
moreover, he was a son-in-law of Scipio Africanus and a relative by
marriage of Aemilius Paullus, with whom he had served during the
war against Perseus. But the fact remains that the Senate, with its
main attention focused on Africa, had not paid sufficient attention
to the implications of Andriscus' invasion of Macedon. Nasica found
that Andriscus had even penetrated into Thessaly; and though on his
own initiative he raised troops from Rome's Greek friends and
drove Andriscus back into Macedon, his report to the Senate made
it clear that only Roman troops could do the job properly.[6]

The Senate, despite its African preoccupation, now took his advice
and duly sent out a legion in 149 under the praetor Publius Juventius
Thalna. He, however, made the fatal mistake of under-estimating
Andriscus—whom he doubtless regarded, with customary Roman
arrogance, as an incompetent upstart—and paid for it with his life
and the loss of most of his troops. It was a serious defeat, for it gave
encouragement to Andriscus and those of his followers who were
prepared to rate his chances high. But the euphoria of the victory
did not last. A larger Roman army of two legions under the praetor
of 148, Marcus Caecilius Metellus, took care of that. Aided by a
Pergamene fleet, Metellus drove Andriscus to battle near the site of
Perseus' defeat at Pydna, and the rising was soon over. Andriscus
escaped to Thrace, but found little sympathy there among his disappointed allies, who delivered him to Metellus. Andriscus'
brief adventure, despite its trivial accomplishment, nevertheless
found its imitators: even during the war, one Alexander tried to
climb on the bandwaggon by claiming to be another 'lost' son of
Perseus, until he was chased into Dardania by Metellus' legions;[7]
and a few years later, in 143, yet another crank claimed, as Andriscus
had done, to be the long-dead Philip, son of Perseus, and he had to
be suppressed by the quaestor Lucius Tremellius.[8]

But these were unimportant matters. The war with Andriscus—

conventionally called the 'Fourth Macedonian War'—ended with
his defeat at Pydna. Metellus boasted about it by calling himself
'Macedonicus', though Paullus, who had defeated a real king, had
not bothered with such ostentation. Moreover, the limited 'freedom'
which Paullus had bestowed on Macedon also ended with Andriscus'
defeat. The Senate soon afterwards at last reached the decision,
which had long been looming, that Macedon was too important to
Rome to be left to the Macedonians. And thereafter a Roman governor was permanently resident. Illyria also seems to have come under
the surveillance of the governor of Macedonia, as the new province
was called.[9] It was not long before the Romans began to build that
major symbol of Roman administrative control and long-term interest, a trunk road through Illyria and Macedonia. This highway, the
via Egnatia, ran right across the Balkans from Apollonia and
Epidamnus to Thessalonica.[10]

II The Greeks

After Perseus' defeat at Pydna, the states and cities of Greece lay
firmly in the hand of Rome's friends. Any who seriously doubted the
wisdom of their policies had merely to look at the fate of the deportees to find their doubts stifled. There were, nevertheless, men remaining after the deportations who hated Callicrates and his fellow
pro-Roman partisans for what they regarded as supine acceptance of
Roman dictation. Polybius records that in 165, when the festival of
Antigoneia at Sicyon was being celebrated—the festival honoured
the Macedonian king Antigonus Doson, Perseus' great-uncle—many
bathers at the public baths refused to use the same bath-water as
Callicrates and his friend Andronidas. Yet despite their unpopularity
illustrated by this incident, the immediate reason for which was
resentment at the failure of an Achaean embassy to Rome to secure
a decision on the fate of the detainees,[11] the rule of Callicrates and
his party in Achaea was comparatively light.

Elsewhere in Greece, Rome's friends looked upon the Roman
evacuation as a signal for them to play the tyrant. The most notor-
ious of them was Charops in Epirus, who carried out such a reign
of terror that when he travelled to Rome to explain his activities,
Marcus Aemilius Lepidus the *pontifex maximus*, and Charops'
patron Aemilius Paullus—who had himself looted from the Molossians—refused to let him even enter their houses; and the Senate,

no doubt on their advice, sent some envoys to investigate. We do not know about their report; nor do we hear any more about Charops, apart from the fact that he was on his way to Rome again, perhaps in 158, when he died at Brundisium.[12] In Aetolia the civil war which Lyciscus had tried to settle in 168 by killing off 500 of his opponents with Roman help, seems to have simmered on even after the Romans' departure. It boiled over again, probably in 160, and this time Lyciscus was himself a victim, after which, says Polybius happily, 'affairs in Aetolia were in good order and the civil war died down'. The same beneficial effect he attributes to the deaths of Rome's friends Mnasippus in Boeotia and Chremas in Acarnania at about the same time, though we have no details by which we can check his inevitably rather biased judgment.[13]

It was Callicrates who, of all the leading pro-Roman politicians, lived the longest. And despite Polybius' attempt to tar him with the same brush as Charops, Lyciscus and the others, it seems clear that Callicrates' period of supremacy in Achaea was mild and peaceful by comparison; and that apart from those of his opponents who had fallen to the initial black-listing in 167, the Achaeans lived a more peaceful and prosperous life under Callicrates' guidance than they had under that of his opponents who had, quite unrealistically, wished to see Achaea as a world power with an independent foreign policy. Even to his remaining political opponents Callicrates seems to have been reasonably humane, though he got no thanks for it from the exiled Polybius. A series of Achaean embassies to Rome, beginning in 166, kept up a constant enquiry about Roman intentions regarding the detainees. Callicrates cannot have wanted these detainees to be released (by definition, they were his political opponents) and, had he wished, he could no doubt have prevented the embassies from setting out. But, adept politician that he was, he realized that there was no real chance of the Senate's agreeing to their release, and he preferred that the Senate should incur the odium of refusing the Achaeans' request rather than he himself—not that, even so, he escaped all odium, as the bath-water incident and the overall picture of his activities in the pages of Polybius illustrate.

Many of the detainees were already old men in 167, and by 160 a good number had died. Of those who survived into the 150's, the most distinguished by far was Polybius the historian, who took every chance of making friends among the Roman governing class, and in particular with Aemilius Paullus' son, Scipio Aemilianus. Their friendship became so close that it was partially as a result that the remaining Achaean (and probably other Greek) detainees were eventually repatriated in 150, after seventeen years of detention. By then, except for Polybius, they were politically unimportant at home; and Polybius' friendly attitude was personally vouched for by Scipio. Achaea had been comparatively peaceful in their absence, and there was no reason to think that the return of a few old men would now make any difference to this: as Marcus Cato succinctly put it, 'why are we wasting time discussing whether a few old Greeks should be buried by Greek or Italian undertakers ?'[14]

The question of the detainees was not the only matter which brought Achaeans to Rome in the years after Pydna. A smouldering dispute with Athens sent envoys from both states to Rome in 160 and 159. Athens, as a result of her staunch friendship for Rome—which, since Athens was militarily feeble and had no independent pretensions, had never been doubted by the Romans—had done well out of the post-Pydna settlement. It had received the once-Athenian islands of Lemnos and Delos (which latter was now to become a free port), and the territory of the ravaged Boeotian city Haliartus.[15] It was with Delos that trouble began, for the Athenians wished to put their own colonists on to the tiny island, and accordingly expelled many of the resident Delians to make room for them. A Delian appeal to Rome achieved nothing—though Demetrius, the priest of the temple of Sarapis, won his own private appeal against an arbitrary Athenian decision to close his temple[16]—and the refugee Delians evacuated the island and sought sanctuary in Achaea, where they were granted citizenship. Many of them immediately used their new citizenship to invoke the standing inter-state legal convention between Athens and Achaea to press suits for damages for dispossession. The Achaeans were sympathetic; the Athenians, not surprisingly, were hostile to the idea, and insisted that they would only accept a Roman ruling on whether the convention was applicable to the expelled Delians who, of course, had not been Achaean citizens when they were dispossessed. The Senate sat on the fence in this dispute between its two good Greek friends, stating only that 'the arrangements which the Achaeans had made for the Delians should stand'. We hear no more about the case, but it is difficult to believe that the Delians, eager for revenge, would be satisfied with this evasive reply.[17]

Another issue which affected relations between Athens and Achaea adversely was the Oropus affair. Possession of the border town of Oropus had traditionally been a bone of contention between

Boeotia and Athens; and when the Boeotian League was suppressed in 172, Athens seemed finally to have won this particular struggle. In 164, for some unknown reason, the Athenians sacked Oropus, whose refugee inhabitants in due course appealed to Rome. The Senate decided that the Athenians had been wrong, but referred the decision about damages to Sicyon, a member-city of the Achaean League. By the time the Sicyonians dealt with the case, the Delian affair must also have been well underway, with the result that when the Athenians did not put in an appearance at the hearings, the Sicyonians condemned them to the enormous fine of 500 talents. Athens again appealed to Rome, this time sending three of the most famous philosophers then resident in Athens, Carneades, Diogenes and Critolaus. They appeared before the Senate in 155 and, despite the boorish pride of Marcus Cato, who objected to all philosophers on principle and to these three in particular because of the enthusiastic reception they had had in Rome for their public lectures, they persuaded the Senate to reduce the fine to 100 talents. By this time it was ten years since the original sack of Oropus, and the Athenians were now determined not to pay even this reduced fine; and in due course they managed to reach an agreement of some kind with the Oropians. But in 151 another dispute broke out in which the Oropians were again ravaged by the Athenians, and an Achaean army arrived too late to stop the destruction, though it apparently managed to restore and rehabilitate some, at least, of the plundered Oropians. As with the case of Delos, we hear no more about this affair. But the two incidents make a fair illustration of how a highly civilized city-state such as Athens could act as brutally and unconcernedly as a Charops towards those placed under its control by the Roman settlement; and both cases show the Achaeans, despite being governed by the party of Callicrates, whose harshness Polybius' personal fate caused him to inveigh against, apparently taking the humanitarian part of the victims of Athenian aggression.[18]

III The Achaean War

In 149 Callicrates died while travelling to Rome.[19] His career had been long: it was thirty years since he had first appeared at Rome to explain to the Senate his vision of the future, almost twenty since the purges after Pydna had left the main lines of his policy unchallenged. He had indulged his political and humanitarian instincts in allowing frequent embassies to Rome about the detainees, and in the (to Rome unimportant) affairs of Delos and Oropus; but as recently as 153 he had persuaded the Achaeans not to risk the Senate's displeasure when the League's council expressed an inclination to help Rhodes in a war which she was currently fighting in Crete.[20] In Callicrates' well-proven political philosophy, the only wars which the Achaeans could safely involve themselves in were either trivial ones (as over Oropus) or those fought with Roman approval or under Roman standards (as against Andriscus). His philosophy was not spectacular, but it worked and was proved to be safe.

Unfortunately for Achaea, it died along with its chief exponent. Callicrates' reason for undertaking the arduous journey to Rome in 149 was primarily that another dispute—after nearly thirty years of peace—had broken out between the League and Sparta, and Callicrates perhaps wished to use his influence to persuade the Senate to let the Achaeans settle it themselves. He may also have wished to assure Rome of Achaean loyalty now that another war with Macedon could be forecast. But his sudden death left the direction of Achaean affairs in the hands of men who were too young to have lived through the troubles of Philopoemen's time, and who therefore did not fully understand (as Callicrates did) the real attitude of the Roman Senate towards Achaea and the reasons for Callicrates' cautious policies. Such a man was Diaeus, who was travelling to Rome with Callicrates on his fatal journey; he was the son of that Diophanes who had opposed Philopoemen in the 180's and had paved the way for Callicrates. But the father's caution had not been inherited by the son, and Diaeus immediately on his return misrepresented the Senate's decision—that it would send envoys to investigate—and gave the Achaeans the misleading impression that the Spartan affair had been wholly left to Achaean discretion.[21]

Menalcidas, on the other hand, who had represented the Spartans at Rome, told them on his return to Sparta that they had been freed from the League. And in this he seems to have had advance knowledge of how the Senate was actually thinking, for when, late in 148 or early in 147, Lucius Aurelius Orestes arrived in Achaea to try to settle the dispute, he met representatives of all the Achaean communities at Corinth and declared that the Senate had decided that not only Sparta but Corinth and two other towns should no longer be members of the League.[22] But events in Achaea and the attitudes which developed from them had outrun the Senate's slow deliberations; for 148 had witnessed open warfare between the League's troops and Sparta, despite the intervention of Roman envoys on their way to Asia whom Metellus in Macedonia persuaded to visit Achaea.[23]

Thus when Orestes made his announcement, Achaean feelings about Sparta were already running high; and the Corinthians not only showed no inclination to be separated from the League, but even promoted (so they thought) the League's cause by arresting all Spartans whom they could find in their city. The Senate's delayed decision was clearly a miscalculation, and it may have been partly due to the death of Callicrates, for there Rome as well as Achaea had lost a good friend, whose sensible advice over the past thirty years had prevented many mistakes on both sides. No doubt seeing capitulation to Spartan requests for independence from the League as the easiest way out of the Achaean tangle, and reminded of how little trouble there had been with Boeotia since the League was split up in 172, the Senate seems to have determined to try the same solution in part in Achaea. But in Achaea it did not work so easily, for there only Sparta wanted separation. Orestes returned to Rome, having failed to achieve his purpose and with a hostile report to deliver.

Relations between the League and Rome now deteriorated still further. Another group of Roman envoys late in 147 indicated that the Senate had dropped its decision about the separation of the four cities and tried to be conciliatory. But Critolaus, who was then chief magistrate of the League, seems to have been determined to have a violent confrontation, perhaps thinking that since Rome was currently committed to wars both in Africa and in Spain she would not trouble to intervene to prevent the Achaeans from dealing with Sparta. He might have been right had he treated the Roman conciliators with any respect. But his obstructionist tactics made his motives immediately suspect; and when he persuaded the Achaeans to declare war on Sparta as soon as the Romans had left, their decision was tantamount to declaring war also on Rome.[24]

If Critolaus realized this (and he seems to have), he was not perturbed by it, for he spent the winter propagandizing both in Achaea and in central Greece, where the Theban Pytheas, calling himself 'Boeotarch'—the title held by the chief magistrates of the long-suppressed Boeotian League—promised him support, for Thebes too had recently felt the rough edge of Roman arbitration when Metellus had tried to censure Thebes for various acts of authoritarian brutality recently committed. No Greek state in 147 could refuse Roman arbitration and hope to get away with it. After

Pydna, Rome regarded herself as patron of the whole Mediterranean world, and all states as her clients, with the consequent moral obligation to do her bidding and to accept her arbitration. And by 147 Rome was prepared to punish violations of this moral obligation with force if necessary.

The rebels never stood a chance; and Polybius who, as a contemporary of the events and long-time student of Roman affairs, fully recognized this, condemns them for a madness which might have destroyed the whole of Greece.[25] But it was a madness which, to us at this distance, is at least partially comprehensible: for the new generation of politicians had been brought up under the protective shadow of Callicrates, safe in the peace he had won; and after his death there was nobody left who had both his prestige in Achaea and his sensible understanding of Roman attitudes. The recently returned exiles were regarded as exhausted and out of touch; Callicrates' close friend Andronidas (and some others who, like Callicrates, understood Rome) had not been politically prominent, and thus after Callicrates' death had not the ear of the people; Diaeus, Callicrates' protégé, had the ear of the people but had not yet developed a satisfactory understanding of Rome. There was thus nobody who had the necessary combination of qualities to prevent the moral obligations of the client-patron relationship from being once again misunderstood, this time disastrously.

First Metellus, moving in from Macedonia, then the consul of 146, Lucius Mummius, defeated the small emergency forces which the Achaeans and their rebel allies raised. Critolaus was soon killed; Diaeus fled and committed suicide.[26] The war was over almost as soon as it had begun (though that did not prevent Mummius from claiming—and getting—a triumph for his trivial victory over misled clients). In Achaea the bonds of *clientela* had proved insufficient, after the death of the one man who both understood them and had the influence to put them into effect, to keep the Achaean League true to the kind of loyalty which, after Pydna, the Roman Senate expected. In the wake of the defeat of Critolaus and Diaeus, Corinth was ravaged and looted by the Roman and Pergamene troops —by an ironic accident these latter were commanded by a general called Philopoemen—and the property of the leaders of the rising was sold off. As after the defeat of Perseus, famous works of art, indiscriminately collected by the troops, were battered and broken en route to Rome. 'Old Masters' were even used as draught-boards. The lesson of the devastation was clear: the Achaean League was now a defeated enemy and, after Pydna, defeated enemies deserved little consideration.

It was, in the end, partly due to Polybius' influence at Rome that some of the statues, decorations, and works of art from other places in the Peloponnese were saved the fate of those at Corinth—particularly representations of the two most famous politicians of the League, Aratus and Philopoemen, and of the Achaean mythological hero Achaeus.[27] For the ten senators sent out late in 146 as commissioners to draw up the settlement after the war knew Polybius personally and were prepared to humour him in such (to them) trivial matters. But it was not just to please Polybius that the commissioners had troubled to travel from Rome: they had important work to do. Greece was not yet turned into a Roman province, as Macedon was. It simply was not sufficiently important to merit a Roman governor of its own. But all remaining Leagues throughout Greece—the chief one being, of course, the Achaean—were now suppressed (though some were revived soon afterwards as convenient administrative units); and those places which had been particularly active in the 'Achaean War' were placed formally under the surveillance of the governor of Macedonia. Other cities and states were left 'free', though as we have seen in the case of the four 'free' Macedonian republics after Pydna, this no longer necessarily meant that such states were immune from taxation. There were, of course, some especially privileged communities which were both 'free' and 'immune'—Sparta, for instance, was one—but our information after 146 is so slight that a complete list cannot be compiled. It seems that in Achaea Polybius acted as some kind of semi-official mediator in the details of the new Roman settlement, and won approval both from the Romans and from the Achaeans for his statesmanship in so doing. But the details are again uncertain.[28]

What is clear from all this is that nowhere in the Balkans could there now be the slightest pretence that any Greek community was independent, in any real sense of the word which had been known until then. 'Freedom' (*libertas*) now meant freedom to control internal affairs so long as this was done in a way that did not bother Rome; it did not mean freedom to have an independent foreign policy; nor did it mean freedom from taxation, unless such a privilege (*immunitas*) was explicitly granted. It had taken a foolish and bitter war to instil this knowledge; but none could now fail to understand *clientela*. Yet by now the Senate too had learned from its experience, that *clientela* alone was an insufficient mechanism for controlling the Greeks, and that the detailed stipulations of what it required had to be spelled out to the legalistic Greeks in every case. Greece as a whole had descended to the status, now that it too had suffered military defeat, which Macedon had reached after Pydna, which Aetolia had reached as long ago as 189. In Greece as a whole, the 'Achaean War' marks the point at which Rome finally and unambiguously decided to rule.

CHAPTER XVIII
ASIA AFTER PYDNA

I Pergamum

IN Asia, as in Europe, Perseus' defeat at Pydna was a decisive event, for the change in Rome's attitude which it brought about was felt not only in the Balkans but wherever Roman influence prevailed. The war had begun when it did, as we have seen, because of the complaints of Rome's most faithful friend in Asia Minor, king Eumenes of Pergamum. And in the course of the war Pergamene troops and a Pergamene fleet worked in close conjunction with the Roman commanders. Yet by the end of the war the Senate's attitude to Eumenes had ceased to be friendly, to the extent that some Romans even encouraged his brother Attalus to consider supplanting Eumenes with Roman support; and when Eumenes came to Italy in person to try to heal the breach, the Senate refused even to allow him to remain on Italian soil.

The reason for the sudden breach seems to have been that news soon leaked out after the war that in 169 Eumenes had secretly negotiated with Perseus. It was alleged that he had offered either to withdraw his forces from the Roman alliance (which he may have had to do anyway if the war had continued beyond 168, since Pergamum was again having trouble with its Galatian neighbours in Asia Minor), or to try to mediate a peace, if Perseus paid him 500 or 1,500 talents respectively. Eumenes' motives are obscure—so obscure, indeed, that many modern scholars have regarded the whole thing as a later invention to justify Rome's subsequent treatment of Eumenes, though Polybius had talked to some of Perseus' friends and felt compelled to believe in the negotiations, despite his own initial doubts; and we should probably follow him in his belief.[1] Eumenes cannot, as Polybius points out, have wanted a victory for Perseus. But, it seems, he may have over-estimated his influence at Rome if he thought the Senate would accept his good offices as negotiator now that the war was in progress. If he was in a position of having to withdraw his troops soon in any case because of the Galatians, he might well have relished the idea of making Perseus pay him for doing so! But whatever his reason, it is difficult to believe that he was being deliberately disloyal to Rome, for his kingdom had been largely made what it was through Roman aid and favour, and he had always seemed to recognize this.

Yet the Roman interpretation of his secret contact with Perseus in the middle of the war could hardly be favourable to Eumenes. A Roman client's duty was to aid his patron unquestioningly—as Eumenes had hitherto seemed to know very well—not to undertake secret negotiations with the enemy and try to take personal profit from Rome's discomfiture. Nor was it even appropriate for him to offer mediation—particularly in this war for which Rome wanted no mediator, since its whole purpose was to destroy the enemy beyond the point of recovery. When a leading ally is found in secret and possibly profitable contact with the enemy, the fact can lead to only one *prima facie* interpretation, that the contact is treasonable to the alliance. And although nothing came of these secret negotiations, and Eumenes neither withdrew his military support from the Romans nor made any suggestion that they should negotiate with Perseus, the fact that he seemed to have thought of both of these things and had hoped to obtain payment for it was sufficient, in Roman eyes, to brand him—despite his loyal past—as unreliable and a potential troublemaker.[2]

Thus when Eumenes' brother Attalus, who was personally well-known to and well-liked by many Romans, came to Rome in winter 168/7 on Eumenes' behalf, to congratulate the Senate on their victory and to explain about the Galatian unrest, on the purely personal level he met an extremely favourable reception. Many senators urged him—as they had apparently in the 180's urged Philip's son Demetrius—to think of the throne for himself; and although Attalus seems to have toyed with the idea, representatives from Eumenes, who argued that to divide the kingdom's internal loyalties would simply weaken it in the face of the Galatians, persuaded him not to go ahead with the Senate's suggestion. So, like Flamininus' scheme with Demetrius of Macedon, the Senate's second attempt to supplant a reigning king whom they regarded as unreliable with a nominee of their own whom they liked and encouraged, failed completely. Aenus and Maronea, those two long-standing bones of contention between Pergamum and Macedon, were again formally declared free, no doubt this time chiefly as an indication to Attalus that the Senate was annoyed at his unwillingness to co-operate with Rome against his brother.[3]

The next winter (167/6) saw a further deterioration in relations with Eumenes. During 167 Eumenes' hostile neighbour, king Prusias II of Bithynia, had himself travelled to Rome to congratulate the Senate on Rome's victory over Perseus, and had received an extremely warm reception. Shortly after this, news reached Rome that Eumenes himself was on the way. The Senate had nothing to say to Eumenes, and did not want to listen to him. Accordingly, it passed a decree that no king should himself address the Senate. As Polybius points out, this general order had in fact the specific purpose of stopping Eumenes; and it was duly presented to him by a quaestor when he reached Brundisium. The contrast with the reception of his opponent Prusias a short while before could not have been more insultingly emphasized, and Eumenes had no alternative but to return to Pergamum.[4]

By severing its good relations with Eumenes (and with Rhodes, as we shall soon see) the Senate was in effect admitting that the policy which it had followed in Asia Minor up to this time, of relying on the loyalty of the two most powerful states, Pergamum and Rhodes, had failed, and that the time had come, now that Macedon was defeated, for a more direct show of Roman interest in Asia Minor. The power of Pergamum had been built up by Rome's dispensation: the Senate now presented itself with the problem of how to dismantle it, while at the same time not involving Rome in direct administrative responsibilities; for it was still unwilling to undertake territorial supervision even of the much closer Balkans. Again, however, an old-established political pattern was to hand, taken from Rome's Balkan experience: the establishment of a balance of power. In the Balkans after 196 Rome had not allowed any single state—not even the Achaean League—to attain the kind of predominance in its own area which Eumenes had established in Asia Minor after Magnesia. Each state, however friendly, had been checked from becoming too powerful by Rome's maintaining another state whose interests conflicted: in central Greece the Aetolian League had been balanced against defeated Macedon; in the Peloponnese Sparta had balanced the Achaean League. In most of Asia Minor Eumenes, until the war with Perseus, had been, in effect, Rome's viceroy; there had been no power to counterbalance him, for Rhodian interests were complementary rather than conflicting.

The Senate now began to encourage other Asian powers to become strong enough to trouble Eumenes—though not so strong, of course, as to trouble Rome! Prusias' friendly reception in 167, sharply contrasting with Eumenes' blunt rebuff, was the first stage in the process. The Galatians—also lukewarm clients of Rome after their defeat by Manlius Vulso in 189—could serve as an appropriate power bloc to the east of Pergamum; within the kingdom itself, Attalus might yet respond to the Senate's invitation, and he might still be assured of the Senate's support if he stirred up his lethargic dynastic ambitions.

Eumenes' Galatian trouble was in fact rapidly quelled by a battle which he fought for himself, though the terms of the settlement after it were dictated by Rome. By them Eumenes was effectively prevented from benefiting from his victory, since Rome allowed the Galatians to keep their autonomy, as long as they remained peaceful.[5] Prusias was also an immensely useful agent for Rome, since he immediately began to accuse Eumenes of continuing to interfere in 'autonomous' Galatia; and hints were even dropped that Eumenes was building up an alliance with the Seleucid king, Antiochus IV of Syria, against the interests of Rome.[6] This was just the sort of thing the Senate wanted to hear, for it was unlikely to be dangerous to Rome—Antiochus was also a Roman client—and it gave an excuse for the Senate's retaining an interest in Pergamum's internal affairs: and although Eumenes' brothers, Attalus and Athenaeus, had a friendly reception at Rome in 165/4, the Senate remained suspicious of Eumenes and even sent out an ex-consul, Gaius Sulpicius Galus, in 163 to investigate the affairs of Pergamum. Galus' interpretation of his instructions—for which he doubtless had senatorial approval in principle—was to go to Sardis and invite all comers, however disreputable, to make complaints, however scurrilous and unfounded, against Eumenes.[7] It was a procedure highly reminiscent of that of the Roman envoys who in 185 at Tempe had similarly invited complaints against Philip V of Macedon. Unfortunately, we do not hear the result of this session at Sardis. But there can be no doubt that, whatever the detailed complaints and decisions, Galus' mission served to broadcast in Asia Minor the continuing disfavour with which Rome viewed Eumenes. Yet it may not have had altogether the desired effect, since Polybius mentions that the Greeks of Asia Minor actually became rather better-disposed towards Eumenes. And their reason is not far to seek, for they will naturally have regarded him as their only real defender against the barbarians, both the Galatians and the Romans.[8]

Eumenes died in 159 or 158, without ever restoring his good relations with Rome. He was succeeded by his brother Attalus. The Senate could now afford to relax its attitude towards Pergamum for, although it had not been in any way responsible for Attalus' succession, it could hardly disapprove of it, since it had continued to encourage Attalus' aspirations even while Eumenes was alive. Attalus, through his frequent visits to Rome and his friendship with leading senators, understood what Rome wanted from a client, and was apparently prepared to comply. An interesting document has survived from his early years which nicely illustrates his developing attitude to Rome. We have noticed that the Senate had encouraged and preserved the Galatians to form a balance of power with Pergamum. Eumenes obviously could not afford to simply ignore this development, and one of his ways of keeping in touch with Galatian affairs was through Attis, the high-priest of Cybele at Pessinus, a Phrygian temple state with which Pergamum had long maintained good relations. Attis was a Galatian, and at this time seems to have acted almost as a Pergamene agent, thus adding some substance to Prusias' allegations of Eumenes' interference in Galatia. When Eumenes died he was apparently contemplating more vigorous action in Galatia, for which he had been negotiating with Attis. This situation Attalus inherited. He soon wrote a letter to Attis, which a fortunate accident has preserved, in which he explained his attitude to Eumenes' project: that after due consideration, he had been persuaded by his council of state—particularly by one Chlorus, who unfortunately is not otherwise known—that Rome was bound to be interested in any Pergamene military operations in Galatia, and therefore should be constantly consulted before any action was taken to support Attis.[9]

This was a recognition of the political facts of life which would have done credit to Callicrates of Achaea; and Attalus could thank Chlorus (and his own good sense in taking his advice) for preventing him from continuing with Eumenes' planned adventure into Galatia, which would certainly have incurred Roman suspicion and quickly made the Senate regard Attalus also as 'unreliable'. Attalus reaped immediate benefits from his decision. When in 156 Prusias attacked Pergamum, doubtless relying on Rome's favour towards him and recent hostility towards Pergamum, the Senate, once it had ascertained the facts, had no hesitation about interfering diplomatically to stop Prusias' aggression; and a stream of Roman envoys passed between Rome and Asia Minor on this issue until in 154

Prusias was forced to accept the terms proposed by the Romans, that he make restitution to Attalus and to damaged Greek cities for the trouble he had caused.[10] The episode was a salutary lesson to both kings that it was advisable to keep on the right side of Rome: Prusias learned the hard way that Rome's favour was strictly limited, and that it certainly did not include supporting him in an aggressive war which, if successful, might upset the whole balance of power in Asia Minor. It was Prusias' turn to learn the moral obligation required of a Roman client, as so many states and kings had learned before him. Attalus was thus made gratifyingly aware of the benefits which might accrue from dutiful acceptance of the principle of clientship, which his adviser Chlorus had so accurately spelled out for him in connection with the projected Galatian activities.

Attalus remained for the rest of his life true to this principle and therefore a good friend of Rome. This does not mean that he did nothing on his own initiative, that he was a complete puppet of Rome, as some have thought. But it does mean that he consulted Roman interests in what he did do. If in 149 he went further than a good client should in encouraging and helping Prusias' son Nicomedes to overthrow his father, his personal interest could be cloaked by the argument that Nicomedes had already won favour at Rome and seemed to be the 'Roman candidate' for the Bithynian throne, just as Attalus himself had once been the 'Roman candidate' for the Pergamene throne. And in due course Nicomedes was indeed recognized as king of Bithynia by the Senate.[11] Thereafter Attalus contributed a fleet to Metellus for the war against Andriscus and troops for the 'Achaean War', some of the spoils from which duly found their way to the loyally receptive coffers of Pergamum.[12] So, when in 138 Attalus died and was succeeded by his nephew, Eumenes' son Attalus III, Pergamum had for twenty years acted as a loyal client of Rome within the broader framework of the balance of power in Asia Minor erected by the Roman Senate after the battle of Pydna.

The last of the kings of Pergamum is briefly summed up by Strabo thus: 'Attalus, named Philometor, was king for five years, died of disease, and left the Romans his heirs.'[13] In his brief reign Attalus III achieved the dubious reputation of being both a crank and a tyrant: he was deeply interested in his herb garden and tested the medicines he manufactured on condemned criminals—some of them apparently worked well! But a persistent tradition also regards him as cruel and bloody in his political life. It is nevertheless the last of Strabo's details which chiefly concerns us. We do not know exactly why Attalus III bequeathed his treasure and his kingdom to Rome, though there was precedent for it in 155, when Ptolemy VII Physcon, then restricted to Cyrene by internal Egyptian dynastic machinations, made a will in favour of Rome if he had no children. His purpose was to gain Rome's favour and to secure himself from personal attack by his brother, Ptolemy VI, who wanted Cyrene.[14] Ptolemy Physcon's will was never executed because he recovered Egypt and had children. But Attalus III of Pergamum had no children; and the persistent rumours about political purges, and the civil war which broke out immediately after his death, both suggest that Attalus, like Ptolemy Physcon, might have viewed his will as the surest way of retaining Roman support and of discouraging a palace revolution.

Attalus' death in 133, after a mere five years of rule, suddenly raised for Rome the whole question of the Senate's foreign policy towards Asia Minor. Attalus' will had been made in Rome's favour: would the Senate simply use the opportunity to continue its recent practice and appoint a suitable candidate for the throne, or would it see fit to turn Pergamum into a formally administered province, as it had recently done with Macedon and with Africa? As it happened, the decision was not taken on purely foreign-policy considerations, for the news of Attalus' death arrived at Rome in the middle of a political and constitutional crisis. The young tribune of the plebs, Tiberius Gracchus, had just passed a new land law, and he needed funds to make it work—funds which he had every reason to believe the Senate would not make available from normal sources. The news of Attalus' death was thus a god-sent opportunity and, pre-empting the Senate's traditional claim to decide all matters of finance and foreign policy, Tiberius persuaded the People to accept Attalus' will. His reason was purely financial, but the effect of his action was, of course, strategic. Although Tiberius was killed in a riot later in the year, the decision which he had stimulated stood. Given time, the Senate might have itself reached the same decision, for there is no sign that its determination wavered during the difficult war and settlement which followed. But what is most significant for our theme is that Rome had now taken the decision, even if thrust upon her by a weak king and a vigorous tribune, to undertake direct control of a province in Asia Minor.[15]

II Rhodes

Pergamum was not the only Asiatic state which was misled by the length of time Rome took to deal with Perseus, into thinking that Rome was in serious difficulties. Rhodes made the same mistake, and it had equally serious results. We have already seen that Rhodes had found difficulty in maintaining control over Lycia and Caria, which it thought had been granted as a gift by Rome in 188. The terms on which the grant was made had been quickly disputed; and this dispute, coupled with Rhodes' providing of transport for Perseus' Seleucid wife Laodice in 178, had affected the smoothness of Rhodes' relationship with Rome; this in turn had favoured the development of a group at Rhodes, led by Deinon and Polyaratus, who began to look to Perseus rather than to Rome for outside friendship.[16]

Until 169, however, the pro-Roman group led by Hagesilochus had managed to retain control of affairs, had apparently satisfied the Roman envoys who visited the island in 172, and in 171 obeyed the request of the praetor Gaius Lucretius for a few ships.[17] But as the war dragged on, and its end was not in sight by the winter of 170/169, Deinon and Polyaratus began to attract a much larger popular support. The internal situation may also have been aggravated by the disruption of Rhodes' traditional grain trade with Egypt through the current war which was going on in Egypt between Antiochus IV and Ptolemy VI. Hagesilochus and his party therefore in 169 decided to send envoys both to Rome and to the new consul Quintus Marcius Philippus in the Balkans, to assure the Romans of the constancy of Rhodian support and to ask the Senate for permission to import grain from Sicily to replace the Egyptian grain not currently available. Hagesilochus himself led the envoys to Rome, where he received a most friendly welcome and was given the permission he sought to import Sicilian grain.[18]

But it was the embassy to Philippus, led by Agepolis, which had the greatest effect at Rhodes, for its mission was much more quickly accomplished than Hegesilochus'. Agepolis was greeted with the utmost cordiality by Philippus—Rhodes was far too important to offend in the middle of a major war—when he explained the Rhodians' current difficulties, no doubt emphasizing the disruption which the Egyptian war had caused; and Philippus even took Agepolis aside and suggested that it would be appropriate if Rhodes offered to mediate in 'the current war'. When this suggestion was disclosed on

Agepolis' return to Rhodes, Deinon and Polyaratus chose to interpret it as a confession of Roman weakness in the war with Perseus—
whereas, in fact, Philippus almost certainly meant by 'the current
war' the war in Egypt between Antiochus and Ptolemy; and by
suggesting Rhodian intervention he hoped merely to be able to avoid
the necessity of Roman diplomatic action which, before the final
defeat of Perseus, might prove embarrassingly ineffective.[19] But
Philippus' suggestion had put mediation in the air at Rhodes, and
Deinon and Polyaratus both had larger things in mind than mediation
in Egypt (though Rhodian diplomatists were duly sent there): they
thought of nothing less than saving Perseus by mediating between
him and Rome! And not only did they think of this but, by insisting
that Philippus' suggestion to Agepolis was a tacit confession of
Roman weakness, they even managed to swing the balance of
Rhodian public opinion on to their side and persuaded the Rhodians
to try their policy. Thus when Perseus and Genthius sent representatives to Rhodes during winter 169/8, they had a very friendly reception and received the assurance that Rhodes intended to dispatch
mediators to Rome and to the Roman commander in the field. The
mission to Rome was led by Agepolis and it set out in spring 168.[20]

The project would have been wrong-headed at the best of times: a
client state had no right to offer arbitration to its patron, and as a
result of the Lycian affair, Rhodes was already suspected of not being
fully aware of the moral obligations of its clientship. But in 168 of all
years, when Perseus had already been driven back into Macedon and
when Aemilius Paullus was to defeat him by the middle of June, it
was nothing less than crazy. The Rhodian envoys to Aemilius Paullus
were told brusquely that Paullus fully expected the war to be over in
a couple of weeks, and they could wait until then for their answer.[21]
But the culmination of the tragic farce came at Rome. For by the
time the Senate was ready to receive the Rhodians, the news of
Pydna had already arrived, so that Agepolis had to abandon his
prepared speech and content himself with tamely saying that,
although they had come to mediate, they were glad that the war was
over and congratulated Rome on her success. The Senate, however,
was not satisfied with this, and made it perfectly clear that it knew
quite well that Rhodes had latterly favoured Perseus and had decided
on mediation simply because it was the most suitable way of helping
Perseus. The envoys were then dismissed, without knowing whether
or not the Senate intended that Rhodes should now be treated, like
Genthius, as an ally of Perseus and open enemy of Rome.[22]

The doleful return of Agepolis to a depressed Rhodes marked the end of the brief predominance of Deinon and Polyaratus who, after desperately trying to escape, in due course joined their fellow 'unreliable elements' from the rest of Greece in Italian internment camps.[23] But the Rhodians were nevertheless made to pay for their belated foolishness in trusting these men, for even Rome's friends in Rhodes during the years of peace had not been over-assiduous in fulfilling their moral obligations as clients. After the return of Agepolis, two more embassies were frantically sent off to Rome in quick succession. While they were there, during winter 168/7, a group in the Senate, largely consisting of men with eastern experience who knew Rhodes' great prestige in the Greek world—and perhaps including the devious Quintus Marcius Philippus—was firmly in favour of demolishing the power and prestige of Rhodes through war, as Paullus had demolished Perseus and Anicius had destroyed Genthius. Their irresponsible urge for war was soon stopped by Cato, who pointed out that Rhodes had not actually *done* anything against Rome's interests, but had only thought about doing it; and it was a bad legal principle to punish somebody for just thinking about possible action.[24]

But the danger had been close, and the Rhodians' envoys were pleased enough to be able to report home that they had avoided war. Having crossed that hurdle, the Rhodians determined to indicate the sincerity of their regard for Rome by asking for an alliance—which they had not so far had, preferring, as Rome did also, to remain free friends. But the time had come, it seemed, when a firm written statement of the conditions of the relationship was indispensable; and to make the point very firmly, Rhodes' senior statesman, the eighty-year-old Theaedetus, was sent to Rome with a large gift. But the Senate still refused to be impressed. It apparently distrusted the Rhodians even when bearing gifts; and it did not soften its attitude when Theaedetus died while still in Rome waiting for a reply to his request.[25] Indeed, the Senate's attitude was still distinctly hostile to Rhodes, and in the very year of Theaedetus' visit and death (167) it passed a decree which set free all parts of Lycia and Caria which it had 'granted' to Rhodes in 188, and on controlling which Rhodes had in the meanwhile spent much time, money and effort. It was a major blow to Rhodian prosperity and aspirations. Nor was it the only such blow, for at the same time the Senate gave Delos to Athens with the stipulation that it should become a free port. Whether or not this provision was specifically directed against Rhodian trade we cannot tell; but it certainly had its effect on the revenues which Rhodes collected from her own harbour dues, which rapidly fell from a million to 150,000 drachmae per year. Nor was even this the end, for Caunus and Stratonicaea, two mainland towns which had belonged to Rhodes before Rome's intervention in Asia Minor, took the opportunity offered by Roman irritation with Rhodes to revolt. Exiles from these places, annoyed at Rhodes' repressive measures, appealed to the Senate in 167 and were in Rome at the same time as Theaedetus in winter 167/6. The Senate promptly passed a decree declaring them also free. It had no legal, or even moral, right to do this. It was an act based quite simply on Rome's superiority in power. But it worked. Rhodes was too weak and worried to resist, and had no alternative but to comply.[26]

But Rhodes' agony was coming to its end. It was not the Senate's aim, once Cato had prevented a war, to weaken Rhodes beyond the point of political and economic viability; but only to demonstrate what was expected of a dutiful Roman client in the changed political conditions after the defeat of Perseus. And in winter 165/4 the Senate at last yielded to the constantly repeated request for a formal alliance.[27] But by then it did not matter much; for Rhodes, like so many other Greek states during these years, had learnt her lesson. Ironically, the 'free and equal' alliance marked the end of Rhodes' power as an independent state: she would not, of course, have been given it if the Senate had thought that the implications of the client-patron relationship had not been digested. Never again would Rhodes operate an independent foreign policy; never again would the Rhodian navy be strong enough to keep the Aegean free from pirates. The Senate might, in time, regret the growth of the pirate menace; but it never seems to have regretted its text-book demonstration of how to cut an unreliable client down to the size it regarded as appropriate.

III Syria and Egypt

The war with Perseus, as we have seen, changed Rome's attitude towards the Balkans and Asia Minor, where the Senate had for long claimed important Roman interests. But it also changed Rome's attitude towards powers much farther afield, in areas where Rome had recently shown only marginal interest, Syria and Egypt. Egypt had for a hundred years maintained a distant friendship with Rome;

the Ptolemies had consistently been on good, if not particularly close, terms with the Senate. Syria had become a client of Rome through Antiochus III's defeat at Magnesia; but in the subsequent settlement the Senate had been quite content with ensuring that Asia Minor was safely in the hands of its friends Eumenes and Rhodes and had made no further territorial restriction on Antiochus. An additional safety factor for Roman interests was the presence of Antiochus' son, also called Antiochus, at Rome as a hostage, where he was well treated and is supposed to have become an admirer of the Roman way of life.

Apart from this contact and the regular collection of instalments of indemnity, the Senate showed little interest in the enormous eastern kingdom which Antiochus retained even after the peace of Apamea. It was therefore possible for Antiochus III himself to begin, and for his son and successor Seleucus IV to continue, to consolidate and rebuild Syrian power without Roman interference. And when Seleucus was assassinated in 175, his brother Antiochus, only recently released from being a hostage at Rome, established himself firmly on the throne of his fathers as king Antiochus IV, with the aid of Eumenes of Pergamum. There is no sign that the Senate had anything to do with Antiochus' unexpected elevation, but it could scarcely be worried by it since Eumenes, Rome's chief watchdog in Asia, had actively promoted it. Diplomatic exchanges were quickly made, and the Senate was assured of Antiochus' goodwill towards Rome when he paid off the remainder of his father's indemnity.[28]

Egypt also had internal troubles. The native Egyptians had been in sporadic revolt for many years (though they seem to have been quieter during the 170's), and the court had had severe dynastic problems. These came to a head again in 176 when Ptolemy VI Philometor—a child at the most ten years old, and a nephew of Antiochus IV of Syria—lost his mother (Antiochus' sister), who had been regent for him. The regency then descended to two court officials, the eunuch Eulaeus and one Lenaeus who, the hostile tradition records, had once been a slave. Perhaps attempting to divert attention from the weakness of the court by starting a foreign war, perhaps simply misjudging Egyptian strength and Syrian weakness, Eulaeus and Lenaeus quickly made it clear that they intended to fight their ward's uncle for possession of the territory of Coele-Syria, which Egypt had lost in 200 after holding it against constant Syrian attacks throughout the third century B.C. As it turned out, this projected expedition was a major miscalculation, and after much diplomatic activity during which Antiochus, late in 170, complained about Egypt to Rome, Antiochus made a pre-emptive strike in spring 169. He had little difficulty in invading Egypt or in defeating Egyptian opposition; and he quickly came to terms with his young nephew the king, once Eulaeus' and Lenaeus' influence was broken. When a Roman envoy, Titus Numisius, reached Egypt, both Antiochus and Ptolemy Philometor agreed that the war was over. Numisius obviously could not mediate in a non-existent war, and had no alternative but to return to Rome.[29]

But the war was not over, despite appearances and claims. For Antiochus did not hold Alexandria; and to confuse matters still further, the Alexandrians proclaimed Philometor's sister-wife Cleopatra and younger brother Ptolemy Physcon to be joint monarchs with Philometor. By the autumn of 169 Antiochus had laid siege to Alexandria. He failed to capture it, however, before the winter and, leaving garrisons in Egypt, he returned to Antioch. This was a decisive mistake. For during the winter Cleopatra and Physcon reached agreement with Philometor, Antiochus' protégé, that all three should rule jointly in the interests of the Ptolemaic dynasty.[30] By this agreement, which Antiochus' presence might have prevented, he lost all claim to be the representative of Philometor's interests. The three reconciled siblings now appealed to Rome against Antiochus, whereupon the Senate, which had earlier refused to act on an appeal by Cleopatra and Physcon alone,[31] sent envoys led by the ex-consul Gaius Popillius Laenas, a seasoned eastern diplomat whom we have already seen in action in the Balkans the previous winter. But Popillius' instructions seem not to have been straight-forward. To obtain the utmost effect from his mission, he was to wait to see whether Aemilius Paullus reached a quick decision in Macedon before going on to Alexandria; and this time he spent on Delos.[32]

As we know, the Senate's faith in Paullus was not misplaced, and shortly after the decisive battle on June 22, 168 Popillius and his colleagues set out for Alexandria, travelling via Rhodes (where they succeeded in thoroughly frightening the Rhodians). They found Antiochus at Eleusis, just outside Alexandria. In one of the most famous scenes in Roman history the Senate's post-Pydna attitude was demonstrated to the world. Handing Antiochus written instructions from the Senate to leave Egypt at once with his army, Popillius even refused him time to discuss the demands with his advisers; and when the king protested too much, Popillius arrogantly drew a circle in the sand around Antiochus with his cane and demanded an answer before he left the circle. The implication for Antiochus was clear; and Antiochus chose peace. His army duly withdrew into Syria.[33]

It was a shattering blow to the prestige of the Syrian king, for it indicated that Rome's view of her intimate interests now extended as far as Syria and Egypt. Antiochus had not been a dutiful client, though his years as a hostage at Rome must have made him aware of what Rome expected from her clients; but, not unlike Demetrius of Pharos long ago, he had not thought that the Senate was much concerned with Syrian and Egyptian affairs. It was his misfortune to be one of the first to discover that after Pydna *all* powers in the Mediterranean area, east and west, attracted Roman attention—indeed, that the Roman Senate was not only interested in their activities but was prepared to regard them all alike as Roman clients. This was the lesson of the 'day of Eleusis', and it had emerged inevitably from the Roman decision to weaken Macedon and from the Senate's consequent hard-line attitude to its friends in the east. It was in Syria and Egypt that the Senate's sudden leap of active interest was most striking; but it was just as much a direct result of the attitude which brought about the war with Perseus as any of the other effects of that attitude which we have considered.

Hereafter Antiochus and his descendents were self-admitted clients of Rome; and the Senate lost no opportunity of interfering in the various succession-crises which overcame the dynasty after Antiochus' death in 164—not so much to make certain that a friend of Rome was always on the throne, but rather to ensure quite simply that the Seleucid kingdom would remain weak. Thus when Antiochus died, his son Antiochus V, who was still a child, was preferred by the Senate to the adult Demetrius, son of Seleucus IV, who was currently a hostage at Rome.[34] The Senate also capitalized on the kingdom's vulnerability at the death of Antiochus IV to weaken it still further by burning Syria's warships and hamstringing her war elephants. When, a little later, Demetrius escaped from Rome with the encouragement of Polybius and the connivance of his Roman friends, and established himself on the throne at Antioch, he failed to obtain the Senate's formal acknowledgment of his kingship, and had to suffer from its constant interference and its encouraging all kinds of dissident elements in his kingdom. Pydna therefore marked the end not only of the independent power of Macedon, Illyria, Pergamum and Rhodes, but also of Syria. The one major difference was that in Syria the Senate was not much concerned to keep a friend in control of what power there still was; for as long as Syria remained weak, it was too far away from Italy to matter very much to Rome.[35]

After Popillius had saved Egypt from Antiochus, Rome's attitude to the Ptolemies was much the same as it was to the Seleucids, except that in Egypt the dynasty created its own weaknesses through constant internal disputes, and accordingly did not require much Roman effort to keep it feeble. The two brothers Ptolemy Philometor and Ptolemy Physcon, both Rome's close clients through being saved from Antiochus by Popillius, occupied Egypt, Cyrene and Cyprus in various combinations and divisions over the next twenty years. Constant disputes between them engendered frequent appeals to Rome; and Roman decisions, normally in favour of the brother who was currently the weaker, were sufficient to remind the two brothers of their obligations as clients and of Rome's overriding supremacy of power.[36] Neither in Syria nor in Egypt did Rome ever care sufficiently during this period to contemplate military intervention in favour of its friends of the moment. The Senate sensibly did not want to get involved (except diplomatically) in the petty power-struggles of the eastern courts. It was enough for Roman purposes that the power-struggles continued, that they kept Syria and Egypt weak, and that they allowed Rome to feel more secure than she had felt since first becoming involved in affairs east of the Adriatic. After Pydna there was no part of the Mediterranean coastline which was not held by a client of Rome who knew that he was a client of Rome. For the Senate that was sufficient. It did not everywhere require direct territorial control to exert Roman dominance.

CHAPTER XIX

AFRICA

I Before Pydna

WE last looked at African affairs in 201, when the Hannibalic war ended. By that settlement Carthage was effectively destroyed as a Mediterranean power: she was turned into a Roman client, and moreover—on a pattern which Rome had already used elsewhere—her aspirations even in north Africa were curbed by Rome's grateful gifts of territory and rights to her uncompromising friend Massinissa. As we saw, Massinissa was not only protected and encouraged by being confirmed in what he already possessed at the end of the war, but had his ambitions stimulated by the explicit provision in the peace treaty that he might legitimately possess himself of all territory which had belonged to his ancestors. It was a vague, emotive phrase, though at first sight it looked like a just recognition of Massinissa's services. But in practice it took little account, perhaps deliberately, of north African conditions. For Massinissa's ancestors (and Massinissa himself) were raiding barbarians, who doubtless would have been able to claim that most parts of north Africa had 'belonged' to them at some time or another.

The limiting factor on Massinissa's aggression was therefore not a precise territorial boundary: in practice it amounted to nothing more than uncertainty about how widely the Senate would allow Massinissa to interpret 'ancestral belongings'. If Massinissa chose to press claims which the Roman Senate regarded as acceptable, it would no doubt support Massinissa's contention that they were covered by the treaty. If it thought that he had gone too far, it would not support him and would protect Carthage, Rome's new African client. Immediately after 201 it yet remained to be tested to what extent Rome still wished to punish Carthage by encouraging Massinissa against her, and therefore to what extent the Senate would allow Massinissa to encroach on what Carthage had hitherto regarded as her territory, under the 'ancestral belongings' clause.

Characteristically, Massinissa seems to have begun to test Roman intentions almost at once. In 195 Roman envoys were in Africa to investigate Hannibal's post-war activities and a territorial dispute which had already arisen with Massinissa. We hear nothing about the territorial dispute, though Hannibal was made to flee to the court of Antiochus III.[1] But in the light of subsequent events, we may assume that the Roman envoys reached no decision, a result which meant that in practice Massinissa retained the territories on which he had encroached. He seems to have been encouraged by Roman suspicion of Hannibal's motives in seeking refuge with Antiochus—with whom Rome was at the time engaged in 'cold war'—and of Hannibal's remaining influence at Carthage, even after his exile, to make bigger encroachments on the rich and fertile coast of the 'Lesser Syrtes' (in the area generally known as 'Emporia'). In 193 this dispute also came to Rome's notice when the Carthaginians appealed to the Senate against Massinissa. Massinissa based his claim on the dubious argument that the particular area in question had always belonged to the strongest African power—until recently, of course, Carthage, but now Massinissa. Massinissa was clearly using this dispute to test further the Senate's attitude to his 'ancestral belongings'. The Senate sent out envoys led by Massinissa's friend and patron Scipio Africanus (who was now, of course, also Carthage's patron). They came, they saw, but by reaching no positive decision, they allowed Massinissa to conquer—although, as Livy points out, Scipio's influence could have ensured that this dispute between his own clients was settled by a nod from him. The reason for his indecisiveness can only have been disreputable: that Carthage had a good case against Massinissa, but that by leaving the dispute formally undecided, Rome's (and Scipio's) good friend Massinissa would again retain the disputed lands.[2]

It is thus clear that Rome was still hostile to Carthage and favourable, far beyond the bounds of fair dealing, to Carthage's opponent Massinissa. And unfortunately for Carthage, the way in which these disputes in 195 and 193 were dealt with by the Senate's envoys set a pattern for the future which, despite the passage of time and the continuing peaceableness of the Carthaginians, the Roman Senate continued to employ. The incomplete nature of our source material prevents us from tracing all subsequent applications of the pattern; and not until 182 do we hear of another territorial dispute coming to the attention of the Roman Senate. This time it was of exactly the sort that the 'ancestral belongings' clause of the treaty had made likely. Massinissa's father Gala had at one time occupied some Carthaginian territory; Syphax had driven Gala out and restored it to Carthage in the last years of the Hannibalic war. Massinissa, now claiming his 'ancestral belongings', had again expelled the Carthaginians. Whose claim was the most just? The Senate does not seem to have even tried to decide. We hear that again Roman envoys failed to reach any decision on the spot, and referred the whole matter back to the Senate, apparently without even making a recommendation. And although we do not know the final result of the case —as with the other disputes—it is clear that Massinissa once more retained possession of the disputed lands.[3] The Senate seemed to be forgetting in all this that Carthage's defeat had made her also a Roman client, and that she too had moral claims to fair dealing from her Roman patron. Where stood Roman good faith in these post-war disputes between her African clients?

Only when the war with Perseus was threatening did the Senate show any inclination to give Carthage a fair deal; and that seems to have been only because of suspicion that Carthage, unless conciliated, might take the opportunity of obstructing Rome by supporting Perseus. Ironically, Massinissa seems to have brought this unwonted exhibition of Roman fair play—the last thing he can have wanted—upon himself; for in 174 he took advantage of Rome's suspicions of Perseus to accuse Carthage of conspiring with him— and there may indeed have been some Carthaginians who sympathized with Perseus, for his relationship with Rome was ominously similar to Carthage's own. But there is no indication that the Carthaginian government actually did (or even planned to do) anything with Perseus beyond exchanging envoys.[4] Massinissa however was satisfied to have sown suspicion—suspicion which, he anticipated, would keep Roman favour for him. He then attacked Carthaginian territory and captured some seventy towns and forts.

The Senate discussed this in 172, and decided that the time was not ripe for driving Carthage to desperation by yet another unfair non-arbitration. A final decision was postponed, as of habit, and the treaty principle of 'ancestral belongings' restated; but although we do not know exactly what effect this had on the practical state of affairs in north Africa, we may reasonably assume that this time the principle worked in Carthage's favour and that Massinissa was not left in complete control of all the territories which he had occupied.[5] Indeed, this most recent arbitration may well have produced Massinissa's attitude in 171 which Livy records, that on the outbreak of war with Perseus Massinissa recognized that if Rome won he would not be able to expand, since Rome would not allow him to use violence on Carthage; but if Rome lost, she would not be able to protect Carthage, and all north Africa would be Massinissa's.[6] Now Rome's protection of Carthage had not been the most conspicuous feature of their relationship over the past thirty years; yet if Livy's description of Massinissa's attitude in 171 is correct, he can only have taken this view through being recently warned by the Senate. And this warning seems most likely to have been implicit in the arbitration, at the outcome of which Massinissa will naturally have been disappointed.

Thus, it seems, only when Rome began to be aware that Carthage might still constitute a threat to her activities elsewhere, and that in the circumstances it was unwise to be seen to be consistently unfair to Carthage, did the Senate attempt to check Massinissa's encroachments. Before the war with Perseus, Massinissa had emerged from every dispute the winner, until he misjudged the situation in 172/1, overplayed his hand, and stirred up Rome to be conciliatory to Carthage. Both Carthage and Massinissa will have been desperately interested in the outcome of the war with Perseus; for if Rome won, it would leave her power quite unchallenged throughout the Mediterranean, and (contrary to what Massinissa seems to have thought in his disappointment in 171) it would remove all requirement for the Senate ever again to be conciliatory to Carthage.

II After Pydna

During the war with Perseus both Carthage and Massinissa expended great efforts in sending supplies to the Roman armies in the Balkans.[7] But after Pydna Massinissa was the first and most successful exploiter of his patron's gratitude. In 168/7 he sent one of his sons, Masgaba, to Rome to congratulate the Senate on its victory and to remind the senators of Massinissa's dutiful clientship during the war. Indeed, Masgaba went so far in adulation as to propound an exaggerated and false theory of what (he claimed) clientship meant to Massinissa: that he regarded his kingdom as Rome's and his enjoyment of it as that of a tenant.[8] Even if our source is accurate, it is difficult to see in this apparent definition of Massinissa's idea of clientship more than the exaggerated flattery which Masgaba thought the Senate would like (particularly after Pydna); and he was not the only royal visitor to Rome at the time to take this view, for in 167 Prusias of Bithynia earned Polybius' scorn for his excessively humiliating and insincere self-abasement before the Senate. Thus Masgaba's speech is unlikely to represent any real misinterpretation by Massinissa of the nature of clientship, for Massinissa had had more than thirty years to learn it, and had in that time, unlike many of the Greek states, shown no deviationist tendencies.

The Senate was nevertheless pleased with Masgaba, as it was pleased with Prusias, thus proving the practical justification of their flattery. But it turned down Massinissa's request to be allowed to travel to Rome himself, since he was already over seventy, and the Senate had no desire to risk his life unnecessarily and add a new African problem to its already complex eastern responsibilities. Masgaba was given presents, and the Senate politely deprecated his too effusive view that Numidia was really Roman property (as Masgaba had doubtless expected). Masgaba's reception at Rome encouraged Massinissa, after the shock of Roman fairness in 172/1 had temporarily shaken his faith in Roman partiality towards him; and he at once began another series of territorial disputes with Carthage about 'Emporia', a piece of which he had already occupied in 193. The remaining parts of the Emporia were particularly rich and fertile, and at some time in the past Massinissa had even tacitly acknowledged Carthage's right to it, since he had asked her permission to pursue a fugitive into the area. But this was no concern to the Senate, as Polybius acknowledges. If even before Pydna Carthage had been treated unjustly, the brutalization of the Senate's attitude which the war with Perseus had brought about could surely not favour Carthage. Accordingly, the Roman decision ran true to form, and was more unfairly discriminating than ever: when the appeal reached the Senate, it firmly decided against Carthage; and to add insult to injury, it even insisted that the Carthaginians pay Massinissa 500 talents as compensation for loss of revenue from the disputed territories from the time the dispute had begun.[9]

Such manifest injustice made Carthage seethe; and since Carthage was allowed under the treaty with Rome to defend her own boundaries (though not to advance beyond them)[10] it seems likely that it was the dispute about the Emporia which stimulated the government to build up stocks of weapons. For if Massinissa could be so arbitrarily and unjustly awarded the Emporia, lands even closer to Carthage, perhaps even the city itself, no doubt seemed in danger from the depredations of the turbulent old sheikh. Their fears proved only too true; and the next years saw Massinissa attempting to encroach on the rich lands of the Bagradas valley. He had seen how Eumenes had finally persuaded Rome to destroy the remaining power of Macedon; and, but for Eumenes' stupid misjudgment during the war, he would no doubt have seen Eumenes profiting from Rome's success. Massinissa seems to have seen himself as an African Eumenes —but with the crucial difference that he was prepared to do his own fighting.

The Carthaginians could scarcely fail to be aware of the close resemblance of their current situation to that of Macedon in the years before the defeat of Perseus. As Philip had done, so they had yielded in every respect to Rome's suspicious unfairness. Yet all they had received for their co-operation was the restriction of their territories (and consequent diminution of the wealth from them), and the building up of their chief antagonist Massinissa. In Macedon when Philip had died Perseus had not had the long-suffering patience to continue his father's bitter but sensible policy: his more aggressive attitude was self-defeating, for it resulted in war and the deliberate suppression of the Macedonian monarchy and the central government from which Macedon derived its strength. After Massinissa's seizure of the Emporia, a change of attitude occurred at Carthage, which in its way was as important for Carthage's future as Perseus' succession had been for Macedon's; and it was also to prove self-defeating for the same sort of reasons.

We have seen that Carthage now probably began to re-arm, clearly with the intention of resisting Massinissa if he made further encroachments on Carthaginian territory. This firmer attitude seems to have stemmed from the strengthening of influence at Carthage of a more militant group of politicians who derived their support from the People and who cultivated popular favour.[11] Their strengthening came chiefly at the expense of the conservative group which since 201 had seen that in the last resort Carthage had no alternative but to do Rome's bidding, and had therefore accepted humiliation after humiliation. A generation which had not experienced the terrible pressures of war with Rome and which did not fully comprehend the supremacy of Roman power—as in Achaea a few years later—seems to have come to the forefront and determined to cry halt to Massinissa's activities while Carthage still had the wealth and strength to resist.

This did not mean, in the first instance, abandoning the traditionalists' appeals to Rome; but it did mean trying to make these appeals

more effective. We know of a series of Roman envoys who went to
Africa in the early 150's, but nothing of the outcome: only that by
about 153 Carthage had not only laid up stocks of weapons but had
also built some warships (under the treaty she was allowed to have
ten triremes). But it was a bad time for 'hawkish' self-assertion, for
such activity (whether or not the new politicians realized it), even if
not contrary to the treaty, was almost certain, given the post-Pydna
attitude of the Roman Senate, to attract hostile Roman reaction. It
had, after all, been the military preparation for effective self-defence
of Philip and Perseus which had first aroused Roman suspicions
to the level at which they could be exploited by the Macedonian
kings' Greek enemies. For a defeated enemy to be seen to be
making preparations for war was sufficient in itself, it seems, to condemn him in the eyes of the Senate of preparing to make war on
Rome.

The Senate was wrong again; its suspicions, as those of Philip
and of Perseus, unfounded. But after Pydna Rome was so strong that
she herself would not suffer much from acting on the Senate's mis-
apprehensions: only those on whom suspicion fell would do so. The
Senate, throughout the second century, had progressively lost
patience with its clients who did not or would not acknowledge
Roman authority. In the case of Macedon, the kingdom had been
dismembered as a result of Roman impatience; and Macedonian
affairs must have been fresh in the minds of the Roman envoys of 153
when they set out for north Africa on yet another mission of arbitration. This time they were led by the blunt octogenarian Marcus
Porcius Cato, and Cato's mission turned out to be one of the most
critical events in the whole history of Romano-Carthaginian relations.[12]

Few men can disregard the experience of a lifetime when facing a
situation superficially similar to one they have met before; and both
the Roman environment, with its deep consciousness of past Roman
history, and Cato's own character and interests (he was himself both
an old man and a historian) made it impossible that he would look
upon Carthage in 153 without being influenced by his lively sense of
historical precedent. Cato was not in principle a war-monger: it
was he who, in 167, had prevented the wilder men in the Senate from
declaring an unnecessary war on Rhodes. But neither was he (or
any of his colleagues in the Senate) an advocate of peace at any price.
Old enough to have fought in the Hannibalic war and to have shared
contemporary attitudes to and fear of Carthage; old enough to have

been a senator throughout the second century and to have participated in and been influenced by the crucial debates in which Roman policy was formulated in those years, Cato, in turning his attention once again to Carthage in 153, obviously could not discard this experience: it was part of him, as it was part of every man of his age, and inevitably it conditioned his attitude.

In the circumstances, the Carthaginians could not have chosen a worse time to harden their attitude towards Massinissa. When Cato and his colleagues reached Carthage they were immediately impressed by the wealth and power of the client city and by its ready availability of manpower of military age. Carthage was again strong. This fact alone was sufficient to revive old fears. But when the Carthaginians chose this occasion to refuse Roman arbitration, holding that Massinissa was this time patently in the wrong, that there was no room for any arbitration, and that Massinissa must be made to withdraw, Cato added a feeling of outraged Roman patronage to his first impressions of Carthage's power. So although Massinissa eventually volunteered to withdraw from the disputed territory, no arbitration was made and Cato and his colleagues returned to Rome to report to the Senate.[13] There could be no question but that Cato's mind was made up. If in the 170's Perseus' Macedon had seemed to present a potential trouble-spot for Rome and needed to be brutally suppressed for the peace of mind of the Senate, in similar circumstances in the 150's Rome's oldest enemy now again seemed to be feeling her strength and proving recalcitrant to her client's duty. Cato's conclusion was straightforward: the two cases, he would have argued, were parallel; and what had been effectively accomplished in the one should now be accomplished in the other. Macedon's power had largely lain in the unity created by its monarchy: the monarchy had been destroyed. Carthage's power, it seemed, lay chiefly in her strategic commercial site: Carthage therefore must be destroyed.

This latter was a phrase which the Senate was to hear much of in the next three years; for Cato's embassy to Carthage had convinced him that the destruction of Carthage should be the chief aim of Roman policy, and he accordingly lost no opportunity of reminding the Senate of his view. From the beginning he had some support among those who were prepared to accept his view as authoritative or who shared his lively awareness of the past. He was not, however, unopposed; and it was not until 149 that war was formally declared. The person primarily responsible for causing the Senate to delay for nearly three years was Publius Cornelius Scipio Nasica, son-in-law of Scipio Africanus and a relative by marriage of Aemilius Paullus. Nasica argued firmly that Carthage should not be destroyed for, he argued, such a war would not accord with Roman traditions of only fighting 'just wars'.[14] The concept of the 'just war' had, of course, already been badly strained in connection with the war with Perseus, but that did not mean that Nasica regarded it as a lost cause; and Polybius confirms the pattern of the argument when he says that the reason why the Senate delayed so long was because it wanted an excuse which would placate foreign opinion.[15]

Polybius represents the proponents of this policy as deliberately holding back until a suitable pretext presented itself, although, he says, the Senate had in fact already decided on the general desirability of war. But this does not necessarily signify that Nasica himself used such a cynical argument. The widespread net of the client-patron relationship, through which Rome still essentially directed her relationships with the eastern Mediterranean states, depended for its smooth functioning to a great extent on the mutual acceptance of moral obligations and on mutual fair play. We have seen how the war with Perseus and its aftermath had weakened these relationships, with Rome in many cases conspicuously failing to support her clients or being excessively suspicious of them. But failure to support was one thing: deliberate and unprovoked aggression on a peaceable and conciliatory client was another and an entirely different matter. The moral and political effect of an attack on Carthage such as Cato was proposing might heavily strain the whole basis of the overseas client-patron structure, on the effective operation of which, in the last resort, Roman peace of mind depended. Nasica's opposition to Cato, therefore, had a firmly practical political purpose, and was not solely based either on simple moral grounds or on a cynical regard for the effect on foreign opinion.

Unfortunately for Carthage, Nasica was fighting a losing battle in the Senate; and the Carthaginians themselves gave him no help. For in 151 they supplied his (and their) enemies with more ammunition when, in a desperate attempt to fend off Massinissa, they crossed their present boundaries (thus technically breaking their treaty with Rome) and pursued Massinissa into Numidia.[16] It did not matter that in the event they were severely defeated and that Massinissa proved perfectly capable of looking after himself. The fact was that they had now added a breach of their treaty to their refusal to do their client's duty by accepting Roman arbitration. Nasica found the ground cut from under his feet by the very people he was trying to help. It was now more than ever difficult for him to argue that there was still no 'just cause' for war, for technically there was. Morally, Nasica could still argue, a war would not be just even now; and politically it might still have the dangerous effect in the east which he had envisaged all along; and it seems that he may have continued to set out this argument even after war was formally declared early in 149. But the Senate had traditionally allowed itself to interpret 'just cause' in exactly the narrow technical sense which the Carthaginians had now made possible. And for those senators who had only accepted the part of Nasica's argument which stated that 'just cause' was necessary to conciliate foreign opinion, without thinking what this meant in practice, the technical 'just cause' was sufficient. Cato's persistence at last won the day: his fears and his estimate of Carthage's wealth and power, which had received sympathetic attention in the Senate when he brought back his news in 153 of Carthage's hard-line attitude, now seemed to be confirmed when this hawkish attitude had actually produced a breach of the treaty. When the independent African town of Utica, wishing to demonstrate its dissociation from the Carthaginians' foolish posturing, offered unconditional surrender to Rome later in 150, perhaps while Nasica was away in the Balkans investigating Andriscus, a suitable base for military operations was made available to the Romans; and the Senate at last accepted Cato's view. Early in 149 war was declared.[17]

III The Province of Africa

Even after the declaration of war, Nasica may have continued to urge moderation. And now, though it was too late, the Carthaginians helped him to help them. For the news of the Roman decision caused the immediate collapse of support at Carthage for the hard-liners, who had never themselves seriously considered that war with Rome might result from their firmer attitude towards Massinissa. Their leaders were condemned to death and a placatory embassy was sent to Rome. But even when the Carthaginians offered unconditional surrender after the war had begun, Nasica could not persuade the Senate to stop the embarkation of the army for Africa.[18] Unconditional surrender was always interpreted by the Romans on each occasion as it suited them: the result, as it had often been in the east and as it was now with Utica, might be the friendship and goodwill of the Roman Senate and People. But it might also mean that every legal obstacle to the fulfilment of Roman demands was removed: so it had been with the Aetolians, so it had been with Perseus, so it was now to be with Carthage.

Realistically, if disreputably, not putting forward the full Roman demands all together in case Carthage, as the Aetolians had done, should effectively withdraw its surrender when it realized the full implications of its action, the Romans progressively weakened and disarmed Carthage until it seemed that the final demand could be stated without running the risk that Carthage might refuse it: that the city of Carthage should be abandoned and the population moved at least ten miles from the sea, thus effectively destroying the maritime trade from which so much of Carthage's wealth had derived. It was this final demand which Cato's policy had required, the final demand which could not fail to shatter Carthage's strength, just as the suppression of the Macedonian monarchy and of Macedonian unity had shattered the strength of Macedon. Too late, it seemed, the Carthaginians realized that they had been vainly led by hopes of fair treatment from their all-powerful patron. All hope of it was now belatedly abandoned. Rome's final demand was rejected by a desperate people, whose expectations of fair treatment had been cynically exploited by the Roman consul Lucius Marcius Censorinus. His treatment of Carthage in these details of the negotiations was as brutally cynical as Cato's initial conception of the need to destroy Carthage; and it did not have the excuse of a traditionalist political attitude to explain it.[19]

It was three more years before Carthage was finally destroyed. When the proud old city fell, it was to the son of the destroyer of Macedon, Publius Cornelius Scipio Aemilianus. They were three years in which the desperate Carthaginians not only preserved their city, but even secured a string of victories against successive Roman commanders; they were three years in which Carthage's long-standing enemy Massinissa, because of whom she was fighting Rome for her very existence, at last died. Had he died at eighty-five instead of ninety, as Carthage might reasonably have hoped, the war with Rome might conceivably have been avoided altogether, if Massinissa's kingdom had been split up among his numerous children. But at eighty-five Massinissa was still fathering children and fomenting trouble; and after fifty years of conciliation Carthage's brief but disastrously timed hard-line attitude had provoked Rome to war. These ironies no doubt added to Carthage's determination to fight to the end.[20]

It was a bitter but glorious finale to the history of Rome's greatest enemy: Carthage perished with a bang, not a whimper. Early in 146, with the city in flames and the cultured Roman commander Scipio Aemilianus quoting Homer to his Greek friend Polybius as he looked at the fires, the end had come. What remained of the city of Carthage after the fire was razed and curses were pronounced against any future settlement of the site. All towns in Africa which had continued to support Carthage were also brutally destroyed; the rest of Carthage's territory, with the exception of towns such as Utica which were rewarded for having joined Rome in time by being declared free, became a formally administered tax-paying Roman province.[21] Africa was to see no divisive experimentation such as Macedon had experienced after the defeat of Perseus; for by 146, as we have seen, the Macedonian experiment had failed, and Macedon too had become a Roman province.

By 146 the two old men who had chiefly destroyed Carthage were both dead. Cato died at Rome very soon after the outbreak of the war, without living to see the full degradation of Roman good faith to a client which his policy had implied. Massinissa too had died during the war, and thus never recognized that his policy had, in the last resort, failed him. No doubt if he had realized that his final provocation of Rome would produce a formal Roman province in Africa, his attitude towards Carthage would have been more cautious; but as it was, the vigorous and unscrupulous old sheikh died while his hopes were still alive. Massinissa's kingdom was divided by Scipio Aemilianus—to whose discretion Massinissa had tactfully left it—among Massinissa's numerous sons:[22] for now that Rome intended to take a direct stake in the administration of north Africa, a too strong and united Numidia on the borders of the Roman province was more a liability to Rome than an asset.

So ended Rome's chief African problem. The solution of it, as we have now seen, fits neatly into the developing pattern of Roman policy towards her overseas allies and friends throughout the second century B.C. It is not inappropriate that, just as this survey of Rome's rise to world power began with her first overseas venture, her first conflict with Carthage, so it should conclude with the final conflict with Carthage. For by 146 there was no longer any single power of the well-established Mediterranean world which Rome could regard as her equal. By 146 Rome's world power was established.

IV Conclusion

The story of Rome's expansion does not, of course, end in 146 B.C. Many of her most famous and far-reaching conquests had not yet been made, had not even been contemplated: Gaul, Germany, and Britain were as yet barely within the Roman sphere of awareness, still less were they the integral parts of the Roman empire which they eventually became. Rome was still only a Mediterranean power— though, by a pardonable conceit, most civilized men of the time would have regarded the Mediterranean coastlands as 'the world'. Nevertheless, Rome did in due course expand beyond the Mediterranean basin; the process of consolidation of Roman overseas interests which we have seen developing in the 120 years of this survey continued. But its essential pattern did not change very much. More directly administered provinces were acquired, more client kings and states on the fringes of Roman territory or of Roman interests were accepted into the web of mutual obligation which protected Rome in such cases. But by 146 the major innovations had taken place. By then Rome had acquired a direct interest in every part of the Mediterranean. There could be no turning back.[23]

ABBREVIATIONS

Most modern works cited in the notes are given in an abbreviated form: those abbreviations which might cause difficulty are listed here. For full bibliographical details of works cited in the notes and the full titles of books, the bibliography should be consulted. The exception is that for some works which are mentioned only once, the full bibliographical details are given in the notes where they are cited.

ABAW	*Abhandlungen der Bayerischen Akademie der Wissenschaften*, Philos.-Hist. Klasse
AJPh	*American Journal of Philology*
CAH	*Cambridge Ancient History*
CPh	*Classical Philology*
CQ	*Classical Quarterly*
CR	*Classical Review*
Ditt. *OGIS*	W. Dittenberger, *Orientis Graeci Inscriptiones Selectae*, Leipzig, 1903–1905
Ditt. *Syll.*	W. Dittenberger, *Sylloge Inscriptionum Graecarum*, ed. 3, Leipzig, 1915–1924
FgrHist	F. Jacoby, *Die Fragmente der griechischen Historiker*, Berlin–Leiden, 1923–
HSPh	*Harvard Studies in Classical Philology*
ILS	H. Dessau, *Inscriptiones Latinae Selectae*, Berlin, 1892–1916
JRS	*Journal of Roman Studies*
ORF	H. Malcovati, *Oratorum Romanorum Fragmenta*, ed. 3, Torino, 1967
PACA	*Proceedings of the African Classical Associations*
RD	R. K. Sherk, *Roman Documents from the Greek East*, Baltimore, 1969
RE	Pauly-Wissowa-Kroll, *Real Encyclopädie der classischen Altertumswissenschaft*
RhM	*Rheinisches Museum*
SDAW	*Sitzungsberichte der Deutschen Akademie der Wissenschaften zu Berlin*
TAPhA	*Transactions and Proceedings of the American Philological Association*

ROME IN 264 B.C.

1. Livy x.10.12.
2. Livy, *periochae*, xi.
3. A table giving details of the composition and competence of all the Roman assemblies will be found in Taylor, *Roman Voting Assemblies*, 4–5. The *comitia centuriata* seems to have been originally the assembly of the Roman People in arms—hence the name of the units, *centuriae*, which is that of the tactical unit of the Roman army. But any original connection with the army had long been lost by this time.
4. Justin xliii.3.4; 5.3. Cf. Diodorus xiv.93.4.
5. Livy viii.17.10; Justin xii.2.12.
6. Strabo v.3.5.
7. Pliny, *Historia Naturalis*, iii.57–8, attributes the detail to Clitarchus, who probably wrote around 300 B.C. and may even have been present in person at Babylon in 324.
8. Polybius xxx.5.6–8.
9. As long as we do not assume Roman political interest in Rhodes at this date there is no need to follow Holleaux, *Rome, la Grèce*, 30–46, in rejecting Polybius' information on the *amicitia*: see Schmitt, *Rom und Rhodos*, 1ff.
10. Livy, *periochae*, xiv; Dionysius of Halicarnassus, *Roman Antiquities*, xx.14.1; Zonaras viii.6.11.
11. Valerius Maximus vi.6.5; Zonaras viii.7.3; Livy, *periochae*, xv; cf. Polybius ii.12.7.
12. On the Carthaginian background, see Picard, *Carthage*; Warmington, *Carthage*.
13. Polybius iii.22–3. Modern scholars have questioned the genuineness of this document, which cannot have come to Polybius' notice much before 150 B.C. But Polybius says that it was written in very difficult Latin, some of which he could hardly understand (i.e. it was very archaic); and since he does not say this about his second treaty, which probably dates from the mid-fourth century (see below), thus implying that he could understand it more easily, the first treaty's extremely archaic language makes Polybius' date for it seem reasonable. Furthermore, we know that the Etruscans, who had ruled Rome until 509/8, had had commercial treaties with Carthage (see Aristotle, *Politics*, iii.9.6–7, 1280a 38f.); and it would be normal practice for the Carthaginian government to try to secure from the new Roman government respect for its predecessor's agreement (or something similar). Thus the balance of the evidence seems to favour the genuineness of Polybius' first treaty and his date of 509/8 B.C. This dispute and the associated one about the dates of Rome's other treaties with Carthage are reviewed by Walbank, *Commentary*, i.337f. For the so-called 'treaty of Philinus' see below, p. 17.

14. Polybius iii.24, does not give the date of his second treaty; but Livy (vii.27.2; cf. also Diodorus xvi.69.1) mentions a treaty in 348, though he does not give its terms, which is probably the same as Polybius' second treaty. This treaty may have been renewed in 306 (Livy ix.43.26).
15. Polybius iii.25; see Walbank, *Commentary*, i.349f.

NOTES TO CHAPTER II

THE FIRST PUNIC WAR

1. The word is derived from *Mamers*, the Oscan form of Mars.
2. Polybius i.6.8f.
3. Polybius i.10.1–2.
4. Polybius i.10.3–9; see Badian, *Foreign Clientelae*, 33–5.
5. This is Polybius' version (i.11.4–5). A later, almost certainly false, Roman tradition gave the honour of the expulsion to a Roman tribune, Gaius Claudius (Zonaras viii.8).
6. Polybius i.11.7–12.4.
7. Polybius i.14. The surviving fragments of Philinus' work are collected by Jacoby, *FgrHist* no. 174; on his use by Polybius see Walbank, *Commentary*, i (index).
8. Polybius iii.26.2f., with Walbank, *Commentary*, i.354f.
9. Polybius iii.25.1–5. See chapter I, above p. 10.
10. Livy, *periochae*, xiv.
11. Livy xxi.10.8.
12. See Warmington, *Carthage*, 47f.
13. Polybius i.17.3–6.
14. Polybius i.17.2; 17.6 (two consuls imply four legions, since each consul normally commanded two legions).
15. Polybius i.17.6–19.15.
16. Most of our information about triumphs comes from the official Roman list (the *acta triumphalia*), much of which has been preserved. Hence the absence of any name from the list (where the stone is not accidentally broken) indicates that the person concerned was not awarded a triumph. The list is published by A. Degrassi, *Fasti Consulares et Triumphales*, in *Inscriptiones Italiae* xiii.1.
17. Polybius i.20.1–8.
18. Zonaras viii.10; Orosius iv.7.7; cf. Polybius i.20.7. See Heuss, *Historische Zeitschrift* 1949, 488f.
19. Polybius i.20.13–14.
20. Polybius i.20.9–16. His account may have come from Fabius Pictor, the first Roman 'annalist', who was a contemporary of the Second Punic War and who, even in Polybius' estimation (cf. Polybius i.14.1f.)—though it did not prevent his using Fabius!—liked to exaggerate Rome's achievements for his Greek readers: see further the chapter by Badian, 'The Early Historians', in Dorey (ed.), *Latin Historians*. The whole incident of Rome's

using the Carthaginian quinquereme is also often regarded as legendary, but the outline is plausible.

21. For the *corvus* see Thiel, *A History of Roman Sea Power*, 101f.; H. T. Wallinga, *The Boarding Bridge of the Romans* (Groningen, 1956), *passim*.

22. The limited number of Carthaginian personal names makes necessary this kind of descriptive periphrasis to avoid confusion.

23. Polybius i.21.4f. A later copy of the inscription from the *columna rostrata* which recorded the victory, has survived: see *ILS* no. 65; also, with translation into English, in *Remains of Old Latin* (Loeb Classical Library), iv. 128–31; translation alone in Lewis and Reinhold, *Roman Civilization*, i.152.

24. Polybius i.24.5–7; Zonaras viii.11–12; *acta triumphalia*.

25. Polybius i.25.1–6.

26. Polybius i.25.5–28; see Walbank, *Commentary*, i.82f.

27. Polybius i.31.4–8. Polybius makes Regulus' motive for opening negotiations the fear that another commander might replace him, and thus take the glory for ending the war. But this may be simply Polybius' own interpretation in the light of later well-attested examples of this. Philinus—not a man to depreciate the Carthaginians—is probably the basis of Diodorus' account (xxiii.12.1) and of other accounts which make the Carthaginians sue for terms, and is more likely to be right on this. Dio Cassius (frg. 43.22-3) purports to give the details of Regulus' proposal—though Philinus, to judge from Polybius' version, made a feature of the excessive Roman demands—but since no other source gives them it is difficult to believe that Dio's account represents the truth.

28. See, for instance, Cicero, *De Officiis*, iii.99–100; Livy, *periochae*, xviii; full references in Klebs, *RE* ii.2, 'Atilius' no. 51.

29. Diodorus xxiv.12; cf. (e.g.) Aulus Gellius, *Noctes Atticae*, vii.4.1.

30. Polybius i.36.5f.

31. Polybius i.40; cf. Diodorus xxiii.21; coins illustrated in *British Museum Coin Catalogue*, Roman Republic, i.155–6; ii.357, 570.

32. Polybius i.42.8f. The battle of Drepana is the occasion when later legend made Claudius throw overboard the sacred chickens—which provided a bad omen by refusing to eat—with the exclamation, 'then let them drink' (cf. e.g. Cicero, *De Natura Deorum*, ii.7; Livy, *periochae*, xix). Since neither Polybius nor Diodorus mentions the incident, it is most likely to be a later invention attempting to explain the Roman defeat by blaming Claudius' impiety rather than his incompetence!

33. Polybius i.56f.

34. Polybius i.59.8f.

35. Polybius iii.27.1–6; cf. i.62.8–63.3. See Walbank, *Commentary*, i.126f.

36. Polybius i.63.4–64.6, with Walbank, *Commentary*, i.128f.

37. Cf. Mommsen, *Römisches Staatsrecht*³, ii, 1. 570f.; Heuss, *Historische Zeitschrift* 1949, 508f.

38. On this and what follows see Badian, *Foreign Clientelae*, 37f.

39. See above, chapter I, p. 4.

40. Cicero, 2 *Verr.*, iii.13 (Mamertines); Polybius i.16.9 (Hiero).

BETWEEN THE WARS

1. See chapter II, p. 22.
2. For details of the war see Polybius i.66f.
3. Polybius i.79.1–5.
4. Appian, *Libyca* 5; Zonaras viii.17. These late authors reflect the material of earlier writers whom they used as sources.
5. Polybius i.83.11.
6. Polybius i.83.6–8; cf. Eutropius ii.27; Valerius Maximus v.1.1.
7. Polybius i.83.11.
8. For discussion see Walbank, *Commentary*, i.149–50.
9. Polybius i.88.8–12; iii.10.1–4; 27.7–8; 28.1–4; see Walbank, *Commentary*, ad locc.; *CPh* 1949, 15f.
10. See *CAH* vii.804–5.
11. Appian, *Libyca*, 5; 86; Zonaras viii.18; see Walbank, *Commentary*, i.150.
12. Polybius i.83.6–9; iii.28.
13. Livy xxii.54.11; cf. xxi.40.5.
14. See Dell, *Historia* 1967, 344f.
15. Polybius ii.8f. For further discussion of this Illyrian war see Badian, *Studies in Greek and Roman History*, 1f.; Walbank, *Commentary*, i.153f.; for a different view, which I do not find convincing, see Hammond, *JRS* 1968, 1f.
16. Polybius ii.8.7f. Later annalistic writers found the theme congenial and developed its rhetorical and platitudinous possibilities: see Dio Cassius, frg. 49.3f.
17. Polybius ii.8.8.
18. Polybius ii.8.12–13; Dio Cassius, frg. 49.3.
19. Appian, *Illyrica*, 7; Dio Cassius, frg. 49. See Holleaux, *Rome, la Grèce*, 23 n. 6.
20. Polybius ii.11.1; 7.
21. Full discussion of this in Badian, *Studies*, 23f.; Dell, *CPh* 1967, 94f.
22. Polybius ii.11. The alleged Roman intervention in the 230's on behalf of the Acarnanians (Justin xxviii.1-2) has been firmly shown to be apocryphal by Holleaux, *Rome, la Grèce*, 5f. See also Oost, *Roman Policy in Epirus and Acarnania*, 92f.
23. Polybius ii.12.1–2; *acta triumphalia*; cf. Walbank, *Commentary*, i.164–5.
24. Polybius ii.12.3, calls it *phoros*, a word which means tribute: from Teuta's point of view, of course, it was effectively tribute.
25. Polybius ii.12.3. On this 'protectorate', see Badian, *Studies*, 6f. On the geography, see Hammond, *JRS* 1968, 1f.
26. Dio Cassius, frg. 53.
27. Appian, *Illyrica*, 7.
28. Polybius ii.12.3.
29. Polybius ii.12.4.
30. Zonaras viii.19. Zonaras also reflects later Roman annalistic embroideries of these first Roman contacts with the famous Greek cities. He says that at Corinth one of the Romans called (impossibly!) Plautus, 'Flatfoot', won the

stadion, the most important foot race; and at Athens that the Romans were given Athenian citizenship and admitted to the famous Eleusinian mysteries. Neither of these details is at all plausible, and both should be firmly rejected as Roman inventions. There is no good evidence that the embassies had any political significance.

31. Polybius ii.12.5–6.
32. Polybius i.65.1–2.
33. On the Gauls and Rome's earlier wars with them see Polybius ii.14f., with Walbank, *Commentary*, i.172f.; also Scullard, *History*, 76f. and 167f.
34. Polybius ii.21.7; Cicero, *de inventione*, ii.52; Valerius Maximus v.4.5; see also Walbank, *Commentary*, i.192.
35. Polybius ii.21.8. It is often thought that Polybius inserted this judgment in the light of his experience of the Gracchan crisis in 133 B.C. (on which see any standard Roman History). But book ii was probably published twenty years before 133, and it therefore seems more likely that Polybius is here reflecting the opinion of Fabius Pictor (with which his own political inclinations would make him sympathize) since his attitude towards Flaminius is consistent throughout this book and book iii.
36. Polybius ii.21.8–9.
37. Polybius ii.22f.; see Walbank, *Commentary*, i.194f.
38. Livy, *periochae*, 20; Solinus v.1.
39. Polybius ii.32f., especially 33.6f.
40. e.g. Plutarch, *Marcellus*, 4.2–5; Zonaras viii.20.
41. Polybius ii.34–5; Plutarch, *Marcellus*, 6–8.
42. Livy, *periochae*, 20 (decision); Polybius iii.40.5 (218).

NOTES TO CHAPTER IV

THE CAUSES OF THE WAR WITH HANNIBAL

1. Polybius ii.1.7–8.
2. Diodorus xxv.10. Though a final identification is impossible, Acra Leuce has recently been placed in the Baetis valley (with some plausibility) by Sumner, *HSPh* 1967, 205f., a major study of Rome's relations with Spain at this time. But see my critical comments in *Latomus* 1970, 28f.
3. Polybius ii.13.1–2.
4. Massilia had probably become a formal ally with a treaty before 218 (Livy xxi.20.8). This status may have resulted from her co-operation in the Gallic crisis (cf. Polybius ii.32.1).
5. Dio Cassius, frg. 48. The text is damaged and may in any case be unreliable. It is certainly poor evidence for serious Roman interest in Spain at this date: see *Latomus*, 1970, 32f. On Massilia at this time see Kramer, *AJPh* 1948, 1f. (though much exaggerating Roman 'party' differences).
6. Polybius ii.13.7. This seems to exclude its having been a treaty formally delineating mutual spheres of influence.
7. Polybius (ii.13.3f.) explains the Ebro treaty as Rome's making the best of a bad job since she could not afford to fight Hasdrubal in face of the Gallic

threat. However, the treaty was never followed up after the Gallic crisis had passed, and Polybius' clearly anachronistic motivation is probably his own (or his source's) later interpretation of the Ebro treaty: see *Latomus* 1970, 34f.

8. Polybius ii.36.

9. Polybius iii.11; cf. Livy xxi.1.4; Appian, *Hannibalica*, 3; cf. Walbank, *Commentary*, i.314–15; my discussion of 'the wrath of the Barcids' in *Latomus* 1970, 26f.

10. Cf. Dio Cassius, frg. 48.

11. Polybius iii.13–14, especially 14.9.

12. The date and nature of Saguntum's relationship with Rome has produced a large modern bibliography (for which see Walbank, *Commentary*, i.357, on Polybius iii.30.2, up to 1956). Polybius (iii.30.2) cites the arbitration as evidence of Rome's friendship with Saguntum, but he does not make it clear whether or not he thinks the friendship was *created* by the arbitration. He also says: 'It was agreed that the Saguntines, some years before they had dealings with Hannibal, placed themselves under Rome's protection.' It is odd that he cites no evidence of this beyond the arbitration; but the context suggests that 'those who agreed' were the Carthaginians. We are therefore probably justified in assuming that the arbitration, which was only a short time before 220 (Polybius iii.15.7), had originated the friendship. For further discussion see Badian, *Foreign Clientelae*, 49f.; Astin, *Latomus* 1967, 37f. (criticizing the views of Hoffmann, *RhM* 1951, 69f.; Scullard, *RhM* 1952, 209f.; and Walbank, *Commentary*, i.168–72; 333–4 etc.); Errington, *Latomus* 1970, 41f.

13. Polybius iii.14.10. We can discard the 'interpretation', which is clearly influenced by the myth of 'the wrath of the Barcids'.

14. Polybius iii.15.1–5.

15. Polybius iii.15.6–7.

16. Polybius iii.15.8–13. Polybius' discussion may be ignored as invented after the event.

17. Polybius iii.17.

18. The names are given by Livy (xxi.18.1), but cf. Dio Cassius, frg. 55.10 for Marcus Fabius. Discussion in Scullard, *Roman Politics*, 274; Sumner, *PACA* 1966, 24 n.63.

19. Polybius iii.20.6f. Third-century examples are: in 266 Quintus Fabius was handed over to Apollonia for an outrage on envoys (Dio Cassius, frg. 42); in 236/5 Marcus Claudius Clineas was handed over to the Corsicans for making an unauthorized peace which the Senate wished to disown (Zonaras viii.18). For other examples see Walbank, *Commentary*, i.312.

20. Polybius iii.21.

21. Polybius iii.29.4f. The Roman account of negotiations in 203 and 202 makes the Carthaginians accept this interpretation: Polybius xv.1.7; 17.3. Were they just trying to please the Roman commander when it no longer mattered? It certainly must not be taken as evidence for their real attitude in 218.

22. Polybius iii.21.1 (explicitly). His reasons seem to be supplied from the later arguments about justification which he records in iii.29.

23. Cf. Appian, *Iberica*, 7; *Hannibalica*, 2.

24. Polybius iii.30.3.

NOTES TO CHAPTER V

THE WAR WITH HANNIBAL IN ITALY

1. Polybius iii.34.4–6. The chief ancient sources for this chapter, which it will be impractical to cite for every detail, are Polybius iii.34–118 (to Cannae, after which Polybius' book survives only in isolated fragments); Livy xxi–xxvii; Appian, *Hannibalica*. Modern accounts of the war are numerous, though the most detailed discussions are not in English: but see Hallward, in *CAH* viii; Scullard, *History*, 186f.; discussion of the effects of the war in Toynbee, *Hannibal's Legacy*, ii; problems which arise from Polybius' account are discussed in Walbank's *Commentary on Polybius*.

2. Polybius iii.40.2. Livy's chronology of the events of 218 is confused and quite unreliable.

3. Polybius iii.40.3–14.

4. Polybius ii.24f., with Walbank, *Commentary*, i.196f.

5. Polybius iii.56.4. This was Hannibal's own figure which he recorded on a bronze plaque in the temple of Juno on the Lacinian promontory in southern Italy, near Croton. Polybius had seen the plaque with his own eyes. Other figures which Polybius gives for the other parts of the march (50,000 foot and 9,000 horse at the Pyrenees (iii.35.7); 38,000 foot and 8,000 horse at the Rhône (iii.60.5)) may be exaggerations by Roman sources.

6. Polybius iii.77.4–7; 85.3–4; Livy xxii.58.1–2.

7. Polybius iii.41–9.

8. See the massive bibliography and discussion in Walbank, *Commentary*, i.382f., to which add Walbank's damaging criticism of Sir Gavin de Beer's book, *Alps and Elephants* (London, 1955), in *JRS* 1956, 37f.

9. Polybius iii.47.6f.

10. Polybius iii.60.8–13; Livy xxi.39.

11. Polybius iii.61–74; Livy xxi.39–56.

12. Livy, *periochae*, xx.

13. Livy xxi.63.7.

14. Details in Livy xxi.63.

15. Polybius iii.77–85; Livy xxii.1–8.

16. Polybius iii.77.4–7.

17. Polybius iii.85.3–4.

18. Livy xxii.9; Polybius iii.86.8f.

19. It is not clear whether this description is meant to be friendly or unfriendly —i.e. 'the man who delayed in order to prepare the ground for later victory', or 'the man who prolonged the war unnecessarily'. In the next century Fabius had become a hero and his tactics were widely approved (which they were not at the time) because it was then clear that they had worked. The epic poet Ennius had no doubt what the epithet meant when he described Fabius, in a famous phrase, as 'the man who saved the Republic by delaying' (*unus qui nobis cunctando restituit rem*); but Ennius' phrase is poor evidence for the contemporary reaction to his policy which gave Fabius his nickname.

20. Polybius iii.103.1–5; Livy xxii.25–6.

21. Polybius iii.104–5. Fabius' part may have been exaggerated by his kinsman, Polybius' source, Fabius Pictor; but the outline will be correct.
22. Livy xxii.34–5. On the elections see Scullard, *Roman Politics*, 49f.; Dorey, *RhM* 1959, 249f.; on Aemilius in Illyria, see chapter VIII below.
23. Polybius iii.107.7.
24. Polybius iii.107–17; Livy xxii.44–53. The mountainous modern bibliography on all matters concerning the battle is discussed by Walbank, *Commentary*, i.435f.
25. Livy xxii.61.14.
26. Livy xxii.51.1–4.
27. On events in Spain see chapter VI below.
28. Livy xxxi.1.1–5.

NOTES TO CHAPTER VI

THE WAR WITH HANNIBAL IN SPAIN

1. On this, see chapter V above. Modern bibliography for the war in Spain is basically the same as that for the war in Italy: but see additionally, Sutherland, *The Romans in Spain*; Scullard, *Scipio Africanus in the Second Punic War*; *Scipio Africanus: Soldier and Politician*.
2. Polybius iii.76.1.
3. Polybius iii.76.2–13.
4. Polybius iii.95–6; Livy xxii.19–20; cf. Sosylus (= *FgrHist* no. 176) frg. 1.
5. Polybius iii.97.1–3.
6. Polybius iii.98–9; Livy xxii.22. Both authors exaggerate the importance of the incident; but it is probably authentic in outline. There is no need to reject it altogether (as Beloch, *Hermes* 1915, 361, suggested) as a confused duplication of Publius Scipio's capture of New Carthage and the Carthaginian hostages there in 209. The outline is quite plausible.
7. Livy xxiii.26–9.
8. Many of the details of the events of these years, as recorded by Livy (xxiii.49f. and xxiv.41f.) are unlikely to represent more than (at best) intelligent guesswork at filling out received outlines; at worst they may be sheer invention. We have no means of checking their authenticity.
9. Livy xxv.32–6.
10. Livy xxv.37–9.
11. Livy xxvi.17–19.
12. Polybius x.2–5; Livy xxvi.18–19. The story that Scipio and his brother were aediles together in 213 is wrong in several details (see Walbank's discussion in *Commentary*, ii.199–200) and probably represents some later embroidery of Scipio's youth when his mature activities had made him a legend.
13. Livy xxii.53; Dio Cassius, frg. 57.28.
14. For another discussion of Scipio's election, in possible party-political terms, see Scullard, *Roman Politics*, 65f.
15. Livy xxvi.19–20.

16. Polybius x.6–20; Livy xxvi.41–51. For discussion of the technical problems arising from the attack, see Scullard, *Scipio Africanus in the Second Punic War*, 56f.; *Soldier and Politician*, 39f.; Walbank, *Commentary*, ii.191f. (also citing earlier bibliography).

17. Livy xxvii. 7.1–6; 17.

18. Polybius ix.11; x.36.

19. Polybius x.34–8; Livy xxvii.17.

20. Livy xxiv.48–9.

21. Polybius x.38.7–40; Livy xxvii.18–19.

22. For discussion of different views of Hasdrubal's march see Scullard, *Scipio Africanus in the Second Punic War*, 114f.; *Soldier and Politician*, 82f.

23. For details of these events see Scullard, *Scipio Africanus in the Second Punic War*, 120f.; *Soldier and Politician*, 86f.

24. See chapter IX below.

25. Livy xxviii.17–18; 35.

26. Polybius xi.33.7–8; Livy xxviii.38. On possible party-political reasons for Scipio's election, see Scullard, *Roman Politics*, 75.

NOTES TO CHAPTER VII

THE WAR WITH HANNIBAL IN AFRICA

1. Livy xxii.31 (217); xxiii.21 (216); xxiii.41.8–9 (215); xxv.31.12–15 (211); xxvii.5.1; 8–15 (210); xxvii.29.7–8 (208); xxviii.4.5 (207).

2. Livy xxiv.48.

3. Livy xxvii.4.5–9.

4. Livy xxvii.19.8–12.

5. Livy xxviii.16.11–12.

6. Livy xxviii.17–18.

7. Livy xxviii.35. This meeting is sometimes regarded as apocryphal; but it is not unreasonable in itself and accords well with Scipio's established technique of diplomacy by personal contact.

8. For a different view of Scipio's strategic aims, see Scullard, *Scipio Africanus in the Second Punic War*, 160f.; *Soldier and Politician*, 108f.

9. Livy xxviii.38.4. It was argued that because Scipio was a private citizen vested with military command (*privatus cum imperio*) and not a regular magistrate he could not be awarded a triumph—an honour which had previously been awarded only to magistrates. But this argument was merely making up rules to suit the political occasion; for there were no written (or even unwritten) rules about what honour a *privatus cum imperio* might be awarded, since the situation was quite unprecedented: there never had previously been a *privatus cum imperio* who deserved a triumph. Since for all other purposes the Senate had treated Scipio exactly as if he had been a normal magistrate, it can only have been sheer legalistic obstructionism which invented this 'rule' specifically to prevent his well-earned triumph.

10. For an attempt to discuss this opposition in party-political terms, see Scullard, *Roman Politics*, 75f.

11. Livy xxviii.40–2. The details of the speech will almost certainly be Livy's own invention, but the outline may be authentic.
12. Livy xxviii.43–5.
13. Livy xxix.3.6; 5.1.
14. Livy xxix.23–33.
15. Discussed in detail by Scullard, *Scipio Africanus in the Second Punic War*, 176f.; *Soldier and Politician*, 116f., and every standard History of Rome.
16. Livy xxx.19.12–20.4.
17. Livy xxx.16; Appian, *Libyca*, 32.
18. Livy xxx.21–5; Polybius xv.1–2; Appian, *Libyca*, 34–5.
19. Cornelius Nepos, *Hannibal*, 6.3, mistakenly says that the battle was fought 'at Zama' (*apud Zamam*), and it is customarily but, strictly speaking, wrongly, called 'the battle of Zama' as a result.
20. For details of the battle the chief sources are: Polybius xv.5f., with Walbank, *Commentary*, ii.445f.; Livy xxx.29–35; Appian, *Libyca*, 39–47.
21. Polybius xv.14.9; Appian, *Libyca*, 48.
22. Livy xxx.37; Appian, *Libyca*, 55.
23. Polybius xv.18; Appian, *Libyca*, 54. See Walbank, *Commentary*, ii.466f.

NOTES TO CHAPTER VIII

EAST OF THE ADRIATIC

1. Polybius iii.16.1–4.
2. Dispute about the purpose of this Illyrian war and the nature of the Roman involvement has produced many modern discussions. I follow in outline the view of Badian, *Studies*, 1of. For a different (and, to me, less convincing) view, see Hammond, *JRS* 1968, 1f.; also Holleaux in *CAH* vii.822f.
3. See chapter III above.
4. See chapter IV above.
5. Polybius iv.16.6–10.
6. Polybius iii.18.1.
7. Appian, *Illyrica*, 8.
8. Dio Cassius, frg. 53, preserves a later invented annalistic version which actually has Demetrius rebuked by the consuls and ignoring their remonstrances.
9. Appian, *Illyrica*, 8. The authenticity of this charge has been defended by Dell, *Historia* 1970, 3of.
10. Polybius iii.18–19.
11. On the site of Dimallum, see Hammond, *JRS* 1968, 12–15.
12. Polybius v.101.1–2; 108.1–9.
13. Polybius v.102.5f. On Philip at this time see Walbank, *Philip V*, 64f.
14. Polybius v.104.10–11. For discussion of the speech see Walbank, *Philip V*, 66; cf. H. H. Schmitt, 'Hellenen, Römer und Barbaren' in Jahresbericht des Gymnasions, Aschaffenburg, 1957–8, 38f.
15. Livy xxii.33.3; 5.
16. Polybius v.109.

17. Livy xxiii.32.17.

18. Livy xxiii.38.7.

19. Polybius vii.9. The later annalistic version in Livy (xxiii.33.10–12; cf. Appian, *Macedonica*, 1) exaggerates the specific nature of the document by reproducing an invented interpretation stimulated by Roman fearful imagination. Thus he adds that Philip was to cross to Italy with as many ships as he could raise (200 is mentioned as a possibility); that Italy and the city of Rome after the war should belong to Carthage—a typical Roman exaggeration of Hannibal's war aims—and that after the conquest of Italy Hannibal should cross over to the Balkans and help Philip to conquer his neighbours there. None of this is in Polybius—nor was it in Philip's treaty with Hannibal!

20. Livy xxiv.40. See Walbank, *Philip V*, 75f.

21. Polybius viii.13–14b; Livy xxiv.12.3; 13.

22. Livy xxvi.24. For the epigraphic fragment, which deals in detail with the cases of cities which fell into Roman or Aetolian hands by various methods, see G. Klaffenbach, *SDAW* 1954, no. 1; *Supplementum Epigraphicum Graecum* xiii, no. 382; *Inscriptiones Graecae* ix.1, ed. 2, no. 241; text also in *JRS* 1956, 153. The date, circumstances and implications of the treaty have been endlessly discussed and can pass without further discussion here. For the most part I follow Badian in *Latomus*, 1958, 199f.; but see also A. H. McDonald, *JRS* 1956, 153f.; Walbank, *Philip V*, 83f.; *Commentary*, ii.11–13; Lehmann, *Untersuchungen zur historischen Glaubwürdigkeit des Polybios*, 10f. (with bibliography up to 1966); Dahlheim, *Struktur und Entwicklung*, 181f.

23. See Badian, *Latomus* 1958, 205f.

24. See Walbank, *Philip V*, 84f.; Errington, *Philopoemen*, 49f.

25. Livy xxix.12; cf. Appian, *Macedonica*, 3.

26. Livy xxix.12.

27. Despite Livy's phraseology, this does not mean that Rome physically occupied these places: as before, they remained 'free friends' of Rome, and Livy calls them 'Rome's' merely because he wants to show clearly that they were no longer Philip's.

28. The authenticity of Livy's list of *adscripti* to the treaty on the Roman side has been widely discussed: see McDonald, *JRS* 1937, 180f., to which add (selectively): Balsdon, *JRS* 1954, 32f.; Badian, *Foreign Clientelae*, 102f.; Petzold, *Die Eröffnung*, 11f. Athens and Ilium have often been regarded as Roman annalistic inventions, Athens for justificatory reasons, because Philip's attack on Athens in 201 was one of the events which brought about Rome's next intervention in the east in 200 (see chapter X below), and the patriotic annalists liked to have an obvious *legal* right for Rome: Ilium for romantic patriotic reasons because Roman legend, by this time well-established, connected the origins of Rome with the fall of Troy, and Ilium was on the site of Troy. These arguments (and others which we have not room to discuss here) do not seem to me to be cogent. Athens was an important city, and may have preferred, in accepting such guarantees of peace as the treaty provided, to be associated with distant and unambitious Rome rather than with close and imperialistic Macedon; Ilium was effectively under the control of Attalus of Pergamum and may perhaps have provided some men

or ships for Attalus' fleet, or indeed, have been deliberately introduced into
the war by Attalus to flatter Rome's pride in her Trojan origin: see on this,
Schmitt, *Untersuchungen zur Geschichte Antiochos' des Grossen*, 291–2.

NOTES TO CHAPTER IX

THE EFFECTS OF THE WAR WITH HANNIBAL

1. By 190 B.C., this kind of result was accepted at Rome as normal Roman
   practice; and Lucius and Publius Scipio, when trying to persuade Prusias of
   Bithynia to become a Roman friend, were able to list a long series of dynasts
   whose fortunes had been made by their friendship with Rome (Polybius
   xxi.11).
2. Livy xxviii.4.10.
3. Livy xxxi.50.11.
4. Appian, *Iberica*, 38.
5. For these see Scullard, *History*, 282f.; Toynbee, *Hannibal's Legacy*, ii.252f.
6. It is a gross overstatement when Toynbee (*Hannibal's Legacy*, ii.35) says that
   the traces of Hannibal's devastation can still be seen in southern Italy. For a
   reasonable view see Yeo, 'The overgrazing of ranchlands in ancient Italy',
   TAPhA lxxix, 1948, 275f.
7. On this see further Toynbee, *Hannibal's Legacy*, ii.115f.
8. Livy xxvii.9–10; xxix.15.
9. Livy xxvii.21.6f.; 24; 38.6; xxix.36.10; xxx.26.12 (Etruria); xxviii.10.4–5
   (Etruria and Umbria).
10. On this see further Badian, *Foreign Clientelae*, 141f.

NOTES TO CHAPTER X

THE RETURN TO THE EAST

1. Livy xxx.26.2–4; cf. 42.2–10. See Badian, *Studies*, 22–3.
2. Livy even includes these men in the Carthaginian ranks at Zama: xxx.33.5.
   Polybius, whose account Livy is generally following, does not mention them:
   xv.11. See Balsdon, *JRS* 1954, 34f., for a defence; but Dorey, *AJPh* 1957,
   185f. is conclusive against their being officially sponsored.
3. Polybius, xviii.1.14; Livy xxxiii.33.3. See Badian, *Studies*, 22–3; Balsdon,
   CQ 1953, 163–4; *JRS* 1954, 35. For a different view, reviving that of Holleaux, which had many followers in the past, see Oost, *CPh* 1959, 58f.; see
   also the triangular discussion between Badian, Dorey and Oost in *CPh* 1960.
   Oost's view seems (to me) an unconvincing interpretation of what Polybius
   says.
4. Livy xxxi.3.4. On his activities (and alleged Macedonian complaints about
   them) see Livy xxx.42.2–10.
5. Livy xxxi.29.4; cf. Appian, *Macedonica*, 4. For a discussion of the authen-

ticity of this Aetolian embassy see Badian, *Latomus*, 1958, 208f., who argues against it; Dorey, *CR* 1960, 9, who defends it. But even if it is historical it seems to have had no effect on Rome's actions, and therefore perhaps does not much matter.

6. Livy xxxi.3.3f.; cf. 5.5. This information about Laevinus was rejected by Holleaux (*CAH* viii. 156 n.1) on the ground that it is a mistaken Roman annalistic reminiscence of Laevinus' activities in the First Macedonian War. Discussed in detail also by Petzold, *Die Eröffnung*, 77f., and rejected as an annalistic fabrication (as Petzold rejects much of the annalistic material, often without adequate reason). Most subsequent writers, by omitting the incident altogether, seem to have tacitly accepted its falsity. Yet the information is circumstantial, and there seems to be no good reason why it should not be substantially correct.

7. These events are all obscure in detail, and I have presented without argument what seems to me to be the most likely course of events. For more detailed discussion see Holleaux, *Études*, iv.211–325; Walbank, *Commentary*, ii.497f.; cf. *Philip V*, 112f. The relevant fragments of Polybius are in book xvi.

8. The exact date is difficult to establish, but early 201 seems most likely: see Pritchett, *The Five Attic Tribes after Cleisthenes* (Baltimore, 1943), 33.

9. This was recorded on an inscription on Cephisodorus' tomb, which was seen in the second century A.D. by the traveller and guide-book writer Pausanias: i.7.7. Another inscription concerning Cephisodorus was published with a translation in *Hesperia*, 1936, 419f.

10. Livy xxxi.14.6–10. The time of the attack on Athens is undated, but this seems most likely: see Balsdon, *JRS* 1954, 36–7.

11. Livy xxxi.1.10–2.4. The part played by Athens in bringing about the Roman declaration of war has often been suspected of being a defensive invention of later Roman writers. But, as I have tried to show, it seems possible to accept it in outline without necessarily making it a major Roman consideration: see also Balsdon, *JRS* 1954, 35f. Appian, *Macedonica*, 4, says that the Rhodians brought with them a rumour of a 'pact' between Philip and Antiochus III of Syria to divide the Egyptian Empire between them (Ptolemy V, a mere boy, had come to the Egyptian throne in 203); and Holleaux and many subsequent writers who followed him have seen in this 'pact' (which Polybius also mentions, though he does not make Roman knowledge of it a cause of the war) the chief cause of the war, for, he argued, it stimulated in the Senate a fear of Antiochus. This is not the place to discuss all the arguments, but it seems most likely that the 'pact', as recorded by Polybius and Appian, was an invention of later writers through their misunderstanding the nature of a local agreement between Philip and Antiochus' representative in Asia Minor, Zeuxis, and through Rome's objection to Philip's capturing various Egyptian possessions in the Aegean after he had been asked not to make war on the Greeks: Egypt was also a convenient friend of Rome. For full discussion, see Magie, *JRS* 1939, 33f.; Schmitt, *Untersuchungen zur Geschichte Antiochos' des Grossen*, 226f.; Errington, *Athenaeum*, 1971.

12. Livy xxxi.2.3–4.

13. Livy xxxi.4.4 (elections); 5.5f. (Aurelius' report and 2nd Athenian embassy); 6.1 (provinces).

14. For discussion of the Roman reasons for taking the decision see Badian, *Foreign Clientelae*, 62f.; McDonald and Walbank, *JRS* 1937, 180f. (the longest discussion in English of most of the matters dealt with in this chapter); Balsdon, *JRS* 1954, 30f.; B. Ferro, *Le origini della seconda guerra macedonica* (Palermo, 1960).

15. Livy xxxi.6.3–6.

16. Polybius xvi.27.2–5.

17. Livy xxxi.7.1–8 (Livy's speech cannot be regarded as authentic: it will be his own imaginative reconstruction).

18. Polybius xvi.27.4–5.

19. Polybius xvi.25–7; Livy (following Polybius), xxxi.14.10f.

20. Livy xxxi.9.1–5.

21. Livy xxxi.16f.

22. Livy xxxi.8.3–4. A decision of the fetial priests concerning Rome's ritual declaration of war allowed Sulpicius to declare war either by announcing the Roman decision to the king in person or by announcing it at the first fortified post in his territory. The Senate then allowed Sulpicius to send anybody he liked to do this, including, if he wished, anybody who was not present in the Senate (i.e. the envoys who were already in the Balkans). The envoys will no doubt have soon heard about this decision; but since, until the siege of Abydus, they made no attempt to contact Philip directly, and only then (according to Polybius: xvi.34.2) because they realized the true seriousness of the siege, Sulpicius obviously cannot have relied for the formal declaration of war on one of them visiting Philip (nor, it seems, were they *instructed* to do so by Sulpicius). In fact, of course, it did not matter much, since the fetials had allowed Sulpicius to arrange the formal declaration when he arrived in Illyria, if he wanted to wait until then.

23. Polybius xvi.29–34 (siege of Abydus); 34 (Aemilius at Abydus).

NOTES TO CHAPTER XI

THE SECOND WAR WITH MACEDON

1. Livy xxxi.28.1–4. On Amynander, see Oost, *CPh* 1957, 1f.

2. Livy xxxi.29–32. Livy's speeches are unlikely to be authentic.

3. Livy xxxi.25. On the relations of the Achaean League with Philip and Rome at this time, see Aymard, *Les Premiers Rapports de Rome et de la Confédération Achaienne*, 13f.; Errington, *Philopoemen*, 75f.

4. Livy xxxi.39–47. On the details of the events of the year, see Walbank, *Philip V*, 141f.; Hammond, *JRS* xlvi 1966, 42f.

5. Livy xxxii.6. Valerius Antias, one of the Roman writers used by Livy, felt compelled (? by misplaced patriotism) to invent a successful battle for Villius in order that a Roman commander should not be seen to have achieved nothing. But not even Livy seems to have believed this.

6. Plutarch, *Flamininus*, 1; Livy xxxi.4.3.; xxxii.7.9 (quaestorship).

7. For an attempt to analyse his support, see Scullard, *Roman Politics*, 97f.

8. Livy xxxii.7.8–12.

9. Livy xxxii.10.1–8. On the development of Roman policy, see Badian, *Foreign Clientelae*, 69f.

10. Livy xxxii.10–18. On the Aous gorge battle, see Hammond, *JRS* 1966, 45f.; on the year's campaign in general, see Walbank, *Philip V*, 151f.; on the war in Epirus, see Oost, *Roman Policy in Epirus and Acarnania*, 45f.

11. On this background, see Errington, *Philopoemen*, 70f.

12. Livy xxxii.19–23.

13. Livy xxxii.25; 38–40.

14. Cf. Livy xxxii.32.5–8.

15. Balsdon, *Phoenix*, 1967, 177f., thinks this business about Flamininus' friends was invented by someone who 'pictured Roman politics (about which he was not well informed) in the image of a hellenistic court' (181). But Polybius recorded this, and even if his source was not well informed, Polybius himself was, and he would obviously be able to correct any fundamentally false impression given by his less well informed sources.

16. Polybius xviii.1–12; cf. Livy xxxiii.32.9–37 (based on Polybius). For modern discussion see Walbank, *Commentary*, ii.548f. (with full bibliography up to 1965).

17. Livy xxxiii.3–10; Polybius xviii.18–27.

18. Polybius xviii.34–9; Livy xxxiii.11–13.

19. Polybius xviii.42 (Rome); 44 (terms in detail). For full discussion see Walbank, *Commentary*, ii. 604f.; Dahlheim, *Struktur und Entwicklung*, 83f.

20. Polybius xviii.45.1–6.

21. Polybius xviii.45.7–12.

22. Polybius xviii.46; Livy xxxiii.32–3.

NOTES TO CHAPTER XII

ANTIOCHUS THE GREAT

1. Polybius xvi.27.5. For a more detailed discussion of the interpretation of the events of this chapter, see Badian, *Studies*, 112f., whose outline I have broadly followed.

2. Livy xxxii.8; 27.1; xxxiii.20.8f.; cf. 34.2.

3. Livy xxxiii.20.

4. Polybius xviii.39.3f.

5. Polybius xviii.47.1–4; Livy xxxiii.34.1–4.

6. Polybius xviii.49–52; cf. Livy xxxiii.39–41.

7. Livy xxxiv.22–40.

8. See Scullard, *Roman Politics*, 196.

9. Livy xxxiv.43.

10. Livy xxxiv.48.2–52.12.

11. Livy xxxiv.57–9. This interpretation (essentially that of Badian, *Studies*, 126f.) has been challenged by Balsdon, *Phoenix*, 1967, 187f., though not (it seems to me) convincingly.

12. Ditt. *Syll*. no.585, line 45.

13. Livy xxxv.12–13. On Achaea and Nabis, see Errington, *Philopoemen*, 92f.

14. Livy xxxv.13.4–17.2. This exchange was even less than usually satisfactory since Antiochus was distracted by the death of a son; but had he been ready to make concessions, he could obviously have authorized Minnio, who represented him in the discussions, to make them.
15. Livy xxxv.32–3.
16. Livy xxxv.31; 34–9.
17. Livy xxxv.42.
18. Livy xxxv.43.6.

NOTES TO CHAPTER XIII

INTO ASIA

1. Livy xxxv.46.
2. Livy xxxv.48–50.2. The date of the treaty is not certain, but see Badian, *JRS* 1952, 76f.
3. Livy xxxv.47.5–8.
4. Livy xxxvi.1–3.
5. Livy xxxv.51.1–5. See Badian, *Studies*, 139 n. 100.
6. Livy xxxvi.5.1–8; Polybius xx.3 (Elis and Epirus); Livy xxxvi.6 (Boeotia).
7. Livy xxxvi.8–10 (Antiochus' campaigns); 4 (Philip's offer to Rome); 11.1–4; cf. Polybius xx.8 (Antiochus' marriage).
8. Livy xxxvi.11.5–16.11.
9. Livy xxxvi.17–21; Plutarch, *Cato Major*, 13–14. On topographical aspects of the battle, see W. K. Pritchett, *Studies in Ancient Greek Topography* (Berkeley-Los Angeles, 1965), 71f.
10. Livy xxxvi.22–4 (siege of Heraclea); 26 (Thoas to Antiochus).
11. Polybius xx.9–11; Livy xxxvi.27–9 (from Polybius).
12. Livy xxxvi.30; 34–5.6. (Naupactus and truce); 42–5 (naval action).
13. Livy xxxvii.1.7–10; 2.2–3.
14. Livy xxxvi.35.8–14 (Epirots and Philip); xxxvii.1.1–6 (Aetolians).
15. Polybius xxi.4–5; Livy xxxvii.6–7.7.
16. Livy xxxvii.8–17; 21.5–24; 26–31.4.
17. Polybius xxi.10; Livy xxxvii.18–19 (Eumenes); Polybius xxi.11; Livy xxxvii. 25 (Prusias).
18. Polybius xxi.13–15; Livy xxxvii.34–6.
19. Livy xxxvii.37–44.
20. Polybius xxi.16–17; Livy xxxvii.45.
21. Livy xxxvii.49–50. On the Aetolians' rebuff see chapter XIV below. On the party-groupings see Scullard, *Roman Politics*, 134f.
22. Polybius xxi.24.1–3; Livy xxxvii.55.1–3 (ratification in Rome); Polybius xxi.42; Livy xxxviii.38. The exact relationship between the treaty-terms as ratified at Rome and the full written treaty as finally sworn by Manlius in Asia more than a year later are not altogether clear in the sources. However, it seems reasonably clear that even on the terms of the treaty Manlius and the commissioners were given some discretion. In the last resort only the final treaty really matters, however the terms were arrived at, and the terms are fully recorded (though there is dispute about some geographical details:

see McDonald, *JRS* 1967, 1f.). On the naval clauses see McDonald and
Walbank, *JRS* 1969, 30f.

23. Polybius xxi.18–22.1; cf. Livy xxxvii.52–3.
24. Polybius xxi.22–3; cf. Livy xxxvii.54.
25. Polybius xxi.24.5–15; Livy xxxvii.55.4–56.
26. Polybius xxi.45; Livy xxxviii.39.

NOTES TO CHAPTER XIV

PEACE IN THE EAST

1. Livy xxxvii.49.
2. Livy xxxviii.1–7; Polybius xxi.25–8.
3. Polybius xxi.29–30; Livy xxxviii.8–10.
4. Polybius xxi.31–2; Livy xxxviii.11 (final peace treaty). Livy's Latin of this
   last clause—the '*maiestas* clause'—is a translation of Polybius' Greek and
   may possibly not accurately represent the original: *imperium maiestatemque
   populi Romani gens Aetolorum conservato sine dolo malo* (xxxviii.11.2). Many
   modern scholars have regarded this clause as typical of a new type of treaty
   which they have christened *foedus iniquum* ('unequal treaty'); but Badian,
   Foreign Clientelae, 25f. and 84f., has shown that the clause was not recognized by contemporaries as having any great importance; and that the
   clause on which the Senate really based its power—and on which it had
   insisted all along—was that the Aetolians should have the same friends and
   enemies as Rome. He argues—and I have followed him—that the '*maiestas*
   clause' was simply a way of trying to come to terms with the Aetolians'
   failure to understand the moral obligation of the client-patron relationship
   by trying to formulate a legal definition of what clientship should mean.
5. The date is not absolutely certain: see Badian, *JRS* 1952, 76f.; on the
   circumstances and on the whole of this section in detail, see Errington,
   Philopoemen, 90f.
6. Livy xxxvi.35.7; Plutarch, *Philopoemen*, 17.4.
7. His statue, with a verse inscription proclaiming this, was set up at Megalopolis: Pausanias viii.30.5.
8. Polybius xxii.10.
9. Polybius xxiii.17.5–18.2.
10. Polybius xxiv.8–9.
11. Polybius xxiv.10.
12. Polybius xxii.5. Polybius, probably using Rhodian sources for this infor-
    mation, presents the Rhodian interpretation of the Roman commissioners'
    decision as being what they in fact intended; but this is very improbable,
    since in 178/7 (Polybius xxv.4.5) the Senate explicitly denied that Lycia had
    been granted as a gift. Now while the Senate's motives in 178/7 are far from
    being wholly straightforward and fair, it seems most unlikely that it would
    issue an explicit denial of a matter which had been written into the terms of
    the settlement, and which could, if necessary, be looked up in the relevant
    documents; and indeed, the whole long dispute between Rhodes and Lycia

would be quite inexplicable if the exact meaning of the 'grant' had been explicitly spelled out in the terms of the settlement. Polybius must therefore have distorted the facts through using Rhodian source material here. For more detailed discussion of Rhodian affairs during these years, see Schmitt, *Rom und Rhodos*, 84f.; P. M. Fraser and G. E. Bean, *The Rhodian Peraea and the Islands* (Oxford, 1954), 107f.

13. Polybius xxiv.15.13.
14. Polybius xxv.4.2.
15. Polybius xxv.4–5; Livy xli.6.8–12.
16. Polybius xxv.6.
17. On aspects of Macedonian affairs during these years, see further: Walbank, *Philip V*, 186f.; Badian, *Foreign Clientelae*, 92f.; Edson, *HSPh* 1935, 191f.; Walbank, *JHS* 1938, 55f.
18. Livy xxxviii.40–1.
19. Polybius xxii.6; Livy xxxix.24.6–14.
20. Livy xxxix.25–6; for discussion of details see Walbank, *Philip V*, 223f.
21. Livy xxxix.27–9.2 (Thessalonica); Polybius xxii.11.1–4; Livy xxxix.33.1–4.
22. Polybius xxii.13–14; Livy xxxix.34.
23. Polybius xxiii.1–2; 3.4–9; Livy xxxix.47–8.1.
24. Polybius xxiii.8; Livy xxxix.53.10.
25. Livy xxxix.53.12–16. Perseis may have been on the site of modern Prilep.
26. Livy xl.3–5; Polybius xxiii.10.
27. Livy xl.5–16.3; cf. Polybius xxiii.11.
28. If the letter was authentic, Livy's allegation that it was a forgery will have come from the apologetic Roman tradition which was hostile to Perseus and highly favourable to Demetrius. This bias will have reached Livy through Polybius, who perhaps picked it up at Rome during his exile there. It accounts for Livy's and Polybius' highly favourable picture of Demetrius (whose actions, in fact, suggest that he was really rather a vain, gullible and incompetent youth) and highly unfavourable one of Perseus, who is depicted as leading the 'plot' against Demetrius—whereas in fact he was fighting for his unchallengeable right to succeed his father, which Demetrius was treasonably questioning. Roman self-interest will have procured the distortion.
29. Livy xl. 20.3–24.8.
30. Polybius, again followed by Livy, throughout his account of these years depicts Philip as preparing war against Rome, a war which Perseus merely inherited. Again, this is a distortion of the true picture which was first promulgated by Eumenes of Pergamum when he spoke to the Senate in 172 and successfully persuaded it to declare war on Perseus (see chapter XV below). It suited both immediate Roman propaganda and subsequent Roman patriotic historiography, for it seemed to provide an equitable defence of Rome's uncompromising attitude to both Philip and Perseus, an attitude which eventually drove Perseus into war to the death. There is no good reason for believing that Philip ever had serious thoughts of again fighting against Rome, despite much serious provocation: but there is reason for thinking that the Senate would not have minded very much if Philip had decided on war and had thus given it the chance to ensure Demetrius' succession or (after his death) to destroy the Macedonian monarchy. Philip

wisely did not yield to his frustration, and it was left to Perseus to bear the brunt of Rome's developing hatred. The war which followed was not planned by Philip and inherited by Perseus: but to say that it was was the only way the Romans could justify (even to themselves) their eventual brutal war-mongering.

NOTES TO CHAPTER XV

PERSEUS

1. Livy xl.58.8. The most recent biography of Perseus is P. Meloni, *Perseo e la fine della monarchia macedone*. There is no full-scale treatment in English, though all standard histories of Rome deal with the events.
2. Polybius xxv.3.
3. Polybius xxv.4.8; Livy xlii.12.3–4.
4. Livy xlii.12.3–4.
5. Livy xl. 57.7–9.
6. Polybius xxv.6.2–6.
7. Livy xli.19.4–6. The Bastarnae were eventually driven off by the Dardanians and suffered enormous losses when the ice on the frozen Danube broke up as they were crossing (Orosius iv.20).
8. Livy xli.22.2–3.
9. Livy xli.22.4–8.
10. Livy xlii.2.1–2.
11. Livy xlii.5.
12. Livy xli.23–4 (Achaean debate in 174); xlii.6.1–2 (Marcellus). On Achaea at this time, see Errington, *Philopoemen*, 205f.
13. Livy xlii.10.11–12.
14. Versions of Eumenes' speech are given by Livy, xlii.11–13, and Appian, *Macedonica*, 11.1–2.
15. Livy xlii.14.1 (Senate's reaction); 40.1–11 (Quintus Marcius Philippus' arguments to Perseus later in 172); Ditt. *Syll.* no. 643; Sherk, *RD* no. 40; translation in Lewis and Reinhold, *Roman Civilization*, i. no. 71 (an inscription from Delphi recording a Roman letter to the Amphictyonic council, in which these very charges are specified); Polybius xxii.18 (Polybius' view of the causes of the war). For further discussion see chapter XIV note 30.
16. Livy xlii.14.2–4.
17. Livy xlii.15–17, presents the Roman version of these two incidents and inevitably has swallowed the propaganda whole.
18. Livy xlii.19.3–8; 25.14; 26.2–7.
19. Livy xlii.18.2–3; 36.8–37. Livy's chronology of the events of 172 is very confused as a result of his attempt to combine information received from Polybius and from his Roman annalistic sources. In particular, the chronological relationship between the missions of Sicinius and of Marcius Philippus is doubtful. Also adding to the confusion is the fact that the Roman calendar in 168 (and probably in 172) was something like $2\frac{1}{2}$ months ahead of the Julian year (i.e. March 15th, the beginning of the Roman official year,

probably fell actually some time in late December of the Julian year). The details of the calendar confusion in the second century B.C. cannot be discussed here: see A. K. Michels, *The Roman Calendar* (Princeton, 1967). For the case before us I have accepted the widely followed view of Walbank, *JRS* 1941, 82f.

20. Livy xlii.37–8.7.
21. Livy xlii.37.5–6 (Perseus' letter to Corcyra); 38.8–43.3.
22. Livy xlii. 36; 47–8.4; Polybius xxvii.6. On the chronology and Philippus' duplicity, see Walbank, *JRS* 1941, 82f.
23. The details are in Polybius xxvii.1–2.10; 5; Livy xlii.43.4–44; 46.7–10.
24. Polybius xxvii.3–4; Livy xlii.45–6.6.
25. Livy xlii.30.8–11.

NOTES TO CHAPTER XVI

THE END OF THE MACEDONIAN MONARCHY

1. Livy xlii.37.6.
2. Livy xlii.49.
3. Livy xlii. 50–4.
4. Livy xlii.56–60.
5. Polybius xxvii.8; Livy xlii.62.
6. Livy xlii.60.8–9.
7. Polybius xxvii.15; cf. xxviii.4.6. For discussion of Epirus see Oost, *Roman Policy in Epirus and Acarnania*, 73f.
8. Livy xlii.63.3–12 (Haliartus and Thisbe); xliii.4.5–7 (general); 6.1–3 (Athens); 7.5–11 (Chalcis).
9. Livy xliii.4.5–13 (Abdera); 7.5–11 (Chalcis).
10. We know about Coronea from a fragmentary inscription: Sherk, *RD* no. 3 (though dated there to 170 rather than the end of 171: see Livy xliii.4.11, *priore anno*).
11. Livy xliii.4.11–13 (Hortensius); 8 (Lucretius); Sherk, *RD* no. 2=Ditt. *Syll.* no. 646; translation in Lewis and Reinhold, *Roman Civilization*, i. no. 123 (Thisbe); Livy xliii.17.2 (decree on contributions).
12. Livy xliii.11.
13. Polybius xxviii.3–5; Livy xliii.17.
14. Polybius xxviii.8–9; Livy xliii.19.13–20.3 (Perseus and Genthius); xliv.1–16 (events of year).
15. Polybius xxviii.12–13.
16. Polybius xxix.3–4; 10–11; Livy xliv.23 (Genthius and Rhodes); Polybius xxix.5–9; cf. Livy xliv.24–5 (Eumenes). Some scholars have refused to believe that Eumenes could have been so stupid, and therefore reject the substance of Polybius' report. But cf. Scullard, *Roman Politics*, 286–7; below, chapter XVIII, p. 242f.
17. Livy xliv.30–2.5.
18. Livy xliv.33–46; xlv.4–8; Plutarch, *Aemilius Paulus*, 12–27.
19. Livy xlv.17 (appointments); 18 (decision on principles of settlement). A

fragment of a speech in this debate by the senior senator Marcus Porcius Cato has survived, in which he argued that 'the Macedonians should be free because they cannot be protected'. (*ORF* p. 61 = Scriptores Historiae Augustae, *Hadrian*, 5.3.)

20. Polybius, a contemporary who was personally deeply affected by the change, was well aware of its importance when his original scheme for his work made his account of Rome's rise to world power end in 167. Although he later continued his writing until 146, he rightly did not change his mind about the decisiveness of the year 168 (see Polybius iii.1–5).

21. Livy xlv.18.

22. Some have thought that Philippus' experience will have certainly made him one of the settlement commissioners, and his name was accordingly added to the list in Livy (xlv.17) by Weissenborn; thereafter it regularly appears in modern texts and translations. There is, however, no manuscript authority for it.

23. Livy xlv.29–30; 32.1–7.

24. Polybius xxx.10; Livy xlv.27.5–28.6; Plutarch, *Aemilius Paulus*, 28.

25. Livy xlv.28.6–8; 31.1–2; cf. Polybius xxx.11.

26. Polybius xxx.13; Livy xlv.31.3–11.

27. Polybius xxx.13.8–11.

28. Livy xlv.31.15.

29. Livy xlv.26.3–11 (Anicius); Polybius xxx.7.1–4.

30. Livy xlv.34.1–9; Polybius xxx.15; Plutarch, *Aemilius Paulus*, 29. The amount of booty taken from Epirus is uncertain: Livy says that each cavalryman received 400 denarii from the sale, each infantryman 200 denarii. But Plutarch says that each man received only 11 drachmae (about 13 denarii); and since Paullus was accused on his return to Rome of being parsimonious with booty, Plutarch's figure has sometimes been regarded as possibly correct. However, the accusation of parsimony was concerned with the enormously rich booty from Macedon, all of which Paullus kept for his triumph, and it is probably irrelevant here. On the whole, Livy's more circumstantial account seems more likely to be right. If so, we cannot tell why Plutarch's information is so diverse.

31. Polybius xxx.12 (Charops). For a rather different interpretation of Charops' influence see Scullard, *JRS* 1945, 58f.; Oost, *Roman Policy in Epirus and Acarnania*, 83f. The apologetic tradition on Paullus reaches its peak in Plutarch, *Aemilius Paulus*, 30, a passage which says explicitly that the Epirus affair was 'contrary to his respectable and honourable character'. As a comment on the career of the man who had already stripped Macedon of so much booty as to allow the abolition of the Italian land-tax, and who had stripped the Greek states of many thousands of their most respectable citizens, it is ludicrously inappropriate.

32. Livy xlv.35.5–41; Plutarch, *Aemilius Paulus*, 30–4; 38.

NOTES TO CHAPTER XVII

EUROPE AFTER PYDNA

1. Polybius xxxi.2.12.
2. Polybius xxxi.17.2.
3. Cassiodorus, *Chronica Minora* ii.130; for the coins see B. V. Head, *Historia Numorum* (ed. 2, Oxford, 1911), 238.
4. Polybius xxxv.4.10–11.
5. The sources for Andriscus' background are late and fragmentary: Zonaras ix.28; Diodorus xxxi.40a; xxxii.15; Livy, *periochae*, xlviii–l.
6. Zonaras ix.28; Diodorus xxxii.9a; 9b; Polybius xxxvi.9.
7. Zonaras ix.28.
8. Livy, *periochae*, liii.
9. Cicero, *In Pisonem*, 86; 96.
10. Strabo vii.7.4 (322–3). On the few surviving details of the first settlement of the province of Macedonia, see J. A. O. Larsen, 'Roman Greece', in T. Frank, *Economic Survey of Ancient Rome* (Baltimore, 1933–40), iv.303. On its date (146), see Morgan, *Historia* 1969, 422f.
11. Polybius xxx.29.
12. Polybius xxxii.5.4–6.9.
13. Polybius xxxii.5.1–3.
14. Embassies: Polybius xxx.29.1 (166/5); 32 (165/4); xxxii.3.14–17 (161/0); xxxiii.1.3–8; 3 (156/5); 14 (155/4); xxxv.6 (150 and Cato's quip). On Polybius and Scipio Aemilianus: Polybius xxxi. 23–4.
15. Polybius xxx.20.
16. Ditt. *Syll.* no. 664=Sherk, *RD* no. 5. Translation in Lewis and Reinhold, *Roman Civilization*, i. no. 124.
17. Polybius xxxii.7.
18. Pausanias vii.11.4–8; Polybius xxxiii.2 (=Aulus Gellius, *Noctes Atticae* vi.14.8–10); cf. Plutarch, *Cato Major*, 22; Ditt. *Syll.* no. 675; cf. Larsen, *Greek Federal States*, 485–7.
19. Pausanias vii.14.8.
20. Polybius xxxiii.16.
21. The longest account of the Achaean War and of events leading up to it is by Pausanias, vii.12–16.
22. Orestes apparently claimed that these towns were comparatively recent acquisitions by the Achaean League (Pausanias vii.14.2), but except for Heraclea-by-Oeta, which probably became Achaean after 167, this was nonsense. Sparta had been Achaean for nearly fifty years, Corinth and Orchomenus for nearly 100. The Roman historian used by Dio Cassius (frg. 72) bettered Pausanias' version by arguing that these towns had once belonged to Philip V: but this was quite irrelevant, and in the case of Sparta plain wrong! Justin (xxxiv.1.5) claims that Orestes was intending to break up the League altogether, but this is unlikely, although some Achaeans may have believed it. At this time it was sufficient merely to weaken it.
23. Pausanias vii.13.2. This was probably the embassy of Marcus Licinius, Aulus Hostilius Mancinus and Lucius Manlius Vulso (Polybius xxxvi.14.

1–6) whose combined physical and intellectual deficiencies provoked Cato to describe it as 'the embassy with no feet, head or heart'. No wonder it failed in Achaea.

24. Polybius xxxviii.9–11.
25. Polybius xxxviii.3.8–13; 18.7–12.
26. Polybius xxxviii.15–18.
27. Polybius xxxix.3.
28. Polybius xxxix.5. For discussion of the settlement as a whole see J. A. O. Larsen, 'Roman Greece', in T. Frank, *Economic Survey of Ancient Rome* (Baltimore, 1933–40), iv.303f.; S. Accame, *Il dominio romano in Grecia* (Rome, 1946).

NOTES TO CHAPTER XVIII

ASIA AFTER PYDNA

1. Polybius xxix.5–9. See Scullard, *Roman Politics*, 286–7; Badian, *Foreign Clientelae*, 102f. On the Pergamene affairs of this chapter see also Hansen, *The Attalids of Pergamum*, 114f.; McShane, *The Foreign Policy of the Attalids of Pergamum*, 177f. (to be used very cautiously).
2. Part of the later Roman tradition, recorded by Valerius Antias and taken from him by Livy, depicted Eumenes as actually withdrawing from the war, and contrasted his conduct with that of his brother Attalus who remained loyal to Rome (Livy xliv.13.12–14; 20.7). The facts do not support this version.
3. Polybius xxx.1–3.
4. Polybius xxx.18; Livy xlv.44.4f. (Prusias); Polybius xxx.19 (Eumenes).
5. The battle is mentioned in an inscription: *Die Inschriften von Pergamon* (Ed. M. Fränkel, Berlin, 1890–5), no. 165. The Roman settlement is mentioned by Polybius, xxx.28.
6. Polybius xxx.30. See also Polybius xxxii.1 (161/0) for Prusias' continuing campaign against Eumenes and Attalus.
7. Polybius xxxi.1.2–8; 6.
8. Polybius xxxi.6.6. There are some contemporary inscriptions which may support this view, for they are full of praise for Eumenes, even calling him 'Saviour' (*Soter*)—possibly because of his victory over the Gauls (see Ditt. *OGIS*, nos. 305; 763). But these may be misleading, since the places where the texts originated (Sardis and Miletus) were subject to Eumenes' influence.
9. Most of the dossier of correspondence of Eumenes and Attalus with Attis has been preserved, since much later it was engraved on the walls of the temple at Pessinus, though many of the documents are fragmentary since the stones are broken: the whole extant dossier with translation may be found in C. B. Welles, *Royal Correspondence in the Hellenistic Period* (New Haven, 1934), 241f.; text alone in Ditt. *OGIS*, no. 315; translation of Attalus' letter in Lewis and Reinhold, *Roman Civilization*, i.317 (though the heading is misleading).
10. Polybius xxxii.15; xxxiii.1.1–2; 7; 12–13; Appian, *Mithridatica*, 3. On this war, see Habicht, *Hermes*, 1956, 101f.
11. Appian, *Mithridatica*, 4–7; cf. Polybius xxxvi.14–15.

12. Strabo xiii.4.2; Zonaras ix.28 (Andriscus); Pausanias vii.16.1 (Achaea). At vii.16.8 Pausanias adds the information that in his time (2nd cent. A.D.) Corinthian spoils could still be seen at Pergamum.

13. Strabo xiii.4.2.

14. The text of Ptolemy's will can be found in *Supplementum Epigraphicum Graecum*, ix, no. 7; translation in Lewis and Reinhold, *Roman Civilization*, i. 318.

15. Plutarch, *Tiberius Gracchus*, 14; Ditt. *OGIS*, no. 338; 435 (=Sherk, *RD* 11); translation in Lewis and Reinhold, *Roman Civilization*, i.321; Sherk, *RD*, 12 (*senatus consultum de agro Pergameno*). On the settlement and details of Roman rule see Sherk's commentary on *RD* 11 and 12; Rostovzeff, *Hellenistic World*, ii.811f.; Hansen, *Attalids of Pergamum*, 148f.; Magie, *Roman Rule in Asia Minor*, 147f.

16. On the background, see above chapter XIV. The most complete discussion of Rhodes' relations with Rome is by Schmitt, *Rom und Rhodos*. On events in this section, see also the brief account by Badian, *Foreign Clientelae*, 100f., and all standard histories.

17. Polybius xxvii.3; Livy xlii.45 (172); Polybius xxvii.7; cf. Livy xlii.56.6 (171).

18. Polybius xxviii.2; 16. On the Rhodian grain trade see Casson, *TAPhA* 1954, 168f. Livy xliv.14.8-15.8, seems to have transposed to 169 the hostile embassy of 168 (on which see below). Since Livy or his source (probably Claudius Quadrigarius: see 15.1) was quite capable of making such a mistake himself without malice aforethought, we probably should not read into its chronological misplacement a deliberate attempt by Roman annalists to blacken the Rhodians by putting their hostile embassy a whole year too soon (though the content is a different matter: see note 22 below).

19. Polybius xxviii.17. The interpretation of the phrase, 'the current war', has been much disputed, since Polybius, who was probably in Philippus' camp at the time of Agepolis' interview, does not bother to explain its point of reference, being interested only in Philippus' motives. Moreover, in view of the fact that the Rhodians did try to mediate at Rome shortly afterwards, and that Polybius thought it possible that Philippus meant deliberately to put them in a position where Rome could easily take offence and punish them, many modern scholars, like Deinon and Polyaratus, have thought that Philippus meant by 'the current war' Rome's war with Perseus. However, this seems unlikely, for Rhodes did send mediators to Egypt (Polybius xxviii.17.5.); and Philippus had said explicitly that the Rhodians were the most appropriate people to undertake the mediation, a consideration which their long-standing trading connections with Syria and Egypt make perfectly comprehensible, but which was by no means applicable to Rome's war with Perseus. Thus, since Polybius is, on his own admission, constructing his explanation solely to explain what happened afterwards, we need not regard it as good evidence, since it represents only his opinion, not hard fact. The most recent discussions are by Schmitt, *Rom und Rhodos*, 145f.; J. van Ooteghem, *Lucius Marcius Philippus et sa famille* (Brussels, 1961), 90f.; Briscoe, *JRS* 1964, 68f.

20. Polybius xxix.4.7; 10-11; Livy xliv.23.5-10; 29.

21. Livy xliv.35.4-6.

22. Polybius xxix.19; Livy xlv.3.3-8 (from Polybius). Livy, xliv.14.8-15.8,

under 169, following a Roman source—probably Claudius Quadrigarius (15.1)—has an account which presents the Rhodian attitude as much more hostile than does Polybius' version; and while the chronological aberration is probably a simple error (see note 18 above) the general account, which has the Rhodians (ludicrously!) threatening to fight whichever party refused mediation (i.e. Rome), was clearly written up after the event to exaggerate the Rhodians' offence in order to provide further justification for Rome's subsequent harsh attitude.

23. Polybius xxx.6–9.
24. Polybius xxx.4; Livy xlv.20.4–25.4. The fragments of Cato's speech may be found in *ORF* 62f. The opposition to Cato was led by the praetor Manius Juventius Thalna, who may have been an associate of Philippus': see Scullard, *Roman Politics*, 216f.; 287.
25. Polybius xxx.5.4–10; 21.
26. Polybius xxx.5.11–16; 21; 23–4; 31 (Lycia, Caria, Caunus and Stratonicaea); 20; 31.10–12 (Delos and Rhodian loss of income).
27. Polybius xxx.31 (including speech of Astymedes).
28. For more detailed discussion of what follows see: Mørkholm, *Antiochus IV of Syria*, 22f.; Bevan, *The House of Seleucus*, ii.115f. On Egypt at this time the standard discussion is still that of W. Otto, *Zur Geschichte der Zeit des 6. Ptolemäers* (*ABAW* 1934); but see also Mørkholm, *Antiochus IV*, 64f.; Bevan, *The House of Ptolemy*, 282f.
29. Polybius xxvii.19; xxviii.1 (embassies at Rome); xxix.25.3–4 (Numisius); xxviii.18–23; Diodorus xxx.15–18 (events of war). Cf. Mørkholm, *Antiochus IV*, 64f.
30. Polybius xxix.23.4; Livy xlv.11.1–7.
31. Livy xliv.19.6–14.
32. Polybius xxix.2; Livy xlv.10.2.
33. Polybius xxix.27; Livy xlv.11–12.8.
34. Polybius xxxi.2.
35. Polybius xxxi.11–15 (Demetrius' escape). On Rome's attitude see Badian, *Foreign Clientelae*, 107–8; on Syrian affairs after Antiochus IV see Bevan, *House of Seleucus*, ii.128f.
36. On Rome's attitude see Badian, *Foreign Clientelae*, 108f.; Bevan, *House of Ptolemy*, 286f. It was during these disputes (in 155) that Ptolemy Physcon had the bright idea of securing himself against his brother by drawing up a will in favour of Rome, though it was never executed (for references see note 14 above). We have seen how his action was later imitated by Attalus III of Pergamum (and subsequently by other eastern kings).

AFRICA

1. Livy xxxiii.47.3–10.
2. Livy xxxiv.62. On the territory concerned and the source problem, see Badian, *Foreign Clientelae*, 295 note N; Walsh, *JRS* 1965, 149f.

3. Livy xl. 17.1–6; cf. 34.14.

4. Livy xli.22.1–3.

5. Livy xlii.23–4; cf. xliii.3.5–7.

6. Livy xlii.29.8–10. The passage is probably based on Polybius' contemporary analysis.

7. Livy xliii.6.11–13.

8. Livy xlv.13.12–14.9.

9. Polybius xxxi.21.

10. Roman defensive historiography tried to deny Carthage even this right by inventing a clause in the treaty of 201 by which (it was alleged) Carthage was prevented from waging war against Roman allies in any circumstances: Appian, *Libyca*, 8.4; cf. Livy xlii.23.3–4.

11. See Appian, *Libyca*, 68; 70. Modern writers normally call them 'democrats', but they seem to have been so only in the sense that they derived their support from the favour of the people.

12. For further recent discussion of Cato's mission and the outbreak of war, see: Astin, *Scipio Aemilianus*, 48f.; 270f.; Badian, *Foreign Clientelae*, 130f.; Hoffmann, *Historia* 1960, 309f.; Walsh, *JRS* 1965, 149f.; Scullard, *Roman Politics*, 240f. On Polybius' view of the outbreak of war, see Walbank, *JRS* 1965, 1f.

13. Plutarch, *Cato Major*, 26; Appian, *Libyca*, 69; Livy, *periochae*, xlviii.

14. On the argument between Cato and Nasica see the works cited in note 12 above, where all versions, ancient and modern, are discussed at length. Zonaras ix.26, says that Nasica also visited Carthage at about this time; if he is right it is most likely that Nasica had accompanied Cato, but Zonaras (or Dio, his source) may simply have made a mistake.

15. Polybius xxxvi.2.

16. Appian, *Libyca*, 70–3.

17. Appian, *Libyca*, 75.

18. Appian, *Libyca*, 74; 76; Polybius xxxvi.3f.

19. Appian, *Libyca*, 77–93.

20. On the events of the war the chief source is Appian, *Libyca*, 93f. On Massinissa, see Polybius xxxvi.16.

21. Appian, *Libyca*, 135. For Scipio's conversation with Polybius, see Polybius xxxviii.21; Appian, *Libyca*, 132; Diodorus xxxii.24, on which see Astin, *Scipio Aemilianus*, 282f.

22. Appian, *Libyca*, 105–6; Zonaras ix.27.

23. On some subsequent developments, see E. Badian, *Roman Imperialism in the Late Republic* (ed. 2, Oxford, 1968).

BIBLIOGRAPHY

THIS bibliography is not intended to be comprehensive. Its purpose is twofold: to list the main ancient sources and to indicate where they can most easily be found, both in the original languages and in English translations; and to list modern works which I have found helpful (many of them are specifically cited in the notes for various details) and which anyone studying the period in more detail might also be expected to find useful. Most of these modern works are in English, since I have had an English-speaking readership particularly in mind; but I have also included some of the more important works in other European languages, for scholarship is international and it would be invidious to omit major works simply because they are not written in English. I have also tried to categorize modern books and articles in order to indicate more clearly their specific point of view. This sub-division is to some extent arbitrary and sometimes unrealistic; but readers should bear in mind that the categories are not intended to be mutually exclusive.

I The most important ancient sources

Polybius of Megalopolis (*c.* 200–*c.* 118 B.C.). Wrote *Histories* (in Greek) in forty books, much of which has been lost. Careful and critical—though at the mercy of his written sources for periods which his own experience did not cover—Polybius' mainly contemporary information (much of which is preserved in Livy's Latin, for Livy used Polybius' material) is the invaluable basis on which the history of this whole period is laid. Standard text: T. Büttner-Wobst (Teubner, Leipzig, 1902–1904); text and translation into English (6 vols.) by W. R. Paton (Loeb Classical Library, Heinemann-Harvard, London–New York, 1922–1927); translation into English (2 vols.) by E. S. Shuckburgh (Macmillan, London–New York, 1889; reprinted by Indiana University Press with introduction by F. W. Walbank, 1962); selections in English translation by M. Chambers, with introduction by E. Badian (Washington Square Press, New York, 1966).

Livy (*c.* 59 B.C.–A.D. 12 or A.D. 17), born at Padua and lived at Rome. Wrote *History of Rome from the Foundation* (in Latin) in 142 books, of which only thirty-five survive. Livy used Polybius and Roman 'annalistic' writers as source material, and his work is the chief surviving source for much of the period covered by this book. Standard texts: W. Weissenborn, M. Müller, W. Heraeus, O. Rossbach (Teubner, Leipzig, 1875–1909); R. S. Conway, C. F. Walters, S. K. Johnson, A. H. McDonald (Oxford Classical Texts, 1914–1965) (books 1–35 only); text and translation into English (14 vols.) by B. O. Foster, F. G. Moore, E. T. Sage, A. C. Schlesinger, R. M. Geer (Loeb Classical Library, Heinemann-Harvard, London-New York, 1919–1959) (only vols. v–xiv cover our period); selections translated by A. de Sélincourt, 'The Early History of Rome' (books i–v) (Penguin Books, 1960); 'The War with Hannibal' (books xxi–xxx) (Penguin Books, 1965).

Appian of Alexandria (*c.* 95–*c.* 165 A.D.), wrote (in Greek) *Roman Affairs* in twenty-four books, of which only nine have survived complete. Appian seems to have used mainly Roman writers as sources, who were not always very accurate. He is our main source only for the Third Punic War (of the events covered in this book), but he often adds interesting details about other sections. Standard text: P. Viereck and A. G. Roos (ed. 2 with corrections by E. Gabba, Teubner, Leipzig, 1962–); text and translation into English (4 vols.) by H. White (Loeb Classical Library, Heinemann-Harvard, London-New York, 1912–1914) (only vols. i and ii cover our period).

Diodorus Siculus of Agyrium (lived at the end of 1st cent. B.C.), wrote (in Greek) *Universal History* in forty books, of which only short fragments survive of the books covering our period, some of which, however, provide useful details. Standard text: L. Dindorf (Teubner, Leipzig, 1886–1888) (the more recent Teubner text of F. Vogel and C. T. Fischer (1888–1906) does not include our fragments). Text and translation into English (12 vols.) of the whole extant work by C. H. Oldfather, C. H. Sherman, C. B. Welles, R. M. Geer, F. Walton (Loeb Classical Library, Heinemann-Harvard, London-New York, 1933–1967) (only vols. xi and xii, by F. Walton, concern our period).

Dio Cassius of Nicaea (*c.* 160–230 A.D.), wrote (in Greek) *Roman History*, from earliest times to 229 A.D., in eighty books, of which those covering our period survive only in small fragments, some of which, however, provide useful details. Standard text: P. Boissevain (Weidmann, Berlin, 1895–1931); text and translation into English (9 vols.) by E. Cary (Loeb Classical Library, Heinemann-Harvard, London-New York, 1914–1927) (only vols. i and ii cover our period).

Zonaras (12th cent. A.D.), Byzantine monk who wrote (in Greek) a short *History of the World*, in eighteen books, for which he made use of Dio Cassius (among others) for our period. His text is useful in filling out Dio's fragments (though it is very much abbreviated and only rarely adds much of value). The relevant sections will be found in Boissevain's edition of Dio Cassius, and text and translation into English in E. Cary's Loeb Classical Library volumes of Dio Cassius.

Plutarch of Chaeronea (*c*. A.D. 46–after 120), moral philosopher who also wrote *Lives* of famous Greeks and Romans, some of which fall into our period (Fabius Maximus, Marcellus, Aemilius Paulus, Cato Major, Philopoemen, Flamininus). Plutarch recognized that he was writing lives, not histories, and he was more interested in depicting the character of his heroes than in testing the accuracy of all the information he collected. Nevertheless, he preserves much good information that would not otherwise have survived. Standard text: C. Lindskog and K. Ziegler (Teubner, Leipzig, 1914–1935); some volumes have been re-edited by K. Ziegler (Teubner, Leipzig, 1960–); text and translation into English (11 vols.) by B. Perrin, (Loeb Classical Library, Heinemann-Harvard, London-New York, 1914–1926).

II Modern Works

(a) Books

(i) About sources

A. Degrassi, *Inscriptiones Italiae*, xiii, 1, Rome, 1947.

T. A. Dorey (ed.), *Latin Historians*, London, 1966.

F. Jacoby, *Die Fragmente der griechischen Historiker*, Berlin-Leiden, 1922–.

G. A. Lehmann, *Untersuchungen zur historischen Glaubwürdigkeit des Polybios*, Münster, 1967.

N. Lewis and M. Reinhold, *Roman Civilization*, 2 vols. New York, 1951–5.

F. W. Walbank, *A Historical Commentary on Polybius*, vols. i and ii, Oxford, 1957–67.

P. G. Walsh, *Livy*, Cambridge, 1963.

(ii) General

Cambridge Ancient History, vols. vii and viii, Cambridge, 1928–30.

M. Cary, *The Geographic Background of Greek and Roman History*, Oxford, 1949.

O. Meltzer and U. Kahrstedt, *Geschichte der Karthager*, Berlin, 1879–1913.

H. H. Scullard, *A History of the Roman World, 753–146 BC*, ed. 3. London, 1961.

G. De Sanctis, *Storia dei romani*, 4 vols. Turin etc. 1907–64.

A. J. Toynbee, *Hannibal's Legacy*, Oxford, 1965.

(iii) Rome and Roman Foreign Policy

A. E. Astin, *Scipio Aemilianus*, Oxford, 1967.

E. Badian, *Foreign Clientelae*, Oxford, 1958.

E. Badian, *Studies in Greek and Roman History*, Oxford, 1964.

E. Badian, *Roman Imperialism in the Late Republic*, Oxford, 1968.

W. Dahlheim, *Struktur und Entwicklung des römischen Völkerrechts*, Munich, 1968.

M. Holleaux, *Rome, la Grèce, et les monarchies hellénistiques au IIIe siècle av. J.-C. (273–205)*, Paris, 1921.

D. Magie, *Roman Rule in Asia Minor*, Princeton, 1950.

Th. Mommsen, *Römisches Staatsrecht*, ed. 3. Leipzig, 1887–8.

K. E. Petzold, *Die Eröffnung des zweiten Römisch-Makedonischen Krieges*, Berlin, 1940 (reprinted, Darmstadt, 1968).

H. H. Scullard, *Scipio Africanus in the Second Punic War*, Cambridge, 1930.

H. H. Scullard, *Roman Politics, 220–150 BC*, Oxford, 1952.

H. H. Scullard, *Scipio Africanus: Soldier and Politician*, London, 1970.

A. N. Sherwin-White, *The Roman Citizenship*, Oxford, 1939.

H. E. Stier, *Roms Aufstieg zur Weltmacht und die griechische Welt*, Köln-Opladen, 1967.

C. H. V. Sutherland, *The Romans in Spain*, London, 1939.

L. R. Taylor, *Roman Voting Assemblies*, Ann Arbor, 1966.

J. H. Thiel, *A History of Roman Sea Power before the Second Punic War*, Amsterdam, 1954.

(iv) External States and their Relations with Rome

A. Aymard, *Les Premiers Rapports de Rome et de la Confédération Achaienne*, Bordeaux, 1938.

E. R. Bevan, *The House of Seleucus*, London, 1902 (reprinted, London, 1966).

E. R. Bevan, *The House of Ptolemy* (originally *A History of Egypt under the Ptolemaic Dynasty*, London, 1927), New York, 1968.

R. M. Errington, *Philopoemen*, Oxford, 1969.

E. V. Hansen, *The Attalids of Pergamum*, Cornell, 1947.

J. A. O. Larsen, *Greek Federal States*, Oxford, 1967.

R. B. McShane, *The Foreign Policy of the Attalids of Pergamum*, Urbana, 1964.

P. Meloni, *Perseo e la fine della monarchia macedone*, Rome, 1953.

O. Mørkholm, *Antiochus IV of Syria*, Copenhagen, 1966.

S. I. Oost, *Roman Policy in Epirus and Acarnania in the Age of the Roman Conquest of Greece*, Dallas, 1954.

G. Picard, *Carthage*, London, 1964.

M. Rostovzeff, *A Social and Economic History of the Hellenistic World*, Oxford, 1941.

H. H. Schmitt, *Rom und Rhodos*, Munich, 1957.

H. H. Schmitt, *Untersuchungen zur Geschichte Antiochos' des Grossen und seiner Zeit*, Wiesbaden, 1964.

F. W. Walbank, *Philip V of Macedon*, Cambridge, 1940.

B. H. Warmington, *Carthage*, London, 1964.

(b) Articles

(i) Rome and Roman Foreign Policy

A. E. Astin, 'Saguntum and the Origins of the Second Punic War'. *Latomus*, xxvi, 1967, 37f.

E. Badian, 'The Treaty between Rome and the Achaean League'. *JRS*, xlii, 1952, 76f.

E. Badian, 'Aetolica'. *Latomus*, xvii, 1958, 199f.

J. P. V. D. Balsdon, 'Some Questions about Historical Writing in the Second Century B.C.' *CQ* NS iii, 1953, 158f.

J. P. V. D. Balsdon, 'Rome and Macedon, 205–200 B.C.' *JRS*, xliv, 1954, 32f.

J. P. V. D. Balsdon, 'T. Quinctius Flamininus'. *Phoenix*, xxi, 1967, 177f.

J. Briscoe, 'Q. Marcius Philippus and *nova sapientia*'. *JRS*, liv, 1964, 66f.

J. Briscoe, 'Eastern Policy and Senatorial Politics: 168–146 B.C.' *Historia*, xviii, 1969, 49f.

T. A. Dorey, 'The elections of 216 B.C.' *RhM*, cii, 1959, 249f.

R. M. Errington, 'Rome and Spain before the Second Punic War'. *Latomus*, xxix, 1970, 25f.

A. Heuss, 'Der erste punische Krieg und das Problem des römischen Imperialismus'. *Historische Zeitschrift*, clxix, 1949, 457f. (reprinted in series 'Libelli', Darmstadt, 1964).

W. Hoffman, 'Die römische Kriegserklärung an Karthago im Jahre 218'. *RhM*, xciv, 1951, 69f.

W. Hoffman, 'Die römische Politik des 2 Jahrhunderts und das Ende Karthagos'. *Historia*, ix, 1960, 309f.

F. R. Kramer, 'Massilian Diplomacy before the Second Punic War'. *AJPh*, lxix, 1948, 1f.

A. H. McDonald, 'The Treaty of Apamea (188 B.C.)'. *JRS*, lvii, 1967, 1f.

A. H. McDonald and F. W. Walbank, 'The Origins of the Second Macedonian War'. *JRS*, xxvii, 1937, 180f.

A. H. McDonald and F. W. Walbank, 'The Treaty of Apamea (188 B.C.): the Naval Clauses'. *JRS*, lix, 1969, 30f.

G. Morgan, 'Metellus Macedonicus and the Province Macedonia'. *Historia*, xviii, 1969, 422f.

H. H. Scullard, 'Charops and Roman Policy in Epirus'. *JRS*, xxxv, 1945, 58f.

H. H. Scullard, 'Rome's Declaration of War on Carthage in 218 B.C.' *RhM*, xcv, 1952, 209f.

G. V. Sumner, 'Roman Policy in Spain before the Hannibalic War'. *HSPh*, lxxii, 1967, 205f.

G. V. Sumner, 'The Chronology of the Outbreak of the Second Punic War'. *PACA*, ix, 1966, 4f.

F. W. Walbank, 'Roman Declaration of War in the Third and Second Centuries'. *CPh*, xliv, 1949, 15f.

F. W. Walbank, 'Political Morality and the Friends of Scipio'. *JRS*, lv, 1965, 1f.

(ii) External States and their Relations with Rome

L. Casson, 'The Grain Trade in the Hellenistic World'. *TAPhA*, lxxxv, 1954, 168f.

H. J. Dell, 'The Origin and Nature of Illyrian Piracy'. *Historia*, xvi, 1967, 344f.

H. J. Dell, 'Antigonus III and Rome'. *CPh*, lxii, 1967, 94f.

H. J. Dell, 'Demetrius of Pharus and the Istrian War'. *Historia*, xix, 1970, 30f.

T. A. Dorey, 'Macedonian Troops at the Battle of Zama'. *AJPh*, lxxviii, 1957, 185f.

T. A. Dorey, 'The alleged Aetolian Embassy to Rome'. *CR*, x, 1960, 9.

C. F. Edson, 'Perseus and Demetrius'. *HSPh*, xlvi, 1935, 191f.

Ch. Habicht, 'Über die Kriege zwischen Pergamon und Bithynien'. *Hermes*, lxxxiv, 1956, 90f.

N. G. L. Hammond, 'Illyris, Rome and Macedon in 229–205 B.C.' *JRS*, lviii, 1968, 1f.

N. G. L. Hammond, 'The Opening Campaigns and the Battle of Aoi Stena in the Second Macedonian War'. *JRS*, lvi, 1966, 39f.

D. Magie, 'The "Agreement" between Philip V and Antiochus III for the Partition of the Egyptian Empire'. *JRS*, xxix, 1939, 32f.

S. I. Oost, 'Philip V and Illyria, 205–200 B.C.' *CPh*, liv, 1959, 158f.

S. I. Oost, 'Amynander, Athamania and Rome'. *CPh*, lii, 1957, 1f.

F. W. Walbank, '*Φίλιππος τραγῳδούμενος*'. *JHS*, lviii, 1938, 55f.

F. W. Walbank, 'A Note on the Embassy of Q. Marcius Philippus'. *JRS*, xxx, 1941, 82f.

P. G. Walsh, 'Massinissa'. *JRS*, lv, 1965, 149f.

GLOSSARY

AEDILE Junior Roman magistrate. Four were elected each year, two by the *comitia tributa* (the 'curule aediles') and two by the *concilium plebis* (the 'plebeian aediles'), to serve for one year. The duties of the two kinds of aediles were indistinguishable, and were concerned with routine matters of the administration of public buildings and streets, temples, archives, public games, traffic, the market and the water supply. Of little political importance in our period, though an important stage in a public man's career.

AS Small Roman monetary unit, originally one pound of copper, but gradually devalued until by 89 B.C. it was a mere half-ounce. The details of the devaluation are obscure, but for most purposes the *as* was replaced by the sestertius, which was introduced during the war with Hannibal and was worth two and a half *asses* at first, but later became four *asses*.

CENSOR The senior Roman magistrate, two of whom were elected, normally every five years, by the *comitia centuriata*, and who served for eighteen months. They did not have *imperium*. Their duties were concerned with public morals, the leasing of public property, listing the citizen population (the *census*), selecting entrants to the Senate and expelling unsuitable members, and the performance of various religious functions.

CLIENTELA The relationship between free client and free patron, whereby each freely undertook certain unwritten extra-legal moral obligations to support the interests of the other. Current at all levels of Roman social life, *clientela* began to be used during our period by Rome as a public relationship between the state of Rome and free overseas communities (some of whom did not understand what the relationship implied). Hence we find 'client kings' and 'client states' growing under Rome's patronage and protection, with the same kind of obligations to fulfil.

COMITIA CENTURIATA Voting assembly of the whole Roman People, organized into 193 units called 'centuries'—by this time the term had nothing to do with either numbers of one hundred or with the tactical unit of the Roman army—but arranged timocratically (i.e. the rich were given a built-in advantage). The premier Roman assembly which elected the magistrates with *imperium*—consuls and praetors—and the censors, which voted on matters of public safety and which declared war and ratified peace treaties.

COMITIA TRIBUTA Voting assembly of the whole Roman People, organized into thirty-five voting units (tribes) based on territorial divisions. Elected quaestors, curule aediles, held some trials and might legislate about anything except declarations of war and ratifications of peace treaties.

CONCILIUM PLEBIS Voting assembly of the Roman plebs, arranged in thirty-five voting units (tribes), like the *comitia tributa*. Passed *plebiscita*, which after 287 B.C. had equal validity with laws; elected tribunes of the plebs and plebeian aediles, conducted some trials, and most kinds of business might be transacted by it.

CONSUL Senior Roman magistrate, two elected each year by the *comitia centuriata* to be joint heads of state for one year. They held *imperium* and were the principal commanders of armies in wartime and the chief officers in other civilian administrative spheres. The most important political post in the state.

DEDITIO IN FIDEM Unconditional surrender, the procedure which was required of any community which threw itself on Rome's mercy. More usually offered by defeated enemies, *deditio* was nevertheless sometimes offered by communities and states which wished to involve Rome in their defence. It was one of the chief ways by which states became Roman clients, since Roman discretion allowed widely varying actions after *deditio*.

DRACHMA Standard small Greek monetary unit, used throughout the Greek eastern Mediterranean, though minted on different standards in different places. 6,000 to the talent.

IMPERIUM Roman term for supreme administrative authority, the power to coerce Roman citizens (including the imposition of the death penalty) and the right to command Roman armies. Held by consuls, praetors, dictators and Masters of the Horse.

LATIN RIGHTS Partial Roman citizenship widely held by Rome's Italian allies. Originally held only by Latins (hence the name), the rights were later widely extended throughout Italy and even overseas. Holders of Latin Rights had the right to trade and, in practice, to marry with Roman citizens, and the right to reside in Rome if they desired.

LEGION   Standard large unit of the Roman army, normally in our period 4,200 infantry and 300 cavalry, accompanied by something like the same number of Italian allies. Rome's regular annual levy was four legions (two for each consul), but more could be raised if emergencies threatened. The numbers of men in each legion will also have varied from time to time.

MAGISTRATE   The technical term for all elected officers who conducted the business of the Roman state.

PRAETOR   Roman annual magistrate with *imperium*, though of lower rank than the consuls. In 264 there were two annually elected by the *comitia centuriata*, whose duties were chiefly concerned with administering justice, but who also had the right to command armies. As Rome acquired provinces, so the number of praetors was increased, since after 227 praetors were regularly appointed as provincial governors. With the creation of the Spanish provinces in 197 the number of praetors reached six, two of whom normally remained at Rome.

PROMAGISTRATE   These officers—proconsuls and propraetors— were normally regularly-elected magistrates whose term of office was extended by the Senate after its normal termination, for the performance of specific duties. They retained *imperium*, but technically they exercised it 'in place of' (*pro*) a consul or praetor, depending on their own grade. This was the Roman method of obviating the chief disadvantages of the system of annually elected magistrates.

PROVINCIA   Originally the sphere in which a Roman magistrate exercised *imperium*. But as Rome acquired overseas territories which were governed by magistrates with *imperium* (normally praetors), so the term *provincia* came to be used to describe the territory concerned.

QUAESTOR   Junior Roman magistrate without *imperium*. Eight were elected annually by the *comitia tributa*. Duties were primarily concerned with finance.

SENATE   Body of about 300 distinguished Romans, selected by the censors; originally the advisory council of the kings of Rome, but later the advisory council of the annual magistrates, most of whom were members of the Senate. Membership was virtually for life. In so far as Rome had a government in the modern sense, the Senate was it. In particular, the Senate was the body which (though technically acting only as adviser to the magistrates who asked its opinion) formulated Roman policies in the spheres of home and foreign policy (though the *comitia centuriata* retained the right to declare war and make peace), it controlled finance, and in wartime appointed generals to their commands and in peacetime arranged the provinces for the governors.

STRATEGOS   The title of the chief annual magistrate of some Greek states, in particular the Achaean and Aetolian Leagues. The word means 'general', and while the *strategos* was the chief army commander, he was also president of the civilian aspects of the life of the state.

TALENT   The largest Greek unit of weight and money. Divided into 6,000 drachmae.

TRIBE   The population of many ancient Greek and Italian states was divided into tribes, the most important function of which was to serve as voting units. Tribes were often arranged on a purely geographical basis, like modern constituencies. At Rome the thirty-five geographical tribes formed the organization of the *comitia tributa* and the *concilium plebis*.

TRIBUNE OF THE PLEBS   Annual Roman officers, ten of whom were elected by the *concilium plebis* as representatives of the plebs. Their duties were to defend the lives and property of plebeians. Each tribune had the right to veto any act performed by magistrates (including his colleagues), to initiate legislation in the *concilium plebis*, and to convene the Senate.

TRIBUNE OF THE SOLDIERS   Junior officer of a legion, six of whom served with each legion. Like other Roman magistrates, tribunes of the soldiers were elected by the People (in the *comitia tributa*).

TRIUMPH   Civic celebration of military success, normally awarded by a decree of the Senate. The triumph took the form of a public procession headed by the magistrates and the Senate, in which were paraded the spoils (including prisoners) of the victorious campaign, and in which the victorious legions took part. Triumphs were jealously coveted and were often the subject of political wrangles.

policy (though the *comitia centuriata* retained the right to declare war and make peace), it controlled finance, and in wartime appointed generals to their commands and in peacetime arranged the provinces for the governors.

STRATEGOS. The title of the chief annual magistrate of some Greek states, in particular the Achaean and Aetolian Leagues. The word means 'general', and while the *strategos* was the chief army commander, he was also president of the civilian aspects of the life of the state.

TALENT. The largest Greek unit of weight and money. Divided into 6,000 drachmae.

TRIBE. The population of many ancient Greek and Italian states was divided into tribes, the most important function of which was to serve as voting units. Tribes were often arranged on a purely geographical basis, like modern constituencies. At Rome the thirty-five geographical tribes formed the organization of the *comitia tributa* and the *concilium plebis*.

TRIBUNE OF THE PLEBS. Annual Roman officers, ten of whom were elected by the *concilium plebis* as representatives of the plebs. Their duties were to defend the lives and property of plebeians. Each tribune had the right to veto any act performed by magistrates (including his colleagues), to initiate legislation in the *concilium plebis*, and to convene the Senate.

TRIBUNE OF THE SOLDIERS. Junior officer of a legion, six of whom served with each legion. Like other Roman magistrates, tribunes of the soldiers were elected by the People (in the *comitia tributa*).

TRIUMPH. Civic celebration of military success, normally awarded by a decree of the Senate. The triumph took the form of a public procession headed by the magistrates and the Senate, in which were paraded the spoils (including prisoners) of the victorious campaign, and in which the victorious legions took part. Triumphs were jealously coveted and were often the subject of political wrangles.

INDEX

This index aims to be a reasonably complete collection of proper names, but is to some extent selective. Romans are cited by their family name (*nomen*), with cross-references for the most important third-names (*cognomina*).

THE MEDITERRANEAN WORLD

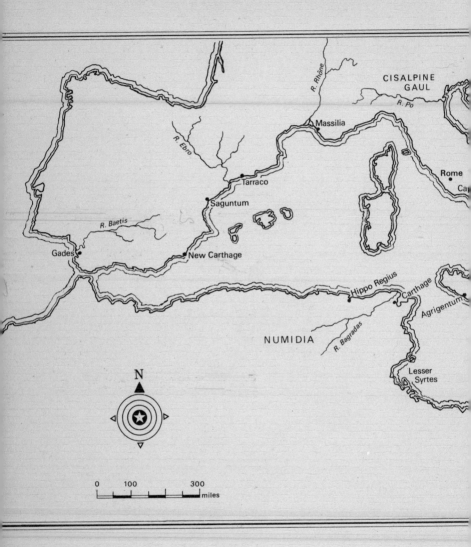

CISALPINE GAUL

R. Rhône

R. Po

Massilia

Rome

Ca

R. Ebro

Tarraco

Saguntum

R. Baetis

Gades

New Carthage

Hippo Regius

Carthage

Agrigentum

NUMIDIA

R. Bagradas

Lesser Syrtes

N

0   100   300
miles